WEYERHAEUSER ENVIRONMENTAL BOOKS
William Cronon, Editor

Weyerhaeuser Environmental Books explore human relationships with natural environments in all their variety and complexity. They seek to cast new light on the ways that natural systems affect human communities, the ways that people affect the environments of which they are a part, and the ways that different cultural conceptions of nature profoundly shape our sense of the world around us. A complete list of the books in the series appears at the end of this book.

PUMPKIN

The Curious History of an American Icon

CINDY OTT

UNIVERSITY OF WASHINGTON PRESS
Seattle and London

Pumpkin: The Curious History of an American Icon is published with the assistance of a grant from the Weyerhaeuser Environmental Books Endowment, established by the Weyerhaeuser Company Foundation, members of the Weyerhaeuser family, and Janet and Jack Creighton.

© 2012 by the University of Washington Press
Printed and bound in the United States of America
Design by Thomas Eykemans
Composed in Sorts Mill Goudy, courtesy The League of Moveable Type
Display type set in Poplar, designed by Barbara Lind
16 15 14 13 12   5 4 3 2

University of Washington Press
PO Box 50096, Seattle, WA 98145, USA
www.washington.edu/uwpress

Library of Congress Cataloging-in-Publication Data
Ott, Cindy.
Pumpkin : the curious history of an American icon / Cindy Ott. — 1st ed.
    p. cm.—(Weyerhaeuser environmental books)
ISBN 978-0-295-99195-5 (hardback)
1. Pumpkin—History.
2. Cooking (Pumpkin)—United States—History.
3. Pumpkin growers—United States—History.
I. Title.
SB347.O88 2012   641.5—dc23   2012011199

CONTENTS

NOT BY BREAD ALONE

William Cronon

HE BEST WORKS OF HISTORY OFTEN ENCOURAGE US TO REVISIT
familiar times, places, people, and things in ways that help us see the
past and even the world today with entirely new eyes. Edmund Morgan's classic *American Slavery, American Freedom* directed our attention to
the paradox that the Declaration of Independence—which has served as
a symbolic beacon of freedom and democracy from the moment Thomas
Jefferson first drafted it—was in large measure the creation of wealthy Virginians whose lives were utterly dependent on the profoundly unfree and
undemocratic institution of slavery. In Morgan's hands, this surprising
fact became a means for understanding not just the American Revolution,
but the contradictions of race and class that have bedeviled the United
States since before its founding. In a very different but no less revelatory
way, Dava Sobel's little volume on *Longitude* asked readers to take a closer
look at the north-south east-west lines we see every time we encounter a
map or a globe in an effort to help us recognize the practical and mathematical challenges those lines have historically posed for navigation. From
that small beginning, she tells an unforgettable tale about mariners on the
high seas who found it nearly impossible to determine their east-west position until an eighteenth-century English inventor finally devised a clock
that didn't lose time even after many weeks at sea. The world we inhabit is
filled with things like these that we typically take utterly for granted. Only
when we ask how they came to be—only when we inquire about their histories—do we recognize how strange and wondrous they truly are.

In the book you now hold in your hands, Cindy Ott performs just such
a minor historical miracle with a plant you've probably known your entire

life without giving it a second thought. *Pumpkin: The Curious History of an American Icon* takes a long, close look at this colorful American vegetable—though, in truth, those misshapen orange globes with stems are really fruits—and by so doing reveals just what a quirky and surprising role it has played in the cultural history of the United States.

Pause for a minute to reflect on the moments in a typical year when your own life intersects with that of the pumpkin. Sometime in October, especially if there are children in your household, someone will likely make a trip to the local grocery store or perhaps to a farm in the surrounding countryside to purchase some of these large orange vegetables. Back at home, the family will cut them open, scoop out their seeds, and with varying degrees of artistry carve faces on their sides which, come Halloween, will welcome trick-or-treaters to the front door by flickering candlelight. Then, a few weeks later, someone will purchase cans of pumpkin from a large display at the local supermarket—which barely stocks the stuff during the rest of the year—in order to serve pumpkin pie at the traditional Thanksgiving feast. The same ritual might possibly be repeated at Christmas if your family is especially fond of this seasonal dessert, but in most households, no one will see or eat such a pie until another year has passed.

For millions of American families, these seasonal appearances of the pumpkin are so familiar that they seem almost natural, which is no doubt why we rarely give them much thought. It takes a scholar of unusual wit and insight to step back from these seemingly timeless American rituals to ask, "But . . . isn't this *strange*? Why would such an attractive and productive vegetable—a plant that in other parts of the world is often consumed year round—be relegated to just two annual appearances in American households, one of them not culinary at all? When did people in this country start doing this, and how did this plant come to play such a peculiar role in American popular culture?" Once she poses these questions—and once the reader has grasped their full oddity—it's hard not to keep reading in spite of oneself. Pumpkin stories begin pouring forth so abundantly from Ott's pages that they rival the plant itself in their fecundity. Read this book, and you'll never see pumpkins in quite the same way again.

Let me offer just a few hors d'oeuvres for the intellectual feast that lies ahead. We all know that the reason pumpkin pie plays such an important role at Thanksgiving is that the Pilgrims and their Wampanoag neighbors dined on it when they gathered in Plymouth, Massachusetts, for a harvest celebration that has ever since been ritually reenacted on the fourth Thursday in November. Unfortunately, what we all "know" turns out to be wrong in most of its particulars. Harvest celebrations like this one have ancient antecedents on both sides of the Atlantic, so this kind of gathering hardly originated at Plymouth. Furthermore, the idea of a special meal for the purpose of giving thanks emerged during the sixteenth century as a feature of the English Reformation, in which Days of Feasting and Days of Thanksgiving were meant to honor special acts of divine providence—and also to replace what Protestants saw as the too-frequent celebrations that typified the ritual calendar of the Catholic Church.

As for the Pilgrims, we have no idea of the date on which they held their feast, only that it took place sometime during the autumn of 1621. Thanksgiving celebrations began to be a regular feature of the New England calendar later in the seventeenth century, but not on any predictable date. By the early nineteenth century, different states chose different dates for these feasts, and not until 1863, in the midst of the Civil War, did Abraham Lincoln regularize the holiday as the final Thursday in November—a date that in 1941 Congress redefined as the *fourth* Thursday in November to anticipate those rare occasions when the month contains five Thursdays. (Canada celebrates its own version of Thanksgiving—which obviously has nothing to do with the Pilgrims—on the second Monday in October, though that particular date wasn't finally resolved until 1957.)

Just as it took quite a while for Thanksgiving to migrate to its present place on the U.S. national calendar, so too did pumpkins take rather more time than we might imagine to find their way onto Thanksgiving menus. There are only two documents from Plymouth that make any mention at all of that first Thanksgiving celebration, and neither of them says a word about pumpkins. Although the pumpkin itself originated in the western hemisphere, it had made its way to Europe within three decades of Columbus's first voyage—a full century before the Pilgrims landed in Massachusetts—and its distinctive appearance had already been depicted on a fresco in Rome by 1518. Ott notes that, much like the early American colonists, Europeans were quicker to recognize the visual appeal of this vegetable than they were its culinary possibilities, and her playful discussions of the diverse and changing roles pumpkins have played in European and American art are among the unexpected treats readers will discover in this book.

Although we can be pretty sure that American colonists were eating pumpkin soon after they arrived here—it was too easy to grow and too prolific a source of food for them not to have done so—their failure to distinguish it from other gourds, squashes, and melons makes it hard for us to know for sure just how they prepared it. One thing we do know is that the dessert with which Americans now end their Thanksgiving meals would have been unrecognizable to the Pilgrims, whose ovens simply weren't up to the task of making a modern pie crust. The first recipes we have for something akin to what we would today call pumpkin pie appear in French and English cookbooks during the second half of the seventeenth century, and probably migrated to the American colonies in the eighteenth century. Not until 1796, when Amelia Simmons wrote *American Cookery*, the first cookbook published in the new United States, did recipes for sweetened "pompkin" baked in a pastry crust appear in print on this side of the Atlantic. Even then, as Ott persuasively argues, it would not be until well into the nineteenth century that pumpkin pie would take its canonical place at the end of the Thanksgiving meal. Before then, pumpkin was more likely to appear on the table in beer than for dessert.

Unexpected details like these are among the special pleasures of Cindy Ott's book, but they serve a much deeper and more important purpose for her larger argument. Pumpkins contribute to modern American culture not just as pies but as jack-o'-lanterns. I will leave to Ott the strange tale of how Washington Irving's famous *Legend of Sleepy Hollow* helped the pumpkin become as canonical to American Halloween as it is to American Thanksgiving—even though the pumpkin hurled at Ichabod Crane by the headless horseman in that story was just an ordinary vegetable with no carved face on it at all. But the jack-o'-lantern is an especially striking example of a lesson that Ott wants us to remember not just about pumpkins, but about all the other nonhuman organisms that touch our lives, whether the primary uses we make of them are for food or fiber or fuel or anything else. Such organisms, she insists, are not just material objects but cultural icons. They are freighted with human meanings. If we think of them only as food, and if we imagine that the value of such food consists solely of the profits it earns or the nutrients it supplies, we'll miss much of what is most interesting about it, for it nourishes our minds and hearts as much as it does our bodies.

Today, American farmers grow more than a billion pounds of pumpkin worth more than a hundred million dollars each year. Since so much of that crop is devoted to the ritual celebrations associated with just two national holidays, it would be hard to find more striking proof that culture is just as important as ecology or economics if we truly wish to understand changing human relationships with the natural environment. In their very different ways, both the jack-o'-lantern and the pumpkin pie serve in the modern United States as symbols of the pastoral harvest, of food that, despite all the industrialization and technological manipulation it has endured, still has deep roots in the farm fields to which so many American families make pilgrimages when they purchase pumpkins each October. The desire to sustain such rituals has equally deep roots in American popular culture. This outsized orange vegetable is now a symbol of America's rural past—even if what we believe it says about that past has as much to do with myth as with history. *Pumpkin: The Curious History of an American Icon* shows how a plant that we ignore for most of the year is all the more important to the popular culture of the United States and to the imaginations of its citizens precisely because we pay attention to it so occasionally. By reencountering it at harvest time, we remind ourselves of where we come from—though, as Cindy Ott so playfully reveals, the story of where we come from, like that of the pumpkin itself, is a good deal more complicated than we think.

ACKNOWLEDGMENTS

ONE OF THE GREAT PLEASURES OF RESEARCHING AND WRITING about pumpkins is that so many people have had a story to contribute. Studying the topic has introduced me to a wide range of wonderful people and interesting places, from midwestern pumpkin farmers to custodians of rare plant dictionaries, and from the humblest of produce auctions to the most prestigious university libraries. I would first like to thank my dissertation committee members at the University of Pennsylvania's American Civilization Program, including Robert St. George, Mel Hammerberg, Christa Wilmann-Wells, and Janet Theophano, not only for their support and guidance but also for their unfailing interest in my general well-being during the earliest phases of this project. Professors Anne Spirn and Elizabeth Johns were also important mentors and wonderful teachers. Bob and Anne have never hesitated to provide letters of support over the years. I am grateful to the University of Pennsylvania and the American Civilization Program for their financial assistance, including the University Fellowship and the Dissertation Fellowship.

For taking time out from their hectic farm schedules, I thank David Ackerman, Todd Butler, John Lewis, and Maureen Torrey—pumpkin producers all. Dave Newhauser, the production manager at Libby's, graciously spent nearly a whole day with me, showing me both field and factory production at the height of packing season. That day was one of the highlights of my research. I thank Mike Badgerow of Morton, Illinois, Ned Harden of Circleville, Ohio, and Vera Edwards of Spring Hope, North Carolina, who kindly shared their experiences and enthusiasm for their respective hometown pumpkin festivals. My sincere thanks to Gary Lucier, agricultural economist at the USDA, and Raymond J. Samulis, county agent 1, professor 1, and county department head, Cooperative Extension of Burlington County, New Jersey Agricultural Extension Station, for their assistance in helping me with facts relating to the production and business of pumpkins. Finally, Maryland farmer David Heisler has helped guide my interest and developing expertise in picking and selling pumpkins from the beginning. He and his family are both mentors and dear friends.

When I was not out in the field investigating pumpkins during the early years of my research, I was probably at the Smithsonian Institution. My pre-doctoral fellowship gave me access to the institution's fabulous resources and allowed me to touch base with old friends from my years working at the Archives of American Art and Department of Anthropology. Rayna Green, Charlie McGovern, Pete Daniel, John Fleckner, and Bruce Smith provided much support and guidance, along with my close friends Liza Kirwin, Karen Weiss, Peggy Feerick, Darcy Tell, Matt Wray, and Judy Throm. Anyone who knew and worked with Garnett McCoy at the Archives of American Art knows what a special privilege that was. His admirable mix of great intelligence, thoughtful insight, and lack of pretense is a model to us all. I want to thank the kind and helpful librarians at the National Agriculture Library, especially Sarah Lee, and the Library of Congress's Rare Book and Special Collections Reading Room staff. I also thank Karl and Sarah Struble and the Circleville clan for their care and assistance. Thanks to my friends at the environmental nonprofit Rachel's Network—Winsome McIntosh, Thu Pham, Elaine Broadhead, and Irene Crowe—who cheered me on while I worked on the first draft of this book, and to Axel Jansen, who was a great companion in and outside academia.

Some of the most important influences of my academic career and the best friends I've ever had resulted from my time at Yale University. My professors John Demos, Howard Lamar, Harvey Weiss, and Bill Cronon (more on Cronon later) continue to inspire. Peggy Burns, Phil Deloria, Marsha Hoem, Gunther Peck, Gul Pulhan, Carlo Rotella, Sam Truett, and Louis Warren are some of kindest and most creative people I know. Gunther had a particularly strong hand in getting this manuscript to publication by commenting on an early version and by supporting my career with letters of recommendation. Jenny Price, Tamar Besson, Emily Greenwald, Laura Katzman, and Sabine Zubragel generously offered their great advice, humor, and encouragement throughout the writing process and the rest of life's trials and tribulations; they are like family to me. Any success I have in producing engaging prose with a strong point I owe to Jenny, who has been a devoted reader and critic of all of my work. A special thanks to Jeff O'Toole, who means the world to me.

At each step in my career, I have been fortunate to make wonderful friends of my talented colleagues. At Montana State University and the Museum of the Rockies, these include Rob Campbell, Aiden Downey, Jody Rasker, Deborah Schuerr, Brett Walker, and Yanna Yannakakis. Jack Horner has always made me feel as special as one of his dinosaur finds, and he is as important to me as a golden pumpkin. There is no person I have more fun with on the back roads of Montana, or anywhere else for that matter, than Bill Yellowtail. It is one of life's gifts that I can call him my friend.

A year as a visiting assistant professor in the history department at the University of Nevada–Las Vegas offered unimaginable creative inspiration in a city that surprised me. Special thanks to the talented Joerg Lemke, Brigitte Hoffman, Anatoli Akerman, Santa Fe and the Fat City Horns, and Michael Grimm. At UNLV, I thank Andy Kirk, Gene Moehring, and the National Park Service's Dave Louter. Thanks to Elizabeth Nelson for her shared interest in cooking, eating, and talking about food and, along with Ethan, Phoebe, Cyrus, Jasper, and Chance, for immediately making their wonderful home like my own.

At Saint Louis University's American Studies department, I have the most remarkable colleagues anyone could hope for. Matt Mancini, Susanne Wiedemann, Ben Looker, and Jonathan Smith produce thoughtful work, cheer each other's successes, and laugh at each other's jokes. They, especially Matt and Susanne, were invaluable in helping me get this book to press. I would also like to thank my graduate assistants Mark Koschmann, Rebecca Odom, and Melissa Ford. I am grateful for the SLU Mellon Faculty Development Grants that supported my summer writing and research, and international conference presentations; and to the SLU College of Arts and Sciences, which generously funded the book's illustrations.

Although I rarely see them outside academic conferences, my times with Paul Sutter, Thomas Andrews, Ann Vileisis, and especially Neil Maher are a highlight of my year. Catching up with Christof Mauch as he dashes around the world is always a special pleasure. I have him to thank for my Fulbright and for many great times together discussing work and all else. I thank Donald Worster for inviting me to present a book chapter at the Kansas University Nature-Culture Seminar in 2009 and for being not only a great role model for all historians but also really good company. I also want to add a word of appreciation to Michael Pollan, whose work has been so inspirational.

I am grateful to the folks at the Weyerhaeuser Environmental Books series for so enthusiastically caring for my manuscript at every stage of the process. Thanks to Julidta Tarver for accepting it and for then handing it off to Marianne Keddington-Lang, whose talent, critical eye, and level of good cheer are unsurpassed and much appreciated. A special thanks to Warren Belasco for his sharp yet supportive review of the manuscript. Thanks to Tim Zimmerman for his assistance with the many illustrations and to Jane Kepp for her great copyediting. It was a long time ago, during a seminar at Yale, that Bill Cronon first inspired me to think about writing history as creating compelling and engaging stories that make people question their assumptions. His commitment to bringing the study of history outdoors, beyond the classroom and library stacks, made history more fun. It also encouraged me to see the field as an exploration not simply of the past but of the world around us today. His integrity and friendly disposition are unmatched. It is a thrill to have my book as a part of his series, for personal as well as professional reasons. For all of the above, I am very grateful to Bill.

As the youngest of four sisters, I am showered with words of wisdom and unconditional support. Much love and thanks to my sisters Susan, Judy, and Debi, and to my nieces Kirsten, Jennifer, Jessica, and Lauren, my grandniece Maira, my brothers-in-law Bruce, Gregers, Robert, and Wolfgang, my nieces' partners Marco and Knut, and the Swarr family. They didn't always know what I was doing, exactly, but they always offered their love and encouragement. For their devotion, hours of great company on trail walks, and patience while I finished one more sentence, I am grateful to Sam, Georgia, Rain Dog, Shiloh, and Lola.

I will always be thankful to James Barter and Pamela Cobb, who made this book possible in the most basic way.

Finally, I dedicate this book to the person whose intelligence, imagination, determination, and love are the guiding inspirations to me for all my life—my mother, Dorothy Welch Ott (1918–1994).

PUMPKIN

INTRODUCTION

I N THE FALL OF 1995 I HELPED A FRIEND, DAVID HEISLER, SELL PUMP-kins in front of his farmhouse in Comus, Maryland—more a cross-roads than a town—about forty miles northwest of Washington, D.C. Heisler had grown up on a nearby dairy farm that had since been sold to developers and divided into large estates. Intent on keeping his tractor a useful piece of equipment instead of merely a yard ornament, he raised fruits and vegetables on a couple of acres adjacent to his house and on fields near his boyhood home just down the road. In the summers, with-out any fanfare, he dropped off peppers, green beans, and corn at the local Safeway grocery store for resale. Later in the season, the piles of pump-kins he set around his yard amid crates of local apples, Indian corn, and colorful squash became an autumn spectacle. His pumpkin stand drew crowds of thousands every weekend in October. From about ten in the morning until sunset, carloads of visitors wandered the pumpkin patch. They playfully held up specimens of different sizes and shapes for their companions' inspection and took pictures in the middle of the patch before leaving with armloads of pumpkins and bags of other fall produce.

After my immersion in the pageantry of the pumpkin stand for five weekends in a row, I no longer just walked, drove, or turned magazine pages past pumpkins but rather stopped, stared, and wondered what the fuss was all about. I thought not only about the crowds flocking to the fall stands but also about the time-honored pumpkin pie at Thanksgiving dinner. Unlike most people around the world, who eat pumpkin uncer-emoniously throughout the year, Americans eat it hardly at all, except at this one national holiday feast. Instead of eating fresh pumpkins, they set them in front of their houses as decorations every autumn and carve them into jack-o'-lanterns for Halloween night. Small towns across the coun-try hold annual festivals named in the pumpkin's honor, though few have any real historic ties to the crop. Suddenly, pumpkins—from farm-grown meaty orbs to hollow plastic jack-o'-lanterns—struck me as fascinating objects.[1]

As customers loaded pumpkins into their cars at the fall stand, I sometimes asked them why they had made the long trip to buy pumpkins, even though they purchased squashes, which are botanically identical, in their local grocery store. They usually responded with a chuckle, not having really thought about it before. They considered the pumpkin simply a holiday decoration with little symbolic import or relevance to their personal values. When I asked Mike Badgerow, of the Morton, Illinois, Chamber of Commerce, why the town held an annual pumpkin festival, he provided a typically vague response about the pumpkin's seemingly indefinable allure: "There's just something about a pumpkin that is appealing."[2]

What the appeal is, exactly, and why it matters, is the subject of this book. The pumpkin is a natural object with a history.[3] From ancient foragers to present-day urbanites, people have transformed the vegetable, propagated it, cooked it, carved it, bought and sold it, ascribed personalities to it, and told stories about it. It is as much an idea as a plant type: common custom and popular knowledge and usage have influenced its physical form, definitions, and meanings over time.[4] Yet the object itself plays a vital role in the story.[5] It participates in a two-way dynamic: the pumpkin influences its own meanings and uses, and in turn, people's ideas shape its physical form.

Salt, potatoes, sugar, bananas, and corn all have their own histories and have been the subjects of recent books.[6] But none of them compares with the spectacle of the pumpkin, which can produce hundreds of pounds of fruit and a twenty-five-foot expanse of vines on a single plant. For centuries the pumpkin's huge size, animated growth, and malleable flesh have made it both a staple crop and a formidable cultural symbol. What makes the pumpkin a particularly provocative topic through which to investigate the cultural history of nature is its almost complete lack of utilitarian function in contemporary life. Apples, bananas, corn, and watermelons offer their own storybooks of lore and fable, yet part of their allure is their succulent flesh and functional uses.[7] Not so the pumpkin. Nearly two hundred years have passed since the pumpkin last played a role in everyday American life, yet its outsized physical presence inspires deep human attachments.

In order to understand Americans' desire for pumpkins, I read agricultural journals, women's magazines, cookbooks, botanical dictionaries, and seed catalogs; interviewed farmers and agricultural scientists; attended pumpkin festivals and giant pumpkin weigh-ins; studied paintings, prints, poetry, fiction, and films; scanned the aisles of retail stores; and read popular and academic literature. I pursued the connections among cultural ideologies, plant biology, and economics, from the precolonial era when American Indians first propagated the vegetable, to contemporary times when pumpkin stands draw huge crowds of customers. Answering the central question—why so many Americans will drive thirty miles to buy a vegetable they do not even eat—opens up a deeper story about how Americans employ nature, art, and history to create personal and national traditions and about the unexpected effects those traditions have on the world around them. *Pumpkin now is an art expression*

The history that unfolds is as remarkable for what it reveals as for what it does not. Although it may surprise many Americans today, who are taught in grade school that eating pumpkin pie at Thanksgiving is a reenactment of the Pilgrims' famous 1621 feast, no one at the event mentioned pumpkins at all.[8] Although the sheer volume of poems, paintings, and political tracts featuring pumpkins in every generation is astonishing, none of the early sources held out the orange, ribbed vegetable as anything special. Until the nineteenth century it was just another form of squash. The story of how it became *the* pumpkin and how it gate-crashed the Pilgrims' fête centuries later tells as much about how Americans have built a sense of national identity as it does about the vegetable itself. Popular memories of the pumpkin can veer far from its actual history, and the point of this book is not only to squash those myths but also to show *oh. my. god.* their power to establish a sense of American identity and to transform the material world. *Does the pumpkin fit with/construct our ID?*

How Americans have eaten pumpkin is one key part of the story; why they turned it into the Halloween jack-o'-lantern is another. Carving a face on a pumpkin tells something about how Americans have imagined wild nature while, conversely, the act expresses ideas about human nature. The history behind the making of the jack-o'-lantern pumpkin unites African American and Irish American folklore with age-old beliefs about the pumpkin's wild nature.[9] Few people probably think much about why they call a small child "pumpkin" or a foolish person a "pumpkinhead," or why

Cinderella rides off to the ball in a pumpkin, but each usage comes out of a long history of employing the vegetable to critique human behavior. Bringing together many such disparate histories shows too that the ways people value nature depend not only on how they think and interact with the natural world but also on how they think about and act toward each other.

The pumpkin's economic status is as central to its reputation as its natural capacities, though not in the way we normally think of the value of a crop. Because it grows like a weed and produces massive quantities of oversize fruit, historically the pumpkin was a food people could rely on when times got tough. American Indians held festivals in honor of the vegetable, but Europeans and American colonists were less than enthusiastic. They stigmatized the pumpkin as food for the rural poor. Yet as early as the 1650s, some recollected "times wherein old *pompion* was a saint"—a romantic, bygone age uncorrupted by market pursuits, when families subsisted off the land. Pumpkin pie appeared in the first American cookbook, published just after independence, because it was a native food tradition but also, already, because of what it meant.

Both celebrating and bracing themselves against the effects of modernization and capitalist expansion, Americans have long turned to nature and rustic rural life as refuges and as sources of powerful stories to explain who they are. The American agrarian myth—the idea that farming inculcates good values of hard work and self-sufficiency and therefore promotes good citizenship—found expression in art, literature, political philosophy, and farm and land policies for generations, and also in this humble yet ubiquitous crop.[10] The pumpkin's natural proclivities made it a potent harvest symbol, and its economic status as a subsistence crop endowed it with power as an agrarian icon for a nation of people who liked to think of themselves as farmers at heart, even as they moved into big cities and built more factories.

Turning an uninspiring pumpkin stew into sweet pumpkin pie, therefore, was as much a political process as a culinary one. The history of the pumpkin follows women who guided other women's efforts in the kitchen, such as Amelia Simmons, who wrote the first American cookbook, and Sarah Josepha Hale, who spearheaded efforts to make Thanksgiving a national holiday, as closely as it follows men such as Thomas Jefferson and Henry David Thoreau, who either farmed pumpkins themselves or wrote eloquently about them. The pumpkin's quaint agrarian symbolism may seem innocent and innocuous, but it has never been devoid of political tensions. Many southerners' preference for sweet potato pie over New England pumpkin pie suggests their cultural biases toward the vegetable and the ideological dimensions of people's appetite for food.[11]

How the pumpkin inspired its uses and meanings is only half the story. The popularity of the pumpkin as a symbol of quaint farm life is not simply ideological. In order to get close to nature, create a heritage, and foster a sense of community, Americans have depended on the actual, physical pumpkin. The pumpkin's history is compelling not only because of the powerful stories and traditions the vegetable has inspired but also because people's ideas about it have altered the pumpkin itself and, ironically, revitalized the very thing it has long symbolized—the small family farm. The natural peculiarities of the crop, its meanings, and market conditions have all encouraged its production by small-scale growers for local markets at the turn of the twenty-first century.

The romantic agrarian fables, imagery, and holiday rituals that so many Americans have used to forge a sense of national identity and heritage may be nostalgic responses to modernization, but they are hardly peripheral to real-world economics and agriculture. In fact they have changed the natural world and the way markets and farms operate. My approach and findings counter works in environmental history that tend to make the economy the driving and primary cause of human-nature encounters or equate the rise of capitalism with environmental destruction and the loss of meaning.[12] Instead, interactions between people and nature are a complex dynamic that moves in multiple directions.

The cultural history of the pumpkin contradicts these common narratives of the decline of rural communities and of people's alienation from nature under the forces of capitalism. The pumpkin's increasing economic value arose out of the deep meanings Americans invested in it, and its increased commodification helped rejuvenate small-scale farmers and small rural towns rather than undermine them. Although histories of literature, art, and consumer culture often find themselves on separate shelves from agricultural and environmental histories, here I offer evidence that romance for an era of premarket agriculture is inextricably linked to the economic realities of modern capitalism and American farming.

Americans' historic migration from the country to the city and their embrace of new forms of technology might have distanced them from the natural world, but they maintained deep connections to it through the resources they used and the stories they told. Reexamining American history through an object like the pumpkin helps draw connections among seemingly disconnected worlds. Pumpkins showed up in seed catalogs, science journals, commodity reports, and cookbooks but also in folktales, *he'll prob speak a lot Po l* paintings, and sentimental short stories—sometimes disguising political texts. The pumpkin enables us to see how economics, the natural world, and storytelling influence each other, a connection that has important implications for rural communities at the turn of the twenty-first century.

Every year, farmers plant thousands of acres of pumpkins, and consumers spend millions of dollars buying them. No one needs to tell pumpkin-stand customers, festival organizers, and farmers like David Heisler what is pleasurable about a field of golden pumpkins, but I hope to help them articulate what the appeal is all about. Perhaps this book will encourage others to seek out the deep stories hidden in common, everyday things and to appreciate the power of the meanings of those things to make profound changes in the world around them.

ONE

CORN, BEANS, AND
JUST ANOTHER SQUASH

10,000 BCE to 1600

I T WAS MOST LIKELY COLD THAT DAY IN NOVEMBER 1621 WHEN
English colonists and resident Indians gathered to celebrate the newcomers' first successful harvest in Plymouth, Massachusetts, at a fête
that Americans now commemorate as the first Thanksgiving. According
to Edward Winslow, one of two participants to leave a written record of
the day, "Amongst other recreations, we exercised our arms, many of the
Indians coming amongst us, and among the rest their greatest King Mas-
sasoit, with some ninety men, whom for three days we entertained and
feasted."[1] Although more than half the Plymouth settlers had died from
disease and starvation within their first year on American soil, the survi-
vors reportedly had more than enough food to go around that autumn.
In addition to "a good increase of Indian corn, and our barley indifferent
[but] good," Winslow wrote, there was "as much fowl, as with little help
beside, served the company almost a week . . . and five deer."[2]

And what of the famous pumpkin pie? For most Americans, pumpkin pie is reserved for Thanksgiving, one of the most treasured of family
gatherings and beloved of national holidays. Yet no one mentioned dining
on pumpkin at the feast that day in Plymouth—not a word about it. William Bradford, the colony's first governor and the only other chronicler
of Plymouth's early settlement days, poetically inventoried the crops the
immigrants had propagated: "All sorts of roots and herbs / Our gardens
grow, / Parsnips, carrots, turnips of what you'll sow, / Onions, melons,
cucumbers, radishes / Skirets, beets, coleworts, and fair cabbages."[3]

In Ireland + old Europe, radish
are carved for Halloween.

9

Neither he nor Winslow said anything about pumpkins, although by "melons" he might have been referring to the pumpkin native to the Americas. Colonists used botanical nomenclature from their homeland indiscriminately for varieties new to them. To throw the familiar history of the pumpkin into more confusion, at the time a pumpkin was not necessarily the round, ribbed, orange vegetable that most Americans know today. But what was it, and how did the Indians, Winslow, and his compatriots think about it and use it? What were the origins of and motivations for their customs?

The cultural history of the pumpkin starts thousands of years ago with a small, round fruit the size of a hardball. Without hyperbole, one can say that the planting of the first pumpkin (*Cucurbita pepo*) seed was one of the most significant acts in American history. The pumpkin was possibly the first plant in the Americas that people brought in from the wild, cultivated, and bred for human use. Planting pumpkins marked a major shift from nomadic hunting and foraging to a settled, agricultural way of life, propelling the development of large-scale settlements.

Initially, Native Americans living across North and Central America gathered wild pumpkins, squashes, and gourds that thrived in moist soils near rivers and creeks. Archaeologists have found no wild progenitor of the orange field pumpkin, but they have discovered its oldest domesticated seeds at Guilá Naquitz, a cave in Mexico's Oaxaca highlands. The seeds date from 10,000 to 8,000 years ago, 2,000 years earlier than the oldest corn or bean seeds yet found.[5] About 5,000 years ago, American Indians living in eastern North America independently domesticated a related group of yellow and green squashes (also *Cucurbita pepo*), from which zucchini, patty pan squash, acorn squash, and ornamental gourds originated.[6] Butternut squash and winter crookneck (*Cucurbita moschata*) developed from different strains. Their oldest remains, uncovered in northwestern Mexico, date back 6,900 years.[7] Buttercup and Turk's turban squashes and ancestors of giant pumpkins (*Cucurbita maxima*) did not enter North America until the eighteenth century, when they arrived on the eastern seaboard aboard ships from South America.[8] Cucumbers and melons, the sweeter and more succulent members of the Cucurbitaceae family, are native to India and Asia, respectively, and were an established part of European diets before American colonization.[9] The domestication of cucumbers and melons dates from at least 4,000 years ago.[10]

The ancient ancestors of the pumpkin were small, hard-shelled orbs about three to four inches in diameter. Although Americans today commonly refer to the pumpkin as a vegetable, it is by definition a fruit, because, like apples and berries, it is a seed packet encased in flesh and develops from a flower. Precolonial Native Americans used hard-shelled gourds for containers and even musical instruments, but they raised pumpkins and squash for food. Because the ancient fruit was thin and bitter, Indians probably first gathered and planted it for its seeds. Over the centuries, agriculturists selected and bred plants for larger seeds and sweeter, fleshier fruit.[11] Why, one wonders, was one of their first projects in plant domestication a small, hard, bitter fruit? If the seeds were higher in nutritional quality, then why did they breed for the flesh?

One currently popular thesis regarding the origins of agriculture is that ancient foragers desired abundant, reliable, and stable food supplies, whether in times of stress or times of security.[12] Some scientists believe that people chose pumpkins because they added variety to the diet.[13] Others contend that pumpkins and squashes were early domesticates because of their ease of propagation.[14] In the river valleys of the Americas, pumpkins sprout quickly and produce abundant crops at prodigious rates. The pumpkin, by its very nature, drew the attention of early horticulturists.

The evolution of the pumpkin from the hard, bitter orb to the fleshy pumpkins and squashes that the Indians gave Captain John Smith and other European explorers and settlers is not fully mapped out. It was a long process involving thousands of years of agricultural experimentation and adaptation.[15] Scientific data on the prehistoric development of pumpkins, squashes, and gourds are continually being updated as ethnobotanists develop new research methods and make new archaeological findings. As a result, dates and trajectories of plant movements seem as elusive as the plant varieties themselves.

In the American Southwest, by 2500 BCE Indians were cultivating the Mexican trinity of corn, beans, and squash (of which the field pumpkin is one variety), but the crops were latecomers in other parts of the continent.[16] Indian communities in what is now the eastern United States initially domesticated native plants such as summer squash, but by the end of the Mississippian period, about 1200 CE, they also grew corn, winter squash, pumpkins, and beans, which they had obtained through travel or trade.[17] In an 1876 interview, Esquire Johnson, a Seneca Indian from New

York State, offered an example of how historic crop exchanges worked. His ancestors had eaten nearly "unpalatable" wild squashes until soldiers returning from "ancient wars with the southern Indians" brought back sweeter and more succulent varieties. "All these things they found on their war expeditions and brought them here and planted them and thus they abound here," he explained.[18]

By the time Europeans arrived on American shores in the late fifteenth century, the Cahuillas and Pueblos in the far Southwest, the Cherokees in the Southeast, the Ojibwas along the Great Lakes, the Mandans of the Great Plains, and the Iroquois in the Northeast all propagated the vegetables. Pumpkins and squashes were never major parts of the diets of Indians of the Pacific Northwest, which was rich in other food sources, nor were they important among many of the nomadic groups, which lacked permanent settlements, but they still traded for squashes and pumpkins.

Descriptions of the Indians' propagation and use of pumpkins of various shapes, colors, and sizes were common in European travel accounts of North America.[19] Christopher Columbus recorded seeing *calabazas* in Cuba on his voyage of 1492.[20] Cabeza de Vaca, during his trip along the Florida coast in 1528, noted that "maize, beans and pumpkins [grow] in great plenty."[21] In describing the Iroquois and Ottawas in the Great Lakes region around 1670, the French Jesuit Claude Allouez reported, "All these Nations have their fields of Indian corn, squashes, beans, and tobacco."[22]

Relying on the words and images of non-Indian observers to describe native traditions has its perils because of historical prejudices against American Indians.[23] Nevertheless, such writings are some of the few means available for documenting colonial Indian customs. By all accounts, many Indian communities relied on squashes and pumpkins as basic food sources, crops second only to corn in Indian economies, oral traditions, and rituals. Pumpkins and squashes were dependable, prolific, and, in many opinions, tasty. Although Indians believed all natural objects were sacred, their origin histories and ceremonial lives attest that they considered pumpkins and squashes especially so because the fruits were so vital to their diet and therefore to their survival. Yet while all forms of squash had a special status among Indian crops, the orange field pumpkin had no special status among squash. American Indians from Canada to Florida cultivated, prepared, and thought about the field pumpkin no differently from any other squash.[24]

And with good reason. The pumpkin is botanically indistinguishable from summer and winter squashes and from gourds. They all belong to the *Cucurbita pepo* species, which means they can crossbreed, producing a mix of forms. That happens at the time of pollination. Most cucurbit plants are monoecious, meaning that both male and female flowers form on the same stem. A tiny round fruit at the base of the female flower differentiates it from the male flower. The white and yellow tubular-shaped flowers require pollination by bees or other insects, unless a grower manually pollinates them. Bees can travel up to ten miles between fields, which can lead to cross-pollination of fruits.[25] When someone discriminates one type from another, therefore, the definition is based on common custom rather than natural fact.

Judging from historical descriptions and archaeological evidence, Indians in eastern North America propagated field pumpkins, gourds, patty pan squash, yellow summer squash, acorn squash, and various intermixed forms of winter and summer varieties. The motley collection of New World squashes ceremoniously set at the foot of an Indian leader in a 1621 engraving from Caspar Plautius's *Nova Typis Transacta Navigatio* vividly depicts both the variety of squashes and the esteem in which American Indians held the vegetable in the seventeenth century, as well as the fascination it engendered in Europeans. In the illustration, the leader's regal air derives not only from his tall turban and long cape but also from the large quantities of pumpkins and squashes that encircle him. The ring of dancers surrounding the royal personage and his bounty signal the high status of both man and crops.

The way Indians named plants helps put the colonists' cultural classifications, and our own, in perspective. The linguistic record offers some clues that Indians differentiated between summer squash, which have more tender flesh and ripen in early summer, from winter squash, which have harder, thicker rinds and ripen in autumn. In the Algonquian language, pumpkins and squash were called *isquoutersquash* or *askutasquash*, from which the word *squash* is derived.[26] The term means "to eat raw" and more likely connotes a summer squash than a winter one. In describing the crops that Indians propagated in coastal Rhode Island in the 1640s, Roger Williams noted, "Askuta squash, their vine apples, which the English from them call squashes, are about the bigness of apples of several colours . . . sweet light wholesome refreshing."[27] According to reports by

Plate from Caspar Plautius, *Nova Typis Transacta Navigatio,* 1621. The ring of dancers surrounding this Native American leader and his bounty of squashes and pumpkins signal the high status of the man and the crops. Yet American Indians at the time of European contact had no special reverence for the orange field pumpkin. Courtesy Smithsonian Institution Libraries, Washington, D.C.

Captain John Smith, who lived in Virginia from 1606 to 1609, and Robert Beverly, who visited the colony in 1705, southeastern Indians used the word *macocks* to identify summer squash.[28] Thomas Hariot, in 1585 Virginia, reported that the local Indians used the term *macoqwer* or *macocks* for "several forms called by us Pompions, Mellions, and Gourds."[29] It was difficult, in other words, for non-natives to document Indians' perceptions of the differences among squashes. Still, there is no indication that Indians imagined an orange field pumpkin differently from other winter squashes that filled the same dietary and medicinal needs.

Many pumpkin and squash producers, such as the Iroquois and Hurons of the Great Lakes region, the southern New England native communities, and the Choctaws in the Mississippi Valley, lived in semipermanent villages. In the early 1600s, French Jesuits reported that Huron towns near Quebec each contained 50 to 100 houses, with 20 towns located in a 25-mile radius.[30] Many of the settlements were probably mere shadows of their former selves. Diseases introduced by the Europeans and their livestock, including a viral hepatitis epidemic lasting from 1616 to 1619 and a smallpox epidemic in 1633 along the East Coast, decimated Indian populations. Some researchers estimate that foreign viruses killed up to two-thirds of native populations as the viruses spread across the continent.[31]

Before the period of major dislocation, most Indian peoples followed an annual pattern of movement. In both the Northeast and the Southeast, agricultural production was often part of a mixed economy of hunting, fishing, trading, and gathering. Communities commonly moved from winter homes in protected lowlands to summer residences that abutted farmland and water sources for fishing: the Great Lakes in the case of the Iroquois and Hurons, and the Atlantic coast and its estuaries in the case of the southern New England and some Virginia Indian communities. Farmland was communal in most Indian societies, but many groups recognized private use and privileges over specific lots.[32] Men were responsible for the major clearing of the land before cultivation, and women were in charge of crop and food production. The Indians' shared practice of multicropping fields, their gender division of farm labor, their lack of fencing and clear property lines, and their consumption of pumpkin and squash were anathema to the new European residents, just as the Europeans' appearance, social customs, and farming traditions were to the Indians.[33]

The Iroquois nicknamed squash, corn, and beans De-o-ha-ko, the "Three Sisters," and the Onondagas named them Tune-ha'kwe, meaning "Those We Live On," because of the crops' significance as economic and dietary staples and because of the interconnected ways in which the Indians used them.[34] Nicolas Perrot noted in about 1700: "The kinds of food which the savages like best, and which they make most effort to obtain, are the Indian corn, the kidney-bean, and the squash. If they are without these, they think they are fasting, no matter what abundance of meat and fish they have in their stores."[35] Pumpkins and squashes were probably some of the first seeds Indians planted in the spring and the last crops they harvested in the fall, because of the plants' long growing season—up to 125 days for winter varieties, in comparison with 75 days for corn. Like squashes and pumpkins, corn and beans are easy to cultivate and produce large yields per acre. Together, they provide complementary nutrition and flavors. Furthermore, squash plants have a symbiotic relationship with corn and beanstalks.[36] Each contributes beneficial nutrients to the

[Handwritten margin note, top right]: Pumpkin not special enough to outweigh the diseases

[Handwritten margin note, middle right]: Sacred Trinity / Why always 3??

[Handwritten margin note, lower right]: But they saw only squash. Pumpkin not yet born

soil, and each serves a practical use for its partners. Cornstalks can serve as vertical poles on which bean and squash vines can climb, conserving space in the field. In turn, the canopy created by the broad leaves of the squash plants helps prevent the spread of weeds that can impede the corn and beans' growth.

Samuel de Champlain described the Indians' multiple cropping technique while he was in and around Quebec in the 1610s. He wrote, "With the corn they put in each hill three or four Brazilian beans, which are of different colors. When they grow up, they interlace with the corn, which reaches to the height of from five to six feet; and they keep the ground very free from weeds. We saw there many squashes and pumpkins, and tobacco, which they likewise cultivate."[37] Like Smith, Champlain separated pumpkin from squash, but he did not state how or why he, or Indians, did so, nor did he indicate what he meant by "pumpkin." Like the other travelers, he could just as likely have meant a crookneck winter squash.

Theodore de Bry's 1590 engraving of the Indian village of Secotan, on Roanoke Island in present-day North Carolina, is probably the first visual depiction of an American pumpkin patch. De Bry based the print on one of many drawings John White made during his trip with Thomas Hariot to document the Virginia colony six years earlier.[38] The pumpkin patch is at the center of what the artists portrayed as a vibrant and stable agricultural community. Huts line one side of a central pathway and dense cropland the other. Villagers are seen both at work and at play. Some are in the woods hunting with bows and arrows, some tend a fire, others sit down for a meal, and one group participates in a ceremonial dance. The plot that White had left bare but identified as "wherein they use to sow pompions," de Bry filled with massive, round, orange pumpkins and deep green foliage.[39] The illustration suggests the significance of the pumpkin to Virginia Indians' livelihoods, the wonder with which Europeans viewed the vegetable, and its importance as a distinguishing feature of the Americas.

In most Indian communities it was as common for corn, beans, and squash to share a cooking pot as it was for them to share a plowed field.[40] A half-cup of cooked pumpkin has fair nutritional value, with approximately forty-one calories, significant amounts of vitamin A, and lesser levels of vitamin C, iron, and potassium.[41] Although corn was "the sole

Theodore de Bry (Belgian, 1528–1598), *The Towne of Secot*, engraving, 1590, made from a watercolor drawing by John White (English, c. 1540–c. 1593), 1585–86. Because of the pumpkin's importance in many American Indians' diets, it figured prominently, along with corn and beans, in many creation stories. Library of Congress Rare Book and Special Collections Division, Washington, D.C., LC-USZC4-5267.

stuff of life," as the Jesuit priest Hierosme Lalemant noted in the 1640s, pumpkin and squash were nearly as ubiquitous at meals.[42] They could be counted on to fill a soup pot when fish did not jump or corn did not grow. When the French missionary Gabriel Sagard stayed in a village on Lake Huron in 1623 and 1624, some residents offered him soup for which, he observed, "one first cooked some shredded meat or fish, together with a quantity of squash, if so desired."[43] Nicolas Perrot reported that the Indians of the Great Lakes had "in especial a certain method of preparing squashes with the Indian corn cooked while in its milk, which they mix and cook together and then dry, [a meal] which has a very sweet taste."[44]

Another style of preparing pumpkins was to roast them, either whole, halved, or sliced, in the hot cinders of a fire.[45] Louis Armand Lahontan wrote, "Commonly they are baked in ovens, but the better way is to roast 'em under the Embers as the Savages do."[46] Indians also boiled pumpkin into a thick, savory sauce.[47] They pounded dried pumpkin into flour, combined it with a sweetener and suet, baked it in a pan, and served it as bread or cake.[48] Thomas Hariot mentioned that Indians in Virginia added ground nuts to cooked pumpkin to make it taste better.[49]

One of the greatest assets of pumpkin and winter squash was their ability to be preserved over the winter, when other food items were scarce. Jesuit sources from the 1630s to the 1720s noted the lack of meat in Indians' diets.[50] Probably reflecting earlier traditions, Father Joseph Lafitau remarked in 1724 that the Iroquois stored pumpkin in bark-lined underground pits, where "their fruit keep perfectly sound during winter."[51] In their memoirs from the 1680s and 1690s, the Frenchmen Lamothe Cadillac and Pierre Liette recalled how Indians near the Great Lakes preserved the vegetable for winter use.[52] Indians scraped out the pumpkin to remove the seeds and stringy innards. They then cut it into slices, strung the slices together, and hung them from racks to dry in the sun. The dried pumpkin provided lightweight, convenient nourishment on trips. Packed like beef jerky, it could be carried for months with little fear of spoilage.

The famous Philadelphia botanist John Bartram offered a rare report of Indians living along the Eastern Seaboard eating squash flowers in the 1740s. Western tribes fried the fresh or dried flowers and ate them alone or used them as flavoring in soups, but these practices seem to have been less common in the East than in the Southwest.[53] While visiting the Onondagas, members of the Iroquois confederacy, in New York in 1743, Bartram ate a meal of "three great kettles of Indian corn soup, or thin hominy, with dry'd eels and other fish boiled in it, and one kettle full of young squashes, their flowers boiled in water and a little meal mixed." "This dish was but weak food," he editorialized.[54] Like most native foodstuffs of the time, pumpkins and squashes served a dual function as nourishment and medicine. Cherokees and Iroquois consumed the ground seeds to provoke urination, treat kidney ailments, and rid the intestinal system of worms. Other Indians applied the crushed seeds, pulp, and leaves to flesh wounds, making use of nearly all the components of the plant for their health and nutrition.[55]

When the French missionary Jean de Brébeuf, at the Huron village of Ihonatiria, remarked in 1636 that "the squashes last sometimes four and five months, and are so abundant that they are to be had for almost nothing," he summed up the vegetable's value as a commodity to Indians.[56] Squashes and pumpkins did serve as objects of trade among Indian peoples, as Esquire Johnson noted, and between Indians and Europeans, as attested by reports of French colonists in Louisiana bartering European goods for pumpkins in the early 1700s. Yet squash never acquired the exchange value that corn did.[57] Corn was vital not only as a foodstuff but also as a central currency, especially after the arrival of Europeans.[58] Indians valued pumpkins and squashes less for their exchange value than as trustworthy food sources that they could count on when other foods failed.

American Indians' oral traditions chronicle the meanings Indians ascribed to pumpkins and squashes and the deep reverence they felt for them. Although it is difficult to date these stories, they presumably flourished in the precolonial and colonial eras, when pumpkin and squash production thrived in the East. Many American Indian creation stories portrayed the earth as a mother, and some communities depicted corn, beans, and squash as her daughters. For the Iroquois, each of the three plants was a guardian spirit that, if separated from the other sisters, would perish.[59] They perceived squash as a life-sustaining force and personified the vegetable as a maiden of great beauty. According to one tale, the Great Spirit created the squash and her sisters at the beginning of time to provide food to sustain the human race.[60] In another Iroquois creation tale, the Great Spirit walked the earth in the guise of a woman. Wherever she stepped, squash sprang up on her right, beans on her left, and corn in her footprints. In still another tale, corn and squash sprouted from the body of a sacred being or from the grave of a deceased woman. Seneca and Huron variations of this oral tradition have squash sprouting from the woman's abdomen and head.[61]

Squash was a sacred ingredient in the Green Corn ceremony, a thanksgiving rite among the Iroquois and Cherokees that predates the colonial period.[62] The Iroquois also held an annual feast of squash. To indoctrinate the Indians, the Jesuit missionary Jacques Marquette tried to construe their 1672 squash festival in terms of his own religious beliefs. He noted: "I cheerfully attended their Feast of Squashes at which I instructed them and called upon them to thank God, who gave them food in abundance while other tribes, who had not yet embraced Christianity, had great difficulty in preserving themselves from hunger."[63]

John Bartram, during his visit to the Onondagas, recorded in his journal the following story:

[margin note: Women are associated with squash, although important to men esp] We perceived a hill where the Indians say corn, tobacco, squashes were found on the following occasion: An Indian [whose wife had eloped] came hither to hunt, and with his skins to purchase another [wife]. Here he espied a young squaw alone at the hill; going to her, and inquiring where she came from, he received for an answer that she came from heaven to provide sustenance for the poor Indians and if he came to that place twelve months after he should find food there. He came accordingly and found corn, squash, and tobacco, which were propagated thence through the country, and this silly story is religiously held for truth among them.[64]

This version of the Onondagas' origin story conveys the significance of pumpkins and squash in their cosmology, the depth of belief in the vegetable's ties to the birth and survival of their culture, and the chronicler's cultural biases. The Onondagas derived deep meaning from pumpkins and squashes because of the vegetables' significance in their daily sustenance. And like all other Indian communities, they considered a field pumpkin to be just another squash. — *[margin note: You said they differentiated earlier!!]*

American Indians introduced the pumpkin to European explorers and colonists, who regarded it with the same mix of wonder and disdain with which they viewed much of North America. Just as they envisioned many Native American cultures, animals, and plants, so the colonists interpreted squash and pumpkins in terms of what was familiar to them. After the vegetable arrived in Europe, botanists and lay people alike developed a lexicon and uses for American pumpkins and squashes that suited Europeans' definitions of nature, their taste in art, their common foodways, and their perceptions of the Americas.

[margin note: European Cultural Fascination] The word *pumpkin* originated in Europe. It is a derivation of the French *pompion*, which comes from the Latin *pepo,* meaning to ripen, or "cook by the sun."[65] In his 1727 *Practical Kitchen Gardiner*, Stephen Switzer explained that the word *pumpkin* had "several Greek roots which imply its aptitude to grow large and swell well."[66] Before Europeans colonized the Americas and encountered American varieties of pumpkins and squashes, a pompion connoted to them a large fruit, melon, or gourd. The

Roman naturalist Pliny the Elder stated, "When the cucumber acquires a very considerable size, it is known to us as the '*pepo*'."[67]

Along with being one of earliest sources for the pumpkin's linguistic heritage, the ancient Romans established the use of the pumpkin as an astonishingly consistent comical motif for the politician. Instead of canonizing the emperor Claudius after his death, the Roman satirist Seneca transformed him into a pumpkin. In the title of his ode to the emperor, the famous poet playfully substituted the Latin term *apocolocyntosis*, meaning "pumpkinification," for *apotheosis*, meaning deification.[68] Seneca intended the twist to demean Claudius by reducing him to a pumpkin— an empty-headed fruit. The classical scholar A. Palmer wrote that Seneca portrayed Claudius as "a paralytic, pedantic, foolish and cruel man."[69] This Roman legacy survived, and the label "pumpkinhead" has never lost its force as a word to insult a politician.

Europeans resurrected ancient Greek and Roman cultural traditions in the fifteenth and sixteenth centuries, at the same time they expanded their reach around the world. As a result, the images and ideas of the pumpkin depicted in Renaissance works of art, literature, and botanical dictionaries—otherwise known as "herbals"—melded ancient concepts, uses, and botanical types with new ones based on overseas encounters. The profusion of herbals was a response to Europeans' renewed appreciation of ancient cultures, to innovations in the printing press, and to the expansion of worldwide exploration, which added considerably to the catalog of plants.[70] Herbals contain plant descriptions and illustrations, along with medicinal and practical uses for each specimen. Returning voyagers disseminated the first American pumpkin and squash seeds and specimens as exotic gifts to royal sponsors within twenty-five years of Columbus's landing on American soil in 1492. Eventually the seeds circulated to botanists and local market vendors.[71]

In an attempt to bring some order to the overwhelming number of new plants seen by European explorers, herbalists often attempted to fit new discoveries into old prototypes.[72] Europeans initially used terms for the better-known melons and cucumbers interchangeably with terms for the American-type pumpkins and squashes. Jacques Cartier referred to the American varieties he observed on his travels in the 1540s as *gros melons*.[73] Sixteenth-century botanical descriptions and illustrations of fruits that resemble American pumpkins and squashes variously carried

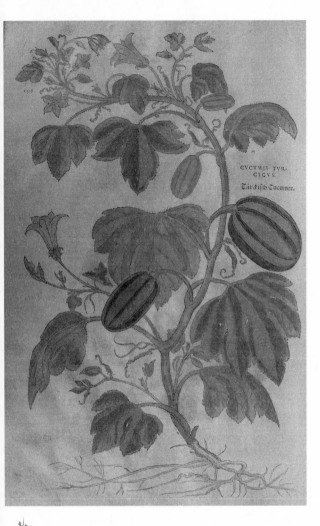

Cucumis turcicus (Turkish cucumber), illustration in Leonhard Fuchs, *De historia Stirpium* (Basel, 1542), 698. This is one of the earliest depictions of an American pumpkin by a European botanist, although Fuchs based its name on what was familiar to him. Courtesy Peter H. Raven Library, Missouri Botanical Garden.

Why and don't trust botanists

the appellations *Melopepo compressus, Pepo maximus oblongus, Cucurbita indica rotundus, Cucurbita major,* and "*Millions or Pompions.*"[74] The generic, oval-shaped, ribbed fruit labeled *Cucumis turcicus* (Turkish cucumber) in Leonhard Fuchs's 1542 herbal *De historia Stirpium* resembles many forms of American squashes and African melons and illustrates the ambiguous and overlapping definitions of newly introduced and more familiar varieties.[75] *Turkish* or *turkie* was a generic term identifying any plant that was exotic in Europe. Europeans at the time often called American corn, or maize (from the Spanish *maiz* after the Taino *mahiz*), "turkie wheat."[76]

Please don't tell me turkey derived from this,

In some cases, as is likely with Fuchs's depiction of the American pumpkin, the naturalists had no actual specimen before them. Their botanical descriptions might have been based on a word-of-mouth exchange rather than firsthand observation. With no other frame of reference, they defined or characterized new specimens by what was familiar to them. In *Theatrum Botanicum*, John Parkinson bemoaned his peers' inconsistencies, complaining of "our modern writers who confound *Pepo*, *Melopepo*, and *Cucurbita*, so promiscuously that it is not possible to find out the distinct certaintie of them all, for some make that *Pepo* that others call *Melopepo*, and others, *Cucurbita*."[77]

Herbalists almost never adopted American Indian terms for the native American vegetables. A rare exception was John Gerarde, in his 1633 herbal, which included "Virginia Macocke or Pompion" as a synonym for *Pepo indicus minor rotundus* (small round Indian pumpkin).[78] Either few colonists knew of the Indian terminology or few cared. This narrow worldview would prove disadvantageous to the colonists, who would initially see American crops through European eyes and suffer the consequences.

Most herbalists relied on the Aristotelian method of description, which divided the world into four elements—earth, fire, air, and water—which in turn corresponded to the four humors—dry, hot, cold, and moist.[79] According to this system, all objects in nature were made up of a combination of the four elements. Sickness was caused by an imbalance in the humors; administering the opposite of the "bad humor" could restore health. For example, the herbalist John Gerarde wrote that the pumpkin was "little, thin, moist and cold (bad, saith Galen). . . . The fruit boiled in milke and buttered, is not onely a good wholesome meat for man's body, but being so prepared, is also a most physicall medicine for such as have an hot stomacke, the inward parts inflamed. The flesh or the pulpe of the same sliced and fried in a pan with butter, is also a good and wholesome meat: but baked with apples in an oven, it doth fil the body with flatuous or windie belching."[80] Although a field pumpkin had blander flesh and a longer growing season than a sweet melon, both were edible when ripe, both had cool and moist properties, and both were rather large fruits. These similarities help explain why Europeans adopted known terminology for the newfound fruit.[81]

Europeans' appetite for new American foods was indifferent at best, and their attitude toward the pumpkin was no exception. It is unclear why Europeans were slow to accept pumpkins and other New World products, such as potatoes, tomatoes, and corn, as part of their diet.[82] Simple unfamiliarity could be one explanation. Another reason might have been Europeans' general queasiness about eating fruits and vegetables. Although the importance of plant products in combating deficiency diseases such as rickets and scurvy was well known, these foods were also known to cause stomach ailments and sickness. In the 1560s, it was even forbidden to sell fresh fruit in the streets of London.[83] Remhert Dodoens's 1586 herbal noted that the pumpkin "eaten rawe and unprepared is a very unwholesome foode, as Galen saith, for it cooleth and chargeth, or lodeth the stromache and overturneth and hurteth the same, by stirring up the pain thereof. But being boiled, baked or otherwise . . . it is not to hurtfull, for it doth coole and moisten the hot and dry stomach, slacketh thirst and cooleth the belly, nevertheless it nourisheth butte little."[84] To avoid the hazards of raw or spoiled produce, most people across Europe cooked or overcooked fresh foods. One-pot meals and stews made with bread, vegetables such as cabbage, onions, and carrots, and (for the lucky ones) meat or fish were common fare for most Europeans, from north to south. Wealthier members of society indulged in more meat and exotic ingredients from abroad.[85]

Europeans valued pumpkins and squashes, like many other products of nature, for food and for medicine. One herbalist recommended eating the seeds for colic.[86] A pile of American pumpkin flowers displayed alongside other edible fruits and vegetables in Vincenzo Campi's 1580 painting *The Fruit Seller* indicates that Italians ate the flowers in this time period, as they do today.[87] On the other hand, the absence of American pumpkins in sixteenth-century Dutch cookbooks, which were expressions of upper-class tastes and culinary habits, hints at either the pumpkin's general lack of appeal or its association with the lower class. *The Shepherd's Demand*, published in Brugge (now in Belgium) in 1513, reported that pumpkins were foods that rural peasants ate.[88]

Just as they admired tomatoes as ornamental plants before they appreciated their culinary uses, many Europeans initially valued the image of the pumpkin more than its meat.[89] During the sixteenth century, artists from Italy to the Netherlands found deep symbolism as well as humor in the prolific vegetable. Their pumpkin imagery was malleable, but it

Giuseppe Arcimboldo (Italian, 1527–1593), *Autumn*, 1573. Oil on canvas, 76 by 63 centimeters. Arcimboldo's portrait of this pumpkin-headed man and William Shakespeare's depiction of Sir John Falstaff as a "gross watery *pompion*" in *Merry Wives of Windsor* transformed the pumpkin from a simple vegetable into a symbol of a man's dimwittedness and self-aggrandizing. Inv. RF1964-32, Louvre/Art Resource, N.Y.

pivoted around the central theme of being on the edge of civilization. As a sign of human nature, the pumpkin embodied unbounded lust or lack of civility; as a symbol of a place, it represented the untamed natural bounties of North America; and as an emblem of a way of life, it stood for a rustic peasant existence. Each cultural meaning informed the others and people's appetites for pumpkins as well.

The first depiction in Europe of an American orange field pumpkin appeared in the frescoes of the Villa Farnesina in Rome, created between 1515 and 1518.[90] Robust, ribbed pumpkins ranging in color from orange to gray fuel the verdant imagery of nature's bounty and fertility in a scene that celebrates the mythical love affair of Psyche and Cupid. The Italian artist interpreted the pumpkin's exuberant size and reproductive capacities as signs not only of nature's abundance but also of human sexuality.

In the tradition of Seneca's "pumpkinification" of Claudius, the Italian painter Giuseppe Arcimboldo, in his famous vegetable compilation portraits, equated the American field pumpkin with a man's mental capacities or the lack thereof. In both *Autumn* (1573) and *Vertumnus-Rudlof II* (c. 1591), Arcimboldo paints an assortment of garden produce to form the outline and features of a man's head and torso. In *Autumn*, the man has a pumpkin head, and in *Vertumnus-Rudlof II*, a pumpkin heart or chest. The artist's strategic placement of the pumpkins suggests his commentary on his subject's empty brain and empty heart. His clever intermingling of human and natural forms highlights their shared qualities. The portraits confounded and delighted the artist's contemporaries and later generations of scholars. Interpretations of these vegetable portraits have ranged from allegories of the universe to "serious jokes" about the Habsburg monarchy.[91]

In a similar vein, William Shakespeare, in his *Merry Wives of Windsor*, written about 1600, characterized Falstaff, who drank and ate too much, as "this unwholesome humidity, this gross watery *pumpion*."[92] (Shakespeare might have had in mind the Asian melon rather than the American pumpkin, for the names and meanings were interchangeable at the time.) Both Arcimboldo and Shakespeare made the pumpkin something to laugh about. They attributed human qualities to the pumpkin, giving it a personality and ascribing its physical traits to a man, making him an empty-headed lout, a man without culture. The artists gave the pumpkin meaning beyond its mere flesh.

Dutch genre painters of the sixteenth century, like the Italian fresco artists, exploited the pumpkin's natural attributes to represent the bounty of nature. Like Shakespeare and Arcimboldo, they also made the vegetable a sign of uncultured behavior, though of a different sort. Instead of associating the pumpkin with men's heads and a lack of intellect or refinement, Dutch artists made it a symbol of peasant women's bodies, sexuality, and unguarded lust. They also more broadly crafted the pumpkin as a totem of a poor, rustic way of life within a rapidly developing urban and merchant society. In the sixteenth century, the Netherlands was a center of economic expansion and imperialism, an international force in the marketplace, and the home of some of the largest and most cosmopolitan cities in the world. The era is known as a golden age of prosperity.[93] The demand for religious art all but vanished as the Protestant Reformation forced out the Catholic Church, which had filled the lavish interiors of its cathedrals with paintings and sculptures. In the early sixteenth century,

[handwritten margin note, top left:] The image of the Pumkin is somehow related to...

[handwritten margin note, middle left:] Common in Europe. All classes relate to foods

[handwritten margin note, lower left:] The head of most body of women, church. Thinks (?)

[handwritten inline note:] Also why it is not a food for the rich?

the Protestant churches that gained power preferred more austere settings for worship. As a result, artists turned to the new class of merchants as patrons as well as to more secular subjects.[94]

At the same time, Dutch urban expansion created ready-made markets in which farmers could sell their goods. Land reclamation projects and extensive canal systems enabled farmers to get their produce to urban markets cheaply and efficiently.[95] Artists such as Pieter Aertsen (c. 1508–75) and his nephew and apprentice, Joachim Beuckelaer (c. 1534–75), were part of an art movement that portrayed the work and pleasures of the peasant classes. These paintings are rich in physical detail and wit. Scenes of the everyday lives of common, rural people were not so much tributes to the rustic peasants themselves as devices by which to celebrate material wealth, communicate moral lessons and literary aphorisms, and illustrate artistic skill. As one historian explained it, artists employed the rustic motif to highlight their own artistic abilities—to demonstrate how they could turn even something as plain and simple as peasant farmers into something great.[96]

A common motif, which appears in paintings such as Aertsen's *Market Scene with Vegetables and Fruit* (1569) and Beuckelaer's *Vegetable Market* (1569), is a buxom peasant woman surrounded by a bountiful harvest. Cabbages, carrots, turnips, apples, cucumbers, peas, and large, eye-catching field pumpkins and squashes overflow from giant baskets and spill haphazardly toward the viewer in an exuberance of natural abundance. The meticulous and realistic style of these genre paintings led some historians to claim that they were "truthful" reflections of peasant life in this time period.[97] Yet as in medieval illuminations, the grouping of produce such as peaches and pumpkins, which ripen at different times of the year and could not have appeared in the markets together, suggests that the images had allegorical meanings. The paintings were visual puns illustrating proverbs from emblem books—collections of old adages and riddles, which were popular at the time—and they made allusions to classical satires that were familiar to most middle-class art patrons. They also communicated more overt moral lessons about the hazards of material wealth and overindulgence.

Staged alongside the women and their voluptuous fruits and vegetables are scenes of sexual titillation and innuendo. In many paintings, men lurk in the background, gazing at the female peddlers and their goods. In

Joachim Beuckelaer (Dutch, 1533–1574), *The Country Market*, undated. This painting is typical of many sixteenth-century Dutch genre paintings in its portrayal of rustic peasant women alongside voluptuous pumpkins and squashes in scenes of sexual titillation and innuendo. Museo Nazionale di Capodimonte, Naples, Italy; Alinari/Art Resource, New York.

Beuckelaer's *The Country Market* (undated), one woman turns seductively toward the viewer, and the other leans toward a male admirer who rests a hand on her breast. The women's open, inviting gestures are as alluring as the succulent pumpkins and melons. In Jean Baptiste Saive's *Market Stall* (1594), a female produce merchant sits surrounded by her bounty. She points one hand to a child and another to a pumpkin, both products of her labor. A man leans suggestively toward her. An embracing couple in the background echoes their encounter.

Like their farm produce, the women are objects of desire and fertility. They are more harlots than goddesses, unlike the mythical and benevolent Earth Mother figures, such as the ancient Greek Gaia and the American Indian Three Sisters. The paintings are playful reminders of the sins of unbounded lust and sexual promiscuity. Rustic peasant women

Welcome to Christianity

communicated these themes well because they seemingly lived closer to nature in the countryside and supposedly were less inhibited and restrained by social mores than middle-class urbanites.[98] Other paintings of the period, such as Johannes Vermeer's *Woman Reading a Letter* (c. 1662–63), which depict women writing letters and maintaining tidy houses, reflect the relatively high status of women in Dutch society, a consequence of their authority and responsibilities in the home.[99] Pumpkins and other produce are absent from these more tranquil, middle-class domestic scenes. Holding pumpkins and cabbages rather than books, as in the market scene paintings, underscored women's eroticism, their reproductive capacity, and their natural drives, which pushed beyond the limits of social decorum and propriety. The pumpkin's sexual development from a female flower, its impressive growth rate, its fertility, and its pregnant-belly-shaped fruit evoked a more libidinous behavior.

At the time when Beuckelaer and Saive painted, even scientists associated women with pumpkins. In keeping with the Doctrine of Signatures, which contended that the physical shape or appearance of a plant or animal was an indication or sign of its use, function, and meaning, the herbalist John Parkinson suggested in the 1630s that the juice of a pumpkin be "applied to private parts to restrain the immoderate lust of the body.[100] Apply opposite to create, same to destroy.

What made the pumpkin a medical antidote for "immoderate lust," an icon of fecundity in Italian frescos, a symbol of rusticity in Dutch genre paintings, and a sign of dimwittedness in Shakespeare's plays was not only its natural attributes and its uses in Europe but also its Americanness ties—its cultural associations. After no more than a handful of Europeans had set foot on North American soil, they seized on the pumpkin as the continent's emblem. It symbolized both the natural wonders of the continent and its perceived primitiveness, because the pumpkin was prolific, unwieldy, and used by Indians. Many Europeans conceived of North America as a paradise of lush vegetation, a virgin land just waiting for civilized people to conquer it and harvest its riches.[101] Captain John Smith noted that other continents were "beautiful by the long labor and diligence of industrious people and Art. This is onely as God made it."[102] Many imagined it as a desolate wilderness that, with faith and ingenuity, could be turned into a garden. Yet as the Englishman George Withers noted, it was a "rude Garden" nonetheless.[103]

We are
Pumpkin

In texts and illustrations, almost nothing was small or ordinary about the North American continent, its inhabitants, or its flora and fauna.[104] Explorers and settlers described its plants and animals in exaggerated proportions, portraying them as bigger and more exotic than they were in reality. William Wood, in *New England's Prospect*, was one of many writers to offer a remark along the lines of "Whatsoever grows well in England grows as well there, many things better and larger."[105] Reports from explorers hired by commercial trading companies extolled the natural abundance and the opportunities that the rich resources promised. De Soto wrote in 1539 that pumpkins in Florida were both "larger and better than those of Spain."[106] Robert Beverly stated, "Their Pompions I need not describe, but must say they are larger and finer, than any I ever heard of in England."[107]

Theodore de Bry's 1591 engraving of the Carolina coast for his *Brevis Narratio*, an account of European explorations of the Americas, echoed the travelers' sentiments.[108] Disregarding scale, the artist filled the landscape with naked Indians pursuing stags, a rafter of turkeys, dense forestland, and two oversize pumpkin plants bearing voluptuous ribbed fruit.[109] De Bry's central placement of pumpkins in his iconic image of North America attests to the vegetable's powerful hold on Europeans' imaginations and its strength as a symbol of the continent.

Pieter Cornelisz van Rijck's *Market Scene* (1622) could almost be retitled *New World Harvest,* because it contains nearly the same plants and animals as de Bry's scene, but van Rijck sets them in a Dutch produce stall.[110] The painting helps illustrate the conceptual and actual leaps of the pumpkin from one continent to the next. Among six oversize field pumpkins and three winter squashes is a pile of Jerusalem artichokes and a live turkey (both also native to the Americas), which dominate the otherwise typical market scene. Van Rijck might have been simply chronicling the use of the native American products in Dutch kitchens at the time. Yet because playing with symbols was one of the genre's main intentions, he more likely chose the animals and vegetables for what they represented—an archaic world.

What European travelogues and visual depictions make clear is that it was not just the pumpkin's natural proclivities that inspired its meanings and uses, but its cultural history as well. Europeans envisioned the pumpkin as inhabiting a symbolic and tangible place on the edge of civilization.

Theodore de Bry, *They Reach Port Royal*, engraving in *Brevis Narratio*, 1591. This illustration of the Carolina coast features objects of nature native to the Americas that intrigued Europeans, including, in the center of the picture frame, the pumpkin. De Bry's depiction of the pumpkin mimics Fuchs's *Cucumis turcicus* illustration, suggesting that de Bry based his drawing not on firsthand observation but on Fuchs's herbal. Library of Congress Rare Book and Special Collections Division, Washington, D.C., LC-USZ62-380.

The pumpkin itself and its land of origin helped inspire the imagery. The sullied associations and pragmatic uses of the pumpkin that developed in Europe before the permanent settlement of the American colonies would shape the immigrants' appetite for the vegetable as much as their hunger would.

TWO

"THE TIMES WHEREIN OLD POMPION WAS A SAINT"

From Pumpkin Beer to Pumpkin Pie, 1600 to 1799

WITH HERBALS IN HAND AND LITTLE MORE THAN HOPE TO GUIDE them, those who took the leap and set off for North America were not fully prepared for the dramatic adjustments they would have to make upon their arrival. When the first English colonists landed on the continent's shores in the early seventeenth century, they had a few mementos and provisions but otherwise little except cultural baggage to sustain them. It was not enough. In a land where native peoples thrived on a plentitude of plants and animals, many colonists suffered because they could not imagine eating the native pumpkins, corn, and shellfish. "Between human beings and foodstuffs in the natural environment," the historian John Bennett wrote, "there exists a cultural screen, which modifies and controls the selection of available food."[1]

Accustomed to a diet of domesticated meats and their by-products, along with European grains and root vegetables, the colonists were unfamiliar with and in some cases repulsed by the wild and cultivated products they encountered. They had both feet on the American continent, but their customs and worldviews were still firmly planted on the other side of the Atlantic. Edward Johnson noted in the 1650s that "a want of English graine, wheat, barley and Rie proved a sore affliction to some stomachs, who could not live upon Indian Bread and water, yet they were compelled to it till Cattle incr'd, and the plows could but go: instead of Apples and Pears, they had Pompkins and Squashes of divers kinds, their lonesome condition was very grievous to some, which was much aggravated by continual fear of Indians' approach."[2]

Equated to a dietary niche

32

The pumpkin's colonial history offers a view of how early Americans thought about and made use of the new natural resources available to them and how they saw themselves in comparison with their Indian neighbors and their way of life back home. Rather than thinking of the pumpkin as merely something to eat, colonists made it a symbol of their identity, separate from that of the world they had left behind. The "lonesome condition" that Johnson identified with the pumpkin—survival in the wilderness and dependence on local resources—while a sign of desperation to Europeans, came to be a point of pride to the colonists. By the time of the Revolution, Americans had turned the pumpkin and pumpkin farming into meaningful emblems of American independence and cultural identity.

But that transition in thinking was a long way off at the time of the first landings. Those initial months on the continent were chaotic for the English colonists. They lacked proper shelter, knowledge of the local environment, and the ability to obtain food. Without the Indians' help, they would not have survived. John Smith recalled of the Virginia colony that "had the salvages not fed us, we directlie had starved."[3] Indians provided the new arrivals with meat, grain, and produce and taught them how to procure the same.[4] Travelers commented on Indians' hospitality, for their custom was to greet visitors with generous amounts of food. Indians made squash and pumpkin common components of their welcoming feasts, because the vegetables were readily available and perhaps also because they had special status as food items. From what is now upstate New York, the Dutchman Harmen Meyndertsz van Bogaert noted in the 1630s, "A woman came to meet us bringing us baked pumpkins to eat.... [We] ate heartily of pumpkins, beans and venison, so that we were not hungry, but were treated as well as is possible in their land."[5] The colonists did not always reciprocate. Edward Winslow's account of the creation of the Plymouth colony described how, in the winter of 1620, settlers stole caches of corn that local Indians had buried for their own winter use.[6] And William Bradford recalled in *History of Plymouth Plantation*, "Others fell to plaine stealing both night and day from ye Indians, of which they grievously complained."[7]

The Pilgrims—and the Indians, judging from Winslow's and Bradford's comments—had something to celebrate when the settlers produced their first successful harvest in the autumn of 1621. Although most

Americans commemorate the festivities as the first Thanksgiving in the land, the Pilgrims themselves would not have considered the occasion a Thanksgiving Day at all. Instead, they thought of the feasting and games as a harvest fête, and the antithesis of the way they observed Thanksgiving Day. In the Pilgrims' time, Thanksgiving was a day of devotion and reflection on God's benevolence during which merriment was specifically disallowed. People were more likely to fast than to feast.[8] Church or civic leaders proclaimed public days of thanksgiving in response to particular events, such as a military victory, the safe passage of a ship, or the arrival of rain, and not on an annual basis or in connection with the fall harvest. The Pilgrims' celebration was also hardly the first of its kind; many predated it. The Spanish explorer Francisco Vázquez de Coronado held a similar feast with local Indians in present-day Texas in 1541. The French Huguenots held a day of thanks after their safe arrival in Florida in 1564. And the English settlers at Jamestown held a solemn Thanksgiving commemorating their successful passage to Virginia in 1619. The commemoration of the Pilgrims' celebration as the first Thanksgiving has less to with historic fact than with national mythologies created generations later.

The English festival Harvest Home was a more likely progenitor of the Pilgrims' event than Thanksgiving, although the chroniclers of the first Plymouth celebration made no mention of the customary Harvest Home parade and effigy figures. Pious Pilgrims might have deemed these rituals too pagan and sacrilegious to include in their event because of their pre-Christian roots. The Hebrew harvest festival known as Succot, or Festival of the Tabernacle, as described in the Pilgrims' well-worn Bibles, also might have been their inspiration. But Bradford and his followers did not necessarily have to turn back to old sources brought from home. Their Indian neighbors, who charitably introduced the colonists to many new customs and goods, might have shared their harvest traditions as well. In any case, no one recorded anything about eating pumpkin at the feast, and pumpkin pie was not the celebrated finale of the Pilgrims' "Thanksgiving" holiday, as later stories would have it.

Whether or not the Pilgrims served pumpkin that day for dinner, the vegetable was a ubiquitous part of colonial life. No evidence exists that colonists in the seventeenth century bred any new pumpkin varieties, but they defined them in new ways, altered their culinary uses, and ascribed new meanings to them. More than a hundred years after Europeans first encountered the pumpkin, their descendants on both sides of the ocean still could not quite get a handle on how to categorize it. They indiscriminately called any and every form of squash a *pompion*. John Parkinson's 1629 herbal *Paradisi i Sole* offers an example, defining a pompion as a "fruit, which is very great, sometimes of the bigness of a man's body, and oftentimes lesse, in some ribbed or bunched, in others plaine, and either long or round, either green or yellow, or gray, as Nature listeth to shew herselfe; for it is but waste time, to recite all the formes and colours may be observed in them."[9] Thomas Hariot, when he wrote that "several forms are of one taste and very good, and do also spring from one seed," recognized the propensity of pumpkins, squashes, and gourds to produce different varieties on the same plant due to cross-pollination.[10]

The color orange, one of the most common physical traits by which Americans identify pumpkins today, played no part in colonial taxonomy. Sources are more likely to define pumpkins as green. John Gerarde's 1633 herbal described the "great round *pompion*" as "oftentimes of a greener colour with an harder barke" than the "great oblong *pompion*."[11] In Joseph Tournefort's 1719–30 *The Compleat Herbal*, the "common pumpkin [has] a hard and lignous Rind, of a green or dark green colour, spotted with white or striated and a soft, white and sweetish pulp, not altogether so insipid as a gourd."[12] One explanation could be that the green pompion was not an American pumpkin at all but a melon or cucumber. Another is that these writers described the fruit in its immature state, before it turned yellow or orange. Jean de La Quintinie's 1699 *The Compleat Gard'ner* supports this assertion: "There are two sorts of Pumpions, the Green and Whitish, but neither of them are fit to be gather'd till they be grown Yellow and the skin becomes tough enough to resist ones nail."[13] The Count de Lahontan's description of a vegetable "as big as our Melons; and their Pulp is as yellow as Saffron," from around 1684, however, closely matches that of a field pumpkin.[14] *A(red): B(orange) — Men are color blind*

Great size, not color or shape, was the most noteworthy characteristic of pumpkins in this time period. Pumpkins, explained La Quintinie, "are the biggest Productions which the Earth brings forth in our climates."[15] John Josselyn referred to the watermelon as "a large fruit, but nothing near so big as a Pompion."[16] Underscoring its value for basic sustenance rather than for display, observers considered pumpkins remarkable not just for the size of their individual fruits, as many people do today, but also for the quantity of fruits produced by a single plant. In *A True Discourse of the Present State of Virginia*, Ralph Hamor noted that pumpkins "propagated in [such] abundance that a hundred were frequently observed to spring from one seed."[17] And Philip Miller wrote with awe in *The Gardener's Dictionary*: "I have measured a single plant which had run upwards of 40 feet from the Hole, and had produced a great Number of side-Branches; so that if the plant had been encouraged, and all the side-Branches permitted to remain, I dare say it would have fairly overspread 20 Rods of Ground which, to some people, may seem like a Romance; yet I can affirm it to be fact."[18] ~Alice ~ *Reason for importance: Fertility*

Many of the native American food items cataloged by Edward Ward, an English traveler to New England in the late 1600s, which included "Fish, Fowl, Bear, Wild-cat, Raccoon, Deer, Oysters, Lobsters roasted or dry'd in Smoke ... Ind-corn, Kidney beans boil'd, Earth-nuts, Chest-nuts, Lilly-roots, Pumpkins, Milions, [and] divers sorts of Berries," would have been utterly foreign to the early European inhabitants.[19] In *New England's Plantation*, Francis Higginson noted in 1630, "The countrie aboundeth naturally with store of good roots of great variety and good to eat.... Here are also store of pumpions, cowcumbers, and other things of that nature which I know not."[20] Until the settlers acquired ample stores of European seeds and livestock, they had to depend on these local resources or perish. Colonists did not eat some foods, however, such as the potato and the tomato, until they were first accepted in Europe. One culinary change that probably elated most settlers was their increase in meat consumption in the colonies. In Europe, wild game was beyond the reach of most people. Hunting wild animals was a privilege reserved for the aristocracy. In the American colonies, wild creatures were literally fair game to anyone who was a good shot.

Since the pumpkin's reputation in Europe was uninspired at best, the colonists might have eaten the vegetable less because they were fond of it than because it grew almost effortlessly and produced high yields. In his 1648 *Good News from New England*, Edward Winslow wrote that "pumpkins there hundreds are." And a colonial song reportedly dating from 1630 expresses how extensively they were put to use:

Instead of pottage and puddings and custards and pies
Our pumpkins and parsnips are common supplies

Aussies don't diff Pump+Sqush, so how do we know

We have pumpkins at morning and pumpkins at noon
If it was not for pumpkin, we should be undone.[21]

In keeping with European culinary traditions, the typical way colonists prepared pumpkins or any other vegetables, even leafy greens, was to boil them down to a thick sauce called "porrage" or pudding, or to toss them into meat stews.[22] Pumpkin pudding was similar to apple butter, although it was both savory and sweet. John Josselyn's 1671 *New-England's Rarities* contains one of the oldest surviving pumpkin recipes, which he called "an ancient New England Standing Dish":

> The Housewives' manner is to slice them when ripe and cut them into dice, and so fill a pot of them of two or three gallons, and stew them upon a gentle fire for a whole day, and as they sink, they fill again with fresh Pompions, not putting any liquor to them; and when it is stew'd enough, it will looke like bak'd Apples; this they Dish, putting Butter to it, and a little Vinegar (with some Spice, and Ginger, Etc.) Which makes it tart like an Apple, and so serve it up with Fish or Flesh: It provokes Urin extremely and is very windy.[23]

The one-pot meal or stew was as common among colonists as among the Indians. Both dishes relied on similar technologies—an open fire and a cooking pot. Instead of the traditional wheat bread, cabbage, and onions that sustained them in Europe, many early colonists made do with Indian succotash, which, in the words of Ralph Hamor, who visited Virginia in 1615, was "a mess of boiled beans, maize, and pompions."[24] The versatile pumpkin could serve simultaneously as cooking vessel and entrée. Parkinson's herbal noted that this method required the cook to "take out the inner watery substance with the seeds, and fill up the place with pippins [apples], and having laid on the cover which they cut off from the toppe, to take out the pulpe, they bake them together."[25] During his visit to New England, Edward Ward wrote rather condescendingly about the colonists' great consumption of pumpkins in the early years of settlement. He commented, "Their provisions (till better acquainted with the Country) being only Pumkin, which they'd cook'd as many several ways, as you may Dress Venison: And is continued to this Day as a great dish amongst the English. Pumpkin Porrage being as much in esteem with the New England Saints, as Jelly Broth with Old-English Sinners."[26]

Most of the first colonists, even if skilled as merchants or craftsmen and aspiring to something more than a homestead in the woods, had to grow corn and pumpkins full-time until the colonies established dependable stores of food.[27] In imitation of the Indians, colonists often planted pumpkins in cornfields. The vegetables were convenient and abundant by-products of the corn crop, the most important early colonial food commodity. John Winters, a Maine farmer, noted in the spring of 1634 that his five-acre farm was "all set with corn and pumpkins."[28] Settlers also planted pumpkins in kitchen gardens with other plants and herbs to use for home consumption instead of to sell in the marketplace.

Initially, farming was a communal enterprise in both the North and the South. Colonial governments attempted to sustain communal economic systems, but private self-interest thwarted their success. Once the colonies were stable and the inhabitants beyond starvation, residents began seeking remuneration for moving to America. When prospects of gold vanished, they turned to animal and vegetable products for sources of wealth and gain. In the South, the original plan to have colonists contribute their crops to a communal repository failed. Land was opened up for private purchase and use, which led to the development of the large-scale plantation economy. In some instances, Virginians barely produced enough food to sustain themselves, because profits from cash crops such as tobacco proved much more enticing.[29]

The northern colonies developed different landscape and economic patterns. They were colonized as religious and social utopias as well as profit-making enterprises. In the North, families broke up the original *landschaft* system, an old European town plan in which communal fields farmed for the common good surrounded a central town, because the settlers preferred to stake out claims of their own.[30] Northern farms, unlike those in the South, remained small-scale, family-run operations because of poorer soil and climate and because settlement patterns remained more centrally controlled. New Englanders, however, were arguably no less interested in profit than their neighbors to the south.[31]

Remarkably, within a quarter century after their founding, the colonies prospered. By 1642, 15,000 acres were under tillage in Massachusetts, and 12,000 head of cattle were being raised.[32] In Virginia, the population soared from 2,500 in 1630 to more than 15,000 by 1642.[33] Between 1650 and 1675, the English population in all the British colonies reached 110,000, whereas the combined population of Plymouth and Virginia in 1624 had been a mere 1,525.[34] The rapid growth from both new immigration and native births created a ready market for farmers and traders. Colonies began to export goods. In the South, tobacco and rice brought the greatest returns. In the North, with its shorter and more inclement summers and less productive land than in the South, timber, livestock, and furs were of primary importance. Wheat was paramount in the middle colonies. The social and economic fabric of colonial life transformed as the opening up of international markets, improved mobility, and the increase in individual enterprises interconnected isolated rural enclaves.[35] There was also more than enough to eat. Pork, beef, milk, wheat, peas, and barley were daily pleasures, no longer dreams of the hungry. Edward Ward wrote in 1699 that pumpkins "were the chief Fruit that supported the English at their first settling of these parts. But now they enjoy plenty of good Provisions."[36]

Pumpkin remains a subsistence food. To decorate with it is to live in comfort

The market that developed for other American crops never materialized for the pumpkin, and the vegetable is hard to find in colonial business accounts. A document titled "Manufacturer and Other Products Listed in the Rates on Imports and Exports Establish'd by the House of Parliament," dated June 24, 1660, notes the export of corn, beans, onions, and potatoes from the colonies, but no pumpkins.[37] Robert Johnson's *Nova Britannia*, a commodities report published in 1609, ignored native products altogether, listing only more familiar crops, such as oranges, almonds, and rice, introduced from Europe.[38]

The pumpkin's cultural affiliations, not just its bland meat, undercut its popularity. Within a few decades of the founding of Jamestown and Plymouth, dining on native pumpkins instead of standard European fare was a sign of dire circumstances, the "lonesome condition" that colonist Edward Johnson mentioned in 1654.[39] Instead of being a food of necessity, it became food for the poor, as it had been in Europe for some time. Europeans ridiculed the pumpkin and the people who ate it as boorish and crude, the antithesis of cultured society. The famous seventeenth-century herbalist John Gerarde called a pumpkin "food utterly unwholsome for such as live idly; but unto robustious and rustick people nothing hurteth that filleth the belly."[40] The herbalist John Parkinson wrote that "the poore of the

Citie, as well as the Country people, doe eate thereof, as a dainty dish."[41] The melon and cucumber were "of much esteeme . . . with all the better sorts of persons; and the [pompion] is not wholly refused of any, although it serveth most usually for the meaner and poorer sort of people."[42]

Many people thought of melons and pumpkins as markers not only of social classes but also of cultural differences between Europeans and American colonists. By accusing Puritans of having "pumpkin-blasted brains," Nathaniel Ward, in his 1647 New England satire *The Simple Cobler of Aggawam in America*, adapted the historic symbolism of Shakespeare's Falstaff and Arcimboldo's pumpkin-headed emperor to ridicule those who had picked up and moved from old England to New.[43] "Pumpkinhead" was a common term of ridicule for colonists.[44] The lowly status of American pumpkin eaters was garnered, in part, from the colonies' image as a cultural backwater. Many Europeans deemed America's early immigrants to be misfits and social outcasts, among them the anarchistic Puritans and Quakers, who challenged social and religious order, and the inmates and roustabouts who were indentured servants and Virginia pioneers. After observing Americans' great consumption of pumpkins during his travels, Edward Ward remarked sarcastically that Americans "have wonderful Appetites, and will Eat like Plough-men; tho very Lazy and Plough like Gentle-men. It being no rarity there, to see a Man Eat Till he sweats and work till he freezes."[45]

People on both sides of the Atlantic identified the pumpkin with crude and unruly behavior and with unchecked human desires. When Pilgrims journeyed to North America to live among what they considered wild men and beasts, they offered proof of their faith and sacrifice. Yet they directed their fears not just toward external dangers but also toward threats from within. They worried that living alone in the wilds, beyond the order of society, might provoke the colonists' wild natural desires and urges. Pious Pilgrims chastised someone who pursued earthly delights or passions rather than more godly and virtuous paths—who, for example, celebrated Thanksgiving with feasts and revelry instead of fasts and prayers—as a worshiper of "St. Pompion."[46] Calling someone a disciple of St. Pompion—a believer in a lowly, laughable vegetable—was also a means of degrading the Anglican dogma and faith.

Two paintings offer visual evidence of the sort of untamed prospects a pompion conjured up for people living in the seventeenth century.

Giovanni Benedetto Castiglione's 1645 *Earth's Fertility* portrays the pumpkin as a symbol of both nature's benevolence and its menace.[47] In the painting, Ceres, the goddess of fertility or grain, holds a cornucopia of fruits and vegetables in one hand and, with the other, points to a cauliflower, an overripe and bursting melon, and, most prominently, a massive orange field pumpkin. The produce represents the natural wealth of the earth that nurtures and sustains humanity. Standing with one foot on the pumpkin, however, is one of several centaurs. The gesture symbolically links the vegetable to these half-men, half-beasts, which embody lust and primal natural drives. The centaurs—and by connection the pumpkin—represent decadence and debauchery, the tawdry side of nature and of people. *We linked the pumpkin with older mythologies, thus it now draws up our imagination*

Bambocciate (Childishness), an undated painting by the Italian artist Faustino Bocchi, pictures the pumpkin's wild nature even more dramatically.[48] The painting is reminiscent of Hieronymous Bosch's work in its portrayal of tiny figures in chaotic mayhem. Bocchi depicts dozens of wild little creatures fighting with abandon in a gruesome battle. Central to *still seen in fiction today* the frenzied scene is a towering pumpkin fortress. Some dwarfs scale ladders to its carved-out windows, others rush its rounded doorway, and one dwarf sits triumphantly atop its stem. By making the pumpkin the object of these beastly little nymphs' desires and conquests, Bocchi imbues the vegetable with the qualities of their world, which is disorderly, unruly, and uncivilized. Both images resonate with the feral qualities of "St. Pompion" and with the popular vision of the pumpkin's native land as, in the words of William Bradford, a "howling wilderness." "The whole countrie," he said, "full of woods and thickets, represented a wild and savage hew."[49]

St. Pompion might call to mind a jack-o'-lantern to readers now, but the pumpkin's transformation into the Halloween totem lay many years in the future. Evidence of colonial Halloween celebrations is scant, although Halloween was a fixture on the annual calendar in many parts of Europe. Known as All Hallow's Eve, the holiday blended the traditions of the ancient Celtic festivities called Samhain, signifying the onset of winter, and the Catholic holidays of All Souls Day and All Saints Day, dating from the ninth century.[50] All Hallow's Eve, or October 31, marked the time when supernatural spirits and ghosts wandered about. During the festivities, participants set bonfires to ward off the evil spirits and offered gifts of food to placate them. In Europe, instead of pumpkins, people displayed hollowed-out turnips lit by candles from within to signify souls lost in purgatory. The holiday was a time of misrule, masquerades, and pranks, when omens were at their most powerful. By the time of the Plymouth landing, the revelry characteristic of Halloween had fused with that of Guy Fawkes Day, a holiday celebrating the foiling of the Gunpowder Plot to blow up the British Parliament on November 5, 1605, and, more generally, the Protestant takeover of Catholicism in England, shifting the holiday toward secular rather than occult or religious meanings.

Catholic colonists of Maryland and Anglican colonists of the South recognized All Hallow's Eve in their church calendars, but the Puritans in the North abhorred both the pagan ritual and Catholic rites as violations of their Calvinist principles.[51] Belief in an active spirit world and the supernatural, however, never lost their hold on New Englanders' imaginations. The Salem witch trials are the most famous example, but every colony had statutes to punish practitioners of magic, and most farmers used astrological charts to guide their planting, plowing, and harvesting.[52] Although Halloween was not much celebrated and St. Pompion was yet to metamorphose into the jack-o'-lantern, the St. Pompion image foreshadowed the pumpkin's later incarnation. For many colonists, the pumpkin represented the holiday's central themes—it was the unsettling face of wild and unruly nature, which could be found in both the world around them and the spirit within them.

A few, like Edward Johnson, contested these disparaging characterizations of the pumpkin. He declared in his 1654 *Wonder-Working Providence of Sions Savior in New England,* "Let no man make a jest at Pumpkins, for with this Fruit the Lord was pleased to feed his people to their good content, till Corne and Cattel were increased."[53] For colonists like Johnson, the pumpkin embodied the more pastoral and bucolic qualities of nature and a primitive way of life. As early as the 1650s, those uneasy about the expansion of cities and industrial development (who were the same group that sought upward mobility) valued the pumpkin as an icon of the simpler, more natural existence they supposedly had left behind.[54] Less than fifty years after the landing at Plymouth, Benjamin Thompson editorialized on the region's state of affairs with a nostalgic look back at the first New England colonists. In the poem "New England's Crisis," he wrote:

The Times wherein old Pompion was a Saint,
When man's far'd hardly yet without complaint
On vilest cates, the dainty Indian maize
Was eat with clamp-shells out of wooden trayes
Under thatent Hutts without the Cry of Rent,
And the best sauce to every Dish, Content
When Flesh was food and hairy skins made coats . . .
when cinmels were accounted noble blood
Among tribes of common herbage food. . . .
These golden times (too fortunate to hold)
Were quickly fin'd away for love of gold.[55]

Thompson described "The Times wherein old Pompion was a Saint" as at once difficult and deprived yet hardy and moral. By referring to "cinmels" (another term for pumpkins and squashes) as royalty among edible plants, perhaps he meant that the pumpkin was a savior when people had little else to eat. He could also have meant that the colonists were living so primitively that their saints were mere pumpkins. Yet instead of calling on the humble pumpkin to criticize uncivilized behavior, as the Puritans did, or to celebrate the colonists' progress, the poet used it to critique society's corruptive "love of gold." He viewed the pumpkin as the antithesis of economic prosperity and modernity, but in a romantic light. By associating the pumpkin with "golden times," Thompson imbued it with the qualities of Elysian fields. He equated it with the mythical, halcyon days before capitalism reigned and greed and avarice were paramount. This interpretation of the pumpkin is just a glimmer of what would become the vegetable's strongest meanings in American culture.

These sentimental ideas did not resonate with southerners as much as they did with northerners, even though pumpkins were grown in the South as in the North. Perhaps because the southern colonies were founded primarily as economic enterprises rather than religious or communal utopias, southerners did not share northerners' nostalgia for the formative early settlement days.[56] For southerners, expanding markets and entrepreneurialism were signs of progress, whereas for some New Englanders these changes meant falling away from the colonies' founding ideals. Northern colonists took notice of the pumpkin because its great size and production rate offered not only feasts for starving bellies but also a strong, vibrant, and unforgettable maternal symbol of these common ideals. Europeans might have made fun of pumpkins and the people who ate them, and some colonists even chided one another as followers of St. Pompion, yet there was something about the pumpkin that was unlike any of the other natural resources that expanded colonial markets and built colonial cities—something with which New Englanders identified. The pumpkin meant something that simple economics could not explain but that would one day make it a valuable commodity. That something was a sense of identity rooted in an agrarian world. Neither corn, tobacco, nor furs carried the pumpkin's symbolic weight.

In the eighteenth century, colonial settlements and economic enterprises stabilized and prospered. The drive for commercial success was predicated on the exploitation of human labor and the land's seemingly limitless natural resources. Populations diversified as Africans toiled as slaves on the plantations of the South and as Germans, Irish, and Scots-Irish immigrants joined English and Dutch farming communities in the North and West. Conservation measures to protect forests in the North reflected at least a limited awareness of the effects of commerce on the land and people.[57] Indians who had survived persistent epidemics still outnumbered Euro-Americans east of the Appalachian Mountains, but warfare, epidemics, and expanding white settlement were displacing them to the west.

While international trade in rice, tobacco, fish, furs, and wheat made family fortunes, there was no profit in pumpkins. Overseas commerce was the route to prosperity, and little demand existed for the American vegetable. In the produce business, pumpkins still sat at the bottom of the market. For example, a long list of vegetable seeds advertised in the March 8, 1793, edition of *Maryland Journal and Baltimore Daily Advertiser* included turnips, carrots, and kale, but not pumpkins.[58] In the late eighteenth century, George Washington grew pumpkins at Mount Vernon—not for sale or for his own consumption but as food for his slaves, an indication of the fruit's low social status.[59] The English herbalist Philip Miller summed up contemporary attitudes toward pumpkins this way: "These plants require so much room to spread, and their Fruit being very little valu'd in England, hath occasioned their not being cultivated amongst us; we having so many Plants, Roots, or Fruits, which are greatly preferable to those for Kitchen Uses; but in some parts of

America, where provisions are not in so great variety, these Fruits may be very acceptable."[60]

Exactly what defined a pumpkin was still difficult to pin down. Jonathan Carver's convoluted phrase, "the melon or pumpkin, which by some are called squashes," reflects the continued overlapping and imprecise descriptions of pumpkins and squashes in the late colonial era.[61] Peter Kalm, one of Carl Linnaeus's students, who traversed the American eastern seaboard in the 1740s, catalogued "pumpkins of several kinds, oblong, round, flat or compresses, crook-neck, small, etc.," leaving the impression that a pumpkin was any number of different forms of squash.[62] With the publication of *Systemae Naturea* in 1735, Linnaeus revolutionized the natural sciences by establishing a standardized classification system that is still in use today, but even he could not bring clarity to the confusing world of the pumpkin.[63] Linnaeus organized the natural world into animal, plant, and mineral kingdoms, which he subdivided into a hierarchy of classes, orders, genera, and species. Abandoning the vague and competing identifications and nomenclature based on earlier notions of Aristotelian humors, the Doctrine of Signatures, and practical functions, he and other scientists relied on morphology, or physical form and structure. In the case of plants, morphology included the basic forms of leaves, vines or stalks, seeds, and fruits. Later scientists designated species not only by their shared forms but also by their ability to crossbreed and produce offspring.[64]

Linnaeus grouped pumpkins, melons, cucumbers, squashes, and gourds all within the order (later family) Cucurbitaceae, or gourds, because, to state it very generally, they shared lobed leaves, oval seeds, monoecious flowers, vines with tendrils, and large, seed-bearing fruits.[65] He established a universal naming system based on a specimen's genus and species, a system known as binomial nomenclature—hence, *Cucurbita pepo*, which encompassed the field pumpkin and other varieties of squashes and gourds. But scientists also classified what were popularly known as pumpkins, summer and winter squash, and gourds into three other species: *Cucurbita moschata, C. maxima,* and *C. ovifera*. They identified no distinct botanical trait or separate species for a field pumpkin.[66]

To add to the confusion, what looked like different types, such as field pumpkins and summer squashes, could crossbreed and produce new forms altogether. In 1716, Cotton Mather described a humorous incident involving pumpkins' and squashes' propensity to cross-pollinate. According to his story, a friend's garden outside Boston was periodically robbed of squashes. "To inflict a pretty little punishment on the thieves," Mather explained, his friend "planted some gourds among the squashes (which are in aspect very like them) at certain places which he distinguished with a private mark, that he might not be himself imposed upon. By this method, the honest man saved himself no squashes by ye trick; for they were so infected and embittered by the gourds that there was not eating of them."[67] Sorting out a clear definition of a pumpkin sounds confusing because it is. The main point is that no botanical difference exists between a pumpkin and other forms of squash. The distinctions Americans have made are based on cultural ideas, not objective evidence.

The shifty nature of the pumpkin family was perhaps one reason pumpkin farming was not a moneymaking venture. The vegetable's value lay in the kitchen cellar, not in the marketplace. Americans raised pumpkins primarily to feed their families rather than to garner wealth. The lack of a market for pumpkins was partially a reflection of the domestic food economy at the time. In the seventeenth and eighteenth centuries, most Americans lived on farms and produced almost all their own food. Wealthy colonists obtained luxury items such as spices and alcoholic spirits through trade, but even the elites produced meat, fruits and vegetables, and beverages at home. In her journal chronicling a trip from Boston to New York in 1704, Sarah Kemble Knight noted that a New Haven justice "had gone into the field with a Brother in office to gather his Pompions," and both Thomas Jefferson and George Washington procured their own harvests, albeit through slave labor.[68]

The ability of pumpkins and squash to thrive in a variety of environments encouraged people to grow and consume them throughout the colonies in spite of the prejudices against the vegetable. Pumpkins were as ubiquitous in Maryland and Virginia as in Massachusetts and Connecticut. British officer Thomas Anburey reported from New York in 1787, "The inhabitants plant great quantities of squashes, which is a species of pompions or melons; the seed of it [is] cultivated with assiduity."[69] Peter Kalm noted in the 1740s, "Each farmer in the English plantations has a large field planted with pumpkins, and the Germans, Swedes, Dutch, and other Europeans settled in their colonies plant them."[70] Indian communities relied on pumpkins and squash as much as ever. Attributing a scarcity of wild game to overhunting, the Jesuit Sieur Aubry stated in 1723 that the Iroquois in and around his Quebec post "seldom have any food but Indian corn, beans, and squashes."[71] After a raid on an Iroquois village in 1779, one soldier noted in his diary: "The fields contain about one hundred acres beans, cucumbers, simblens, watermelons and pumpkins in such quantities (were it represented in the manner it should be) would be almost incredible to a civilized people."[72]

Journals and letters from as far south as Georgia and the Carolinas noted the propagation of pumpkins for domestic consumption.[73] John Lawson recalled seeing "pompions yellow and very large" while touring North Carolina around 1700.[74] One traveler described a South Carolina farm on which forty-five acres were planted in rice for the market, and another forty-five acres were "sowed with Indian Corn, Pease, Pompions, Potatoes, Melons, and other Eatables, for the Use of the Family."[75] Pumpkins were so prodigious in the South that one family in South Carolina named its rice plantation "Pompion Hill."[76] Because New Englanders had fewer varieties of fruits and vegetables to choose from in their colder northern climate, they might have depended on pumpkins more than Southerners. Still, the plant was a common part of farm life throughout the colonies, North and South.

Although few Americans in the twenty-first century can imagine an autumn festival without hundreds of pumpkins resting on haystacks and strewn in fields, corn and wheat, not pumpkins, were historically at the center of American harvest celebrations.[77] Of the few accounts that document community harvest festivals in the colonial period, not one mentions a pumpkin as the symbolic core of the event, even though the vegetable had been used historically as an icon of nature's bounty. By making grain the focus of their festivities, American settlers adhered to traditions long established in Europe. Over many generations and across broad regions, farming communities celebrated the last grain harvest of the season with feasting, dancing, and other merrymaking, along with grain maiden figures or effigies, farming competitions, and the symbolic reenacting of harvest events such as the ritualized cutting of the last sheaf of wheat. Their purpose was to commemorate the good fortune of a bountiful harvest and give thanks to the religious deity who provided it. Like the Pilgrims' and Indians' 1621 celebration; the festivals celebrated the results of a long season's labor and the blessings of an ample store of food.

A Frenchman traveling in Virginia around 1700 considered the harvest season to be the time of "the principal festivals of . . . rejoicing" in that colony.[78] He noted that it was "the custom of the country" to have a big communal feast after the last corn was brought in from the fields. Despite Puritans' dour reputation, they still apparently enjoyed a good party, especially if it came in the guise of work.[79] In *A Trip to New-England*, Edward Ward noted that "husking Ind-corn, is as good sport for the Amorous Wag-tailes in New England, as Maying amongst us is for our Youths and Wenchs."[80] At the end of the 1700s, the poet Joel Barlow described similar festivities in his poem "Hasty Pudding." He wrote: "For now, the corn-house filled, the harvest-home, / The invited neighbors to the husking come; / A frolic scene, where work, and mirth, and play / United their charms to chase the hours away."[81] Communal events brought men and women together not just for work but also for romantic pursuits. The celebration of nature's fertility aroused human desires as well. But even though Europeans historically associated pumpkins with sexuality and fertility, and the colonists made pumpkins a common part of their diet, no one mentioned them in the few records that document these harvest events. In the colonial harvest celebrations, corn was queen, not the pumpkin.

Colonial Americans continued a steady consumption of pumpkins in the eighteenth century because they were inexpensive to produce, grew like weeds, and were durable and versatile as a foodstuff. When people had no apples for pies, barley for beer, or meat for supper, they could substitute the prolific pumpkin. Paul Dudley explained the appeal:

Among the remarkable Instances of the Power of Vegetation, I shall begin with an Account of a Pumpkin Seed, which I have well attested, from a worthy Divine. The Relation is as follows: That in the Year 1699, a single Pumpkin Seed was accidentally dropped in a small Pasture where Cattle had been fodder'd for some Time. This single Seed took Root of itself, and without any Manner of Care or Cultivation; the Vine run along over several Fences, and spread over a large Piece of Ground far and wide, and continued its Progress till the Frost came and killed it. This Seed had no more than one Stalk, but a very large one ; for it measured eight Inches round; from this single Vine, they gathered two hundred and sixty Pumpkins; and, one with another, as big as an half

Peck, enough in the Whole, to fill a large Tumbrel, besides a considerable Number of small and unripe Pumpkins, that they made no Account of.[82]

In addition to its massive output, the pumpkin's late harvest time and its hardiness encouraged its use in the kitchen. Jonathan Carver, during his travels in America in the late seventeenth century, observed: "The crane-neck, which greatly excels all the others, are usually hung up for a winter's store, and in this manner might be preserved for several months."[83]

Peter Kalm provided a good synopsis of the pumpkin's versatility in the eighteenth-century colonial kitchen.[84] Although the cooking methods he described reflect European tastes and habits, American Indian influence is also strongly evident. Kalm reported:

> The French and the English also slice them and put the slices before the fire to roast: when they are done they generally put sugar on the pulp. Another way of roasting them is to cut them through the middle, take out all the seeds, put the halves together again and roast them in an oven. When they are quite done some butter is put in, which being imbibed into the pulp renders it very palatable. The settlers often boil pumpkins in water, and afterwards eat them alone or with meat. Some make a thick pottage of them by boiling them in water and afterwards macerating the pulp. This is again boiled with a little of the water, and a good deal of milk and stirred about while it is boiling. Sometimes the pulp is kneaded into a dough with maize and other flour; of this they make pancakes. yum Some make puddings and tarts of pumpkins.[85]

One source in 1770 noted that Indians in Pennsylvania were "very particular in their choice of pumpkins and squashes, and in their manner of cooking them. The women say that the less water is put to them, the better the dish they make, and that it would be still better if they were stewed without any water, merely in the steam of the sap which they contain."[86] Another technique called for baking the shell in cabbage leaves and then serving the pumpkin whole, with cream poured into the middle.[87] Colonial cooks freely interchanged pumpkins and squash in their recipes. They might specify one or the other but were not consistent.

Besides serving as an entree or a side dish, the adaptable pumpkin made a ready substitute for a multitude of other ingredients. Like Kalm,

Carver observed that Americans used pumpkin "partly as a substitute for bread."[88] Whiter, lighter bread made from refined wheat flour was most desirable. In contrast, heavy, dark breads made from barley, rye, cornmeal, or pumpkin connoted more rustic tastes. Sarah Knight, even though she was hungry after a day's travel, once turned down a tavern's fare, saying, "[We] would have eat a morsell ourselves, But the pumpkin and Indian-mixt bread had such an Aspect."[89] If pumpkin bread did not suit someone's fancy, there were "pompion chips" to whet their appetite. "To make Pompion Chips," a South Carolina recipe book from the 1770s explained, "shave your pumpkin thin with a plain and cut it in slips about the width of your finger, put shreds of Lemon peel among it, wet your sugar with orange Juice and boil it into syrup. Then put in your chips and lemon Peal and let them boil until done."[90] A farmer from the Carolinas constructed an outbuilding, called a "pumpkin house," just for the purpose of drying pumpkin to prolong its longevity and diversify its uses.[91] Kalm remarked of dried pumpkins, "I own they are eatable in that state, and very welcome to a hungry stomach."[92]

Some cooks boiled dried pumpkin down into a thick paste and used it to flavor and sweeten dishes.[93] Throughout the eighteenth century, only the wealthy could afford white cane sugar imported from the West Indies. Shipments arrived in the form of eight- to ten-pound cones, called loaves, that diners shaved off sparingly with sugar shears. As with grains, the whiter and more refined, the better.[94] Molasses, a cheaper by-product of sugar refining, was a common ingredient in many kitchens. At the less desirable end of the sweetener scale were locally produced maple syrup, honey, and pumpkin. They were consumed throughout the colonial period because of the prodigious cost of imports. Sweeteners and spices were important not just as flavorings but also as food preservatives and as ingredients in distilled beverages. The main spices used today for pumpkin pie, including cinnamon, nutmeg, ginger, cloves, and allspice, were also common ingredients in colonial kitchens, and were used to flavor meats, fruits, and vegetables alike.[95] Like molasses, the spices were West Indies imports, but their costs were affordable to many colonial families.

Pumpkin ale and beer were economical substitutes for more popular malt drinks. In an era before sanitized and filtered water, many colonists had a healthy and reasonable distrust of the safety of water, which commonly carried parasites or worse. They deemed cider, beer, and rum to be safer and better tasting than water. They also considered distilled or fermented drinks to be more robust and fortifying than the more insipid natural beverage.[96] One Englishman touring America in 1711 wrote that "ye greatest punishment of all to me is ye drinking allmost allways water, for we cannot afford wine it is dear."[97] Colonists brewed beverages at home or sent ingredients to a malt house for brewing.

Most people associated pumpkin beer, like pumpkin culinary dishes, with the impoverished. Robert Beverly commented that the "poor sort brew beer with molasses, bran, Indian corn malt, and pompions."[98] A lyrical poem exclaimed, "Oh, we can make liquor to sweeten our lips, of pumpkins, of parsnips, of walnut-tree chips!"[99] Most of the references to pumpkin beer are from Virginia, possibly because the vegetable was prolific in that colony, or perhaps because Virginians needed it less as a foodstuff and more as a beverage than people did in other places. The Dutch traveler Adrian van der Donck noted in his New York travel journal that he had heard that colonists there also made "a beverage from it."[100] A recipe for "Pompion Ale," dated 1771, instructed, "Let the Pompion be Beaten in a Trough and pressed as Apples. The Expressed Juice is to be boiled in a Copper a considerable Time and carefully skimmed that there may be no Remains of the fibrous Part of the Pulp. After that intention is answered let the liquor be hopped cooled fermented etc. as Malt Beer."[101]

Pumpkin ale allegedly had a "slight twang," suggesting that its flavor was off-putting in comparison with that of other beers. Yet according to the recipe's author, aging improved the flavor, just as it did with most fine spirits. He explained that "three dozen bottles of this Pompion ale had been filled two years previously. It was greatly improved and the 'Pompion Twang' has acquired something of a Mellowness approaching to Musk which is far more agreeable than before."[102] Virginia plantation owner Landon Carter used pumpkins to make a form of vinegar that he called "Pumperkin." In his diary entries for September 1771 and 1778, he mentioned storing a ninety-gallon cask of pumperkin in each of those years, along with much larger quantities of cider.[103]

Precursors to the sweet pumpkin pie that Americans are familiar with today pop up only occasionally in accounts of eighteenth-century culinary habits. Kalm described a pumpkin dish that consisted of mashed pumpkin mixed with milk, cinnamon, cloves, and lemon peel, but it is unclear whether diners considered the concoction a dessert.[104] Another

Weird

rendition, dating from 1763, called for baking apple and pumpkin slices together with plenty of sugar in "some good paste."[105]

For Thanksgiving celebrants, pumpkin made as undistinguished an impression in the late 1700s as it had in the early 1600s. Within fifty years of the Plymouth celebration, New England colonists had merged Harvest Home and Thanksgiving into an annual autumn holiday, though this tradition still had not taken hold in the South. Each New England colony set aside a day on which to give thanks for the health and well-being of the land by attending church, praying, and eating a family feast.[106] The diarist Juliana Smith recounted pumpkin being served at Thanksgiving dinner in the fall of 1779, though she gave it no special notice. She stated, "Our Mince Pies were good although we had to use dried Cherries as I told you and the meat was shoulder of venison, instead of Beef. The Pumpkin Pies, Apple Tarts and big Indian Puddings lacked for nothing save Appetite by the time we had got around to them."[107] Another colonial version of "Thanksgiving pie" consisted of bear's meat, dried pumpkin, and maple sugar in a cornmeal crust, for which, according to the source, "the colonial wife [was] complimented on her achievement."[108]

Although it is not readily evident from these accounts, the pumpkin was becoming something more than just another squash. As Americans began to sculpt their own sense of identity, which was decidedly not English, the very qualities for which many had chided the pumpkin—its unruly yet bountiful nature, its native roots, its lack of worth in international trade, and its associations with subsistence agriculture—took on new worth and meanings. And as the meanings of the pumpkin changed, so did people's appetite for it. While Benjamin Thompson's poem is the earliest example of sentimental literature about pumpkins, Amelia Simmons's publication of *American Cookery* in 1796 marks the beginning of the transformation of the pumpkin from uninspired side dish into glorified dessert.[109] Sweetening the vegetable was a means not simply of enhancing its flavor but also of celebrating its meanings. Americans have commonly recorded colonists' declarations of independence through acts of civil disobedience and heroic battles, but recipes created in the kitchen are also significant.[110]

As the first cookbook published in the United States, Simmons's *American Cookery* was self-consciously an indigenous and patriotic American text, although one with a New England bias, having been published in Connecticut.[111] Before *American Cookery*, the only published cookbooks available were written by Europeans and printed in Europe, so they did not always reflect or cater to American tastes, products, and sensibilities. The omission of the pumpkin from other popular eighteenth-century cookbooks, such as Eliza Smith's 1727 *The Compleat Housewife* and Susannah Carter's 1802 *The Frugal Colonial Housewife*, possibly reflects the pumpkin's disfavor among wealthier women, toward whom the cookbooks were directed, or a culinary bias against the American vegetable, since these cookbooks were published in London. Even though published cookbooks gained popularity, the most common way in which women exchanged recipes was still through oral tradition or homemade "receipt books."[112]

Little is known about Amelia Simmons, which has led some historians to suggest that she was a fictional creation of the publisher.[113] The title page identified Simmons as "an American orphan." Referring to America as a child was a literary device commonly used to define America's relationship to its motherland, England, during the Revolutionary War period.[114] In the cookbook's preface, Simmons, as the archetypal American or as the embodiment of the nation, described her humble origins and a life predicated on honest labor rather than privilege. She is independent and self-sufficient. And unlike "those females who have parents, or brothers, or riches, to defend their indiscretions"—presumably like European aristocracy—she explained, "the [American] orphan must depend solely upon character." Tying the idea of an indigenous American culture to popular rhetoric about equality, the cookbook's recipes profess to be "adapted to this country and all grades of life."

In contrast to previously published cookbooks, *American Cookery* offered recipes for native American foodstuffs, including pumpkins and corn. America's first national cookbook maintained the pumpkin's status as indigenous American fare while elevating it as an emblem of the nation's culture. And Simmons made a clear distinction between a pumpkin and a squash. Unlike all cooks and culinary observers before her, she cataloged winter squash as a vegetable and pumpkin as a dessert. "A Crookneck, or Winter Squash Pudding" is a recipe for the typical savory colonial porridge, which called for stewing squash—she suggests substituting potatoes, yams, or pumpkins—with apples, bread crumbs, and eggs to create a dish reminiscent of savory bread pudding. The recipe for

"Pompkin," in contrast, is not a form of daily sustenance at all, but a sweet treat. Simmons gave cooks two versions of "Pompkin":

> No. 1. One quart stewed and strained pompkin, 3 pints cream, 9 beaten eggs, sugar, mace, nutmeg and ginger, laid into paste No. 7 or 3, and with a dough spur, cross and cheque it, and baked in dishes 3 quarters of an hour.
>
> No. 2. One quart of milk, 1 pint pompkin, 4 eggs, molasses, allspice and ginger in a crust, bake 1 hour.[115]

The first pie, made with nine eggs and three pints of cream, would have been large, rich, and creamy. It probably had the consistency of cheesecake, and it is likely that Simmons intended it for high society. As Peter Kalm remarked, people "above the vulgar put sugar to [pumpkin]."[116] The second pie, more reflective of everyday fare, calls for molasses, regular milk, and smaller quantities of ingredients. The two recipes suggest that both higher classes and poorer people had begun to use pumpkins to create sweet desserts, a culinary form that showcases the vegetable's symbolic value. Unlike the squash, which remained an unremarkable side dish, the pumpkin was now being touted as something to celebrate and as a pleasant reward. It had taken on greater importance as a symbol than as sustenance.

It is not surprising to find a sugary pie categorized as a dessert, but a pumpkin? Cherries and apples make a lot more sense than this bland-tasting vegetable. Unlike in the past, desperation and starvation are unlikely explanations for cooking with pumpkin in the late 1700s, for the pumpkin was now being prepared with more expensive sweeteners, and plenty of other fruits were available to choose from by this time. But perhaps its blandness is exactly why Americans invested it with such rich meaning. The blank slate made the meanings all the more intense.

Although the pumpkin never provided colonists with surplus wealth or cultural cachet, it always gave them something to eat, and in that lay a story for a new democratic nation. Eating pumpkins signified a family's taking care of itself on its own piece of land, no matter how humble the size, and depending on no one but itself. Growing pumpkins required nothing more than land, honest work, and family. Because the pumpkin produced large yields on minimal plots, wealth and social class were superfluous to its production. Any man, at least any white man, could plant pumpkins, and every woman could transform them into food for the family, nourishing themselves and the nation's democratic aspirations in the process. The pumpkin, therefore, made a strong political statement. It embodied the Jeffersonian agrarian ideal of a nation of self-sufficient farmers. In *Notes on the State of Virginia*, Jefferson famously wrote, "Those who labour in the earth are the chosen people of God, if ever he had a chosen people, whose breasts he has made his peculiar deposit for substantial and genuine virtue."[117] Citizens' economic independence more broadly enabled national independence, because the country did not have to rely on outside sources, England in particular, to sustain itself. With the pumpkin, the nation's citizens were able to provide for themselves. Making the lowly pumpkin—a vegetable Europeans stigmatized as primitive and rustic—a delicacy and publishing a recipe for it in the first American cookbook was a powerful expression of American pride and independence.

Women contributed to this nationalistic discourse and helped celebrate these principles by making pumpkin taste sweeter and better. Transforming pumpkin into a delicious pie was one way women showed their support for these political ideals, and by giving slices to their families and friends they offered others a means to do the same. Simmons was adamant about women's "having an opinion and determination" and serving as "good wives and members of society."[118] Although women lacked a vote and had a limited public voice, the recipes they created and the food they prepared were far-reaching and fundamental for establishing a sense of American identity and independence. Baking pumpkin pie was one vital way to achieve these ends. *To bake pumpkin pie is to be independent*

For most of the colonial period, people dreamed of oranges but fed on pumpkins. Suffering through many hardships, early colonists were likely thankful for the sustenance that pumpkins provided, but their letters and journals indicate that they were equally appreciative of being able to switch to other foodstuffs when they could. Almost everyone grew pumpkins because they produced bountiful harvests without much effort or cost. Yet they offered little economic profit and even less social collateral. Piercing the fog of national memory, we find that the pumpkin may not have had a place on the table at the mythic first Thanksgiving feast. Chroniclers of colonial harvest celebrations wrote nary a word about them. And to further upset the American myth of the pumpkin, the vegetable was indigenous not just to New England; farmers produced them throughout the colonies.

Yet while some Europeans scorned the pumpkin as rural peasant food and others equated it with hedonism, the vegetable triggered a sense of pride and nostalgia in some early Americans. It did more than fill dinner plates; it communicated a set of assumptions about who Americans were and what America stood for in contrast to Europeans. Although a pumpkin was not a pumpkin in the same way Americans define it today—according to what it looks like, the way most people prepare it, and what it means—these historic uses and definitions nevertheless resonate into the present.

The pumpkin's future was anything but destined at the time, however. In the early nineteenth century, while some Americans made it into a dessert, many others tossed it into troughs for their cows and pigs. Although making pie and making fodder out of pumpkins seem contradictory, the acts are more closely related than might be imagined at first thought. The circumstances and ideas that would unite these acts in the next decades explain not only why Simmons made pumpkin pie instead of squash pie but also why American families would soon, at last, begin to serve pumpkin pie at Thanksgiving.

THREE

THOREAU SITS ON A PUMPKIN

The Making of a Rural New England Icon, 1800 to 1860

TASTE—THAT IS, THE QUALITY OF ITS MEAT—WAS THE LEAST likely reason pumpkin became a dessert. Indeed, when most Americans in the early republic sat down to a meal, they did not expect to find pumpkin on their plates. With increasing national prosperity and a greater number and variety of foods available, most Americans could afford to be more particular about what they ate. While they continued to keep winter and summer squashes a part of dinner fare and as a valuable commodity in the marketplace, many people dropped varieties known as pumpkins as daily sustenance. Although little market existed for pumpkins, some farmers kept them in production for livestock fodder, "adding to the solid comfort of barnyard dependents," as one Maryland farmer remarked in 1837.[1] A farmer from Massachusetts summed up the ever-widening gap perceived between a pumpkin and a squash: "It is considered with us that the Winter Squash is not a substitute for pumpkins in our section of the country. The squash is accounted a valuable vegetable for the table, and is also used for pies. The pumpkins I raised for the use of my cows and fatting cattle. They increase and enrich the milk, whether for cheese or butter."[2] – *will usually end up with Ryan's sympathy*

The seemingly innocuous ways in which Americans began to distinguish pumpkins from squashes tell a much deeper story of how they experienced and thought about the transformations going on all around them in American society. Although the United States population remained mostly rural through the end of the nineteenth century, the development of manufacturing in the Northeast, of more extensive national and international markets, and of larger transportation and communication networks, along with the rise in European immigration, impelled dramatic growth in urban centers.[3] The advent of mechanized agriculture and the opening up of western land to American settlement increased the average farm size and revolutionized farm work. These larger economic and technological transformations helped inspire new recipes and new attitudes toward the foods that people ate. *Luxury cuisine*

To figure out why and how a pumpkin began to mean something different from a squash requires connecting the crops' physical attributes, market status, and pragmatic and playful uses. The botanical names C. *pepo*, C. *maxima*, C. *moschata*, and C. *ovifera* had little to do with the ways most people thought about and used pumpkins and squashes. Adding to the age-old confusion over the cucurbit family was the introduction of new varieties, such as the warty, football-shaped Hubbard squash, the huge mammoth pumpkin (both C. *maxima*), the oblong, orange Nantucket pumpkin, and the green autumn marrow squash (both C. *pepo*), that fell into the same Linnaean botanical classifications.[4] "Their common names have so multiplied," a writer in the *Southern Planter* complained, "that a farmer wishing to grow some for his stock, or his table, can hardly tell what to ask for at the seed stores, or what will be the character of this crop when obtained."[5] *Problematic today with some herbal families*

Taste and use were truer indicators of the differences between a squash and a pumpkin than botanical species. If people cooked it for dinner, they most likely called it a squash, whether the vegetable was categorized as *Cucurbita pepo* or *Cucurbita maxima*. The names of new squash varieties denoted culinary appeal, as in the case of the custard squash, or respected status, as in the case of the Commodore Porter Valparaiso squash, which *The Farmer's Cabinet* called "the best of its species."[6] The custard squash, with its round, ribbed shape, is a dead ringer for a pumpkin by today's standards, but nineteenth-century seed catalogs categorized it as a squash, presumably because people ate it. Publications still referred to some old varieties, such as the winter crookneck, or cushaw, which has buff skin and a long curved neck, as both pumpkin and squash, suggesting that the lines people drew between the two were still a bit blurry. Determining that a squash was actually something different from a pumpkin broke with earlier traditions, in which the utility of one was indistinguishable from that of the other. This shift forces one to recognize yet again that the present-day habit of defining a pumpkin or squash simply by its appearance is more ideological and less rational than we might ordinarily assume.

The rapid growth of cities created an equally dramatic rise in consumer demand for food, leading many farmers in the Northeast to reorient their production toward urban markets.[7] Writing in *The Market Assistant* in 1867, Thomas DeVoe stated, "It is not many years ago when the suburbs—or say twenty miles around the City of New York—from Long Island, Westchester, and New York counties, and New Jersey, furnished the city with a plentiful and cheap supply of vegetables."[8] Improvements in roads and the introduction of canals in the early 1800s eased access between towns and their hinterlands. Markets for many perishables, such as dairy products and fresh fruits and vegetables, as DeVoe noted, remained local until the railroad dramatically altered the scale of farming and market access after mid-century.

Despite the great influx of immigrants, the American diet retained its Anglo-Saxon biases.[9] Americans continued to eat a lot of meat, with beef the most popular and pork the most common type they consumed. Fruits and vegetables became more important parts of meals because of new ideas regarding nutrition and also the increased availability of produce due to production and processing innovations. Sugar and wheat, once upper-class indulgences, became common stock in kitchen cupboards as the price of sugar beets, sugar cane, and wheat declined.[10] As a result, Americans heartily consumed sweet pies, cakes, and candies. With improved sanitation, water became safer to drink, and so the consumption of beer and cider as daily beverages—though certainly not as social drinks—declined. Lager beers became the draft drink of choice, and pumpkin brews went the way of homespun.[11]

In keeping with colonial cooking traditions, squash recipes in early-nineteenth-century cookbooks usually called for boiling or baking the vegetable and then mashing it into a savory side dish. For "winter squash or cushaw," Miss Leslie's 1854 *Complete Cookery* recommended, "Pare it, take out the seeds, cut it in pieces, and stew it slowly till quite soft, in a very little water. Afterwards drain, squeeze, and press it well, and mash it with a very little butter, pepper and salt."[12] Ironically, while squash held onto the colonial culinary traditions that once applied to all forms of pumpkins and squashes, it lost the earlier meanings. Because it had more flavorful meat, people ate it on a regular basis, which made it economically viable in the marketplace and a product of urban as well as rural homes. As most winter and summer squash varieties acquired respectability as a food and a commodity, they lost their power as a sign of nature and an old-fashioned, primitive way of life. They were too much a part of the modern, everyday world.

The pumpkin was different. Because the pumpkin—the field pumpkin in particular—became divorced from the expanding marketplace and retained its association with the subsistence farm economy, it remained a powerful symbol of nature and of people living on the edge of civilization, the symbolism long associated with all forms of squash. Popular names for pumpkins reflected the cultural associations that differentiated them from squashes. In contrast to the distinguished Commodore Porter Valparaiso squash were the Jonathan pumpkin and the possum-nosed pumpkin, which evoked images of an unsophisticated country bumpkin and a down-and-out way of life. Jonathan was a nickname for a country rube and was used to poke fun at Americans, specifically New Englanders.[13] In defense of the pumpkin, the *New England Farmer* complained about the biases against the plant: "We believe this crop is more neglected than it ought to be. Whether this is owing to the old cant phrase of 'Brother Jonathan and Pumpkin pie,' used by our transatlantic brethren we know not."[14] The possum-nosed pumpkin got its name from the opossum, a large white rodent stereotyped as a dirty animal because it ate household trash. The animals might have scavenged the compost heaps where pumpkins propagated. By identifying the pumpkin with the seamier sides of the natural world and the country, Americans drew a picture of a way of life that communicated as much about their own cultural attitudes toward nature and rural living as it did about the vegetable itself.

Farming changed broadly and profoundly in the nineteenth century, but most of the great agricultural innovations bypassed the field pumpkin.[15] New machines, first horse-drawn and then steam-powered, aided the plowing of fields and quickened and refined the seeding, hoeing, and harvesting of wheat and other cash crops. Cyrus McCormick's mechanical reaper, John Deere's steel plow, and Eli Whitney's cotton gin increased the outputs of the most profitable crops and compressed farm chores from weeks of manual labor into hours. Developments in biological and botanical sciences encouraged the use of fertilizers and crop rotation in the hope

of increasing yields per acre of wheat, tobacco, and cotton. The geographical distribution of American agriculture also changed. Wheat farming
moved west to the Great Plains with the expanding settlement of European immigrants and the displacement of American Indian populations.
The southern economy continued to rely heavily on enslaved laborers to
produce cotton, rice, and tobacco.

New experimental crop varieties and agricultural practices were
exhibited at agricultural fairs, discussed in farm journals, and disseminated through seed catalogs. The first agricultural fair took place in Massachusetts in 1818, and by the turn of the next century most states and
many counties were holding annual exhibitions to display the newest
developments in the agricultural sciences and the most impressive specimens of plants, animals, and domestic arts.[16] Yet fairs were as much places
of entertainment as of business. According to Susan Fenimore Cooper in
her 1850 memoir of life in New England, "Neither the circus, nor menag-
erie, nor election, has collected so many people as the fair."[17] *Already yearning?*

Organizations such as the Massachusetts Society for Promoting Agriculture and leading horticulturists such as Andrew Jackson Downing and
Thomas Fessenden published journals dedicated to the promotion and
dissemination of agricultural knowledge.[18] Downing's *Horticulturalist* and
Fessenden's *American Agriculturalist* were both national and regional in
scope, and they openly exchanged and duplicated articles and information from competing publications. Articles and letters from *Maine Farmer*
and *New England Farmer* routinely appeared in the Maryland-based
American Farmer and the Buckeye state's *Ohio Cultivator*. Like the fairs,
the journals were sites for the exchange of jokes and social commentary
as much as scientific data. The expansion of commercial nurseries, greenhouses, and seed companies in the early 1800s can be measured by the
exponential growth in the number of seed catalogs published and the
increasing thickness of each new annual issue.[19] Pages devoted to each
of the lucrative varieties of potatoes, onions, peas, strawberries, apples,
pears, and peaches commonly outnumbered pages describing the pumpkin by more than two to one.

The field pumpkin was a secondary crop in every respect. While farmers shipped grains overseas and trucked fresh produce by wagon into
towns, for the most part they left pumpkins behind on the farm. "Parsnips and winter squashes must be retailed," noted one farmer in 1835, but

"pumpkins in any quality would not sell for anything."[20] Although the pumpkin had value in the farm economy as a cheap addition to livestock feed, it lacked the monetary value of the food crops that farmers sold to urban dwellers for home consumption. One clear reflection of the disparity value in pumpkins and squashes was the price of seeds. Seed catalogs usually listed the cost of squash seeds by the ounce, and that of pumpkin seeds by the quart. Thomas Dunlap's 1852 catalog advertised seeds for cheese pumpkins (for domestic consumption) for 12.5 cents an ounce and Connecticut field pumpkin seeds for 37.5 cents a quart.[21] The 1856 *Transactions of the State Agricultural Society of Michigan* reported that the "best winter squash" was worth 75 cents and the "best and largest pumpkin" just 25 cents. Similarly, it valued four squash at 50 cents total and three sweet pumpkins at 25 cents.[22]

Attempts to garner surplus wealth from the pumpkin never materialized. In 1819, after a visit to a German farmer in Indiana, one entrepreneur proposed marketing pumpkin seed oil. "Instead of throwing away or giving to the pigs the seeds of their pumpkins," he suggested using them "for all the purposes of lamp oil and olive [oil]."[23] A year later a British man wrote that he found pumpkin oil "good to use on the axletrees of carriages . . . to prevent friction" and good as a lamp oil because it produced a nice light.[24] Although the entrepreneur projected that "two millions of gallons of such oil could be made annually in the United States," few American farmers, if any, seem to have taken his hook and produced pumpkin oil "on a large scale and for economic uses."[25] Most references to pumpkin oil production appear in domestic advice books, which recommend making the oil as an economical substitute for other oils or as a remedy for tapeworms.

The pumpkin's best attribute was that it produced large yields with little effort. "I presume there is not a vegetable on the face of the earth more easily raised, or that is more productive, when it is considered that they will grow among corn, potatoes, or on any waste of ground, and that the seed of one pumpkin will produce cartloads of fruit," remarked a farmer from New York.[26] Farmers from such diverse states as Ohio, Massachusetts, California, Connecticut, Michigan, Tennessee, New York, Maryland, Maine, and Louisiana raised pumpkins. Many sang the pumpkin's praises for improving the color and quality of milk and butter and for fattening hogs and cows before the traditional fall slaughter. "For early feed for hogs and milch cows they are excellent, contributing to the condition of the first and to the milk of the last in an eminent degree," attested one grower.[27] Others were less than enthusiastic. Some farmers believed pumpkins made poor fodder because they were too watery and insufficiently nutritious.[28]

Although distinctions between some varieties of pumpkins and squashes were still inexact, no one mistook the orange field pumpkin for a squash. The botanist Fearing Burr identified the qualities that made it the quintessential pumpkin: "The term 'pumpkin' . . . as popularly understood, includes only the few varieties of the Common New England Pumpkin that have been long grown in fields in an extensive but somewhat neglectful manner."[29] "Extensive" and "neglectful" describe both the natural proclivities of the field pumpkin and its diminished status as a crop. According to the 1843 edition of John Douglas's seed catalog, the field pumpkin was the "greatest bearer" among all pumpkins and squashes and the poorest tasting of the lot.[30] Farmers cultivated the variety beyond the colonial period less because it was a popular delicacy than because it was cheap, prolific, and required little effort to produce. It was, in other words, a "good, old-fashioned" pumpkin, according to the March 1850 *American Agriculturist*—a holdover from the past, the antithesis of innovation.[31] The yellow field pumpkin became *the* pumpkin—the one artists would paint, poets would laud, and holiday rituals would honor—because it embodied a sense of natural exuberance and an archaic, rural way of life like no other. It defined pumpkinness, and its reputation crept into the names of other produce. An apple variety known as "Pumpkin Sweet," for example, was "little valued, large and showy."[32]

The field pumpkin's natural productivity and lack of economic worth affected the way farmers handled it. In keeping with American Indian and colonial traditions, pumpkins were most commonly propagated in a field of corn or other crops.[33] Farmers probably interplanted pumpkins with other crops because land was too valuable and the return on pumpkins too small to devote an entire field to their production. Some farmers, however, created separate one- to two-acre pumpkin patches, because of their misgivings that the pumpkin plants might disturb the more valuable grains and produce.[34] One farmer mentioned that the pumpkin interfered with his plow and was a nuisance to any sort of mechanized farming.[35] Another planted his pumpkins in areas "so full of grubs and roots as not to admit the plough."[36] Farmers continued to propagate pumpkins in compost and manure heaps, bringing some usefulness to otherwise idle dumps. The seed seller John Douglas used this as a selling point, advertising the fact that pumpkins were "well-adapted for raising on waste-lands."[37] This tradition only exacerbated the pumpkin's lowly reputation.

Because the pumpkin grew almost free of labor in fields cultivated for other purposes, some farmers called it a "stolen crop."[38] Many wrote to journals with testimonies to the pumpkin's prolific production rate and volume of output, telling how hundreds of fruits had developed from a seed dropped "accidentally" in a field and how plants had produced great quantities of fruit "without any particular care" or "with no attention whatsoever."[39] "I happened to be hoeing round a pumpkin vine," explained one character in a story published in *New England Farmer*, "and was about to dig it up, when the old man said, 'Stephen, don't dig it up, my son, let it grow, and see what it will eventually become.' I obeyed, of course, yet could see nothing so very wonderful about it."[40] The young man's antipathy toward the pumpkin's ability to grow like a weed, and the old man's enthusiasm for the same trait, communicates the idea that the pumpkin was a thing of the past and not fully domesticated.

The almost unbelievable testimonials to the pumpkin's production make vivid why people were fascinated with the vegetable and why it gained such symbolic import. One farmer reported that four acres planted with pumpkins yielded "thirty-three ox cart and wagon loads, containing 4427 large pumpkins, and one wagon load of small and broken ones."[41] Another extolled, "On gathering the crop, I counted 1076 sound pumpkins . . . making 53,858 lbs. per acre."[42] Under the heading "Enormous Product," an article in *New England Farmer* reported, "Mr. Moses Holden, of Barre, raised, this season, from a single seed, 34 pumpkins, weighing 653 lbs. that the aggregate length of the different branches of the vine was 636 feet."[43]

Although most farmers corresponding with *American Farmer* measured their pumpkin crops by the size of a plant's entire production, the most talked-about marvel was the mammoth variety, which produced fruits weighing more than one hundred pounds. Although its weight and girth meant that one mammoth alone could feed practically a herd of cattle, the variety served little purpose beyond giving a farmer bragging rights. A mammoth was, as one seed catalog noted, "cultivated as a matter of curiosity more than from its merit."[44] These monstrous vegetables supposedly date back to Mayan times, and they began to appear regularly in seed catalogs in the nineteenth century. In 1822 Samuel Deane, in his book *New England Farmer*, noted that "a new and very large species of pumpkin has lately been introduced into this country, of which it is said more than five hundred pounds can be raised from a single seed"—which suggests that the mammoth pumpkin started to become popular in the early 1800s.[45] The propagation of the mammoth moved the pumpkin toward its identity as a show crop, a visual wonder more than a meaty morsel.

Classified botanically in the genus *C. maxima*, the type was called variously the "mammoth pumpkin," "mammoth squash," "big pumpkin," and "largest squash yet."[46] Perhaps because farmers specified no distinct purpose for the mammoth variety for either livestock feed or dinner fare, nor identified any viable botanical trait to distinguish it as a pumpkin or a squash, early nineteenth-century sources were not concerned about classifying it as one or the other, as later generations of giant pumpkin growers would be.

The mammoth epitomizes the pumpkin's awesome nature. "This is, indeed, a huge and ponderous vegetable," exclaimed an article about a 116-pounder.[47] Farm journals and seed catalogs endlessly reported stories about the enormous weight and size of mammoths. The October 19, 1813, *Commercial Advertiser* carried an advertisement for "a pumpkin weighing two hundred and twenty-six pounds, and measuring seven feet five inches in circumference. It is one of eight pumpkins produced from two seeds, whose weights, added together, amount to one thousand and seventeen pounds. It was raised on the place of D. Gelston, Esq., in the neighborhood of this city [New York]."[48] *New England Farmer* reported that "a Pumpkin, of unusual size, grew on the farm of John Reynolds, Esq., a few miles from Clarksburgh, Virginia, this season; it weighed 320 pounds and measured around the middle six feet."[49] Farm journals chronicled many types of oversize produce, but the mammoths drew the greatest attention. A twenty-ounce apple is impressive, but it cannot compete with a 128-pound pumpkin.[50]

Comstock, Ferre and Company's concern that the huge pumpkins were "always coarse grained and watery" and the *Horticulturalist's* criticism, "They do not keep well after being cut open, smaller kinds are greatly preferable," missed the point.[51] The quality of the variety's meat and its practical applications were irrelevant in the face of its visual spectacle. These "Extravagances of Nature," as an 1819 edition of the *Boston Gazette* called them, were natural marvels with the power to amaze.[52] Although Comstock, Ferre and Company's *The Gardener's Almanac* announced in 1856 that "the rage for mammoth squash we hope has gone by," the hope proved out of touch with popular opinion.[53] The mammoth's popularity was only in its infancy. An American visiting Paris in 1852 bragged that "France can not boast of a Niagara or the biggest pumpkin," thereby equating the pumpkin with one of the nation's most famous natural wonders.[54] Farmers and horticulturists competed to produce larger specimens with every passing year. In 1893 a grower exhibited a 469-pound specimen at the Chicago World's Fair, and mammoths weighing more than 1,800 pounds would win contests in the early 2000s.

Unlike Niagara Falls, which Americans revered, the pumpkin inspired jokes. The animated quality of the pumpkin's growth and its great size were the inspiration for folktales that exaggerated every feature of the naturally enormous plant into hilarious proportions. A pumpkin plant had "leaves as large as a dining table, and a stem as large round as a hoe-handle."[55] A pumpkin vine grew "over the north end of the garden wall . . . passed right under [a] sled, thence over another wall, thence through a cabbage patch and orchard, thence over a piece of meadow a hundred and fifty yards wide, thence down a long hill, and at last crossed a stream of water four rods wide."[56] Pumpkins grew as big as houses, "approaching the size of young mountains."[57] Others were so large that "a stone boat, two oxen and a horse [were] needed to move it from the field."[58]

Many tales imagined the pumpkin as more animal than plant. In one, a quick-growing pumpkin vine chases a farmer.[59] Wrestling with the giant vine, the man finally releases himself from its grip by cutting the vine with a knife. In another, a farmer is so frightened by a creaking and clattering pumpkin "of monstrous size" that he seeks assistance from his neighbors. "They armed themselves with axes, clubs, and pitchforks, and accompanied him to the spot," as if they were about to face a grizzly bear or a mountain lion.[60] The story ends with the farmers' discovery of a sow and her piglets inside the giant pumpkin, a common folkloric motif that makes the vegetable more akin to four-legged than to one-rooted creatures. The pumpkin is as awesome and fearsome as a wild animal, beyond the farmer's control and the confines of the field. Yet it is a silly adversary as well. The pumpkin was a powerful symbol of nature and of agrarian prowess, to be sure, but it also represented an archaic, rural way of life—the life of the country bumpkin—that was the antithesis of the changing times.

Almost the only people who stuck to the tradition of eating pumpkin instead of feeding it to their cattle were "old folks," as *Southern Planter* noted, as well as settlers on the western prairie.[61] "Baked pumpkin and milk, pumpkin-sauce, and dried pumpkin for winter use have had their day and gone out of fashion . . . except for some of the old folks who still prefer baked pumpkin in a milk pan without any pastry," wrote David Wells in his 1855 agricultural yearbook.[62] Nineteenth-century pioneer families in the Appalachians and on the Great Plains relied on the pumpkin just as their colonial predecessors had, to carry them through the first difficult years of settlement.[63] Farm families used pumpkin to stretch out the grain supply and relied on it as a supplement for breads and stews.[64] "To save meal," recalled an Ohio settler, "we often used pumpkin bread, in which, when meal was scarce, the pumpkin was so predominant as to render it next to impossible to tell our bread from that article."[65] An 1819 journal claimed that pumpkin bread was as ubiquitous at the table in Kentucky as pumpkin pie was in New England.[66]

Some people preached the virtues of pumpkin as a sweetener for those living on homesteads isolated from commercial markets and access to more refined sugar. William Kenrick, in his book *The New American Orchardist,* wrote, "In places remote from the seaboard, the making of sugar from pumpkin will probably obtain a preference over that of the beet root; so easily is the pumpkin raised."[67] In *Pioneer History of Ingham County [Michigan]*, a local historian noted that "pumpkin molasses was their usual sweetening."[68] These testimonies about the pumpkin's ability to sustain American pioneers echo those found in colonial stories, in which the pumpkin was known as "the food provided by the Lord until the corn and cattle increased."[69] Its ties to a rustic and primitive way of life continued, even as the stories moved forward in time. These homesteading stories made prime seasoning for the pumpkin's iconic representation of American agrarianism—at least in some parts of the country. *Where not?*

The pumpkin continued to be a feature of southern ways of life, appearing in newspaper accounts of record-setting pumpkin crops in North Carolina, Virginia, and Louisiana; in southern cookbooks and newspapers, which carried both savory and sweet pumpkin pie recipes; and in the names of towns such as Pumpkin, Virginia; Pumpkin Pile, Georgia; and Pumpkintown, South Carolina.[70] A man traveling through Georgia in the 1850s was impressed by one woman's "magical art in the mazes of cookery—being able to set up a pumpkin in as many forms as there are days in the week."[71] Yet for most southerners, pumpkin still meant little beyond being able to satisfy hunger in versatile ways.

In contrast, New Englanders' identity was synonymous with pumpkins. A letter to the editor in the January 11, 1833, *American Farmer* stated, "Having recently traveled through the 'Land of Steady Habits,' or 'Pumpkin Dominion' (I mean the New England States), there was scarcely a family but what, in the article of diet, when forthcoming at stated periods, would bring up the rear with a company or platoon of pumpkin pies."[72] With a bit of jest, a biographer of Horace Greeley identified the abolitionist as "a genuine product of New England soil. He belongs by birthright to the nasal, angular, psalm-singing, pumpkin-growing generation."[73] Another source observed, "One or two dishes are peculiar to New England, and always on the table, toast dipped in cream and pumpkin pie."[74]

Sweet pumpkin pie originated in New England in the late eighteenth century, and nineteenth-century pie recipes mimic those in Amelia Simmons's *American Cookery*, with only minor adjustments in the quantities of ingredients or types of sweeteners used. Bakers might even make pumpkin pie with the sweeter-tasting winter squash, but they still called it pumpkin pie. As the November 1834 edition of *American Farmer* explained, "If Thanksgiving in Massachusetts go not off with éclat, it will neither be for the want of a good proclamation . . . nor for lack of squashes, which every body knows are converted into what is by a figure of speech called pumpkin pie."[75] Pumpkin pie recipes published outside New England often labeled the concoction "New England pumpkin pie," affirming its regional affiliation. Cookbooks provide some clues to its spread beyond the Northeast. For example, the fifty-fourth edition of *Miss Leslie's Complete Cookery*, published in Philadelphia in 1854, was the first to include a recipe for "New England Pumpkin Pie," although stewed pumpkin was present from the first issue in 1800.

Reflecting on New Englanders' particular appetite for pumpkin pie, Susan Fenimore Cooper wrote in *Rural Hours*, "In this part of the world, not only cattle, but men, women, and children—we all eat pumpkins.

Yesterday, the first pumpkin-pie of the season made its appearance on the table. It seems rather strange, at first glance, that in a country where apples, and plums, and peaches, and cranberries abound, the pumpkin should be held in high favor for pies."[76] Cooper hit on the very essence of New Englanders' hunger for pumpkins. It was not exactly logical. Southerners produced and ate plenty of pumpkins, but they did not give them an honored place at the dinner table as their neighbors to the north did. Although Cooper speculated that "this is a taste which may probably be traced back to the early colonists," celebrating baked squash would in fact have been more consistent with colonial food traditions. And yet New Englanders yearned for *pumpkin* pie, even if the recipe recommended squash.

The extensive use of pumpkins in New England's growing dairy industry might offer a practical reason for the tying of the region's name and reputation to the pumpkin, but it hardly explains why people relished food they used as livestock fodder as a treat for themselves. The full explanation leads back to the complicated ways in which Americans have used and thought about nature, rural life, and their relationships to those things. It leads back, too, to growing cultural and political divisions in the United States at the time.

New Englanders came to value the pumpkin more for its meanings than for its meat. Although pumpkin stories may seem more esoteric than market reports, agricultural practices, and culinary habits, they have often powerfully influenced the American environment and economy—and Americans' sense of identity. In the early nineteenth century, many Americans began to reimagine the wild land beyond a community's borders less as a threat and more as a refuge. They began to think of nature as a "place apart" from the place where they worked and lived, an antidote to the hectic pace and crowded confines of the rising industrial centers.[77] Frederic Church's Hudson River School paintings of sublime mountaintop sunsets—paintings that celebrated nature as divine inspiration for the new nation—both influenced and expressed these new attitudes toward nature.[78] The rising popularity of wilderness vacations and of Niagara Falls as a tourist attraction manifested the same way of thinking. In this era, such excursions were accessible only to the wealthier classes, and vacationers self-consciously interpreted their nature trips and romantic sentiments in class terms.

Americans' changing appetite for pumpkins owed much to this larger cultural shift toward viewing nature as someplace beyond town and city borders. The new distinction that many Americans made between a pumpkin and a squash aligned with new ways of imagining rural versus urban places and old-fashioned versus modern ways of life. The status of squash as an urban market crop obscured squash's ties to the country-side.[79] Although consumers were undoubtedly aware of its origins, the vegetable lost its power as a sign of nature because it was so much a part of their daily lives. Nature, as they conceived of it, was out in the country. Farm families embraced these sentiments toward squash just as readily, suggesting that they were equally modern in their outlook.

Squash's flavor, commodity status, and affiliation with the modern world encouraged Americans to think of it as just another table vegetable instead of a totem of rusticity. The pumpkin was gaining considerable cultural status despite its low economic standing. This seemingly contra-dictory development makes sense only when seen within the vast social and cultural transformations of the nineteenth century and the concomi-tant opportunities and anxieties they produced. Henry David Thoreau, no less, called on the pumpkin to articulate the difference and distance between rural and urban life. In *Walden* he claimed, "I would rather sit on a pumpkin and have it all to myself than be crowded on a velvet cushion. I would rather ride on earth in an ox cart, with a free circulation, than go to heaven in the fancy car of an excursion train and breathe a *malaria* all the way."[80] For Thoreau, the pumpkin was an icon of nature, the reverse of all that modern America stood for. Its earthiness and simple wholesomeness represented a place where one might discover oneself, the meaning of life, and, in the case of some New Englanders, a cultural heritage. Yet modern, urbane America inspired mixed reactions, even in Thoreau. Simple and natural could also mean backward and ignorant.

By figuratively sitting on a pumpkin rather than harvesting pumpkins, Thoreau set himself apart from farmers in important ways. His imagined act was one of contemplation, not of work, and his appreciation of nature was a reflection of sensibilities that he believed local country inhabitants did not share. "There is something vulgar and foul in [the gardener's] closeness to his mistress," he bluntly stated.[81] So while he and others like him idealized farming as a virtuous means of communing with nature, they nevertheless looked with disdain on people who made a living off the land, and saw them as socially inferior.[82] As Ralph Waldo Emerson wrote disparagingly in his essay "Nature," one "cannot freely admire a noble landscape if laborers are digging in the field hard by."[83] In his essay "Farming," he opined about the nature of farm labor: "This hard work will always be done by one kind of man; not by scheming speculators, nor by soldiers, nor professors, not readers of Tennyson; by men of endurance—deep-chested, long-winded, tough, slow and sure, and timely."[84] Emerson characterized the farmer as primitive, "as being really a piece of old Nature, comparable to sun and moon, rainbow and flood; because he is, as all natural persons are, representative of Nature as much as these. That uncorrupted behavior which we admire in animals and in young children belongs to him, to the hunter, the sailor—the man who lives in the presence of Nature."[85] *Do I sense envy? Not as disparaging as Thoreau*

And this kind of man, the prototypical rustic inhabitant, was often depicted as a pumpkin farmer. Nineteenth-century literature is rich with pumpkin farmers and pumpkin-headed men, who represent Emerson's and Thoreau's backward and unsophisticated rural type. As in times past, storytellers used the pumpkin to define personal character traits, the kind of wild natural instincts Emerson described. Because of the pumpkin's minimal economic value, its somewhat disreputable status as cheap cattle feed, its reputation as a subsistence crop tied to working for oneself instead of for profit, and its historic wild associations, writers embraced the pumpkin as a ready object with which to define a primitive, natural way of life. Pumpkin farmers were objects of fun and ridicule because they represented so fully the naive and old-fashioned values, habits, and places that seemed so antithetical to those that flourished in the busy metropolises. On another level, pumpkin tales expressed condescension toward American culture in general, and the nagging self-consciousness that North America might still remain culturally inferior to Europe. *Hedge w/ "may" source?*

Nathaniel Hawthorne's *The Scarlet Letter*, the 1850 tale of adultery in colonial New England, made the pumpkin a metaphor for the supposed boorishness and lack of sophistication of American culture. Hawthorne described the garden of the fictional Massachusetts Governor Bellingham:

> Pearl, accordingly, ran to the bow-window, at the farther end of the hall, and looked along the vista of a garden-walk, carpeted with closely haven grass, and bordered with some rude and immature attempt at shrubbery.

But the proprietor appeared already to have relinquished, as hopeless, the effort to perpetuate on this side of the Atlantic, in the hard soil and amid the slow struggle for subsistence, the native English taste for ornamental gardening. Cabbages grew in plain sight; and a pumpkin vine, rooted at some distance, had run across the intervening space, and deposited one of its gigantic products directly beneath the hall-window; as if to warn the Governor that this great lump of vegetable gold was as rich an ornament as New England earth would offer him.[86]

Jab at Columbian goals?

Hawthorne equated the ragged, disheveled condition of the governor's garden with the primitive, backward state of affairs in colonial America. The pumpkin, along with the parochial cabbage, epitomizes the primitive and poor conditions. For Hawthorne, the pumpkin, with its meandering, tangled vines, was antithetical to the English ornamental garden, which was a sign of wealth and refined taste, and which many American elites emulated on their riverfront estates. The passage ends with a succinct description of the pumpkin as both an animated piece of nature not under human control and a sign of false affluence exemplifying American crassness. The pumpkin is a "lump," a cheap substitute for gold, and the only kind of wealth one could hope to acquire.

But it was not, even in it

Although ostensibly pertaining to the world of plants and gardening, A. H. Hovey's and several other horticulturists' descriptions of the pumpkin sound peculiarly like Hawthorne's. "We cannot think of admitting this vegetable into the precincts of the garden where there are cucumbers, melons, etc.," wrote Hovey, for "they would mix and contaminate the quality of the more valuable sorts."[87] An article in an 1854 issue of *American Farmer* concurred that the pumpkin was "of course an ugly concern and if planted in a garden but serves to mar its effect and expression."[88] *New England Farmer* stated, "The summer and winter squashes, if they flower near together, will degenerate; and the neighborhood of the pumpkin will deteriorate the future progeny of both."[89] Finally, an agricultural and literary journal declared that the pumpkin "had no business among flowers."[90]

Classism?

Protect your daughters? ×

These writers offered practical and aesthetic considerations for plant cultivation, yet their statements seem to veer toward class and cultural commentary. Hovey's fear that the pumpkin might interbreed with the more esteemed squash varieties and *New England Farmer*'s use of the word

Knew it! (handwritten note at top)

neighborhood and the phrase "deteriorate the future progeny" might easily have alluded to broader social relations, not just to garden culture.
The farming almanacs might have been reiterating Emerson's and Thoreau's embrace of American class hierarchies by implying that provincial
or poor rural Americans, as represented by the native pumpkin, did not
belong among the more sophisticated and superior, well-bred classes—
the cucumbers and melons. Perhaps the *American Farmer* editors saw
wild, wide-ranging, and undulating pumpkin vines as a metaphor for
uncivilized living and therefore as a nemesis to the ordered symmetry
of most vegetable gardens, here signs of civilization and refinement. To
assume that no correlation exists between the agriculturalists and the literary icons is to miss the larger point that cultural ideas, science, and economics mutually influence each other, and never operate independently.

One of the most famous pumpkins is the one attached to Cinderella. Over hundreds of years, the fairy tale has taken many forms across
many cultures.[91] Charles Perrault's version, published in French in 1697,
was probably the first to incorporate a pumpkin into the story.[92] The
first English translation, which was available to many American readers,
appeared in England in 1729, and an 1811 version may be the earliest one
published in the United States.[93]

As in most contemporary versions of the tale, in Perrault's rendition a
poor, good-hearted young country girl is abused by her stepmother and
stepsisters. She is rescued by a fairy godmother who helps get Cinderella
to a royal ball to meet a handsome prince. The fairy transforms barnyard
animals and objects, including a pumpkin, into elegant and sophisticated
finery and accouterments, with the warning that they will revert to their
former selves at the strike of midnight. The 1811 edition: "Then [the fairy
godmother] said to [Cinderella], run into the garden and bring me a pompion. Cinderella went immediately to gather the finest she could get, and
brought it to her godmother, not being able to image how this pompion
could make her go to the ball. Her godmother scooped out all the insides
of it, having left nothing but the rind, which done she struck it with her
wand and the pompion was instantly turned into a fine coach, gilded all
over with gold." After Cinderella hurried to leave the ball just past the
prescribed hour, she looked for her carriage to carry her home, but in
its place "all she saw was a large pompion lying upon the ground, and a
rat, some mice and lizards running away."[94] The story concludes with the

prince rescuing Cinderella from her impoverished life on the farmstead and bringing her to his palace, where, of course, they live happily ever after.

The pumpkin enjoys a pivotal role as the foil in this rags-to-riches story. Its commonness and lack of sophistication provide the ultimate contrast to the opulent life of the rich and urbane. Moreover, the pumpkin is not just a static symbol but also the vehicle, the carriage, that carries Cinderella to her new way of life. Unlike Cinderella, however, the pumpkin does not remain at the palace. Mimicking Hawthorne's pumpkin, its golden color is less a sign of wealth and success than the opposite: a sign of a primal natural world untouched by cultural accouterments. By returning the pumpkin to the farmstead, the tale separates it from a genteel, cultured way of life. Later American readers would likely interpret the pumpkin's transformation into a golden carriage as a glorification of the vegetable and the poor, hard-working way of life it embodies.[95] Yet if other sources from this time period are a fair indication, the pumpkin was an ambiguous symbol, serving as a marker of both a rural abyss and rural virtue.

"Peter, Peter Pumpkin Eater," a classic nursery rhyme, takes a more jocular approach but employs a similar motif, that of the pumpkin as a container for a woman. It also shares the theme of a woman striking out on her own, but with more scandalous overtones. The poem became popular when American publishers added it to the Mother Goose nursery rhyme book in 1825, and many Americans can still recite it today. Unlike other nursery rhymes, this one is believed to have originated in the United States.[96]

> Peter, Peter Pumpkin Eater,
> Had a wife and couldn't keep her,
> He put her in a pumpkin shell,
> And there he kept her very well.

"Pumpkin eater," or "pumpkin roller," was a derogatory term for a poor, ignorant farmer.[97] The rhyme hints at the man's foolishness even as it notes the woman's wandering ways. Perpetuating themes from sixteenth-century Dutch genre paintings, both the pumpkin and the wife embody unbounded sexuality. Some American folk songs, such as the undated "Finger Ring," played off the rhyme's pumpkin imagery and its theme of women's infidelity. The song goes,

> Wish I had a needle and thread, fine as I could sew,
> I'd stitch my true love to my side and on the road I'd go.
> Wish I had a pumpkin shell to put my true love in,
> Take her out and kiss her twice, then put her back again.[98]

The consistency of the pumpkin-and-woman motif over generations is striking. Carolyn Merchant, in *The Death of Nature*, argued that the scientists and philosophers of the sixteenth- and seventeenth-century scientific revolution demoted the stature of both nature and women by reimagining a spirited Mother Nature as inert material and a machine to be controlled rationally instead of as a powerful force to be appeased.[99] Yet Merchant's chronology does not account for the startling continuity of tales about pumpkins and women. *Other arguments since say they are both relegated to basal desire*

The advent of the Enlightenment and capitalism did not necessarily eradicate beliefs in nature and women's power but reinforced old ideas in new contexts. These early nineteenth-century tales might have expressed men's anxieties about young, single women leaving home on their own for the first time to take jobs in the textile factories in Lowell, Massachusetts, and other New England towns. The women textile workers' powerful labor and reform organizations and successful strikes against male factory owners and managers might have exacerbated a sense of men's loss of control. Putting a woman in a pumpkin meant keeping her tied to the farmstead or perhaps bound to the traditional rules and values of an older way of life that was slipping away. But in these tales, man's ability to control her is not taken for granted. *You are not keeping consistent*

Still, in pumpkin iconography, men fared little better than women. An illustration in the book *Memoirs of a Stomach* is a good place to get a glimpse of the pumpkin's early-nineteenth-century male incarnation.[100] The print is a portrait of gluttony. In it, an androgynous figure sits with fat legs splayed, stomach bulged, and shirt buttons popped. The contents of his latest gorge surround him in nightmarish fashion. Fowl, hams, turtles, eggs, and bottles of spirits chaotically encircle him, as if they have come back to haunt him and his digestive system. And his crown, centrally placed on his head as a totem of his gluttonous ways, is a round field pumpkin. Although corpulence in the nineteenth century could be a sign of affluence, in this case the figure looks more like Shakespeare's Falstaff than President Taft.

Many people apparently thought there was no truer or funnier way to express a man's stupidity than to use a pumpkin. Like the Jonathan variety of pumpkin, numbskull tales conflate country bumpkins and pumpkins. One of many variations on these tales tells how the numbskull mistakes a pumpkin for a donkey or rabbit's "egg."[101] In another, a numbskull ties a pumpkin to his leg in order to be able to distinguish himself from other men sleeping nearby when he wakes up. As he sleeps, someone moves the pumpkin to another person's leg, a trick that confuses the numbskull about his own identity.[102] Similarly, many satirical works, such as Samuel Warren's 1842 *Ten Thousand a Year* and the 1857 poem "Iconoclastes: A Domestic Story," which poke fun at country people, feature a character named Pumpkin.[103]

One of the best-known literary works in which a pumpkin stands in for a man's foolishness is Washington Irving's *The Legend of Sleepy Hollow*, published in 1848 and set in the rural countryside of New York's Hudson River valley.[104] As a central element of the tale, the pumpkin represents the area's rusticity as well as the buffoonery of its main character, Ichabod Crane. In the story, Crane, a silly, gangly, itinerant schoolteacher, spends his idle hours spooking himself by reading local ghost stories, especially a notorious one about the Headless Horseman. According to the legend, the Horseman's head was severed from his body during a Revolutionary War battle fought in the area, and he periodically rides again to reclaim it.

One night, while returning home late from a party down an isolated country road, Crane, who is afraid of his own shadow, is chased by the Headless Horseman. As the apparition rides past Crane, the ghost throws a headlike object at him, terrifying the schoolmaster so profoundly that he runs away and is never heard from again. The end of the tale reveals that the ghoul was actually Brom Bones, Ichabod's rival for the attention of a farmer's attractive young daughter. The head was nothing but a pumpkin, accentuating the Crane character's silliness and perpetuating this age-old association.[105]

About the time of the publication of *Sleepy Hollow*, the pumpkin first appeared in its incarnation as a jack-o'-lantern, although Halloween was not yet a part of Americans' regular holiday calendar. The jack-o'-lantern as a folk character originated in Ireland as a trickster forced to wander the netherworld after being banned from both heaven and hell for his ornery behavior.[106] He had nothing to do with the pumpkin at all. Americans may have merged the Irish jack-o'-lantern with legends about supernatural pumpkins, but another source lay closer to home.

In North America, "jack-o'-lantern" (or jack-ma-lantern among African Americans in the South) was another name for the will-o'-the-wisp—an unsettling and inexplicable light emanating from a darkened forest or dense swamp.[107] A newspaper account published in October 1830 offers a good description: "Two gentlemen saw a globe of light or fire apparently twenty feet above the ground. The light resembled a large lamp, was in constant motion, slowly traveling on a light breeze. . . . This is the first 'Will with a Whisp,' or Jack o' Lantern, of which we have had any credible information for many years."[108] Jack-o'-lantern personified the unknown, bewildering forces that seemingly occupied wild places. For some, it was not simply a spook. Like St. Pompion, it might lead people astray or lure them with its evil ways. "If the victim had an irresistible urge to follow the Jack-O'-Lantern," explained one source, "it would be overcome only by 'flinging [himself] down, shutting [his] eyes, holding [his] breath, and plugging up [his ears].'"[109]

By having a ghost hurl a pumpkin from the dark and sinister woods, Irving combined the pumpkin and the jack-o'-lantern legends, but the pumpkin in his story was not carved into a grinning jack-o'-lantern. One of the earliest examples of the pumpkin as jack-o'-lantern is an 1846 newspaper account called "The Jack o'Lantern," about a young boy taking a pumpkin that a farmer did not "make any use of" and carving in it "the outline of three faces, with their eyes, and noses, and teeth."[110] The article made no mention of Halloween, however, and the story's description of a man's inquisitive reaction to the jack-o'-lantern pumpkin indicates that it was not yet a common phenomenon. Yet the connection made sense.

Nathanial Hawthorne's use of a pumpkin head for the main protagonist in his 1830 story "Feathertop: A Moralized Legend" is another antecedent to the Halloween jack-o'-lantern.[111] The tale also offers a strong social commentary on men's character. Feathertop is a scarecrow resembling "a fine gentleman of the period" made by a bewitched New England farm woman. She uses a pumpkin for the head and cuts two holes for eyes and a slit for a mouth. On his head she places a wig and a hat with a long rooster feather in it—hence the name. "I've seen worse [heads] on human shoulders," she said, "and, many a fine gentleman has a pumpkin head, as well as my scarecrow."[112] As the narrator tells readers, "There was something wonderfully human in this ridiculous shape. . . . it appeared to shrivel its yellow surface into a grin—a funny kind of expression betwixt scorn and merriment, as if it understood itself to be a jest at mankind."[113]

By puffing on a tobacco pipe, the scarecrow comes to life. Without the pipe, "instead of a gallant gentleman in a gold-laced coat, thou wilt be but a jumble of sticks and tattered clothes, and a bag of straw, and a withered pumpkin!" warns the witch.[114] She sends Feathertop off to town to dazzle the locals. Many town folk notice a mysterious and magical quality to the man, but they take it to be an expression of his nobility. Only dogs and children, those ostensibly guided more by their natural senses than adults, are able to see the figure for what he really is. While visiting the daughter of a wealthy merchant, Feathertop accidentally reveals his true identity when his reflection is captured in a mirror. He runs back to the farm and never appears in public again. Hawthorne's tale offers a commentary on charlatans, or good-for-nothing, empty-headed men who pretend to be more than they are.

Like other storytellers, Hawthorne used the pumpkin as a tool to articulate social and class distinctions: between urban intellectuals, guided by culture, and rural workers, guided by nature. When New Englanders cast the pumpkin in terms of such class or social differences, their portraits were usually negative. Farmers were foolish, and rural men and women usually corrupt or immoral. The image of the pumpkin and of pumpkin farmers was much less condescending when New Englanders linked it to their past and adopted it as a symbol of their cultural roots.[115] Many New Englanders embraced the pumpkin as a sign of virtue, finding a sense of heritage and comfort in the old-fashioned, rural way of life it embodied. John Greenleaf Whittier's 1846 poem "The Pumpkin" was "written as receiving a gift of a Pumpkin Pie, By a Yankee." In it, Whittier seamlessly united the jack-o'-lantern, Cinderella, and nature motifs in one vivid rustic scene. Absent is any trace of the demeaning tone found in the literature addressing class and superiority:

> Oh, fruit loved of boyhood! The old days recalling,
> When wood-grapes were purpling and brown nuts were falling!

When wild, ugly faces we carved in its skin,
Glaring out through the dark with a candle within!
When we laughed round the corn-heap, with hearts all in tune,
Our chair a broad pumpkin,—our lantern the moon.
Telling the tales of the fairy who raveled like steam,
In a pumpkin-shell coach, with two rats for her team![116]

In this stanza, the poet imbued the pumpkin with nostalgic recollections of his youth, the natural rhythms of an idyllic farm life, and the magical and mystical qualities of nature. For many Americans in the industrial North, these themes were indelibly linked. The pumpkin evoked a way of life tied to childhood memories of the farm, a place where many northerners were raised but then left for opportunities elsewhere.

One way they held onto that way of life was to indulge in pumpkin pie at Thanksgiving. "The thought of keeping Thanksgiving without a pumpkin pie," wrote a correspondent to *American Farmer* in 1833, "is surely almost insupportable."[117] Northerners served pumpkin pie on any and all occasions, but they came to identify it with Thanksgiving because it spoke to the holiday themes: a bountiful harvest, an idyllic past, and agrarian virtue. New Englanders clearly thought of Thanksgiving as more than just another holiday; they found in the celebration—and the pumpkin—a grand vision of regional identity. "Of all the holidays in the year which are generated among us New England people, there is, perhaps no day in the whole holiday vocabulary, that gives a more general source of satisfaction and joy, than . . . Thanksgiving," explained a November 1825 edition of the Dedham, Massachusetts, *Village Register*.[118]

Celebrants customarily spent Thanksgiving mornings at church, where sermons recounted the blessings and good fortune of the preceding year. Yet family reunions and "universal stuffing," as one contemporary source called it, were also hallmarks of the occasion: "The children and grandchildren return home at this season, to pay their respects and manifest their undiminished love and affection, not to the 'old folks' alone, but also to their roasted turkies and . . . that savory dish, peculiar to New England—that sine qua non of a Thanksgiving dinner—the well filled, deep and spacious pumpkin pie."[119]

Some of the region's most popular and respected writers—John Greenleaf Whittier among them—published quaint stories about Thanksgiving homecomings set in the New England countryside. The tales almost always culminate with an irresistible pumpkin pie. Although authors cast the holiday in a golden hue, they nevertheless made an important distinction between being of the farm and briefly returning to the farm on holiday. Thanksgiving was not a rural holiday per se but a holiday that celebrated cultural ties to rural places and ways of life. New Englanders celebrated simple farm life more as a heritage than as an occupation. Emerson and Hawthorne prove, through their scorn of the region's rural laborers, that "Yankee" was an ambivalent term of endearment. And since most New England farmers were businessmen in pursuit of profit, they enjoyed the holiday's rustic imagery with as keen a sense of nostalgia as urbanites did.

Urban and rural relations were only part of the Thanksgiving story in the early nineteenth century. The saccharine tales also disguised (sometimes poorly) strong political points of view. Some of the most popular storytellers were also ardent abolitionists who were engaged in sectional debates between the North and the South. In 1844, Lydia Maria Child was best known as the author of one of the most popular women's domestic advice books, *The American Frugal Housewife*, when she published her still famous Thanksgiving poem, "A Boy's Thanksgiving Day," now better known as "Over the River and Through the Woods." The familiar verse, "Over the river and through the woods, to grandfather's house we go. / The horse knows the way to carry the sleigh through the white and drifted snow," follows the genre's classic trope—a Thanksgiving visit to a bucolic family home.[120] By ending the last verse with the line, "Hoorah for pumpkin pie!" Child echoed Whittier in "The Pumpkin." Whittier concluded his poem with a pumpkin-inspired blessing that cast a glow on his Yankee homeland and its people:

And the prayer, which my mouth is too full to express,
Swells my heart that thy shadow may never be less,
That the days of thy lot may be lengthened below,
And the fame of thy worth like a pumpkin-vine grow,
And thy life be as sweet, and its last sunset sky
Golden-tinted and fair as thy own Pumpkin Pie!

Although Whittier delighted in the sensual pleasures of baked pumpkin pie, he also cast the vegetable as a sign of a life well lived, a good life blessed with health, longevity, and good fortune. The pumpkin brought together food, farm, family, and New Englanders' sense of place.

The most influential Thanksgiving celebrant was Sarah Josepha Hale, the editor of *Godey's Lady's Book* from 1837 to 1877.[121] Her 1827 novel *Northwood: A Tale of New England* included an entire chapter dedicated to Thanksgiving. She set the novel in a rural New Hampshire village "inhabited," she wrote, "almost exclusively, by husbandmen, who tilled their own farms with their own hands. . . . [They] displayed, in their simplicity and purity of their manners and morals, a model . . . [of] what constituted a 'happy society.'"[122] To bring the image of the idyllic, yeoman New England farm community to full effect, she added, "Among this unsophisticated people, men are esteemed more for merit and usefulness, than rank and wealth."[123] They were a community of pumpkin farmers in the best and most romantic sense.   *Original Am + Fr + E Dream*

In *Northwood*, Hale defined the quintessential Thanksgiving Day, when family members returned to the New England farm of their youth for a celebration of the blessings of country life and family. Pumpkin pie was "an indispensable part of a good and true Yankee Thanksgiving," and among the roast beef, mutton, pork, chicken pie, plates of vegetables, gravies, and puff pastries both sweet and savory, "pumpkin pie occupied the most distinguished niche."[124] Hale led a cohort of New England clergy, editors, and private citizens in advocating for states throughout the country to proclaim an annual Thanksgiving day and for the federal government to declare it a national holiday. Every November beginning in 1846, she transformed *Godey's* "Editor's Table" into a platform to promote the nationalization of the holiday. Although her efforts would not succeed until 1863, the holiday began to catch on beyond New England's borders.

The publication of pumpkin pie recipes and poems in newspapers from Ohio to Nebraska documents the holiday's spread to new settlement areas across the West. "Who that has ever lived in New England will not heartily endorse the sentiment thus gratefully expressed?" wrote the editors of the *Omaha Nebraskan* in the preface to the nostalgic poem "Pumpkin Pies," which declared, "I'm dwelling now 'neath other suns, / And bright are other skies, / Yet memory oft brings back again / the thought of pumpkin pies."[125] Whereas Maryland, South Carolina, North Carolina, and Louisiana had all proclaimed "fast days of thanksgiving, humiliation, and prayer," homegrown holiday rituals—the rural homecomings, the harvest themes, and pumpkin pie—were popularly known as New England traditions.[126] The commemoration of rural virtue perhaps did not resonate the same way in the South, especially at a time when many northerners publicly questioned the morality of the southern plantation way of life based on slave labor.

Some of the most strident critics of slavery were also some of the most prolific writers of pumpkin tales. Whittier was a public spokesman for the antislavery cause, a founding member of the American Anti-Slavery Society, and author of the 1833 pamphlet "Justice and Expediency; or, Slavery Considered with a View to Its Rightful and Effectual Remedy, Abolition," and the 1834 poem "Our Countrymen in Chains!"[127] Child was elected to the American Anti-Slavery Society's executive committee in 1839, became editor of its *Anti-Slavery Standard* two years later, and wrote *Appeal for the Class of Americans Called Africans*, among many other antislavery texts.[128] Although Hale was less politically active than Child and Whittier, *Northwood* was a forceful abolitionist tract. She renamed the novel *Northwood; or Life North and South, Showing the True Color of Both* in 1852 to emphasize the regions' distinctions. The main character, Squire Romilly, sums up the author's own attitudes about slavery: "I feel it is a stain on our national character, and none could more heartily rejoice to see the abomination removed. It will be, it must be; honor, justice, humanity and religion, are all violated in the system of slavery."[129] These three writers' efforts to free slaves did not mean that they believed in the inherent equality of the races. Hale, for example, was a strong proponent of freed African Americans' emigration to Liberia, because she could not conceive of them coexisting with Euroamericans.[130]

What bound pumpkins to abolitionism was the political economy. The writers interpreted agrarian ways of life or modes of production in social and political terms, imagining the small family farm as an antidote to the plantation. Rather than being determined to spread the agrarian way of life itself, they sought to spread the values and sense of morality they saw embedded in it and in themselves. Emerson, who was dismissive of actual farmers, expressed faith in the power of agrarian life to transform the political world: "If it be true that, not by votes of political parties but by the eternal laws of political economy, slaves are driven out of a slave state as fast as it is surrounded by free states, then the true abolitionist is the farmer, who, needless of laws and constitutions stands all day in the field, investing his labor in the land, and making a product with which no forced labor can compete."[131] Hale stated more directly, "I have no doubt many of the slaveholders would rejoice to have the southern states entirely freed from slaves, and cultivated in the same manner we Yankees do in the North."[132] Both writers infused the rural landscape with their political identity and cultural values, even as they saw their region's future as lying in industry, not agriculture.[133]

Whittier, Child, and Hale, some of the most outspoken abolitionists, also wrote some of the period's most popular and cherished pumpkin stories. To them, the pumpkin—and pumpkin farming—so completely embodied New England, as opposed to southern, values.[134] The pumpkin was a naturally abundant crop that exemplified agrarian prowess, yet at the same time it was an unmarketable crop that stood for timeless agrarian values uncorrupted by the pursuit of profit. The quaint musings about pumpkins in the popular press also conveyed political sentiments. To communicate the larger political significance of a New Jersey man's establishing an orchard in the new state of California, one woman correspondent wrote in 1851, "Who does the most good, the leader in wars and insurrections, or the public-spirited individual who benevolently adopts means to provide prosperity with the blessings of pumpkin-pies?"[135] The pumpkin, for that writer, was an icon of a civil society. A southern visitor to Boston made a more direct association between abolitionism and pumpkins when he conceded the futility of enforcing the fugitive slave laws in the North: "As easily could a law prohibiting eating of codfish and pumpkin pies be enforced."[136] *P-Pie is essential + desired*

Eating pumpkin in the early nineteenth century had less to do with economic hardship than with identity politics, and regional distinctions in cuisine had more to do with cultural differences than with divergent climates or access to pumpkins. Amelia Simmons had already made pumpkin much more than simply a dessert to satisfy a sweet tooth. Hale built on this legacy, but she did not identify the colonists as her progenitors. Indeed, the Pilgrims were not even a focus in these early versions of Thanksgiving.[137] Eating pumpkin was instead a way to affirm New Englanders' identity through attachments to a place, a particular landscape, and the simple virtues of farm life. Pumpkin pie was a New England food because it represented New England values. Pumpkin tales suggest that urbanites and even many farmers ridiculed a preindustrial, rural way of life as backward and ignorant; that many believed it was bad for either men or women to follow their natural urges, though for different reasons; that men were insecure about women striking out on their own; and that New Englanders were nostalgic for a rustic farmstead in ways that self-consciously set them apart from southerners. The cultural history of the pumpkin shows us that the ways in which people value nature depend not only on how they think and interact with the natural world but also on how they think about and act toward one another. With all this in mind, the answer to the question "Why the pumpkin?" becomes clearer, if far more complex.

ᴄᴏ— FOUR —ᴄᴏ

"WONDERFULLY GRAND AND COLOSSAL"

The Pumpkin and the Nation, 1861 to 1899

A FTER THE CIVIL WAR, AMERICAN FARMERS WOULD INCREAS-
ingly forsake the agrarian ideal of self-sufficiency in their push
toward maximizing profits on commodity crops.[1] They relied on
banks to extend them credit to expand their operations and purchase the
latest equipment. They depended on railroads and grain operators to con-
nect them to manufacturing centers throughout the country. And with
increasing regularity, farm households became food consumers instead of
producers so that they could devote their land entirely to moneymaking
crops.

Facilitated by federal land grant programs such as the Homestead Act
of 1862 and by the completion of the transcontinental railroad in 1869,
the center of agricultural production continued to move westward. Cattle
replaced buffalo on the midwestern prairie, and railroad towns sprang up
to convey the animals to Chicago slaughterhouses. The invention of the
refrigerated railroad car jump-started the beef industry in the 1870s but
also helped northeastern farmers, who were unable to match midwestern
farm prices, reorient toward dairy production for urban markets. Barbed
wire, windmills, and sod houses marked the presence of homesteaders on
the Great Plains, yet the changing mode of American agriculture made
it difficult for them to compete, much less survive, in international commodities markets.[2]

Feeling hamstrung by the railroads, banks, and grain operators, which
increasingly controlled the flow and profits of agriculture, in the 1860s

farmers mobilized through the Grange and Farmers Alliance to try to regain their independence. They achieved only mixed success because farming and food processing were moving toward greater corporate control. Bonanza wheat farming, which developed in the Red River valley of North Dakota in the 1880s, was a portent of the future, with its industrial form of production, heavy reliance on machines, and dependence on large outside investments.

At the other end of agricultural production, the demise of slavery in the South meant the rise of tenant farming and sharecropping, under which many newly freed slaves and poor whites lived in dire poverty. There was nothing picturesque about subsistence farming. All too many people barely eked out a living on land devastated by the war, and they were often strangled by debt. With this combination of poor sharecroppers, rich middlemen operators, and massive farm businesses, American agriculture was moving in directions that could not have been more at odds with the quaint family farm of lore.

Nor could it have been more different from pumpkin farming. Raising pumpkins remained antithetical to all the new trends in American agriculture. The mode and scale of their production—hand picking a few acres—were anachronistic. "We could wish that we had seen the last of them," wrote the influential agricultural journal The Horticulturalist in 1870. "It is about time that pumpkins were retired from service and entered upon the fossil list."[3] At a value of $2.50 a ton by the end of the century—that is, about a tenth of a cent per pound (rice brought 7 cents per pound)—the pumpkin ranked among the least valuable and useful of farm commodities.[4] The July 1882 edition of American Agriculturalist stated disparagingly, "It would hardly pay to devote land to the production of pumpkins."[5]

Yet a pumpkin, one of the least profitable and palatable of vegetables, appeared prominently on the American Agriculturalist's masthead. Biggs and Brothers advertised pumpkins on the cover of their annual seed catalogs.[6] Agricultural fairs became known as "pumpkin shows" because the vegetable was a key attraction.[7] It was obviously not the crop's economic worth or its promise of financial reward that inspired agricultural trade publications and expositions to feature the vegetable. It was the pumpkin's symbolic value. By placing images of pumpkins alongside bucolic scenes of farm work and outdoor recreation and making the vegetable the cornerstone of their events, publishers and agricultural fair organizers embraced the idea that pumpkin farming was a valuable, uplifting pursuit and the pumpkin an important crop, even if it was not a route to financial success.

The late nineteenth century marks the important shift when the pumpkin's meanings were alienated from its uses. No longer was its symbolism sustained by material and practical functions—that is, by actual farmers raising actual pumpkins for human and animal sustenance. It now thrived on its own without them. The popular literary journal *Harper's Weekly* filled its pages with images and stories of pumpkins, evidence of its public appeal. But the U.S. Agricultural Census, the data-collecting arm of the U.S. Department of Agriculture (USDA), established in 1861 for the purposes of research, education, and regulation, did not even bother to include pumpkins in its reports through the end of the century, a strong indication that the pumpkin lacked status as a commercial crop.

Most Americans valued pumpkins for pleasure, not for profits. They made pumpkins objects of display detached from any practical utility. For example, rather than bragging about the total yield per plant that could contribute to a farm's economy, Burpee's seed company documented the success of its "Genuine Mammoth" with reports of cash prizes won for 200- and 225-pound specimens.[8] Similarly, the 1899 Buckbee seed catalog described new varieties in terms of how they served the pumpkin's expanding ceremonial uses for display and dessert. It touted its "King of the Mammoth," a 469-pounder exhibited at the 1893 World's Fair, for its grandiose size, calling it a "wonderfully grand and colossal variety, astonishing everyone by its mammoth size and heavy weight."[9] It marketed "Pure Gold" for its associations with picturesque farm life and its excellence in sweet pies rather than for its uses as daily food for people or animals. "The pumpkin is a gorgeous fruit, principally celebrated for its services to agricultural fairs. . . . It must be remembered that pumpkins of mastodonic size are valued, like the very fat women and overgrown pigs which are placed on exhibition, rather for their weight and size than for any other quality. . . . Its bigness is all it is valued for," explained a journalist for the *Rocky Mountain News* in 1879.[10] By comparing the pumpkin with a pig and a woman, the reporter underscored the vegetable's reputation as a living creature and its value as a metaphor with which to talk about human relations and gender identity, even as he recognized its complete lack of utilitarian function.

"Desirable Pumpkins," a page from the 1899 H. W. Buckbee Seed and Plant Guide, Rockford, Illinois. Buckbee began to breed pumpkins for holiday display and dessert rather than for practical functions. Special Collections, National Agricultural Library.

Many merchants around the country must have taken notice of the spectacle the pumpkin's great girth aroused at fairs, because they began to display pumpkins in their shops. The vegetables were "highly prized to place in show windows, restaurants, etc.," as Samuel Wilson's 1888 seed catalog noted.[11] Instead of offering pumpkins for sale for food or fodder, merchants used them as marketing gimmicks to draw in customers, thereby infusing the pumpkin with a brand new commercial value never previously achieved for its practical uses. One merchant described how a mammoth pumpkin on public view at a Massachusetts nursery "astonished the gazers." A man was "moved to write a poem about it," he contended, and another "declared that he positively stood in awe of it."[12]

Clothing-store proprietors from St. Paul, Minnesota, to Boston,

Massachusetts, held contests offering merchandise prizes to whoever could most accurately guess the number of seeds in a giant pumpkin on display. A Boston dry goods store owner named Wallenstein, explained an 1890 article in the *Atkinson (Kansas) Champion*, "placed a large pumpkin in his show window and advertised that any person purchasing one dollar's worth of goods should have a guess at the number of seeds it contained, and that the person guessing the number, or the nearest to it, should be entitled to a first prize of a plush cloak."[13] As nine people tied for first place and three for third, the publicity stunt must have worked. The owner of Proprietor Barth, a "St. Paul One Price clothing house," gained a lot of press and customers by displaying a reported ten thousand pumpkins and serving up pumpkin pies to more than seven hundred people in his store.[14] As the *Rocky Mountain News* observed, there was nothing useful about the pumpkin besides the spectacle it aroused. Americans prized the pumpkin for its looks and its meanings, not its meat.

Like New Englanders of a generation before, many Americans in the late nineteenth century celebrated the pumpkin for the very reasons that made it a "fossil" in the world of agriculture: the unruly nature of the plant, which was ill adapted to standardization and mechanization; its minimal economic value in the modern commodities market; and its association with an old-fashioned way of making a living off the land. As Americans erected more skyscrapers, laid more railroad tracks, and diligently pursued wealth and material goods, many felt they were losing their connection to the natural world, an authentic way of life, and their cultural roots. The pumpkin helped them rebuild those connections.

A romance with nature permeated almost every aspect of American middle-class life in this period. It found expression in the birth of the national park and city park movements, the spread of suburbanization, greater participation in outdoor recreation, and the popularity of nature writing and landscape paintings.[15] The families of bankers, merchants, lawyers, and, by the end of the century, those of more modest means sought temporary refuge from urban life by spending their vacations at farmsteads and at resort hotels and cottages in mountain settings.[16] Closer to home, middle-class Americans created picturesque suburban homes with manicured lawns and naturalistic gardens inspired by the work of the popular landscape architects Andrew Jackson Downing and Frederick Law Olmsted.

Frederick Jackson Turner's famous frontier thesis address at the 1893 Chicago World's Fair was but one political manifestation of this pervasive romantic pastoralism.[17] Building on the legacy of Jeffersonian agrarianism, Turner predicated American democratic values on the vastness of the American continent, where generations of independent farmers had broken the soil, supposedly paving the way for civilization. Although more contemporary historians have long since rebuffed this idea as misguided and ethnocentric, this frontier myth rang true for many Americans. Just as Americans believed the frontier was closing in the late nineteenth century, so they began to look more longingly on the agrarian way of life, with which they associated it, and to the pumpkin, with which they had long equated it.

Playing with pumpkins—putting scary faces on them and giving them devious personalities—marked one of the new ways that middle-class Americans found a way to feel connected to nature. The field pumpkin's rusticity, its headlike shape and living flesh, its time of harvest, and its historical connection to the world of wild spirits all captured Halloween's essence and explain why the pumpkin acquired its ghoulish persona. "To add weirdness and quaintness [to your party]," advised a party planner, "have plenty of jack-o'-lanterns made of pumpkins."[18] The danger of the jack-o'-lantern titillated more than it terrified. The fear was part of the fun, just as it was, for example, when hiking the John Muir trail in the newly opened Yosemite National Park.

Newspapers published accounts of people carving and displaying jack-o'-lantern pumpkins instead of feeding the vegetable to cows and pigs. Probably the first image of a pumpkin jack-o'-lantern appeared alongside the article "A Pumpkin Effigy" in the November 23, 1867, issue of *Harper's Weekly*—although the article did not describe the pumpkin that way, nor did it mention Halloween.[19] The engraving depicts a rustic farmstead, and portrays a pumpkin perched atop a fence post, surrounded by the farm boys who have carved it. The streams of light that flow from its jagged, devilish facial features illuminate a frightened girl, her younger sibling, and their terrified dog. In the background, a man loads pumpkins into a barn surrounded by leafless trees, signs of the passing season and rural setting. The darkened sky and gnarled tree limbs echo the mood set by the pumpkin's sinister face. The author of the accompanying article, which included Whittier's romantic ode to the pumpkin, explained to readers:

L. W. Atwater, *The Pumpkin Effigy*, wood engraving, *Harper's Weekly*, November 23, 1867. This illustration is one of the earliest depictions of a jack-o'-lantern pumpkin. Library of Congress, Washington, D.C., LC-USZ62-8391.

"THE PUMPKIN EFFIGY."—[DRAWN BY L. W. ATWATER.]

"The sport of the pastime consists of paring a pumpkin to resemble a human head, and placing a light within to illuminate it, suddenly expose the monster just created to the view of passing persons, frequently to the very considerable horror of some youthful and more timid persons."[20]

An 1887 story in the *Boston Daily Advertiser* told of a group of Harvard students "who stole a prize squash to make a jack o' lantern." Another story covered a group of boys in Newark, New Jersey, who had placed a carved pumpkin over an electric lamppost.[21] "The effect can be better understood than described when one thinks of the huge head of a monster suspended in midair with the rays of a strong electric light streaming from its eyes, nose and mouth," commented the reporter. Jack-o'-lantern pumpkins were still a new enough phenomenon to elicit surprise and astonishment.

Pumpkin lies? (handwritten annotation)

The popularization of Halloween mirrored the development of Thanksgiving and happened at about the same time. In both cases, nineteenth-century Americans reimagined remnants of old rituals to fit their whims and fancies.[22] By the time of the great Irish migration to North America in the middle of the century, Americans no longer celebrated Halloween as the ancient Celtic fête commemorating the onset of winter, when souls of the dead walked the earth. Now it was a night of entertainment, when spirits appeared as sources of eerie fun and playful conjuring. Halloween night in the post–Civil War United States became an excuse for socializing among young adults, a time to recall the magic and mystery of the ancient festivities in a good-humored way. "We are all of us the better for an occasional frolic, and Halloween, with its quaint customs and mystic tricks, affords opportunity for much innocent merriment," declared the authors of "Halloween Romps and Frolics by Two Experienced Entertainers," in the October 1897 issue of *Ladies Home Journal*.[23]

Pagan roots lost, As usual (handwritten annotation in left margin)

With women's magazines to guide them, Americans transformed ancient Halloween festivities into parlor games, and participants began arriving in costume. Activities centered on finding clues to one's future paramour's identity. His initials might appear in an apple rind, or her image in a candle-lit mirror. Creepy stories and decorations of witches, black cats, jack-o'-lanterns, and other spooks amused more than they frightened.[24] "The Magic Halloween," "Halloween Pumpkins," and dozens of other poems like them imagined the pumpkin as a wily creature stalking the night.[25] "The Magic Halloween" chimed:

Once again alive (handwritten annotation in left margin)

> All Hallowe'en, the magic night,
> When folly reigns supreme,
> The pumpkin heads are all alight,
> The stars are all agleam.

"Halloween Pumpkins" playfully warned:

> With pumpkin heads all peering,
> Is it not a fearsome sight?
> For the witching hour is nearing
> Of Hallowe'en midnight!

Rural harvest decorations became backdrops for the more mystical creatures. As one columnist instructed: "Bunches of wheat or grasses over pictures and in vases, ears of ripened corn, and festoons of brilliant cranberries strung upon a thread, will give a suggestion of the country to the scene. Wherever possible, have a roaring, crackling, open-fire."[26] The party planner suggested that in lieu of holding a Halloween party in a "large old-fashioned country barn," the hostess could use her house and let "the old fashioned pumpkin or squash be the chief dependence."[27] She recommended, "Let all the light that is used, either inside or out, come from pumpkin lanterns."[28] Turning the pumpkin into a jack-o'-lantern made it not only a playful spirit but also a party favor, signaling its transformation from an agricultural product into a home decoration, a new use that would eventually change both the actual physical pumpkin and its market value.

One need not look hard to discover where Halloween celebrants, agricultural fair organizers, and journal publishers got their inspiration to embrace the pumpkin as their totem. Picturesque pumpkin images and stories filled the popular press. The cosmopolitan *Harper's Weekly* regularly published sentimental and nostalgic vignettes of country life, with its barnyard dances, cornhusking parties, and pumpkin harvests, which appealed to middle-class sensibilities. Currier and Ives introduced such images into American homes through inexpensive prints, such as the "American Homestead" series, which featured quaint farm scenes in every season. These artists and writers were concerned less with presenting the economic realities of American agriculture than with communicating the belief that small-scale, low-tech farms stood for simpler times and a more natural and virtuous existence. As farms began to exist more in the hands of large-scale enterprises than of small ones, and as labor became more the act of machines than of human hands, these antiquated images lived on in popular culture as symbols of American cultural identity and, in time, as models for late-twentieth-century farm markets.

Many writers gushed unapologetically over the pumpkin because it captured so well both the rustic image of rural life and nature's vitality. "How dear to this heart is the old yellow pumpkin . . . the mud covered pumpkin, / The big-bellied pumpkin that makes such good pies!" cheered a poem published in newspapers from Minnesota to Louisiana.[29] The author of the article "Gone Forever" anxiously viewed the changes happening around him by mourning the passing of the days when pumpkins were a part of everyday life. "They don't grow the same kind of pumpkins now," he sighed. "The sun never shines down on the old cornfield the same way it did thirty odd years ago."[30] As if to relive those mythic days of old, James Whitcomb Riley's 1887 poem "When the Frost Is on the Punkin" recalled the visceral sounds and traditions of a rustic farm at harvest time:

> When the frost is on the punkin and the fodder's in the shock,
> And you hear the kyouck and gobble of the struttin' turkey-cock,
> And the clackin' of the guineys and the cluckin' of the hens,
> And the rooster's hallylooyer as he tiptoes on the fence;
> O, it's then the time a feller is a-feelin at his best,
> With the risin' sun to greet him from a night of peaceful rest,
> As he leaves the house, bareheaded, and goes out to feed the stock,
> When the frost is on the punkin and the fodder's in the shock![31]

Riley's rhythmic cadence reinforces the sense of harmony between the farmer and the natural world. Each seems in tune with the other. The pumpkin, as the centerpiece of the poem, symbolizes this happy union. The poet's use of parochial language, such as "It's then the time a feller is a-feelin at his best," evokes a provincial and unsophisticated small-time farmer. Yet the poet evinces none of Emerson's condescension toward working farmers.

Any number of landscape paintings, such as Winslow Homer's 1878 *Pumpkins among the Corn*, could have illustrated such poems. The typical farm painting of the time revealed little of the regularity or standardization that actually characterized late-nineteenth-century commercial farm operations. Rather, in typical picturesque style, the paintings emphasized the natural irregularities of the setting. Although some paintings of the genre, such as J. Francis Murphy's undated *The Pumpkin Field*, contain no human figures, the insertion of fences or glimpses of distant farmhouses is a benign reminder of the human presence.[32] In Winslow Homer's 1873 *The Last Days of the Harvest*, which was reproduced in *Harper's Weekly*, two young boys lazily shuck corn in a field of bundled cornstalks and pumpkins while two men spear and toss pumpkins into a horse-drawn wagon. Homer places a field pumpkin prominently in front of the boys, making

John Whetten Ehninger (American, 1827–1889), *October*, 1867. Oil on canvas, 32 1/4 by 54 1/8 inches. Quaint images of pumpkin farming like this one showed up regularly in the popular press and in works of fine art and literature in the mid-nineteenth century. Smithsonian American Art Museum, Washington, D.C./Art Resource, New York.

the vegetable both the visual and the thematic focus of the painting.[33] In John Whetten Ehninger's 1867 *October*, four men load pumpkins into the back of an ox-drawn wagon. One stands with a pumpkin in his arms next to a woman who sits passively on a cart to the side. The stoic female sitting in the field could represent nature itself, a contemporary rendition of the mythical Ceres watching over the men's labor. All the figures wear simple country clothes, yet the cleanliness and neatness of their garments imbue them with a sense of dignity. *Dignty + Clan*

The large orange pumpkins in *October* blend into the colors of the fall foliage of distant trees and the more muted hues on faraway hillsides, as if to relate the natural changes in the landscape to the seasonal labor of the farmers. A calmness and serenity in both Homer's and Ehninger's paintings belie the arduous work being depicted. The sexual improprieties that Dutch genre painters associated with rural peasants and with pumpkins are absent from these more earnest and sympathetic views of humble, rural life.

The golden halo that pumpkin farmers enjoyed in these tributes to American agrarianism could still be reduced to a tarnished crown of thorns, however, when pumpkin motifs left the farm. In an editorial that evokes Hawthorne's Feathertop, the ~~New Eclectic Magazine~~ observed: "There is nothing ~~women resent so~~ much as pumpkin manhood—nothing which humiliates them more in their own esteem than to discover that they have been taken in by appearances, and that what they believed was solid wood turns out to be only squash."[34]

Strains of the mean-spirited or ignorant pumpkin man reemerged in political cartoons such as one in the 1863 issue of *Harper's Weekly*, which portrayed Clement Vallandigham, an outspoken critic of President Lincoln and a Democratic candidate for the Ohio governorship, as "an ugly Pumpkin growing upon thy land."[35] In the cartoon, a large pumpkin with a frowning human face sits unhappily on the ground between two men with pitchforks, who personify the states of Ohio and Pennsylvania. The cartoonist is criticizing the "noxious weed" type of politician who keeps returning to the political landscape even after the people try to get rid of him. "I've tossed [him] over into my neighbor's field," says one man to the other, "and he's [returned] and took root, you see, among the . . . thistles." Similarly, a cartoon of the U.S. Supreme Court published in an 1896 edition of *Puck* portrayed the judges as lacking sophistication and erudition by depicting them as farmers surrounded by hard cider, whittling sticks, doughnuts, chewing tobacco, and a pumpkin.[36] The perpetuation of this negative stereotype for men of letters throughout the second half of the nineteenth century underscores the limits of agrarian ideology: pumpkins and subsistence farming were antithetical to modern society—although that could be their charm, too.

Perhaps the most endearing new meaning of the pumpkin was an affectionate association of children with pumpkins. Like previous generations, many Americans in the industrial centers thought of rustic farms as places of their youth, but now they began to depict children and pumpkins together. This development coincided with new attitudes not only toward nature as an escape from modern stresses but also toward childhood as a time of carefree existence. Throughout the colonial period and into the nineteenth century, most people thought of children as small adults whose temptations needed to be strictly controlled. Influenced by the rise of Romanticism and new pedagogical approaches in the nineteenth century, many Americans began to view children as more inherently good than bad. They saw childhood as a time of innocence and purity. For a child to act naturally was considered proper and good. Describing the young pumpkin plant before it burst into great fruit, none other than Henry Ward Beecher noted, "But this pause upon the threshold of active life, this modest reserve, is becoming in both boy and pumpkin."[37] Equating a child with a pumpkin, a potent symbol of nature and vigorous development, was therefore a positive affirmation, as opposed to the negative connotations for adults, who were supposed to be guided by reason.

The artist Worthington Whittredge's 1863 *In the Pumpkin Patch* offers a case in point.[38] A teenage boy rests next to a gigantic pumpkin, with massive leaves, which is growing in a clearing on the edge of a wood. The boy and the pumpkin straddle the boundary between tamed nature—the manicured field—and wild nature—the overgrown vegetation. That the boy lies on the ground next to the pumpkin conflates boy and vegetable. Both the young man and the pumpkin exude a sense of vitality and promise yet also a bit of unruliness and laziness. Just as the boy escapes his chores and his responsibilities to his household, so the pumpkin escapes the confines of the field. The tone of the painting suggests a celebration of the splendors of youth and nature. Whittredge's image is echoed in many of Winslow Homer's paintings that pair young boys with pumpkins, such as *The Last Days of the Harvest* and *Corn and Pumpkins*.

Children's stories at this time began to feature the pumpkin in tales that aimed to teach the difference between virtuous and unruly behavior. Olivia Lovell Wilson's 1887 play *Luck of the Golden Pumpkin* is a good example.[39] In the play, the eldest son of a poor farm family goes into town to sell his prize pumpkin in order to buy his starving brothers and sisters Christmas dinner. He sadly gives the pumpkin to an impoverished stranger, whose request for the pumpkin the boy, out of the goodness of his heart, cannot refuse. At the play's finale, the stranger turns out to be a long-lost wealthy uncle who reciprocates the boy's generosity with a pumpkin filled with gold coins. The play reiterates the adage that hard-working, virtuous people are rewarded with the fruits of their labor. The pumpkin, the catalyst for the farm boy's success, is the embodiment of this theme, as it is in the Cinderella tale. One of the last lines of the play announces: "We owe it all to Mark's golden pumpkins!" Pumpkins are literally as good as gold and no longer a crass, fake "lump of gold," as Hawthorne had it.

Following the model of the animal fable, the novelist and social critic William Dean Howells instilled childlike behavior in the pumpkin, playfully using it to offer a morality tale about blind ambition and the benefits of a humble, old-fashioned rural work ethic. In his 1892 "The Pumpkin Glory," a virtuous young pumpkin stays within the confines of the garden and aspires to be the epitome of domestic harmony—a Thanksgiving pie.[40] Unlike his dutiful brother, a bad little pumpkin wanders off in search of greater fame and glory. He gets his vine twisted in a fence post so that his body droops and becomes lopsided rather than growing beautifully round like his brother's. True to his nature, the wild pumpkin becomes a jack-o'-lantern, but while vainly teetering on a fence post he falls into the squalor of a pigsty and ends up being eaten by a sow. In contrast, the good little pumpkin ends his life by attaining his lifelong dreams of winning first prize at the county fair and occupying an honorable and revered place on the Thanksgiving table as a pumpkin pie.

By the 1890s, Americans saw pumpkins more regularly in tales, prints, and poems than in fields. And these sentimental stories and images, more than the vegetable's flesh, fueled the appetite for eating pumpkin. People craved pumpkin pie because of what it meant. "When properly made," explained the author of "Genuine Pumpkin Pie" in the *Kansas City Journal,* "the pumpkin pie is the embodiment, so to speak, of peace on earth and good will toward men. No man ever plotted treason or formulated dark damnable designs while filling his system with a genuine New England pumpkin pie. . . . If the genuine, thick, creamy, sweet-scented pumpkin pie could be universally distributed it would banish pessimism and cause anarchy to take to the woods."[41] Like this anonymous writer, many Americans believed pumpkin pie possessed deep cultural values and profound goodness and righteousness. Eating pumpkin pie connected people to particular ideologies. Who did not eat pumpkin pie, then, is as important as who did. *Dayum*

Technological innovations that changed the course and character of agricultural production also affected consumption patterns. The development of refrigerated railroad cars by the 1870s and the use of iceboxes in homes increased the availability and sustainability of perishables, from dairy and meat products to fruits and vegetables. The advent of commercial canning, as well as of Mason jars and other hermetically sealing home canning techniques at mid-century, made once-seasonal products edible year-round. Jars of green beans and tomatoes replaced strings of dried pumpkin in house cellars. The use of canned meats and vegetables proliferated during the Civil War as a means of sustaining troops in the field.[42] The industry spread to the civilian market after the war. Canned goods were initially affordable only for the well-to-do, but by the turn of the century, reductions in the costs of manufacturing and materials made the products available to most segments of society.

The transition from the open hearth to the cast-iron stove and lighter steel pots eased the burden of home cooking. New modes of transportation and the development of grocery store chains that standardized the types of foods available to consumers weakened regional differences in foodways. Cookbooks and women's magazines were among the many new publications that proliferated in the late nineteenth century with innovations in the speed, quantity, and cost of commercial printing and distribution systems. Recipes were no longer handwritten notes among family heirlooms but printed documents that women cut out from popular magazines.

Although Americans might have eaten pumpkin pie throughout the year, they associated it most strongly with Thanksgiving. In the early 1860s, the idea of the American nation was anything but certain. With the help of Sarah Josepha Hale's letter-writing campaigns and editorials lobbying for the national holiday, President Abraham Lincoln signed the Thanksgiving Proclamation on October 3, 1863, while the nation was in the midst of the Civil War—a moment when the need for reassurance about the nation's identity could not have been greater. Independence Day and George Washington's birthday were the only two national holidays to precede it. Like them, Thanksgiving was at once a call for national unity and patriotism and an attempt to create a common sense of heritage. It was to be celebrated annually on the last Thursday of November.

In her November 1864 *Godey's Lady's Book* column, "Our National Thanksgiving—A Domestic Festival," Hale editorialized about the special place the holiday would serve in the nation's annual calendar: "'The Birth of Washington,' which brings before all minds the example of the patriot hero and the Christian man; 'Independence Day,' which reminds us of the free principles on which our Government was founded; and 'Thanksgiving Day,' which lifts our hearts to Heaven in grateful devotion, and knits them together in bonds of social affection—are three anniversaries such as no other People have the good fortune to enjoy."[43] At this moment of unparalleled national crisis, Hale's beloved New England holiday and its celebratory pumpkin pie became, like the other holidays, an affirmation of American values and identity. Pumpkins, wrote one poet, "are the joy and pride of a nation."[44] *What they symbolize*

What made Thanksgiving different from the other national holidays was its reliance on food, nature, and traditions connected to the land. Any holiday meal is a "reminder of common origins and common past," as the food historian Harvey Levenstein has observed, yet at Thanksgiving the meal and the food itself embody the holiday ideals and are absolutely essential to creating a sense of shared American identity.[45] The holiday's harvest symbolism brought all the facets of the celebration together. Lincoln's Thanksgiving Proclamation called on Americans to celebrate "the blessings of fruitful fields and healthful skies," defining the harvest as a bedrock of the country.[46] Many Americans made Lincoln's sentiments their own. Timothy Ball's 1898 Thanksgiving sermon proclaimed, "So today we gather, according to the custom of the New England forefathers, to offer our public Thanksgiving and praise to the Giver of seed-time and harvest, for the many blessings that we enjoy, and especially for the fruits of the earth, these varied products of our fertile soil."[47]

In the early nineteenth century, Americans celebrated the nation's natural resources and spectacular scenery to compensate for what they feared was a lack of national cultural heritage relative to that of Europeans. Yet by making the harvest, and the pumpkin in particular, a central symbol of Thanksgiving, Americans made nature a building block of their heritage, not a substitute for it. They began to think of nature as a repository of native, homegrown traditions and an icon of the nation's ancestral roots. By sitting down to a harvest meal, they made these ideas part of themselves in a very real way.

Although many historic examples existed of thanksgivings and harvest celebrations, such as the one held by the Jamestown settlers in 1609, the founders of the national holiday focused on the Pilgrims and their 1621 gathering as the true source of the national holiday meal. The Pilgrims, of course, were not the first Europeans to colonize North America, nor was their harvest feast anything out of the ordinary. And the pumpkin certainly was not. Even though New Englanders maintained the strongest Thanksgiving tradition over the years, the holiday's founders had less historical and more ideological reasons for focusing on Pilgrims and pumpkins.

During the tumultuous years of the Civil War, northerners portrayed the Pilgrims' struggles and successes as a motivational story in the country's own conflict. Thanksgiving devotees held up the Pilgrims, the ancestors of the North, as pious and righteous, in contrast to slave-holding southerners. They therefore lent credence to the northern cause. "Their sacrifices, their heroic example, their pious and purifying influence, thrown loose upon the atmosphere for us to breathe, or embodied in institutions that mould and order our lives, are among the richest blessings that claim acknowledgment upon each recurring Thanksgiving Day," enthused *Scribner's* magazine in 1869.[48] Many writers of children's primers found potent role models in the Pilgrims. The educator Elizabeth Share, of Brookline, Massachusetts, wrote to teachers: "But the most suggestive work of all for Thanksgiving must always be the old, old story of the Pilgrims. Again we find *life*, life in its noblest relations of self-sacrifice and love."[49]

For many Americans, especially in the North, who felt threatened by the influx of new immigrants from abroad, the Pilgrims became emblematic of American society and culture. Owners of colonial revival homes and members of the newly formed Daughters of the American Revolution expressed similar passions for establishing ties to their colonial ancestors and their Anglo-Saxon roots. Just decades before, of course, ardent New England patriots such as John Greenleaf Whittier were decidedly ambivalent about the early New England colonists. And few Thanksgiving enthusiasts acknowledged them, which highlights the contrivance of claiming Pilgrims as the originators of the holiday and the progenitors of American national identity. By the time of Lincoln's proclamation, historical episodes in which desperate New England colonists stole food from Indians had been replaced with scenes of benevolence and good will.

Besides being a celebration of the nation's natural bounty and a reenactment of the mythical Thanksgiving of the Pilgrims and Indians, the holiday was an affirmation of simple American fare (and, by extension, what were thought of as down-home values) and the virtues of rural life, as well as a time for family reunions. Thanksgiving celebrants kept true to the vernacular New England tradition by starting the day off with a church service and ending it with a family feast. Displaying jack-o'-lanterns was also part of the festivities, not just for Halloween. Every autumn until Hale retired from *Godey's Lady's Book* in 1877, the magazine published cozy stories about joyous Thanksgiving homecomings at New England farmsteads. "Let Thanksgiving, our American holiday . . . awaken in American hearts the love of home and country," she proclaimed.[50] She and other magazine editors printed recipes alongside quaint holiday tales as instruction manuals for re-creating not only the meal but also the holiday's "olden-time" spirit.[51]

Reuniting family members on the family farm took on particular significance in the mid- to late 1800s as the younger generations left the homesteads for the war or for life in the cities. Under the title "Thanksgiving on the Farm," the cover of the November 1898 edition of *Ladies Home Journal* featured a collage of rustic images depicting dinner preparations and a dining table full of food surrounded by people, with a field of cornstalks and pumpkins as a backdrop. The November 1869 issue of *Scribner's* stated, "It is a healthy thing for separated families to gather back to the old homes and relight the old altar-fires." The article chastised those "multitudes in the great cities . . . who turn their backs upon the humble, hearty country homes." "Give up all that frets you and all that fascinates you in your city life, and be simple boys and girls again!" it counseled.[52] Judging from the numbers of people who pursued lives away from the farms, country living was more appealing in nostalgic poetry and for weekend retreats than in reality—much the way the pumpkin was more delectable as a holiday treat than as daily dinner fare. And for many Americans who struggled at subsistence levels, this image of farm life offered little comfort.

The bill of fare for Thanksgiving in the November 1888 edition of *Ladies Home Journal* included roast turkey, giblet sauce, celery, mashed potatoes, cranberry jelly, boiled onions, and sweet potatoes, along with the now less traditional chicken pie, boiled fish, roast venison, and cauliflower, with turtle soup as a starter.[53] American cooks took pride in the simple, mostly native fare as an expression of a down-to-earth American character. Some critics sneered at those who incorporated French culinary styles into this all-American occasion. They even objected to the European trend of serving food in courses, rather than family style, in which everything appears on the table at once. In "Puritan Costume Party for Thanksgiving," one writer advised: "You must pile your table with food as if to give the impression of a recent famine. That is not easy to do if you serve in courses, like the French manner."[54]

An engraving by John W. Ehninger for *Harper's Weekly* conveys the way Thanksgiving celebrants directly correlated what they ate with a particular American scene and illustrates why food is such a cornerstone of this national holiday. Entitled *Preparing for Thanksgiving*, the print, a variation on the pumpkin harvest in Ehninger's *October*, casts the main ingredients of Thanksgiving dinner in the typical rustic farm imagery so popular at the time. Farmers load a wagon with harvest vegetables for the holiday meal. A rotund haystack, marker of a bountiful harvest and natural abundance, is echoed in a big pile of pumpkins, and enormous turkeys waddle across the picture frame. By partaking of the holiday meal, diners both emotionally and tangibly became part of the American farming tradition and the natural world. And although this quaint Thanksgiving picture could not have looked more different from industrial forms of agriculture at the time, the ways in which Americans invested their identities in rustic farm life, and in pumpkin farming in particular, began to transform real-life farm economies.

The finale of the meal was—as it still is—the pie. There might be apple, cherry, and coconut cream pies, but by the mid-1800s there was always pumpkin pie, a key ingredient in this national identity-building ritual. The *Chautauquan* magazine referred to Thanksgiving as "the season of pumpkin pie."[55] May Hanks's poem "Pumpkin Is Queen" waxed:

> Thanksgiving day would be a side-play,
> Minus the golden Pumpkin,
> No feast is complete, if they have not to eat,
> A circle of yellow Pumpkin.[56]

The pumpkin became the celebratory end to the Thanksgiving meal and the "national vegetable," as the author of the newspaper article "The American Pumpkin" called it, because it was both a voluptuous symbol of the natural gifts of the American continent and a container of "distinctly American" stories.[57] In the essayist's words, the pumpkin was "emphatically and literally a home industry in all its roots and branches and manufacturers." Late-nineteenth-century Americans celebrated pumpkin pie as a homegrown tradition and as a symbol of the nation with a sense of pride that Amelia Simmons's revolutionary-era pumpkin pie only hinted at. "It has a noble and generous mission to perform and a grateful memory to preserve," continued this paean, as the author traced landmarks in American history through the vegetable. "It is known to have been the early comrade of the Pilgrim Fathers and was a constant companion of the pioneers who followed the star of empire westward. It was a friend in need to the patriots who fought the Revolution," he declared. Although New Englanders had sung the pumpkin's praises for generations, Lincoln's proclamation established a whole new level of meaning. Regional stories about pumpkins became epic American tales. Eating pumpkin was no longer an act of desperation but an act of patriotism.

Consuming a "golden crescent" of pumpkin pie, as described in the children's tale *The Story of Pumpkin Pie*, was one of the most fulfilling ways to partake in the nation's agrarian ideals.[58] Endless poems, children's stories, and magazine articles sang the praises of pumpkin pie as a "golden reminder" of the values and virtues of life on an old-fashioned farm, just as so many popular paintings by Homer and others had done.[59] One Thanksgiving story referred to pumpkin pie as "a moral thermometer." "Pumpkins, you know," wrote the author of "Peppery Pumpkin Pies," "are nourished in sunshine. They are gathered in the glowing autumn days, and brought in the house, golden reminders of the summer sun. If the pies are made by one of a sunny disposition, they will be sweet, juicy, and delicious—in short, such an essence of sunshine, sugar and spice.... But if one ill-natured thought is harbored during their preparation, they are soured and ruined."[60] Pumpkin pie stood for the simple things in life and the bedrock qualities of the American character. Or so many people liked to think.

American writers loved to define themselves as an unpretentious lot in comparison with more sophisticated Europeans. And they often used pumpkin pie to do it. While some writers celebrated the Thanksgiving meal itself, many more called on pumpkin pie to humbly sing America's praises. In "Pumpkin Pie," one poet portrays himself as a modest man who desires nothing more from his homeland than the simple things in life, rather than any exotic riches. He writes:

> Then hail to the muse of the pumpkin and onion!
> The Frenchman may laugh and the Englishmen sneer
> At the land of the Bible, and psalm-book, and Bunyan;

Still, still to my bosom her green hills are dear;
Her daughters are pure as her bright crystal fountains;
And, Hymen, if ever thy blessings I try, Oh!
Give me the girl of my own native mountains,
Who knows how to temper the sweet pumpkin pie.[61]

In a news article titled "He Longs for Pie," the author complains about being unable to find pumpkin pie on the menu at Delmonico's, the St. James, the Waldorf, or the Brunswick—the fanciest and most expensive New York restaurants. He said, "I trust that I shall always be able to eat and value the splendors of French cookery without peptic accompaniment or subsequent regrets, but, as an American citizen, I demand that the national discs of delight, the mince and pumpkin pies, be retained upon their pedestals and flashed under our eager eyes whenever our souls send forth a cry for them."[62] In a similar vein, Margaret E. Sangster wrote "Thanksgiving Pumpkin Pies" in the dialect of a country fellow who takes pride in his plain background, as epitomized by a love of pumpkin pie.[63] He recalls "a thinkin', like a simpleton, of Mother's pumpkin pies," while bemoaning the wealthy, aristocratic life into which he has married. His wife's "French cook costs a fortune, but—*I* favor home-made pies," he states proudly.

The American fairytale "The Pumpkin Giant," published in 1892, turns these sentiments about the simple things in life into a morality play, similar to *Luck of the Golden Pumpkin*.[64] These both sound a lot like Benjamin Thompson's colonial poem about "the times when Pompion was a Saint." In the tale, a poor farm woman makes pies from pumpkins that sprout from the remains of a pumpkin-headed giant who has been slain by her husband. When the local king tries a piece of her pie, he exclaims, "I never tasted anything so altogether superfine, so utterly magnificent in my life. . . . stewed peacock's tongues from the Baltic are not to be compared with it."[65] As in most fairytale endings, everyone lives happily ever after, but this story takes an unusual twist. "Roses in the [royal] garden were uprooted and replaced by pumpkins," it concludes. "All royal parks became pumpkin fields." The tale extols the simple rewards of the pumpkin over the finest delicacies that money can buy. The modest pumpkin farm becomes a mythical landscape of deep meaning that signifies American values.

As the many odes to the pumpkin pie's delicious taste confirm, the pie's appeal was not just ideological but visceral and personal, too. Adding sugar and spices made eating pumpkin not only a symbolic act but a pleasurable one, which by extension sweetened the ideas attached to the vegetable. The 1890 cookbook *Hood's Good Pie* expresses the way these two phenomena—the ideological and the physiological—worked together. The cover depicts three large, voluptuous pumpkins reaching up with their broad, leafy vines and wrapping themselves around a baked pumpkin pie set on a linen-covered table. Whittier's line, "What moistens the lip and what brightens the eye—What calls back the past, like the rich Pumpkin pie?" serves as a caption. In large, bold letters across the top of the cover is the title, *Good Pie*, signifying the tasty flavor, of course, but also the benevolent meanings and values the pie possesses. Eating a slice offers not just nutritional enrichment but cultural enrichment.

In the late nineteenth century, Sarah Josepha Hale encouraged women to take seriously their role as Thanksgiving cooks and hostesses. She wrote in *Godey's Lady's Book*, "It belongs to the altar and the hearth at which woman should ever be present, and the women of our country should take this day under their peculiar charge, and sanctify it to acts of piety, charity and domestic love."[66] Her success in making Thanksgiving a national holiday is evidence enough of how American women used the domestic sphere, particularly the kitchen, to political and patriotic ends, as Simmons did during the Revolutionary War period.

Not everyone, however, thought about women's making pumpkin pies in quite the way Hale did. For example, *Preparation*, an engraving by C. G. Bush for *Harper's Weekly*, depicts a suitor sitting close to a woman and leering over her shoulder as she dutifully prepares Thanksgiving dinner, with the meal's ingredients, including turkeys, apples, and a mound of pumpkins, set before her. "Pumpkin pie a tempting dish to almost any fellow; / So sweet and tender, luscious (yum!)"—a line from the poem "Pumpkin Pie"—could easily serve as a caption. It well sums up the sexual innuendo in the scene and thereby perpetuates old stereotypes about women, pumpkins, and sexuality.[67] While women took their responsibilities seriously, at least some men seem to have had other things on their minds. In his book *Eyes and Ears*, Henry Ward Beecher offered a variation on the same theme when he quickly moved between botanical description and sexual innuendo: "The pumpkin-blossom is large and buxom, open-hearted, a

Cover of the 1890 cookbook *Hood's Good Pie*. Warshaw Collection of Business Americana: Cookbooks. Archives Center, National Museum of American History, Smithsonian Institution.

Ew,11

refuge for bees, that fly into it with open wings, and work around its nectarines in a golden dust, and so overload themselves with sweets as often to forget their homeward duties, and, like sailors in some tropic island, desert their ship to live in the luxury of overmastering sweets."[68]

Regardless of its meanings for men and women, the Thanksgiving holiday was in the hands of northerners, and its themes reflected northern values and ways of life. The Northern bias begs the question of how the holiday was received in other parts of the country and among people who were not "Anglo-Saxons," as Euroamericans were referred to at the time. Whereas white Americans in the Midwest and in the mid-Atlantic regions were quick to see themselves in the rural and colonial Thanksgiving icons, white southerners were, in short, reluctant. "It is a New England custom, said some," noted a Congregational minister who sought to introduce the holiday to his Texas congregation, "and not at all adapted to us."[69] The *Richmond Daily Dispatch,* on February 15, 1865, editorialized sarcastically that "the Day of Thanksgiving, when he [the Yankee] gorges to repletion with turkeys and pumpkin pie, and [honors] the Landing of the Pilgrims, who came to America to be at perfect liberty to deprive everybody else of their liberties, [is one of] his great festival days."[70] Not everyone across the nation embraced the national holiday as his or her own.

The general consensus for the South, based on a variety of sources, is that white southerners were initially unreceptive to the holiday, but by the end of the nineteenth century many had begun to embrace it.[71] Even then, many still considered it a New England transplant versus a "national" tradition. As one observer noted in 1879, "'The Thanksgiving Day' was a New England institution, to commemorate the landing of the Pilgrim Fathers . . . though I dare say that the Southerners heartily wish that the Pilgrim Fathers had gone to the bottom of the sea before they ever landed at all. However, now 'Thanksgiving Day' seems to be the family feast of the year."[72]

Northerners such as the minister in Texas used the holiday stories, harvest symbols, and foods to try to inculcate their values in others. One overt example is the 1892 Thanksgiving celebration at the Hampton Institute, the Virginia school funded by northerners to educate African Americans and American Indians. Goose, potatoes, and "New England pumpkin pie" were served to the students, who had been gathered in an assembly hall with a stage "decorated with symbols of the year's abundance in grains and grasses and golden fruits of the earth," explained the institute's journal, *Southern Workman.* A Seneca Indian girl from New York State stood before the audience and recited the stories of the Pilgrims' first Thanksgiving and of the Thanksgiving held by the Revolutionary War soldiers at Valley Forge. A Winnebago boy proclaimed to the gathering, "I am thankful that by the help of the white race, the Indian and negro races are advancing in civilization and Christianity."[73] The reformers made Thanksgiving and the pumpkin valuable tools of assimilation, with actions that now appear to be rabid testaments to the gross ethnocentrism of the nineteenth-century reform movements.

Many African Americans seem to have readily adopted Thanksgiving on their own. One source stated that "all the negroes learned to look upon it as the holiday of year," and W. E. B. DuBois observed, "On the whole, the Negro has few family festivals. . . . Thanksgiving is coming to be widely celebrated, but here again in churches as much as in homes."[74] Southerners and African Americans did develop their own Thanksgiving food traditions, perhaps reinterpreting the holiday's ideals and symbols. Many substituted sweet potato pie, a regional specialty, for the traditional New England pumpkin pie. In the article "Thanksgiving at All Healing, N.C.," published in the journal *The American Missionary*, Miss K. Le Grange wrote with a sense of regional pride that "not a pumpkin was to be had, so we made a sweet potato pie, which looked just as golden as any New England pumpkin pie that ever was eaten."[75] One explanation for this practice could be that in the South, the image of the pumpkin farmer was more pejorative, denoting a lazy good-for-nothing instead of an inspirational image of the humble and virtuous yeoman. This racist argument against emancipating slaves illustrates the point. "Instead of becoming intelligent husbandmen, working in an orderly way," one critic wrote, "the negroes cut and shuffle about, like vagrants and squatters, enjoying their light pumpkin livelihood in a desultory way."[76]

A derogatory cartoon titled "Thanksgiving Morning in the Johnson Family," which depicts a black family as numbskull characters who mistake a mock turkey, made of a pumpkin body with stick feathers and head, for a real one, reveals the pervasiveness of the stereotype.[77] Pumpkin was a common food for poor blacks in the late nineteenth century for the same reasons that other poor people throughout the centuries had relied on it. But in the case of poor black farmers, depicting them as "pumpkin eaters" was a racial slur without the airbrush of nostalgia. This stigma might explain the popularity of sweet potato pie instead of pumpkin pie to this day in the South.

The deep meanings Americans invested in the pumpkin tell a story not only about people but also about the vegetable itself. The relationship between the physical plant and the stories about it has always been reciprocal, with the pumpkin's physical qualities inspiring meanings and the meanings transforming the plant's uses. The separation of squash from pumpkin is one of the best examples of this. But another major shift began to take place in the late nineteenth century. The cultural iconography began to alter the nature of the plant itself and to infuse market value in the pumpkin for the first time in its long "earthly career," to use a poet's phrase. This shift would foreshadow larger changes to come.

Farmers reacted to elevation in the pumpkin's status by attuning their businesses to take advantage of the new demand. "The Pumpkin Business," a headline in an 1891 agricultural journal, would have seemed an oxymoron just a few years earlier.[78] The farmer featured in the article grew pumpkins to supply his canning factory. "You see, in order to keep his factory going he has to have a pumpkin-ranch," explained the author. The year 1899 was a milestone for pumpkin farming: it was the first year in which the U.S. Agricultural Census recorded pumpkin production. Yet calling pumpkin production a business still required some stretch of the imagination. That year, 3,194 of 614,146 American farmers reported growing pumpkins on a total of 3,341 acres, slightly more than an acre per farm. Judging by these statistics, fewer than 0.5 percent of farmers in the United States grew pumpkins. By comparison, 5,336 farms (about 0.8 percent) each grew eight-tenths of an acre of squash; 18,964 farms (about 3 percent) each grew less than an acre of green beans; and 343,999 farms (about 56 percent) each planted about half an acre of cabbages.[79]

That its cultural affiliations, not its practical uses, spurred innovation is evident in the pumpkin's new names and varieties, such as Burpee's Golden Marrow and Buckbee's Big Gold, first advertised in 1882 and 1899, respectively. One grower's comment that "in many places people will pay more for early pumpkins for pies than they will for any kind of squashes" helps explain the proliferation of new varieties, including Finest Family, Early Sugar, Sweet, Quaker Pie, and Thanksgiving, all of which were small to medium-size pumpkins bred primarily for pie making—each pumpkin approximately two pies' worth—at Thanksgiving.[80] A small advertisement, "Ask for 'thanksgiving' pumpkin at your grocer's," verifies the marketability of the vegetable's new uses and imagery.[81]

Although it might at first seem incongruous that the pumpkin started out as livestock food early in the century and became a treasured holiday dessert by century's end, its cultural history provides some compelling explanations for this development. The two forms of consumption might have been at opposite culinary poles, yet Americans linked them ideologically. As a cheap and prolific vegetable, the pumpkin proved good fodder not only for horses but also for American mythmakers, who self-consciously tried to distance themselves from foreign influences and to shelter themselves from the modern, industrial world. They sought their cultural heritage in the countryside and in hardscrabble settlement stories, in which the pumpkin was a prominent and potent player. Americans ate it up. Events in the nineteenth century set in motion the transformation of a nearly worthless farm crop into a highly marketable icon of American agrarianism.

The 469-pound Buckbee's "King of the Mammoth" pumpkin displayed at the 1893 Chicago World's Fair, an event that celebrated American progress, ingenuity, and modernity and attempted to articulate to the world an American identity, sat across the concourse from the pavilion where Frederick Jackson Turner delivered his now-famous frontier speech. The pumpkin was an awesome natural specimen, but more important, fair organizers featured the behemoth because it embodied the stories Americans liked to tell about themselves, stories that rivaled those of the famous historian himself.

FIVE

JACK-O'-LANTERN SMILES

Americans Celebrate the Fall Harvest

with Pumpkins, 1900 to 1945

J OHN ARATA, A FARMER LIVING NEAR HALF MOON BAY, JUST OUT-
side San Francisco, recounted a day back in the 1930s when he and
his brother were returning to the family farmstead from distant fields
with a wagonload of pumpkins for their hogs. "This car came along with
a couple of well-dressed men" who wanted to buy pumpkins, recollected
Arata, in his eighties when a journalist interviewed him in 2000. "We sold
three or four for $1. We took that home, and our dad said, 'Get the team,
load pumpkins, and go sell them on the road.'"[1] Before long, Arata's father
(and observant neighboring farmers) deemed the pumpkins too valuable to
feed to the pigs and began to produce them for the retail market.

A couple of well-dressed men cruising the countryside in their car and
buying pumpkins seems innocuous, if perhaps peculiar, but this trip and
the men's purchase can tell much about Americans' relationships with
nature and rural life in the first half of the twentieth century. It is a good
guess that the men did not actually *need* the pumpkins. Arata's description leads one to believe that these were not local farmers but people who
lived in a nearby city or suburb, so they probably owned little more land
than a front stoop, much less livestock. It had been years since pumpkins
had been necessary to feed a family, and the spread of canned goods and
neighborhood grocery stores offered much more convenient options than
a distant farm for obtaining fruits and vegetables. It is difficult to imagine
a practical reason for two men in suits to stop in the countryside to purchase pumpkins.

Americans' desire for pumpkins has defied reason and logic since before Amelia Simmons created the pumpkin pie, New Englanders featured it in song, and Abraham Lincoln propelled it into becoming a national dessert. As at these pivotal moments in the pumpkin's history, so in the early twentieth century—just when the vegetable was least useful in the household economy—Americans such as the two "well-dressed men" steeped it in meaning. In 1920, for the first time in history farmers made up less than half the American population.[2] The foundation of American society and its core values, rooted in rural ways of life, were under serious threat. In the words of President Franklin Roosevelt: "The American dream of the family-size farm, owned by the family that operates it, has become more and more remote. The agricultural ladder, on which an energetic young man might ascend from hired man to tenant to independent owner, is no longer serving its purpose."[3] Images of American farmers, dignified and ennobled, which appeared in government-sponsored Farm Security Administration (FSA) photographs of migrant farm workers, in American regionalist paintings of midwestern farm life, and in literary works such as James Agee and Walker Evans's *Let Us Now Praise Famous Men*, about southern tenant farmers, are well-known cultural responses to the dramatic change in status of rural people and ways of life in the first half of the twentieth century.

Some farm families did more than just pose for the cameras. They took advantage of this new incarnation of rural nostalgia by selling a picturesque ideal in which the pumpkin had long been a prime attraction. Farmers of course sold many fruits and vegetables from their roadside stands, but the pumpkin is a particularly powerful crop to follow because demand for it was spurred by its bucolic meanings and symbolic uses in harvest displays and holiday treats, rather than by the needs of daily sustenance, as was the case for strawberries and apples. Pretty pictures and quaint stories of pumpkin farming may seem like superfluous responses to industrialization, having little or nothing to do with actual farm operations, but they propelled two men in suits to stop for pumpkins and thereby altered real places and people in profound ways.

Few American farmers, if any, imagined a family fortune in pumpkins. American agriculture in the first half of the twentieth century is known for its great economic highs and lows, although the overall trend was toward greater consolidation, meaning bigger and fewer farms, and toward increasingly industrial modes of production, signifying greater reliance on machines, synthetic inputs, and capitalization.[4] Although expanding the acreage and intensity of cultivation of farm land offered growers the chance for greater profits, not to mention the ability even to stay in business, farming was a risky enterprise in an ever-fluctuating market. An investment for the future could quickly turn into overextension, debt, and bankruptcy. The late 1910s marked the high point of agricultural output, when World War I fueled overseas demand for wheat and other commodity crops. Farmers' capacity to fulfill this demand was never greater as they got behind the latest gasoline-powered tractors to plant more productive crop varieties on expanding acreage made possible in many regions by water from new, federally sponsored irrigation projects. Although the Midwest still led the nation in grain production, California farmers developed large commercial fruit and vegetable operations.

In this age of mechanization, farmers still harvested pumpkins by hand, but the impracticality of doing so became ever more evident. "The inventor of the corn-cutting device did not take pumpkins into account," explained one observer of the technological changes in 1901, "and as a result the pumpkins have to be plucked before the machine can be used, which is a great nuisance, and besides most of the pumpkins would be still unripe."[5] The newest agricultural machinery, in other words, was rolling over the pumpkin. Adding insult to injury, a 1918 study by the U.S. Department of Agriculture undermined the practicality of the pumpkin's one remaining farm function, that of livestock feed, by determining that "5 to 6 lbs. of pumpkin was equal in food value to 1 lb. of hay."[6] Inefficiency was not the pumpkin's only liability. The demand for pumpkin production was not remotely comparable to that of major commodity crops, which deterred capitalist investment in the crop. For example, in 1919, a peak year in all agricultural output, a mere 1,674 out of 6.5 million American farms grew a total of just 3,056 acres of pumpkins (around 4 acres per farm) within more than 500 million acres of improved farmland across the country.[7]

Although pumpkins failed to make headlines in the annals of agricultural research and commerce, they offered some small-scale producers a chance to sustain their operations in the face of threats by larger, corporate enterprises. Newspaper and magazine articles hint at the profits, however meager, that arose from growing pumpkins for canneries, whose market was primarily the holiday pie trade. "Demand for the Distinctly

American Product Is on the Increase—A Tract of 300 Acres in New Jersey Given Up to Cultivation of the Fruit," announced the *New York Times* in 1902.[8] That same season, another *Times* article weighed in, "The commercial side of pumpkin raising is apparent when a consideration is given to the fact that the farmers supplying a single factory in Northern Ohio, for example, collectively often make as high as $15,000 to $30,000 from the sale of their pumpkins in a season."[9] Because the article did not give the number of participants in this collective, it is impossible to determine the actual economic gain for its individual producers. Nevertheless, consumer desire for pumpkin was stirring. A 1913 edition of the book *Garden Farming* verified this trend: "From an economic standpoint, the pumpkin is not so great value as the squash. During recent years, however, the demand for pumpkin as a filling for pies has led to the canning of this product on an extensive scale."[10]

Dickinson Company laid the cornerstone for the largest pumpkin canning plant in the country when it opened a factory in Morton, Illinois, in 1925, creating opportunities for farmers there. Four years after the plant opened, Libby, McNeil and Libby, a prominent Chicago group established in 1868 that was better known as a canner of meat products, purchased it.[11] Libby's also bought factories in nearby Eureka and Washington, Illinois, where it canned peas and corn along with pumpkin. (By the later part of the century, Libby's would control more than 85 percent of the market in canned pumpkin.) Also in 1925, the Atlantic Canning Company, in Iowa, began to provide local farmers with seeds on credit, so they could grow pumpkins to send to its factory.[12] Under this type of arrangement, farmers became more like company employees than independent entrepreneurs. Unfortunately for many of them, the greatest profits were had at the processing and marketing stages, so the farmers did not benefit from the growth in the food industry nearly as much as the companies that processed and sold the food. Some farmers, as I describe shortly, would develop schemes to get around that limitation.

In the 1920s, American agriculture began a steep decline. The bottom dropped out of the market when World War I ended in 1918 and farmers had no buyers for their surpluses. Together, the rising scale of production and the market downturn squeezed out many farm families, many of whom packed up and abandoned their homesteads for work in the cities. Between 1920 and 1930, rural areas lost 2.5 million inhabitants (the rural segment dropped from 48.6 percent of the U.S. population in 1920 to 43.6 in 1930), even as the total U.S. population grew by more than 17 million.[13]

The financial crash of 1929 and the devastating dust storms of the 1930s radically changed the nation's agricultural landscape. In his groundbreaking 1979 book *Dust Bowl*, Donald Worster argued that the two tragedies were less an unfortunate convergence of natural and economic disasters than the result of the same underlying cause: capitalism.[14] In the all-consuming drive for greater profits, farmers ignored the local ecology, especially the health of the soil, with devastating effects. The same machines and business ethic that plowed profits out of the Great Plains also turned dirt and livelihoods into so much fine dust. The consequences were epic in proportion. Thousands of acres of farmland lay barren, and thousands of farm families, many of them tenants working for large corporate enterprises, were forced to abandon their holdings and head west to California in search of opportunities that did not exist.

Americans turned to education, research, and direct aid to solve their farm problems.[15] Science, technology, education, and government support were hallmarks of Roosevelt's New Deal farm programs. The federal government set up protections to steady the market, such as the Ever-Normal Granary program, which established national storehouses of grain to regulate price fluctuations. Under the auspices of the FSA, the government relocated farmers to new land and taught them more sustainable practices, such as contour farming and soil conservation, based on the latest research at USDA extension stations.

In these dire circumstances, the pumpkin more than held its own. Between 1919 and 1949, pumpkin production, though still extremely modest by any standard, increased by 99 percent, from 3,056 to 5,975 acres.[16] Many farmers, such as the Arata family, grew pumpkins for livestock fodder. But the future was not in livestock, something the Aratas learned firsthand when the two men stopped them on the road. By 1949, the acreage of pumpkins harvested for animal feed was only 31 percent of the total acreage of pumpkins harvested that year. The remaining 69 percent was planted in either "processing pumpkins," for canning, or pumpkins for ornamental use.[17] In other words, the majority of pumpkins grown were destined for holiday uses.

A 1938 guide to the state of Iowa described large fields of pumpkins near Atlantic, Iowa. "They are a variety of sweet pumpkin, the seeds for which are furnished to farmers by the canning company on credit, bringing $5 to $9 a ton. From 10 to 20 tons are produced on an acre."[18] Farmers harvested on average 2.7 acres of pumpkins annually, so these Iowa farmers earned between $180 and $486 from pumpkins per year, exclusive of production costs, at a time when average annual income in the United States was $1,725.[19] Not surprisingly, the USDA's "East North Central" region, which encompassed Ohio, Indiana, Illinois, Michigan, and Wisconsin, where most canning factories were located, held by far the most pumpkin farms and acreage. The mid-Atlantic region, which was geared toward urban commercial bakeries, came in second. California harvested only 627 acres on 95 farms, in comparison with Illinois, with 1,663 acres on 179 farms, suggesting that the expansive new California produce farms did not put their resources into pumpkins. New England, long the hub of pumpkin symbolism, ranked near the bottom, alongside the South.[20]

Consumers' increased desire for pumpkins arose from seemingly contradictory trends: the changing material conditions of American life and the perpetuation of historically powerful ideas about the meanings of nature and rural life. Although the basic recipe for pumpkin pie remained relatively constant, the product that made it to the Thanksgiving table and the way it got there were now radically different than in times past. In the early twentieth century, corporations began to control not only American agriculture but also every stage of the food cycle, from farm to table. They laid the foundation for America's integrated system of food production, manufacturing, and distribution, which still dominates today.[21] The development of new technologies for cleaning, chopping, preserving, and packaging foods greatly increased the types and quantities of foods available to middle-class consumers but dissociated those consumers from the growers, places of production, and natural sources of their food as never before. Flour and sugar refineries, meatpacking plants, and canning factories not only eradicated the need for local sources of most foodstuffs but also changed the very nature of many products. As William Cronon eloquently wrote in *Nature's Metropolis*, consumers went from experiencing the livestock they ate as living, breathing animals to simply encountering them as slices of meat in cellophane wrappers, with no physical trace of the four-legged creatures in evidence, nor of the farmer who raised them nor the place where they were raised.[22]

John Cowan, in the 1906 *Pacific Monthly* article "The Golden Pumpkin Pie," favorably compared pie manufacturing to the production of "armor plate, steel rails, wire nails, locomotives and other necessities of high-pressure civilization." Many consumers, however, simultaneously welcomed the new products and their convenience and felt uneasy about the lack of transparency as to where their food came from, or even what their food was.[23] Concerns over safety were common responses and would foreshadow consumers' fears and responses at the turn of the twenty-first century. Upton Sinclair's castigation of the Chicago meatpacking industry's handling and contamination of meat in his 1906 novel *The Jungle* famously led to the federal testing of food additives—for example, by the "poison squad" organized by Harvey Wiley, who became the first commissioner of the U.S. Food and Drug Administration. It also led to the passage of the Pure Food and Drug Act of 1906.[24] All in all, Americans were much farther removed from the sources and natural states of their food than ever before.

Many people also began to think differently about food because of developments in food science, nutrition, and home economics. With the discovery of vitamins and other chemical compounds, consumers started to judge a food's value more in terms of its component parts, and cooking more in terms of digestibility than in terms of taste and texture. A 1906 advertisement for the Natural Food Company stated, "Thanksgiving Day is a day of thanks in every home where the housewife has nailed the 'pure food' slogan to outer and inner walls. But it is not enough that the food be pure and clean. It should present the maximum of nutrition with the least tax upon the digestive powers."[25] The company's concern for food safety and nutrition certainly took some of the allure out of Thanksgiving dinner for celebrants.

The distribution and retailing of foodstuffs followed the trends in manufacturing as more and more Americans purchased food in stores rather than raising it themselves. And although local butchers and bakers still existed, by 1934 fewer than half of food retail stores were independent.[26] Increasingly, consumers bought their food from local and national grocery store chains, led by the Atlantic and Pacific Tea Company (A&P), which standardized the types of foods available as well as the food shopping experience. In the 1930s, most grocery stores shifted from counter service, in which employees assisted individual customers, to self-service, in which eye-catching labels on canned foods helped to entice purchasers. One retailer enthusiastically supported the switch to canned goods when he advised grocers, "In the majority of cases canned goods deserve pushing as they are more uniform, not to mention the cheapness of the entire line when compared with the actual food value of fresh products placed on the table both from a standpoint of quality as well as quantity."[27] By 1934, according to the U.S. Commerce Department's report "Food Retailing," canned goods accounted for a greater proportion (25.13 percent) of food sales than meats, bakery items, and fresh fruits and vegetables.[28]

The popularity of manufactured products made fresh pumpkin an old-fashioned novelty in American "stream-lined" kitchens.[29] "It appears that canned pumpkin has so displaced the fresh article that the time is not far distant when directions for scooping out seeds, peeling, steaming and draining the big succulent wedges will be as outmoded in the cookery books as instructions on stoning raisins and flouring a cloth for boiled pudding," wrote the author of the newspaper article "Our Thanksgiving Feast" in 1935.[30] Capitalizing on another of the new food manufacturing technologies, the Dry Pack Corporation would introduce a ready-made pumpkin pie mix in 1945.[31]

A 1910 advertisement for the Connecticut Pie Company, a bakery in the heart of Washington, D.C., that rolled out thirty thousand pies a day, including "spicy-deep-rich-big-the real pumpkin pie of Yankee-land Thanksgiving," suggests not only the economic value of pumpkin pie but also the ways in which food preparation outside the home had become big business.[32] Cowan, the same man who promoted commercial pie production, wrote, "And it is largely by his pumpkin pies, baked during the Thanksgiving season, that the aspiring pie manufacturer will be judged."[33] A September 1902 issue of the *New York Times* reported that about three million pounds (fifteen hundred tons) of pumpkins were needed for the creation of pies in New York City alone.[34] This demand probably accounts for the relatively large number of farmers who grew pumpkins in the mid-Atlantic region. When the era's main food authority, Harvey Wiley, defined pumpkin as "a food [that] is more condimental than nutritive," he sanctioned its long-standing use as a dessert instead of as a daily food like the squash.[35] By the mid-1940s, the idea of pumpkin *pie* was so ingrained in consumers' minds that women's magazines published articles such as "Wave Your Magic Wand over Pumpkins," encouraging home cooks to "widen pumpkin's food destiny" by using the vegetable in other savory and sweet dishes, not just in pie.[36]

When people began to buy canned pumpkin from stores instead of growing pumpkins in their fields, the pumpkin became a consumer good, as the agricultural statistics document. Turning the pumpkin into a grocery item detached consumers from the plant and the place where it originated. When manufacturers now began to reformulate the vegetable and package it in a tin can or sell it as a ready-made pie or mix, they intensified this process of abstracting the natural object from its origins. Yet the cultural history of the pumpkin runs contrary to the common story that capitalism and commodification inherently lead people to become disconnected and alienated from the natural world around them. Buying and eating canned pumpkin made many Americans feel a part of nature and rural living, and by doing so they returned profits to small family farmers.

The demographic shift from farms to cities by the mid-twentieth century explains the need for people to purchase pumpkins, but not their desire to buy and eat them in the first place. A 1908 elementary school botany lesson offers some insight into that desire. After stating that she was ambivalent about leading a botanical investigation of the pumpkin's seeds, skin, and innards, the educator explained, "I sometimes wonder if such a procedure might not prejudice the child against the pumpkin and detract just a little from his enjoyment of the real functions of the pumpkin, viz, its use in pies, and for making jack-o-lanterns. . . . [but] to have the child raise a pumpkin from the seed, harvest it and finally follow it personally into a jack-o-lantern or a pumpkin pie, the pumpkin would then have filled a happy mission as a nature-study subject."[37]

The teacher wants her students to focus on the rural roots and the holiday rituals but not on the botanical specifics of the pumpkin itself. The popularity of marking the autumn by displaying and eating seasonal symbols, especially pumpkins and corn, suggests that although harvest time had lost most of its practical implications, for the majority of Americans it still held deep meaning. The highlight of an October 1903 "harvest social" sponsored by a Sunday school, for example, was a reading of Whittier's ode to the pumpkin, after which curtains went up to reveal a cornucopia of food, including pumpkin pie.[38]

Even if new canning and dry-mix technologies made eating pumpkin pie possible at any time of year, Americans still preferred to eat it in the fall and associated it primarily with their beloved Thanksgiving holiday. "Surely a Thanksgiving dinner without pumpkin pie would be an empty sham and a hollow mockery," scoffed Cowan in "The Golden Pumpkin Pie."[39] Like any other viable holiday tradition, Thanksgiving both adhered to old practices and adjusted to new circumstances. Gimbel's introduced New York City's Thanksgiving Day parade in 1921, and Franklin Roosevelt moved the holiday from the last to the fourth Thursday of November in 1936, but modernization did not diminish Americans' patriotic zeal for the old-fashioned pumpkin.[40] "Even the lordly turkey holds not a prouder place at this annual feast of all good things than does the delectable-concoction of the cooks that has come down to us from the Heroic Age of the Republic, endeared by sentiment, hallowed by patriotism, glorified by the recollections of childhood and sanctioned by the traditions of mellow antiquity," summed up one pumpkin enthusiast.[41] From sentimental turn-of-the-century postcards, which depicted rustic New England farm scenes or the 1621 Pilgrim and Indian feast, to 1940s magazine articles about "Extra Special Pumpkin Pie" that quoted Whittier's well-worn lines about agrarian life—"What calls back the past like the rich Pumpkin pie?"—Americans found new meanings and uses for old and familiar holiday motifs, rituals, and symbols.[42]

Americans expressed their continued devotion to the New England colonists in Thanksgiving pageants in which people dressed up as Pilgrims, in children's holiday songs that preached the Pilgrims' heroism and civic virtues, and in rosy-tinted greeting cards of pious colonial men and women with pumpkins in their hands or at their feet. Publications such as the 1918 *What to Do for Uncle Sam: A First Book of Citizenship*, which reported that Thanksgiving was Uncle Sam's favorite holiday, tried to inculcate American values in new immigrants by helping them celebrate the Pilgrims and pumpkin pie as their own.[43]

Roosevelt's nostalgic sentiments about the vanishing American family farm permeated popular art and literature, which gave new life to another major Thanksgiving motif, the rural homestead. Many artists and writers incorporated the pumpkin and pumpkin pie directly into their work. Their general message is familiar: the modest family farm as foundational to American national identity and as a source of core cultural values in times of change and hardship. What is less familiar is how these beliefs actually helped change the fortunes of small family farms.

The federal government played a pivotal role in making that happen. Although New Deal reformers prided themselves on rational approaches to farm economy, their programs were also sympathetic to the small family farm. Besides developing resettlement and education programs designed to keep family farms in operation, from 1936 to 1945 the FSA employed photographers to document the farmers' plight, producing one of the most significant records of rural farm life in America.[44] Through their photographs, Walker Evans, John Collier, Dorothea Lange, Gordon Parks, and Russell Lee turned ordinary people and places into portraits of American virtue. Lange's "Destitute peapickers in California; a 32 year old mother of seven children. February 1936," otherwise known as *Migrant Mother*, portrays a woman surrounded by her children in tattered clothing and is one of the most famous photographs of the era. Rugged and weary, the farmers standing before the artists' cameras were transformed into symbols of hard work, simple living, and old-fashioned values that Americans historically linked to farm life. The purpose of the FSA photographs was both to validate American agrarian ideals and to garner public support for government relief programs.

Americans came across these photographs in *Life* magazine, but they also encountered tributes to farm life while walking into the local post office or government office building. Artists hired by the Works Progress Administration decorated federal buildings from coast to coast with murals celebrating, among other themes, local rural history and culture.[45] Above the mailboxes in the Rockville, Maryland, post office is a mural depicting a bucolic patchwork of local farmsteads at the foot of Sugarloaf Mountain, painted by Judson Smith in 1940. In Chilton, Wisconsin, *Threshing Barley*, by Charles W. Thwaites, portrays muscular men in rolled-up shirt sleeves harvesting a crop.[46]

The landscape photographs in the FSA collection speak as effectively about cultural values as the portraits. John Collier's photograph of a pumpkin field near Windsor Locks, Connecticut, looks like a nineteenth-century genre painting, with a large field of pumpkins stretched before a picture-perfect white clapboard farmhouse. The photographer's inclusion of the dwelling turns a simple farm scene into a broader symbol of cultural identity; the picturesque pumpkin field communicates a sense of the values and character of the people inside the house.

Thanksgiving also had its place in this rich photographic record.

Photographer Jack Delano visited the Crouch family in 1940 and captured humble yet hallowed images of the family's Thanksgiving dinner. In "Pumpkin Pies and Thanksgiving Dinner at the Home of Mr. Timothy Levy Crouch, a Rogerine Quaker Living in Ledyard, Connecticut," the family sits around a table filled with bowls of food. Their image is captured in a mirror that hangs above a sideboard displaying desserts, including most prominently two pumpkin pies. Juxtaposing the family and the pies, the photographer infuses the portrait with a sense of well-being and old-fashioned goodness. The pumpkin pies in particular cast this as a distinctly American scene.

These government-sponsored works of art echoed the themes and politics of famous literary works devoted to the trials and tribulations of working farmers. John Steinbeck's 1936 *The Grapes of Wrath* chronicled the life of the Joad family as they migrated to California in search of work after the midwestern dust storms destroyed their farmstead. James Agee and Walker Evans's 1936 *Let Us Now Praise Famous Men* recounted in words and pictures the plight of southern tenant farmers and sharecroppers.[47] American regionalist painters, including Grant Wood of Iowa, John Steuart Curry of Kansas, and Thomas Hart Benton of Missouri, also contributed to the genre with paintings that valorized and mythologized American small-town and rural life.[48] Wood's 1941 *Spring in the Country* portrays a man and a woman planting their crops with old-fashioned tools and horse-drawn plows. White, puffy clouds promise nourishing rain over their lush, rolling green fields. A church on the far hillside sanctifies this way of life.

The artists, who sometimes dressed the part of their subjects by donning overalls, sought to produce an indigenous American art and painting style. In contrast to abstract art coming from Europe and eastern U.S. cities, their realist-style portraits of American farming turned to the past and to the American heartland. Although critics chastised them for being too conservative and nationalistic, and others debated the genre's modern intent and influences, these painters nevertheless kept the old-fashioned farmer a vital symbol of national identity.

During the two world wars, American artists parlayed the pumpkin's familiar iconography into patriotic symbols of the home front, resurrecting another use for the vegetable. A Thanksgiving postcard published during World War I, for example, depicts an oversize golden pumpkin

John Collier (American, 1913–1992), "Harvest Market near Windsor Locks, Connecticut, 1941." Black-and-white film. Library of Congress, Prints and Photographs Division, FSA/OWI Collection LC-USF34-080974-D.

with "Peace and Prosperity" written across it. The pumpkin embodied the simple things in life found in the classic American dream, such as the rewards of hard work in a land of opportunity, and therefore served to invigorate the war effort.

FSA photographers depicted soldiers on leave sitting down to Thanksgiving dinner with their families during World War II.[49] Magazines and newspapers reported on the great efforts made to serve soldiers in the field some semblance of a Thanksgiving dinner and offered recipes for pumpkin pie that promised to please the serviceman in every American household.[50] Just before the end of the war, the famous American illustrator Norman Rockwell created a cover for the November 24, 1945, edition of the *Saturday Evening Post*, titled *Thanksgiving*, that portrayed a soldier in uniform, just home from the war, helping his elderly yet sturdy mother

Jack Delano (American, 1914–1994), "Pumpkin Pies and Thanksgiving Dinner at the Home of Mr. Timothy Levy Crouch, a Rogerine Quaker Living in Ledyard, Connecticut," 1940. Black-and-white film. Library of Congress, Prints and Photographs Division, FSA/OWI Collection LC-USF34-TOI-042712-D.

or grandmother peel potatoes for Thanksgiving dinner. In keeping with the nostalgic imagery of the scene, Rockwell displayed a big, fresh pumpkin at her feet, even though people at the time commonly used pie filling out of a can. The pumpkin not only represents an important component of a traditional Thanksgiving meal but more broadly communicates the illustration's themes of domestic tranquility and the nation's natural and moral wealth.

Rockwell's painting of this elderly woman in her rustic kitchen, along with FSA photographs of families sitting down to Thanksgiving dinner and magazine articles helping to ensure that GIs got their pumpkin pie, all come back to the idea that women's cooking pumpkin pie was an act of patriotism. Just as bakers of pumpkin pie in the Revolutionary War era made a stand for national independence by preparing the indigenous and homegrown vegetable for their families, and just as Sarah Josepha Hale's disciples in the nineteenth century served up pumpkin pies to instill in homes across the country a sense of national unity based on old agrarian ideals, so women in the mid-twentieth century used their culinary skills toward political ends. Cooking and serving food played an active, not just a supportive, role in national politics. It makes sense that Rockwell, as the standard bearer of Americana, would portray a woman baking pie from scratch with a fresh pumpkin. Yet judging from the popularity of canned pumpkin and bakery pies, many women experienced no contradiction as they took advantage of the most modern manufacturing innovations and conveniences to perpetuate old-fashioned values.

Thanksgiving, of course, is only part of the pumpkin's story. Halloween is much of the rest of it. Unlike Thanksgiving, with its focus on the family and domesticated nature, Halloween reveled in mischief. While the jagged-toothed jack-o'-lantern played foil to the pumpkin pie, it also reaffirmed the pie's expression of the therapeutic value of nature. Instead of finding inspiration in farm life, however, it celebrated the unpredictability of nature as a force beyond human control. Honoring the jack-o'-lantern one night of the year gave a break to Americans who might feel pinned down by regimented work schedules and bureaucracies that dictated the pace and structure of their lives. Like the pie, the jack-o'-lantern was an incarnation of complex, intertwined attitudes toward social norms and the natural world.

Although women still threw elaborate holiday "frolics," with the usual party games such as bobbing for apples, Halloween celebrants in the early twentieth century also took to the streets, making the holiday a more public affair than in decades past. They headed out the door in costume for parades, trick-or-treating, and hooliganism, which ranged from minor pranks such as doorbell ringing to more serious property damage.[51] Despite annual reports of violence on Halloween night in New York City in the thirties and forties, most revelers' actions were playful affronts to social norms.[52] As the master of ceremonies, the wild and mischievous jack-o'-lantern led the charge.

The pumpkin's image adorned tablecloths, mantelpieces, and endless party favors. "Here and there, in the most unexpected corners, jack-o'-lanterns smiled or gnashed their teeth amid great shocks of corn or leered from lofty coigns of vantage," described a columnist for the *Ladies Home Journal* in her October 1903 article "Merry Hallowe'en Larks."[53] Because of the more public nature of the holiday, people embellished their yards with pumpkins. At her 1911 "Halloween housewarming," one woman had "jack-o'-lanterns on the gate-posts, in the spooky corners of the cellars, and in the attic."[54]

Most jack-o'-lantern figures possessed a sinister and wily character. Except for Jack Pumpkinhead, the happy, dimwitted, pumpkin-headed creature with a long wooden body created by L. Frank Baum for his Wizard of Oz series, the jack-o'-lantern depicted in most popular holiday ephemera in the early twentieth century was hardly jovial.[55] Below a macabre head, it had a body, arms, legs, and feet that could be used to great advantage. Rather than being stranded on the doorstep, this jack-o'-lantern was animated and moved about. Holiday greeting cards depicted it driving cars, chasing children, riding on the backs of black cats, dancing with devils and witches, and serenading damsels.[56] It pranced among the stars and cavorted with the full harvest moon. Its body might be made of vegetable parts (with corncob arms and squash legs) or mimic the human form. It moved of its own volition as an independent force and could not be controlled. As a walking personification of wild, natural spirits, this pumpkin was full of vim and vigor. It was as much devilish imp as harvest emblem.

In the 1905 song "The Jack O'Lantern Girl," the lyricist called on classic Halloween themes to editorialize about people, particularly about proper gender roles and age-old anxieties about women who step outside prescribed social boundaries. The real focus of the pumpkin tale was not nature but the corrupting influences of urban life. In this ballad, the jack-o'-lantern personifies an untrustworthy female who is beyond a man's grasp. "The Jack O'Lantern Girl" is an attractive and urbane seductress, not the peasant harlot of bygone years. The cover of the sheet music shows a female human figure dressed in finery, prancing before a group of jack-o'-lantern-headed, stick-figure men in trench coats. The lyrics go like this:

> A sort of Jack O'Lantern Girl I lead them here! I lead them there! A most
> elusive elf am I to capture. Their sorrows deep they tell to me. Each seeks
> the tribute of a tear. Because they say my sympathy, To them is very
> very dear. I hear them all with down-cast eye From which the tears Flow
> unforced. They do not note that as I cry I always keep my fingers crossed.
> A sort of Jack O'Lantern Girl I lead them here! I lead them there! A most
> elusive elf am I to capture.[57]

"Halloween," color postcard, circa 1910s. Like the image on this postcard, most jack-o'-lantern figures in the first half of the twentieth century had a macabre head attached to an animated body. Author's private collection.

While the Jack O'Lantern Girl's wildness and unpredictability perpetuate historical analogies between the pumpkin and women's supposed overt and wanton sexuality, the song also expresses specific anxieties of the early twentieth century. At the time, single women were joining the work force in droves to fill service and administrative positions from office secretary to waitress—for example, the famous Harvey Girls, who worked at the well-known proprietor's national chain of restaurants.[58] The song conveys a sense of the danger, though perhaps also the attractiveness, of a working woman in the city who is not dependent on a man. Writing for *American Kitchen Magazine* in 1902, Hannah Ayer drew on the well-known pumpkin fairytales to speak of this unease about women's striking out on their own: "The famous Peter—pumpkin eater—resorted to a pumpkin to help him out of a dilemma, and as in the case of Cinderella the pumpkin was quite equal to the occasion, and by aid of its shell his wife was kept within bounds. Husbands of later date, like Peter, have been disturbed by their wives reaching outside prescribed boundaries."[59] The Jack O'Lantern Girl is the woman who could not be contained and got away. As a city girl unfettered by tradition and guided by her own free will, she is anathema to the venerable pumpkin pie makers who affirm agrarian and gender ideals by domesticating the pumpkin in the form of a pie.

The Light of the Pumpkin, a 1934 play by John Kirkpatrick, speaks similarly of the corrupting influences of the city. It brings together Halloween and Thanksgiving themes in a story about the recuperative powers of rural places. The play takes place in the country house of an elderly couple who await the Halloween visit of their nieces and nephews from the city. Before their arrival, the old man reflects warmly on his unwavering belief in the supernatural. Life was better when people had a healthy fear of the unknown and the powers that lurked in wild places, he says. The only fears people have nowadays, he notes cynically, are of being hit by a car and being taxed too much. As he speaks, the audience casts its eyes on a glowing jack-o'-lantern with "red, sunken eyes and evil, grinning teeth" in the center of the room.[60]

When the couple's citified, twenty-something relatives arrive, the visitors are initially more concerned with their time schedules than with the old man's tales and traditions. They have been corrupted by modern urban life. Mysterious noises echoing from nearby hillsides, however, and other clattering sounds heard on this bewitching night seem to spook away their jaded ways. "Even the sight of—of that old pumpkin—it did something to me," says the old man's niece. In the play, the jack-o'-lantern embodies both the forces of wild nature and the values of rural places. The characters perceive the jack-o'-lantern to be an antidote to the artificialities of modern life, and the countryside as unrefined yet more authentic than the world where they reside. Produced at the height of popularity of American regionalist paintings and of FSA works of art, *The Light of the Pumpkin* affirmed many Americans' longing for the benevolent influences of wild nature and rural life, and it confirmed the power of pumpkins to fulfill these desires.

Going out and buying pumpkins became as much a part of the seasonal ritual as putting them on display. John Arata's story about selling pumpkins to "well-dressed men" who happened by his family's northern California farm, which began this chapter, sounds like a rarity, but it was not. Similar incidents happened across the country as consumers' demand for fresh pumpkins for the holidays grew and their ability to find them in urban markets diminished. By the 1930s, in New York City, it was probably easier to find a pumpkin in a can than fresh from the vine. According to the *New York Times*: "A survey of the markets might give the impression that pumpkins and cranberries are disappearing. . . . John Egan, who regularly solves such mysteries for the Department of Markets, [explains] 'pumpkins are heavy to ship and take up a lot of room. If there is room on a truck and there are any pumpkins around, they'll put them on the load. But you won't find that many, even around Thanksgiving.'"[61]

Unless, that is, you got in your automobile and headed to the country. The 1910 ad for the Connecticut Pie Company, which shows two men hauling off pumpkins from a cornfield, depicts the classic rustic scene, but businessmen in suits and fedoras replace the farmers in straw hats and overalls. The scene is indicative of the turn in the pumpkin market. As early as 1904, a Michigan state booster optimistically viewed the pumpkin as a key tourist attraction. He asked, "Why not bring renown to Michigan as the 'Land of the Pumpkin Pie?' True, Nebraska is the home of the genuine corn-fed girl, and Kansas is not without glory as the home of the grasshopper; but to have it broadly known that Michigan is the 'Land of the pumpkin pie,' would bring tens of thousands of tourists to our State every autumn."[62]

Unable to compete with the wholesale prices offered by large-scale farms or to afford the prices demanded by rail and shipping companies, some farmers in the early twentieth century began to turn to direct marketing techniques, such as the use of roadside stands, to cut out the middlemen and salvage their family businesses. As many direct farm marketing guides explain, the keys to success were proximity to a large population center and an effective enticement.[63] Contributing to the development of roadside stands in the twenties, thirties, and forties was the proliferation of automobile tourism and the persistent interest in

THE WASHINGTON TIMES, SATURDAY, OCTOBER 15, 1910.

WHEN THE FROST IS ON THE PUMPKIN

—and the pumpkin's in the pie—and the pie is a REAL Connecticut Pie—spicy—deep—rich—big—the real pumpkin pie of Yankeeland Thanksgiving—then, and only then, can you know what true GOODNESS is!

30,000 Connecticut Pies

Are Baked and Sold Each Day

—30,000 of the most delicious, appetizing pies that ever made your mouth water with anticipation and delight.

CONNECTICUT PIES reach every home in Washington, and are ON SALE EVERYWHERE—Restaurants, Cafes, Grocers, etc.

25 Kinds At All Times

Order One Today—a REAL Connecticut Pumpkin Pie

CONNECTICUT PIE CO.

Wisconsin Avenue and O Street N. W.

"We Lead—Others Follow"

"When the Frost is on the Pumpkin," advertisement for the Connecticut Pie Company, Washington, D.C., in the *Washington Times*, October 15, 1910. Urbanites' demand for pumpkins for holiday rituals and food helped spark a new form of rural economic development—roadside farm stands.

native rural culture, as exemplified in art and photographs of the time. Concomitant with vast road improvements and construction, the number of automobiles increased exponentially with every passing year.[64] Buoyed by more disposable income and more free time, many Americans hit the road. While national park tours and cross-country road trips made popular summertime vacations, many people also piled into their new sedans for weekend trips to the country.[65]

Often with no clear destination in mind, families toured the countryside to take in the rural scenery. One 1940s American regionalist–style landscape painting portrays a large sedan pulling a camper along a rural road, with picturesque, rolling farmland and a quaint little farmhouse serving as the backdrop. Such places were tourist attractions. In *Middletown*, their study of Muncie, Indiana, Robert and Helen Lynd reported that the "local paper estimated in June 1935 that 10,000 persons leave Middletown for other towns and resorts every fine Sunday."[66] They noted that these "all-day Sunday motor trips" were important for residents who did not have extended vacations and that some considered these jaunts "a threat against the church."[67] Most people sought not just geographical distance from home but also a less tangible separation or respite from their daily lives in and around urban centers. The automobile gave Americans greater access to and freedom to visit once remote places and people.

Tourists' presence in the countryside propelled the very forces of capitalist consumer culture that city folk were trying to escape and thereby altered the landscape to fit their expectations and desires.[68] Farm families were among a large cadre of entrepreneurs who seized the opportunity to serve the growing numbers of weekend vagabonds. James Agee's "The Great American Roadside," an article in the October 1934 edition of *Fortune*, described this new phenomenon. He called roadside businesses "an American institution which is also a $3,000,000 industry, and which is founded upon a solid rock: the restlessness of the American people."[69] Gas stations, eateries, and motels all offered their own sorts of enticements, which they advertised with increasingly elaborate signage, from giant ice cream cones to massive teapots. A 1929 Massachusetts Department of Agriculture survey of 2,500 consumers indicated that more than 60 percent of the respondents stopped at roadside farm stands because of the displays.[70]

Roadside farm stands served a particular market niche by offering customers not only fresh fruits and vegetables at decent prices but also a chance to interact with local farmers. "For years it has been custom," noted the author of *Meet the Farmer* in 1944, "to stop once each trip at a little roadside stand run by a farmer, to pick up fresh eggs, vegetables, and poultry."[71] Early on, regulators tried to ensure that farm stand operators were indeed the farm proprietors, and they discouraged the sale of nonfarm items such as sodas and cigarettes, presumably to sustain a sense of authenticity.[72] New Jersey, for example, required that operators produce 60 percent of the merchandise sold at the stand.[73] Farmers established cooperative roadside associations, and publications from *Economic Geography* to *First Principles of Cooperation in Buying and Selling in Agriculture* described the stands' economic benefits for small-scale producers.[74] One such publication stated specifically that a New York state farmer's roadside stand had lifted his farm out of the doldrums and helped sustain his operations.[75]

The changes wrought by the new road culture on farm communities inspired a melancholy poem from Robert Frost, who is known for his reverence for the New England countryside and his deep sense of rural nostalgia. Written in 1936, during the height of the Great Depression, the poem "A Roadside Stand" portrays the farm stand enterprise as a confrontation between struggling yet sympathetic farmers and greedy and overprivileged urbanites. He wrote:

> Here far from the city we make our roadside stand,
> And ask for some city money to feel in hand,
> To try if it will not make our being expand,
> And give us the life of the moving pictures' promise. . . .
> The sadness that lurks near the open window there,
> That waits all day in almost open prayer,
> For the squeal of brakes, the sound of a stopping car,
> Of all the thousand selfish cars that pass,
> Just one did stop, but only to plow up the grass.[76]

Frost laments the roadside stand as American farmers' tragic attempt to survive against economic forces and ways of life that seem antithetical to their humble rural existence. His pessimism reflects the deep desire that many people felt (and that he was famous for writing about) to hold onto a more traditional, farming way of life in America. Few practicing farmers, of course, have ever thought of themselves as anachronisms; instead, they have sought ways to modernize and improve their businesses. Although it might seem paradoxical, many of them did just that by taking advantage of the American public's nostalgia for the quaint family farm of lore.

Farmers offered all types of produce for sale, but the pumpkin proved a particularly strong enticement because it was such a potent symbol of both the old-fashioned farm and virile nature. Countering Frost's forlorn perspective on the rise of farm stands, a children's tale from 1937 adapted the old agrarian myth to accommodate the pumpkin roadside stand. In *Peter, Peter, Pumpkin Grower*, by Florence Bourgeois, a boy named Peter plants pumpkins and then creates a farm stand where people stop to buy them. He uses the money he earns to buy a bicycle. The book translates the age-old myth of the American yeoman farmer, in which a strong work ethic brings due rewards, to the new economic opportunity offered by the roadside stand.[77] By choosing the pumpkin to make her point, the author used one of the most popular and recognizable symbols of rural virtue, thereby communicating the idea that these old values could stay intact as the world changed.

Alongside the FSA's more famous images of California farm immigrants and midwestern tenant farmers is a photographic series depicting New England roadside pumpkin stands that reinforces Bourgeois's point. Whereas the focus in the early years of the FSA program was on the hardships of the rural poor (which were also evident in Frost's poem), as World War II approached, the emphasis changed to more optimistic subjects. In a letter to his staff of photographers in 1941, Roy Stryker, the head of the agency, instructed: "Please watch for autumn pictures, as calls are beginning to come for them and we are short. These should be rather the symbol of Autumn . . . cornfields, pumpkins. . . . Emphasize the idea of abundance—the 'horn of plenty' and pour maple syrup over it."[78] In response, photographers John Collier and Russell Lee captured images of farm stands heaped high with piles of pumpkins and squashes. Ironically, many of the photographs were shot in New England, where pumpkin production was meager in comparison with that of other regions but which had a large, concentrated population of urban consumers.[79] These "wayside harvest stands," as the artists identified them, were eye-catching sites of agrarian splendor. Mounds of field pumpkins, crates of crooknecks, and bins of gourds and other squashes enticed the caravans of travelers who passed before them. Unlike the spotless and stylized way in which pumpkins are displayed at stands nowadays, these appear nicked, scraped, and haphazardly piled, suggesting that farmers had not yet begun breeding varieties exclusively for display.

Several photographs document the great draw that these rustic marketplaces had for urbanites. Many are crowded with women in heels and men in suits perusing the fall produce. In one photograph in a series labeled "Farmers along the Mohawk trail in Massachusetts depend on the tourist for much [of] their profit," a farm woman dressed in a simple seedcloth dress and apron stands beside a customer in her Sunday finest who inspects the pumpkins and gourds before her.[80] The two women stand as stereotypes of old and new ways of life—the rural producer and the

Russell Lee (American, 1903–1986), "Roadside Stand near Greenfield, Massachusetts," 1939. Black-and-white film. This image is part of a Farm Security Administration photographic series featuring New England roadside pumpkin stands. Library of Congress, Prints and Photographs Division, FSA/OWI Collection LC-USF33-012448-M4.

urban consumer. The photograph "Sales Promotion at a wayside harvest market" depicts a long-retired Model A with a family made of pumpkins seated inside it.[81] Set beside the road, it is a caricature of the new breed of tourists who clambered their way into the countryside. Another, more picturesque roadside attraction is an old farm wagon piled with pumpkins that recalls nineteenth-century harvest paintings.[82] It is suggestive of the ways tourists were offered a piece of Americana along with vegetables for pies. Farmers used historic motifs as enticements for urban visitors to the countryside, and the photographers exploited these themes to their own ends.

Another new tradition drawing crowds of thousands to the countryside was the pumpkin festival. A "pumpkin show" was now considered an

Untitled Farm Security Administration photograph labeled "Farmers along the Mohawk trail in Massachusetts depend on the tourist for much [of] their profit," made between 1935 and 1942. Library of Congress, Prints and Photographs Division, FSA/OWI Collection LC-USF34-081646-D.

old-time county agricultural fair—sometimes called a "pig and pumpkin show"—in contrast to larger state fairs that displayed the latest innovations in the mechanical arts alongside agricultural products.[83] What is interesting about the fairs devoted to modern innovations and the festivals that celebrated the pumpkin is that they arose out of the same trend. In other words, the pumpkin festival is not a remnant of an historical agrarian tradition. Pumpkins were nowhere to be found at colonial and nineteenth-century harvest festivals. The pumpkin festival got started just when an agrarian way of life seemed to be disappearing.

The Circleville Pumpkin Show, in Ohio, was first held during the third week of October in 1903.[84] Displays of corn fodder and assortments of pumpkins marked the early events, which organizers intended "to get

"Circleville Pumpkin Show—1910." Black-and-white film. The Circleville, Ohio, Pumpkin Show has been held the third week in October since 1903. Pickaway County Historical Society, Circleville, Ohio.

the country folks and city folks together . . . so the city folks would be able to appreciate their efforts."[85] Yet modern food technologies, not just old agricultural practices, inspired the festival. Circleville was home to the C. E. Sears Canning Company, which began processing and packing pumpkins, corn, and other vegetables in 1873. During the fall packing season, Circleville streets were lined with long columns of horse-drawn wagons, all loaded with pumpkins that farmers brought to town for processing.

The Depression, a drought, and the closure of the canning factory all took their toll on the community and threatened the survival of the Pumpkin Show. During World War II it was cancelled altogether. In the late 1940s, even as many farmers moved off their land to seek opportunities in nearby Columbus and beyond, the Pumpkin Show reemerged on

Circleville's yearly calendar, and it has continued as an annual tradition ever since. Circleville was only the first of many rural communities to renew its local identity and its prosperity with the pumpkin and thereby defy the dire predictions of economic demise. Ironically, the expanding consequences of corporate capitalism, including increased wealth, technological innovations, and, adversely, economic pressures on small family farms and rural towns, made pumpkins profitable and pumpkin stands and festivals abundant. As insightful as John Arata's father was in the 1930s about a future in pumpkins, he probably could not have imagined that one day his children and grandchildren would grow something called a "specialty pumpkin" and that thousands of tourists would pay up to $15 each just to visit the family pumpkin farm.[86]

SIX

ATLANTIC GIANTS TO JACK-BE-LITTLES

The Changing Nature of Pumpkins, 1946 to the Present

T HOSE NICKED, CROOKED, AND COCKEYED PUMPKINS ON DISPLAY in bins from the early years of the Circleville Pumpkin Show and pictured in the 1940s FSA photographs of roadside stands are no more. Now, pumpkins—real pumpkins—are as beautifully orange and perfectly round as the painted ones in Ehninger's 1867 bucolic harvest scene and Rockwell's 1945 Thanksgiving illustration. The ideal pumpkin is no longer one that will last through winter or nourish a cow but one that is "smooth and glossy orange-yellow in color with a round shape of good uniformity," as Burpee's 1975 seed catalog advertised.[1] A rise in pumpkin sales has matched the changes in the vegetable's appearance. The U.S. pumpkin harvest of 71,700 tons in 1949 more than doubled to 195,300 tons in 1959 and then leaped to 1.1 million tons in 2007.[2]

The use of pumpkins as livestock fodder, a practice that helped solidify the vegetable's association with small-scale subsistence agriculture in the nineteenth century, plummeted by the mid-twentieth century, from 17,645 tons in 1939 to 794 tons in 1954.[3] After 1954, the U.S. Agricultural Census stopped recording data on the use of pumpkins for animal feed altogether. By 2007, 87 percent of pumpkins were not even eaten but were put on display as Halloween and autumn decorations. The pumpkin's symbolism has become so much more important than its meat that many varieties, such as those sold by Burpee's, have become eye-catching wonders at the expense of fertility and palatability. Pumpkin foods do not even have to contain the vegetable; they can simply take the shape of it.

"Pumpkins mean crisp air and pies and smiles on an October night. Never nutrition," explained an observer in 1979.[4] This light-hearted quotation from an airline magazine nicely sums up the pumpkin's positive associations in the late twentieth century, and the impracticality of it all. The same sense of natural goodness that Americans associate with the pumpkin permeates the cornucopia, so common in seasonal decorations and on greeting cards, and, especially, the new version of the jack-o'-lantern, which has become a kind-hearted natural spirit instead of the wily trickster it was in the early twentieth century or the volatile, frightening pumpkin imp seen in Renaissance art.[5]

An affinity with the natural world permeated all facets of American society and culture beginning in the 1960s, especially among the affluent and expanding middle class. Distressed by widespread pollution and the development and disappearance of wild places, many Americans cast modern society as a villainous abuser of an innocent and life-sustaining natural world. The passage of milestone environmental protection laws such as the Wilderness Act in 1964, the Clean Air Act in 1970, and the Clean Water Act in 1972; an increase in the membership enrollment and political influence of environmental nonprofits such as the Sierra Club and the Natural Resources Defense Council; and the popularity of outdoor recreation, back-to-the-land movements, and natural foods are benchmarks of the modern environmental movement in the second half of the twentieth century.[6] But nature appreciation also took more prosaic and less conspicuous forms, such as attachment to pumpkins.

When most Americans think about communing with nature, they probably do not think about celebrating Halloween, but its festivities say a lot about how Americans imagine the natural world around them. While adult costume parties and parades still define the holiday, they share the night with children walking from door to door in costumes, yelling "Trick or treat!" to be rewarded with candies from their neighbors. The tradition started in the 1920s and became more popular with post–World War II suburbanization and the baby boom. Pumpkins ranging from a single jack-o'-lantern to more elaborate displays greet neighborhood children.[7] Some homes metamorphose into haunted-house extravaganzas, with cobwebs stretched across bushes, faux gravestones planted in yards, paper skeletons hanging from porch rafters, and glowing jack-o'-lanterns perched on doorsteps. Others highlight a country

Spring Hope, North Carolina, October 2000. Like many other American households, this one marks the fall season with pumpkin yard decorations. Photo: Cindy Ott.

feel, with hay bales, pumpkin-headed scarecrows, cornstalks, folk-art-style wooden pumpkin cutouts, and fresh pumpkins piled decoratively near potted mums.[8]

Although the themes of death, the supernatural, and wild nature still figure prominently at Halloween, their representative ghouls are tame and benevolent by historical standards. Jack-o'-lanterns and other Halloween creatures have become childlike cartoons such as Casper the Friendly Ghost or, in other cases, nurturing, New Age caregivers. Greeting cards, toys, and books often portray the jack-o'-lantern with big round eyes and a goofy grin rather than a threatening grimace. And perhaps most significantly, instead of being a two-legged beast, the new jack-o'-lantern has, as one poet put it, "nothing underneath"—it is just a head.[9] Amputating and disembodying this symbol of wild, primitive nature nullifies its danger. Without a body to propel it, the jack-o'-lantern is powerless to act on its own will and wreak havoc.

Replacing the volatile and mischievous creature depicted in early twentieth-century Halloween memorabilia is a comforting and compassionate guardian spirit. A 1999 poem offers a glimpse of this new jack-o'-lantern personality:

> Pumpkin, pumpkin, pumpkin bright,
> When my "Tricks or Treats" are said,
> Will you light me to my bed,
> Kind old father pumpkin head?[10]

The transformation owes much to the rising popular beliefs in the healing power of nature.[11] *Pumpkin Light*, a 1993 children's book, is one of many tales about a pumpkin with magical powers. In the story, a jack-o'-lantern saves a boy named Angus, who was born on a day when "the sun rose like a shining pumpkin." After Angus disobeys his parents, a mean scarecrow turns the boy into a dog, and the only way he can be transformed back is for someone to carve a magic pumpkin into a jack-o'-lantern. The tale's narrator states about Angus, "Sometimes he thought he could almost hear sounds from deep within the pumpkin. As if messages from the sun and the moon somehow entered through the pumpkin's stem to rest among the silent seeds."[12] At the end of the story, Angus's mother carves the pumpkin and thereby returns the boy to his rightful form. In this fairy tale, the jack-o'-lantern offers salvation and restores the human spirit with the power of its natural forces.

This magical character also appears in one of the most popular contemporary jack-o'-lantern tales, *It's the Great Pumpkin, Charlie Brown*, a holiday television special based on the beloved *Peanuts* comic strip by Charles Schulz.[13] The syndicated comic, which ran from 1950 to 2000, follows a boy named Charlie Brown, his dog Snoopy, and the kids in his neighborhood. *It's the Great Pumpkin, Charlie Brown* has aired every year since 1966. In the story, Linus, the philosopher of the group, treks out to his pumpkin patch on Halloween night to await the Great Pumpkin's arrival while the other kids attend a holiday costume party. According to Linus, "The Great Pumpkin rises out of the pumpkin patch, and flies through the air and brings toys to all the children in the world." Alas, to Linus's great consternation, the Great Pumpkin never appears in his patch, but he holds out hope for its return the following year. While Linus's friends ridicule him for believing in a pagan spirit in modern times, the audience feels compassion toward him and his faith in an idyllic supernatural force.

The affiliation of pumpkins with children, dating back to the mid-nineteenth century, remains as powerful as ever, because the two mutually reinforce the themes of natural exuberance and goodness. Photographs of a small child sitting on or holding a pumpkin in a pumpkin patch or dressed up as a pumpkin in a Halloween costume are ubiquitous in calendars, office cubicles, studio portraits, and just about every American newspaper in the month of October. Children's stories meld one with the other. For example, "The Ugly Pumpkin" (1970) mimics the classic ugly duckling tale but substitutes a "lopsided runt" pumpkin that becomes a handsome jack-o'-lantern. *Peter Pumpkin* (1963) is a coming-of-age story about a boy pumpkin learning how to be a man.[14] "Pumpkin" is a common term of endearment for children.[15] A 1995 Libby's advertisement for canned pumpkin includes a photograph of two cheerful toddlers sitting inside a giant pumpkin, suggesting that the contents of the can are as sweet and wonderful as two rosy-cheeked babies.[16] Both the pumpkin and the babies exude happiness and well-being.

As Americans made Halloween spooks sweeter and more benevolent than the frightening supernatural forces that traditionally ruled the night, they increasingly conceived of people as the instigators of mayhem. Jack the Ripper aroused more fears than a jack-o'-lantern.[17] Activities on Halloween ranging from minor pranks such as tossing eggs at cars, covering front-yard trees with toilet paper, and smashing pumpkins to sinister acts of violence such as lacing candy with poison and placing razor blades in apples have superseded invisible threats from above on Halloween night, even though the more serious offenses have never been verified.[18]

In the 1998 movie *Sleepy Hollow,* based on the Washington Irving tale, director Tim Burton resurrected the older, more haunting jack-o'-lantern through the movie's main protagonist, a terrifying and murderous ghost.[19] Deviating from the original tale, the Headless Horseman in the movie stalks and decapitates townfolk in its quest to find its long-lost head. (The film also depicts pumpkins, anachronistically, as glowing jack-o'-lanterns, which did not appear in the original 1832 version of the tale.) While the audience is first led to believe that this wild, supernatural spirit is responsible for all the bloodshed, they discover in the end that a woman is the culprit. The ghost of the Headless Horseman is simply a pawn in her sinister plan to avenge the mistreatment of her family when she was a child. By concluding that the real danger is human acts, not natural or

James Wyeth (American, b. 1946), *Pumpkinhead— Self-Portrait*, 1972. Oil painting, 30 by 30 inches. Private collection.

supernatural ones, the movie reasserts the popular belief that wild nature offers joy and solace while human beings harbor threats of evil and terror.

Contemporary artists, writers, and filmmakers have kept alive age-old negative gender stereotypes, and many of their works corroborate the menacing image of people at Halloween. James Wyeth's *Pumpkin-head—Self-Portrait* (1972) conjures up the Headless Horseman by picturing himself wearing a black overcoat and a large pumpkin head carved into a sliver-eyed, grinning jack-o'-lantern.[20] He stands in a vacant field with a dense white sky overhead, reminiscent of a late autumn day. The setting instills in the character a sense of earthiness and coldness. The painting is both a playful self-mockery and a portrait of the mystery and savagery of the artist's mind.

Quentin Tarantino's black comedy *Pulp Fiction*, released in 1994, features its own disturbing version of this male personality type, one who lies beyond the controls of society and is guided by brute natural instincts.[21] "Pumpkin," played by John Travolta, is a likable common criminal with an evil streak, somewhat simple-minded but also deadly violent. His persona is evocative of several short story characters, such as the protagonist of "Pumpkin," a 1986 story by Bill Pronzini about a man who becomes possessed by "a telepathic evil pumpkin," turns into a madman, and kills his wife.[22] The moral of these stories is that seemingly good people can be capable of evil deeds. The authors use the pumpkin to express the wild and demonic alter egos.[23] Unlike the Great Pumpkin, who personifies the benevolent powers of nature, the pumpkin *man* teems with wrath and danger. Perhaps not quite so evil but certainly troublesome is the pumpkin-headed politician, who persists as a popular motif. During the 1999 Democratic presidential primary, for example, the *Washington Post* published a Jeff MacNelly cartoon called "The Great Debate," which depicted two pumpkins perched on podiums and carved into faces mimicking those of candidates Bill Bradley and Al Gore.[24] After thousands of years and hundreds of generations of political leaders, this pumpkin iconography remains as viable as the belief in the pompousness and buffoonery of politicians remains strong.

Recent scientific studies document what popular writers have said for generations—the smell of pumpkin pie increases sexual desire.[25] When Philip Roth, in *Portnoy's Complaint*, nicknamed the white Anglo-Saxon Protestant girlfriend of his young Jewish male protagonist "Pumpkin," he tapped directly into the familiar gender trope of the promiscuous woman.[26] The female protagonist in Penelope Mortimer's 1963 novel *The Pumpkin Eater*, which became a Hollywood movie based on Harold Pinter's screenplay in 1965, and in Susanna Hofmann McShea's 1992 *The Pumpkin-Shell Wife* offer harsher portraits of pumpkinish women.[27] Like the fabled wife of Peter Pumpkin Eater, these women disregard the rules of society, such as fidelity in marriage, but with direr consequences. In *The Pumpkin Eater*, the central character is chastised by her friends for having several husbands and many more children. Broken marriages and sorrow are her destiny. The fortunes of the New England housewife in *The Pumpkin-Shell Wife* are even grimmer. She is murdered during a venture into New York City to meet her lover.

Alongside the modern-day pumpkin fables about immoral women reaping their just rewards for lecherous behavior, "pumpkin" has also become shorthand for a frumpy woman, like Cinderella before the ball. For example, in the fall of 1999, a Washington, D.C., sports club advertisement for new members said, "This could be the last Halloween you'll have to go as a pumpkin."[28] In a similar vein, at the 2000 American

Academy of Motion Picture Awards, winner Marcia Gay Harden said she felt like "queen for the day," wearing her designer dress and two million dollars' worth of Harry Winston jewelry. Yet "after this is all over," she commented, "I'll turn back into a pumpkin."[29]

When Americans put pumpkins on their front stoops for Halloween, they turn the pumpkin into a sign of friendliness, complicating any simple distinction between benevolent nature and corrupted humanity. On Halloween, many Americans transform their private homes into community spaces by inviting neighbors to come to their doors. The pumpkin serves symbolically as a latchkey because trick-or-treaters usually approach only houses with a lit pumpkin out front. The popular home entertainment specialist Martha Stewart demonstrated how to line a walk with pumpkin lanterns so people could find your door. "You needn't express your artistry with a traditional jack-o'-lantern," advised an article in the October 1998 issue of *Martha Stewart Living*. "Elegant pumpkin lanterns look at home in the most sophisticated settings, and cast a welcoming light for any visitor."[30]

Putting a jack-o'-lantern in front of the house is a neighborly act of good will. Belvedere Street in San Francisco is one of thousands of American streets where residents go all out for Halloween by lining their doorsteps with masses of pumpkins every year. The street is aglow with flickering faces, enticing visitors from all across the city to be a part of the festive event. The sense of community forged with the pumpkin is what makes the teen prank of smashing pumpkins such an effective antisocial act (and a good name for a rock band). Smashing pumpkins destroys not only private property but also this totem of communal togetherness.[31] Americans have turned the pumpkin into an abstract symbol of cultural values—in this case, neighborliness—and they widely rely on the actual, physical pumpkin to communicate their sentiment.

These new ways of thinking about and displaying pumpkins have altered the very nature of the pumpkin itself. "Orange-amental" is how one South Carolina farmer described modern breeds of pumpkins. Emphasizing their aethetic qualities, he said, "I plant sugar babies not because they're the best pie pumpkin—and they are—but because they're small—just the right size and shape for kids; and they're bright orange and have prominent ribs."[32] New pumpkin varieties such as Autumn Pride, Ghost Rider, and Spooktacular—voluptuous in shape, size, and color—call forth romantic yet playful visions of nature and nostalgic memories of autumn. Seed catalogs boast about the cosmetic qualities of the fruits, describing them as "handsome," "uniform and attractive," and "well-colored and classy."[33] A few go a bit overboard. "Words cannot describe this beautiful pumpkin," gushed the 1990 Holmes Seed Company catalog about the Spirit pumpkin.[34] Many modern-day pumpkins are mere façades compared with their botanical predecessors. Some are hybrids with seeds that cannot reproduce; in others, the flesh is inedible.[35] Some fruits are now so large that heavy machinery is needed to lift them. These physical liabilities are of little consequence today, because consumers view the fresh pumpkin more as a decoration than as a meal. People are more interested in its visual effect than its practicality.

The variety Oz was bred to be uniform in shape and color, at the expense of palatability and potency. Its rind is beautiful, but its flesh is dry and stringy and its seeds are infertile. This pumpkin is essentially window dressing in comparison with the varieties that allowed colonial and nineteenth-century farms to thrive. Big Autumn and Autumn Gold have an "early coloring gene" that makes their fruit turn from green to orange before other types do.[36] Growers value these varieties because they require a shorter growing season, which in turn provides a more flexible harvest period. Unlike in times past, when a fresh pumpkin's usefulness spanned the winter months, it now terminates abruptly the day after Halloween, at least for the main consumer market.[37] Changing color prematurely helps ensure that the crop will obtain the essential orange hue during the brief window of opportunity for sales. Even pumpkin stems are now engineered to be attractive and strong, so that people can easily pick up an individual fruit from the marketplace and carry it home. "Get a handle on the pumpkin business," the 1986 Harris Moran catalog said about the Pankow's Field pumpkin, which it advertised as having "remarkably big, sturdy 'handles.'"[38]

Another alteration is the replacement of the Connecticut Field pumpkin with the Howden. In the early 1970s, John Howden, of Massachusetts, developed the Howden pumpkin to be a more standardized version of the antiquated variety. Harris Seeds described it as "a Connecticut Field type but far superior. Its size is more uniform, averaging 20–25 pounds, and the deep-round fruit are quite symmetrical. . . . it is much less apt to produce lop-sided fruit."[39] In testament to the way the vegetable now emulates its cultural image, instead of the other way around, the *Seed Savers 2001 Yearbook* advertised the squat, deeply ribbed Cinderella pumpkin as being "similar to Disney's 'coach' pumpkin." Likewise, the white-skinned Casper pumpkin takes its name from the cartoon ghost.[40] And with a name like Paint-a-Pumpkin, a hybrid with pale smooth skin, how could anyone think of eating it?[41]

In keeping with the maxim that form follows function, Gurney's Seed and Nursery Company, in its 1998 catalog, marketed Jack-Be-Littles and Baby-Boos, miniature pumpkins that weighed no more than a pound, as "charming accent[s] for fall centerpieces."[42] The USDA classifies these tiny new pumpkins as a nonfood item, even though they are edible. Seed companies have reintroduced gourds and squash varieties such as Turk's turban as tasteful additions to fall home decor. "Roadside stands find these ornamental squash command prominent prices for fall decorations," stated the Burpee's seed catalog.[43]

These small, decorative pumpkins and squashes are akin to the endless variety of pumpkin novelties offered for sale every fall. Starting in the early twentieth century, jack-o'-lantern cardboard cutouts, plastic figurines, and tin noisemakers became popular Halloween party favors. By the beginning of the twenty-first century, consumers could stock up on pumpkin welcome mats, every assortment of dinner plate, baking dishes, Pez candy dispensers, candles, T-shirts, watches and earrings, and blinking flashlights, not to mention the sterling silver enameled pumpkin key chain on sale for $225 at Tiffany's in the fall of 2001.[44] Promoting a dizzying mix of natural and artificial qualities, and with no apparent sense of irony, the Cotton Gin's fall 2001 catalog, under the heading "Naturally Country," offered "realistic handcrafted 'faux' pumpkins and gourds [that] will last for years."[45]

If one judges the quality of a metaphor by the size of its image, then the ultimate symbol of nature's abundance, or "Naturally Country," has to be the Atlantic Giant (AG) pumpkin.[46] Developed in the 1960s by Howard Dill, of Windsor, Nova Scotia, its dime-size seeds produce fruits that average between four hundred and five hundred pounds. Some reach almost a ton.[47] An Associated Press photograph of Christy Harp, of Massillion, Ohio, with her 2009 world record 1,725-pounder is typical in the way it depicts the grower's outstretched arms, unable to reach even halfway around the colossal body of orange flesh.[48] A scene of a single

Pumpkins

A Fun-to-Grow Garden Crop!

Pumpkins are the perfect pick for decorating craft projects, pie making, seed roasting and entering in your county fair. **SELECTION TIP:** *For really big pumpkins, if your fair allows squash-type varieties, grow Atlantic Giant. If the rules specify "true pumpkins only," try Prizewinner or the brawny Connecticut Field.*

DILL'S ATLANTIC GIANT *Still the Champion*
Outstanding performer—current record-holder at over 1,000 pounds! Even without special treatment, you get eye-popping 200- to 300-pound squash-type pumpkins with flavorful orange flesh. But if you're set on shooting for the pumpkin-growers' hall of fame, tips for growing giant pumpkins come free with every order. Approx. 10 seeds per pkt. 120 DAYS.

	Size	1 Offer	2 Or More
5727-181	Pkt.	3.98	3.59 Each
5727-341	1/2 Oz.	7.69	6.93 Each
5727-591	2 Oz.	23.09	20.95 Each

BRAGGER'S SPECIAL
4430-351—*Save $1.14!* Get 1 pkt. each of Prizewinner and Dill's Atlantic Giant. They're both huge!
ORDER 1 OFFER, GET 2 PKTS! **1 OFFER** $4.59

HYBRID BUSH SPIRIT *Compact and Extra Early*
GURNEY'S CHOICE Ripens 2-3 weeks faster than most. Its bright orange fruits are smooth skinned and nicely rounded—a real charm to carve. Each weighs 10-15 pounds, filled with sweet orange flesh that bakes up light and delicious. Approx. 25 seeds per pkt. 90 DAYS.

	Size	1 Offer	2 Or More
5738-151	Pkt.	2.45	2.21 Each
5738-561	1/2 Oz.	8.35	7.52 Each

LUMINA PUMPKIN
Ghostly White Fruits
Novel pumpkin is perfect for carving or painting. Grows 8-10 inches tall, weighs up to 20 pounds. Smooth and pure white outside, all fine-grained orange flesh inside. Approx. 15 seeds per pkt. 95 DAYS.

	Size	1 Offer	2 Or More
5708-111	Pkt.	1.89	1.53 Each
5708-371	1 Oz.	4.29	3.87 Each
5708-521	1/4 Lb.	12.87	11.67 Each

CONNECTICUT FIELD
Largest Carving Pumpkin
Folks favor these for really big jack-o-lanterns. Orange-gold fruits weigh 20 pounds or more, have a flattened bottom that won't tip. A great baker, too. Approx. 25 seeds per pkt. 115 DAYS.

	Size	1 Offer	2 Or More
5701-181	Pkt.	1.12	1.01 Each
5701-341	1 Oz.	3.35	3.05 Each
5701-591	1/4 Lb.	10.05	9.12 Each

HYBRID PRIZEWINNER
True, Award-Winning Pumpkins
Exhibition-style fruits, round and covered with smooth and glossy red-orange skin. Easily attains 100-200 pounds, with much larger ones—think 400-pound range—likely. Flavorful flesh is a bonus. Approx. 5 seeds per pkt. 120 DAYS.

	Size	1 Offer	2 Or More
5716-111	Pkt.	1.75	1.58 Each
5716-371	1 Oz.	7.98	7.19 Each

◄ JACK-BE-LITTLE
True Miniature Pumpkin
Not a gourd! Bright little pumpkins color up early, easily fit into the palm of your hand—a charming accent for fall centerpieces. Fruits are smooth skinned, very uniform in size and shape. Properly cured, they last up to 12 months. Compact vines spread 10-12 feet, produce up to 10 edible fruits. Flesh is smooth and sweet. Approx. 25 seeds per pkt. 100 DAYS.

	Size	1 Offer	2 Or More
5717-101	Pkt.	1.50	1.35 Each
5717-361	1/4 Oz.	3.39	3.09 Each
5717-511	1 Oz.	10.19	9.25 Each

BABY BOO
Ghostly Fun for Halloween
All-white fruits 3 inches wide, 9-10 per vine. Approx. 25 seeds per pkt. 95 DAYS.

	Size	1 Offer	2 Or More
5715-121	Pkt.	1.65	1.67 Each
5715-381	1/4 Oz.	4.40	3.96 Each
5715-531	1 Oz.	13.19	11.97 Each

MINI-MIX PUMPKIN SPECIAL
4431-341—*$3.35 value.* You get 1 pkt. each of Jack-Be-Little and Baby Boo. Made-to-order matchup for craft projects!
ORDER 1 OFFER, GET 2 PKTS! **1 OFFER** $2.69

HYBRID AUTUMN GOLD
Colors Up Early
Golden weeks before harvest. Shapely 7- to 10-pound fruits get brighter as time goes by, finally turn deep orange. Produces 3-5 pumpkins per vine. A fine choice for pie making. Approx. 25 seeds per pkt. 90 DAYS.

	Size	1 Offer	2 Or More
5702-171	Pkt.	1.59	1.44 Each
5702-331	1/2 Oz.	3.78	3.41 Each

JACK-O-LANTERN
Bred Especially for Carving
Nice and smooth—no bumps to jar your carving knife. Bright orange 10- to 12-pound fruits balance nicely, won't tip over without a trick-or-treater's help. Approx. 25 seeds per pkt. 110 DAYS.

	Size	1 Offer	2 Or More
5710-171	Pkt.	1.05	95¢ Each
5710-331	1 Oz.	3.15	2.85 Each
5710-581	1/4 Lb.	9.45	8.59 Each

SMALL SUGAR
Flavor Standard for Pie Making
Has sweet, smooth-textured flesh and lots of it—seed cavity is unusually small. Colorful orange 6- to 8-pound fruits can be carved into compact jack-o-lanterns. Approx. 25 seeds per pkt. 95 DAYS.

	Size	1 Offer	2 Or More
5729-161	Pkt.	1.12	1.01 Each
5729-321	1/2 Oz.	1.99	1.80 Each
5729-571	2 Oz.	5.97	5.42 Each

GURNEY'S, Yankton, SD 57079 • 19

Page from Gurney's Seed and Nursery Company's 1998 spring catalog, Yankton, South Dakota. At the turn of the twenty-first century, producers bred pumpkins for display, at the expense of fertility and palatability. The Hybrid Frosty and Bush Hybrid Spirit, for example, produce seeds that cannot reproduce, but their fruits are symmetrical and attractive.

Christy Harp posing with her world record 1,725-pound pumpkin at the Ohio Valley Growers Weigh-Off in Canfield, Ohio, on October 3, 2009. Her world record has since been broken. Photo: Scott Heckel, Canton Repository.

giant pumpkin shoehorned into the back of a pickup truck, or of an adult comfortably nestled inside a single specimen, documents the variety's comically huge size. Every October, images and tales of its production are ubiquitous on television and radio, and in newspapers, including the *Wall Street Journal*.[49] The enormousness of these pumpkins incites hyperbole. When a bystander at a giant pumpkin-weighing contest in Allardt, Tennessee, in 1995 asked how much a pumpkin weighed, someone replied, "I don't know but I hear some boy took a picture of it and the picture alone weighed seven pounds!"[50]

Although many growers might protest, it is difficult to see Atlantic Giants as beautiful. Ribbed with orange to gray skin, giant pumpkins are lopsided, rather obese, fleshy forms. A thick rind, sometimes measuring nearly a foot across, supports their enormous girth, yet the meat is dry, stringy, and practically inedible. The effort growers exert to nurture the plant are rewarded not only by prizewinning pumpkins but also by a sense of virtue that taps directly into agrarian myths about the value of hard work and toiling in the soil. And it is not just the size of the vegetable but the *idea* of the pumpkin that helps growers succeed. The outrageous proportions and orange color say as much about Americans' passion for agrarian life as about the great natural proclivities of the plant. Giant pumpkins are made up not only of DNA but also of cultural values; inside that obese, lopsided vegetable lies the goodness of nature and agrarian virtues.

The only thing small about a giant pumpkin is its seed. Seed selection is one of the most important factors in creating a giant among giants, because of both the seed's natural genetics and the sense of cultural heritage it perpetuates. Almost all the seeds of the heavy hitters originated with Dill, who owned a U.S. patent for his variety. His Atlantic Giant is descended from the Goderich Giant, a cultivar used by William Warnock to produce the pumpkins that received national exposure at both the Chicago 1893 and St. Louis 1904 world's fairs.[51] Growers closely track the lineage or provenance of prizewinning pumpkins, just as if the plants were victorious racehorses. Dan Langevin's 1993 *How-to-Grow World Class Giant Pumpkins* contains full-page genealogical charts for some of the heaviest pumpkins ever grown.[52] Growers identify individual pumpkins by name of grower, year of production, and weight. For example, one grower on a popular AG listserv noted, "In 1995, George Lloyd crossed the 1994 614 Neilly with the 1994 752.8 Craven, producing the 687.5 Lloyd."[53] Some growers bid for seeds at online auctions, paying up to $1,600 for a single top-quality seed from a "stud pumpkin," as the heaviest, better-pedigreed pumpkins are known.[54] The fact that something called a "pumpkin expert" exists says a lot about the vegetable itself. Growers' development of the science of giant pumpkin production and their creation of volumes of instructional materials infuse each individual specimen with a body of knowledge and a sense of biography. Pumpkins such as the "2009 1,725 Harp" come to stand for people, not just nature.

The transformation from seed to prizewinner takes a combination of a human's ingenuity and a plant's natural proclivities. For most AG growers, propagating a giant pumpkin is recreation, not a business.[55] The 2010 record holder, Chris Stevens, is a contractor, and the 2009 record holder, Christy Harp, a high school math teacher. Yet this labor of love is an all-encompassing pursuit. Another grower, Don Block, a factory worker in upstate New York, is a good case in point. For several summers in the 1990s, Block spent countless hours in his garden cultivating giant pumpkins. He weeded, watered, fertilized, pruned, and carefully planned so that his pumpkins stayed healthy and reached their full potential weight. Block commonly trudged out to his patch two or three times a night to check for intruders, both quadruped and biped. When his well ran dry one year, he ran a hose three hundred feet from his pumpkin patch to his brother's well and bathed at his sister's house.[56] Block is one of the thousands of stockbrokers, nurses, mechanics, office workers, and laborers of all sorts (rarely working farmers) who passionately and, some say, obsessively grow giant pumpkins.

Unlike pumpkin farmers in the past, who were laissez-faire about their crop, AG growers incessantly pamper their pumpkins, leaving as little as possible to chance. Giant pumpkins require between 120 and 150 days to reach maturation, and during that time growers chart, record, calculate, and measure every aspect of the plant's environment and development. Success depends on a delicate balance between providing the plant with enough water and nutrients for it to achieve its full potential weight and not overdoing it so that it cracks, rots, or, even worse, explodes before show time. The cultivation of these pumpkins is neither easy nor cheap. Participants commonly speak of skipping summer vacations to tend to their plants. Wayne Hackney, a TV repairman from New Milford, Connecticut, estimated that growing an AG pumpkin "cost me a dollar a pound." But, he added, "it was worth it."[57]

Propagating a giant pumpkin takes personal commitment. Growers must hand-pollinate the female flowers to ensure the desired genetics. Once the fruit begins to set, the grower removes all but the strongest vine, so that the plant's energy is fully directed toward one or sometimes two fruits. Growers often clip and trim vines so that they grow in a direction that maximizes the fruit's expansion. They use all kinds of contraptions to protect the plant in every stage of its development. Seedlings have their own little greenhouses to warm and protect them from chilly spring winds. At the end of the season, blankets and canopies provide each fruit with its own private shelter from the heat of the summer sun. Growers wage constant battles against insects and disease.

Estimates of how much water a pumpkin should consume are variations on the same oversize theme. One grower calculated that he gave his pumpkin three hundred gallons a day. Another claimed to give his eighteen hundred gallons of water at a single serving.[58] Water is so important because a pumpkin turns water into pounds of flesh. Harp's pumpkin gained thirty-three pounds a day during its peak growing time.[59] Another grower watched his pumpkin grow dramatically at a rate of more than an inch every three to four hours.[60] One scientific study found that a giant pumpkin grows as much as eleven kilograms a day, and another recorded pumpkins growing at a rate of one gram per minute.[61] As one expert noted with both awe and trepidation, giant pumpkins "grow so fast they can literally tear themselves apart!"[62] Moving these five-hundred-plus-pound pumpkins from garden to weigh-in at the end of the season is obviously no easy task. Elaborate pulleys and levers have been created just to pick the pumpkins up. Without any mechanical contraptions, five or six people are required to surround and lift it.

Growers of giant pumpkins communicate through a network of organizations, such as the Great Pumpkin Commonwealth, the World Pumpkin Confederation, the International Pumpkin Association, and the Giant Urban Pumpkin Growers of America, now defunct, which was "dedicated to growing and venerating giant urban pumpkins."[63] The organizations have local and regional chapters and hundreds of thousands of members. Growers post messages monthly on dozens of Internet sites dedicated to the "sport." One website, "BigPumpkins.com," received thousands of messages in the summer of 2010.[64] Growers seek and give advice and offer congratulations and condolences to those who pursue the production of scale-breaking, super-sized pumpkins.

The aim of most giant pumpkin growers is to compete in one of dozens of annual pumpkin weigh-offs staged across the continent. Warnock's 403-pounder, presented at the 1903 St. Louis World's Fair, held the world's record until 1976, when a 451-pound pumpkin won the U.S. Pumpkin Contest in Churchville, Pennsylvania. Howard Dill, the only repeat performer, then held the record from 1979 to 1982 with pumpkins weighing just under 500 pounds. Nowadays, a 500-pounder is dismissed as a lightweight among the elites of the sport. In 1996, Paula and Nathan Zahr were

Howard Dill sitting in a patch of Atlantic Giants, the variety he developed in the 1960s. All prize-winning giant pumpkins originated with Dill's Atlantic Giant seeds. Photo: Don Langevin and GiantPumpkin.com.

Growers inspect the underside of a giant pumpkin being lifted for weighing at the World Championship Pumpkin Weigh-Off in Half Moon Bay, California, on October 12, 2009. Photo: PI/Terry Schmitt.

awarded a $50,000 prize for being the first to surpass the coveted 1,000-pound mark, with a 1,061-pound pumpkin, a record that some compared to breaking the four-minute mile.[65] Chris Stevens, of New Richmond, Wisconsin, claimed the world record in 2010 with a 1,810.5-pounder he entered at the Stillwater Harvest Fest and Giant Pumpkin Weigh-Off in Stillwater, Minnesota.[66]

The great lengths to which growers go to produce such fantastically huge, unwieldy vegetables was questioned by one of their own. "We're overfeeding them. We're overwatering them. It's like we're growing a fat person . . . and it is not as healthy as a lean person," said Edward Gancarz, who won the 1990 World Pumpkin Confederation title with an 816-pound pumpkin.[67] His skepticism about the process and the product raises an obvious question. Why do so many people—nonfarmers at that—exert so much effort, and to what ends? What is the fuss all about?

Perhaps it is the contest prize money. Christy Harp won $2,500 for her 1,725-pound effort.[68] Perhaps it is the love of competition and working in the garden. But why a pumpkin? One obvious reason is that the pumpkin is big. It is a thrill to produce such a huge specimen. World record holder Harp said, "I grow giant pumpkins because it's fun being outside and really neat to be able to test nature and see how fast these things can grow."[69] Because the pumpkin is a "live product," to use the words of Howard Dill, its growth is never fully predictable.[70] Even with many human interventions and additives to push plant growth to extremes, the pumpkin is still a natural object that cannot be completely manipulated. Although these qualities are true of almost any plant, the pumpkin's tremendous size, output, and animated growth have made it a particularly powerful object of nature to defy, or "test" in Harp's words, human control. When growers produce the biggest pumpkin possible, they are creating a gigantic plant but also a natural symbol that has deep cultural roots.

If grand size was the only factor that motivated these growers, then a giant squash should be just as popular, but it decidedly is not. As one expert grower noted, "The real show stoppers are the giant pumpkins."[71] Both Stevens's and Harp's pumpkins were pale orange with streaks of gray, and if they had been grayer in color, they would have been disqualified from competition. Dave Stelts, who grew a 1,662-pound, deep orange pumpkin in 2009, said, "We'd like to have them all this beautiful—a nice, shiny, bright orange color. But sometimes they get a little opaque, like you see in the world record-holder for the Harps. But with this one we got really lucky. It turned out a beautiful, shiny orange."[72] Though growers all hope for that vivid orange hue, some AG seed stock produces fruit that is orange, and some turns out bluish gray. Sometimes growers cannot be certain about what they are propagating until the fruit sets. The World Pumpkin Confederation has a rule that for an entry to be considered a pumpkin, "The fruit must be 80% orange to yellow."[73] As one giant pumpkin grower succinctly stated, "Squash are green, pumpkins are orange."[74] Most squashes are barred from pumpkin competitions, even though they are essentially the same vegetable. Competitions that make no distinction between the two types are disqualified from joining in the major weigh-offs. There is no difference between a pumpkin's and a squash's genetics, cultivation, nurturing, and weight—only between attitudes toward them. Squashes compete in size and girth but not in sentiment.

The giant pumpkin harks back to a field of meanings. A recurrent theme in the production literature is the celebration of the growers' work ethic and generosity. *How-to-Grow World Class Giant Pumpkins* referred to a top competitor at the "Big E" (Eastern States Exposition) as "a hard working, devoted family man who contributes much of his time to pumpkin growing organizations, the community and his church."[75] The veneration of the manual labor involved in cultivating giant pumpkins resonates with old agrarian myths about the virtues of working the land. Participants in the world of weekend pumpkin farming conceive of it as a morally and physically uplifting pursuit. By growing a giant pumpkin, someone can be close to nature and live out the agrarian myth in his or her own backyard, on the rooftop patio of a downtown Los Angeles apartment building, or in the thickets behind a museum in an inner-city neighborhood.[76] Pumpkins—historically the least commodified field crop—lend great symbolic weight to growers' endeavors. "Best of all was the simple, irrelevant quality of it all," explained one grower. "You planted and nourished this little seed, and you got this enormous gourd in a fluorescent color that was good for just about nothing except gawking at."[77]

The combination of pumpkins' physical attributes and their historical associations make them quintessential emblems of agrarian prowess. By growing giant pumpkins, suburban and urban dwellers gain access to the farming experience and thereby feel as if they are closer to nature and the mythic American agrarian way of life. Full-time pumpkin farming is impractical and probably inconceivable to most participants. Besides having neither the land nor the equipment to run a full-scale pumpkin farm, what would most of these people do with two hundred 20-pound pumpkins? One 400-pound giant pumpkin, however, suits suburban needs because growers can create the ultimate farm symbol at an incredible scale but in limited space. Giant pumpkins require great skill to produce, while being difficult to move as well as mealy and tasteless. Growing giant pumpkins epitomizes the modern celebration of the symbolism of the pumpkin over its substance. It is no wonder that champion grower Edward Gancarz believed there was something unnatural about the vegetable: it is as much a container of human values as a wonder of nature.

Pumpkins big and small are commemorative objects, like souvenirs. Rather than possessing intrinsic worth, they are valuable as holders of memories, experiences, and ideas. A souvenir fulfills a person's yearning to feel connected to a place, another person, or a way of life unobtainable in any other way.[78] One cannot go back in time, for example, but one can buy an object that represents an earlier time. Most people say they buy and display pumpkins every fall because it is a tradition, and the most famous giant pumpkin grower, Howard Dill, professed simply, "There is always something about a giant pumpkin that has the power to make people happy."[79] But the pumpkin does much more than that. It helps people feel close to nature and rural life, and it creates a sense of community.

Because a souvenir's value derives mainly from the meanings it possesses, it can take any size or material form. That is why a plastic, wooden, or crystal pumpkin may serve the purpose of a real one. The same principle holds true for food. While manufacturers of pumpkin products make nutritional claims, the food's real value derives from what it represents. The importance of the *idea* of pumpkin over its substance has completely outweighed the necessity of a food's containing even a trace of the vegetable.[80] Hence, the product needs only to resemble it. Biting into Jell-O's Halloween Creepy Jigglers, which consist of orange-colored gelatin set in a jack-o'-lantern mold, one tastes the sweetness of sugar but not a trace of pumpkin. Godiva pumpkin truffles are each wrapped beautifully in orange foil and capped with a tiny, curly stem and a green leaf. The candy contains lots of sugar, butter, chocolate, and pumpkin *spice* (cinnamon, ginger, nutmeg, and allspice) but barely a hint of powdered pumpkin. "Linus' Great Pumpkin Cookies" is a Pillsbury's product consisting of a tube of sugar cookie dough with an image of an orange jack-o'-lantern set in it. Home bakers simply slice, bake, and serve the cookies. Each contains a happy jack-o'-lantern face but no trace of real pumpkin.[81]

Of the 13 percent of pumpkins now produced for culinary purposes, 80 percent are sold as canned pumpkin between September and January.[82] An ad in the October 2000 issue of *Cooking Light*, which read "American Spoon Goods brings the . . . mellow taste of autumn with its Pumpkin Chipotle Roasting Sauce," promoted pumpkin as the essence and flavor of fall. Pumpkin inundates restaurant menus, cooking magazines, and grocery stores, both plain and fancy, every autumn. Adding to the traditional pumpkin pie are pumpkin pasta, ice cream, cookies, muffins, and bread, as well as soups served in an edible mini-pumpkin tureen.[83]

Many books and articles about cooking with pumpkin are illustrated with antiquated harvest scenes. *Holiday Pumpkins*, a book of pumpkin crafts and recipes, opens with an image of a picturesque pumpkin field set against a verdant hillside, a view steeped in powerful ideas about the healing powers of nature and American country life.[84] The product "Pumpkin Spice Cookies" epitomizes the deep meanings yet pumpkin-free quality of many pumpkin foods.[85] It consists of a pumpkin-shaped cookie cutter, a small packet of pumpkin spice, and a recipe that calls for flour, sugar, and baking soda—but no pumpkin. The packaging says it all. The cookie cutter is attached to a card with a painting of a pumpkin field dotted with cornstalks, a typical nineteenth-century farm scene. Even some natural foods businesses, such as the online Pumpkin Seed Health Food Store, have built their reputations on the pumpkin's symbolic wholesomeness.[86]

Tapping into the pumpkin's connotation of American heritage, some microbrewers produce a pumpkin beer for sale during the fall season. Although most contemporary brews contain at least a trace of actual pumpkin, many acquire their flavor not from pumpkin but from pumpkin pie *spices*, which were absent from the eighteenth-century beverage.[87] Post Road Pumpkin Ale draws directly on the colonial origin of the beverage in its advertising but presents the drink in a more positive and romanticized light than is probably warranted by its earlier, rather squalid reputation. "In the 18ᵗʰ Century, colonial Americans brewed wonderful and interesting ales by using local ingredients," the label explains. "Pumpkins were favored by brewers for their rich spicy flavors, which melded

"Pumpkin Spice Cookies," cookie cutter and spices, manufactured by Bark and Barkley, Inc., 1995.

perfectly with the malted barley. Post Road brings you a delicious rendition of this traditional American classic."[88] Most colonists would probably have balked at this description; to them, pumpkin beer was a drink of last resort.

All these pumpkin culinary treats, of course, are secondary to the most revered tradition of eating pumpkin pie at Thanksgiving. Echoing *American Farmer* almost two hundred years earlier (and sources from almost every generation in between), the November 2000 issue of *Martha Stewart Living* advised, "For many, without pumpkin pie, it's just not Thanksgiving."[89] Innovations in preparing and serving pumpkin pie have done nothing to diminish the deep sense of tradition and heritage in the holiday dessert. The pie's popularity is matched only by the endurance of these beliefs and meanings. Rows of sentimental holiday cards, dozens of holiday magazines, popular TV programs, children's books, and elementary school programs revere the same colonial New England motifs and country themes that brought the pumpkin and the Thanksgiving holiday to national prominence during the Civil War. The eternal popularity of Lydia Maria Child's famous poem, "Over the River and Through the Wood," speaks to the continued relevance of the countryside and pumpkin pie as sources of national and familial heritage.

Except for those who make restaurant reservations instead of cooking at home, Americans have changed their Thanksgiving celebrations little over the last fifty years. Millions still look forward to family reunions capped by an early evening feast of turkey, mashed potatoes, yams, cranberry sauce, and pumpkin pie—or some modern or other cultural rendition of this classic feast. Pumpkin cheesecake, pumpkin crème brûlée, and, for the vegans, tofu pumpkin pie are novelty twists on the traditional pie recipe, yet "plain old pumpkin pie," as the November 2001 issue of *Bon Appétit* called it, is still "a comforting favorite."[90] Marvelous Market, an upscale bakery in the Washington, D.C., area, marketed its "Pilgrim" pumpkin pie as being "about as traditional as you can get."[91] The pie that Amelia Simmons concocted in 1796 is essentially the same recipe used today. Bakers still mix pureed pumpkin with cream, sugar, cinnamon, and ginger, although the addition of Jell-O, Cool Whip, and a ready-made crust can give the dessert a peculiarly contemporary flavor.[92]

As predicted in the 1930s, the convenience of the can has outweighed strict adherence to culinary traditions, despite some retailers' claims. Fresh pumpkins are more likely to show up on a front stoop than on a kitchen table, and heirloom recipes now require a can opener instead of a knife. Noting the sense of nostalgia and tradition that pie made with Libby's brand pumpkin inspires in her family, a consumer on the "Chowhound" website wrote in 2005, "I have to think the fact that we've had Libby's pumpkin pie every Thanksgiving in my life has something to do with it."[93]

According to company records, Libby's produced 85 percent of the approximately 222,000 tons of canned pumpkin packed annually in the early 2000s.[94] Responding to an increase in pumpkin demand, in 1973 Libby's transferred its pumpkin processing from its Eureka, Illinois, plant, where it also canned corn and peas, back to its Morton, Illinois, plant, which it devoted solely to pumpkin. When Nestlé USA, a conglomerate of food and beverage companies, purchased Libby's in 1991, it sold the Eureka and Washington, Illinois, factories and concentrated all its efforts on processing pumpkin at Morton. The growth in production must have fulfilled the company's wildest expectations. In the 2010s, Libby's rolled out enough cans to produce 90 million pumpkin pies annually.[95]

Libby's developed a special pumpkin variety specifically for canning. The Libby's Select is a hybrid of the Dickinson pumpkin, which is one of the most popular processing pumpkins and the namesake of the family that established the canning factory in Morton. Bred for its thick orange flesh with little concern for its exterior attributes, the Libby's Select is an oblong, slightly ribbed "pumpkin" with beige skin and brilliant orange flesh. In other words, it does not fit the picturesque model. It would be a poor Halloween decoration, but it makes a great pie. Everything about the vegetable is suggestive of a squash, but the company calls it a pumpkin for obvious reasons. *Pumpkin* inspires feelings, meanings, and traditions that *squash* does not.

Libby's advertises that its product is as "pure" as the vegetable on the vine. In one way, it is hard to argue with the company because, as its label ensures, the can contains 100 percent pumpkin, with no additives, preservatives, or sweeteners. Yet as anyone knows who has cooked with both processed and fresh pumpkin, the two forms create quite different results. Canned pumpkin is thicker and more condensed. It produces a stronger flavor that requires fewer spices, and it sets more readily than fresh pumpkin. These differences are the result of canning. At the Libby's factory, after the pumpkins are harvested from the fields, they are literally dumped from tractor trailers onto factory conveyor belts. They are washed and inspected, sliced, and chopped before being cooked, seeds, skin, and all. Next, the pumpkin mush is squeezed through presses to remove some of its water content and then channeled through pulping machines that separate the meat from the fibrous skin and seeds. Then it is pureed, reheated, and pumped into cans. The canned pumpkin is sealed and then cooked again in large pressure cookers before being labeled and packaged for shipment on tractor trailers and rail cars positioned inside the factory. In the words of a Libby's pamphlet, rather than having to "scrub, cut, seed, bake, puree, 'cook down,' stir, and drain, and 'cook down' pumpkin again just to get enough meat (hopefully not too thin or watery) for one pie," bakers can now simply spoon cooked and pureed pumpkin meat out of a can.

The industrialization of pumpkin processing has not prevented Libby's from marketing pumpkin's reputation for old-fashioned, natural goodness. Besides the two cute babies sitting in the pumpkin, another Libby's advertising figure is a grandmotherly-looking woman who appears on the company's website offering a pumpkin pie in her outstretched arms.[96] (Mrs. Smith's, the largest commercial producer of frozen pumpkin pies, also refers to its concoction as an "old-fashioned" creation.)[97] Eating pumpkin, the ads like people to think, is not just good for you but also inculcates family values.

In stark simplicity, the cover of the Thanksgiving 2001 issue of *Time*— two months after the terrorist attacks on the World Trade Center and the Pentagon on September 11—depicted a pumpkin pie with an American flag stuck in the middle of it.[98] During that time of national crisis, the illustration was a poignant reminder of Americans' core values, cultural heritage, and sense of patriotism. When the country faced one of the worst acts of aggression and violence on home soil in its history, it turned again to Thanksgiving pumpkin pie to provide a sense of well-being and security, much as when Lincoln first declared the national holiday during the Civil War. "The Thanksgiving meal is a true gesture of comfort, friendship and love—a holiday feast full of symbolism and hope for the future," wrote the editor of *Bon Appétit* in November 2001. "[It is] a meal that can be a haven of comfort, joy and goodness—the feast of thanks that has stood the test of time."[99]

The pumpkin's meanings do not resonate with all Americans, of course. For some, the *Time* cover might have been illegible. For others, such as southerners who still push aside pumpkin pie for the more regional sweet potato pie, it might have seemed like Yankee bias. Yet one would have to look as far back as the early colonial days, when pumpkin was daily fare, to find a time in American history when the vegetable was more in demand than it is now. Even back then, people ate it more out of necessity than out of choice. Some Americans might view Mrs. Smith's pumpkin pie with Cool Whip as a poor substitute for Amelia Simmons's 1796 version.[100] They might see the Paint-a-Pumpkin as a hollow gimmick in comparison with the Connecticut Field pumpkin, and the giant pumpkin as a worrisome mutation of nature. They might be concerned that processing and packaging farm goods such as pumpkins dislocates consumers from nature and from the people and places that produce their food.[101]

Yet pumpkin farmers from Half Moon Bay, California, to Comus, Maryland, and the residents of small towns from Pumpkintown, South

Carolina, to Keene, New Hampshire, would not be among them. Instead of lamenting modern-day pumpkins and traditions, they have capitalized on and commercialized them. Although creating hybrids that do not reproduce but are easy to paint and scooping out fruit from a can to re-create a colonial recipe might seem to contradict reason and expectation, neither compares to the feat of resurrecting small family farms and rural towns as viable economic enterprises in the twenty-first century.

TIME

Thanksgiving 2001

Next week American families will set their tables, count their blessings and discover how their lives have changed—and how they haven't. Pull up a chair…

By Nancy Gibbs

Cover of *Time* magazine, November 19, 2001. Time Warner, Inc.

SEVEN

PULLING UP A PIG STY
TO PUT IN A PUMPKIN PATCH

The Changing Nature of American Rural Economies,

1946 to the Present

REINTRODUCED AFTER WORLD WAR II, THE CIRCLEVILLE PUMP-
kin Show in Ohio now attracts 300,000 people over a four-day
period at the end of every October. The festival features more than
100,000 pounds of pumpkins on display, a pumpkin pie contest, a 500-
pound pumpkin pie, a giant-pumpkin competition, a pumpkin-decorating
contest, and a Miss Pumpkin and Little Miss Pumpkin contest. Vendors
sell pumpkin-inspired novelties such as pens, hats, bumper stickers,
t-shirts, and artworks. Doughnuts, waffles, ice cream, soups, cakes, even
hamburgers are all made with pumpkin. In no small way, the town of Circleville, population 13,700, celebrates the vegetable.[1]

Hundreds of other pumpkin festivals take place throughout the country during the month of October. Vying for the title of pumpkin capital
of the world are Morton, Illinois (pop. 16,209); Half Moon Bay, California
(pop. 12,586); Keene, New Hampshire (pop. 22,395); and other small towns
that put on annual festivals in honor of "the vaunted orange orb," as one
promoter called it.[2] Roadside stands and pick-your-own (PYO) pumpkin farms line the roads leading out to these towns. The Arata Pumpkin
Farm is now one of fifteen in and around Half Moon Bay that cater to San
Francisco–area residents.[3] Unlike the Aratas' market, which began in the
1930s, most of them got their start in the 1970s and 1980s. Farms such as
these have grown into tourist destinations in their own right by offering
visitors not only local fall produce but also rural attractions designed to
fulfill the most romantic fantasies of life on an American farm.

The Circleville Pumpkin Show, Circleville, Ohio, October 1999. The show is one of hundreds of pumpkin festivals across the country that have helped rural communities survive and hold onto a rural sense of place. Photo: Cindy Ott.

For many rural communities, the pumpkin is at once a catalyst for change and a sign of tradition. It aids local development while symbolizing an unchanging way of life. "We're maintaining our small-town identity. We have Starbucks, and a Gap has come in. We need something to hold onto," a resident of Chagrin Falls, Ohio (pop. 3,641), said about the pumpkin roll that has taken place on Main Street since the 1980s.[4] Pumpkins have helped communities both survive economically and hang onto a rural sense of place. It is remarkable to hear festival organizers and farmers talk about the pumpkin as an embodiment of their values and as a tool for community building. Yet people give no hint that they are talking about an object of nature, much less a farm crop. As Bob Marsh, owner of Bob's Pumpkin Farm near Half Moon Bay, told a reporter without irony, "It's a people thing."[5] Nancy Sporborg, who founded the Keene Pumpkin Festival in New Hampshire in 1991, explained, "What makes the pumpkin festival special, what makes it magic, is all of you [participants]. Every single pumpkin has meaning; it's amazing."[6]

People's ideas of nature are multifaceted, and these ideas can reshape the world in unexpected ways that defy purely economic explanations. While Americans' ideas about and uses for pumpkins have altered the fruit itself, the widespread desire for pumpkins is actually helping to revitalize the very small family farms with which Americans have long identified this iconic harvest symbol. The pumpkin's biology, its meanings, and the market together encourage the growing of pumpkins by small-scale producers for local consumers. The history of the pumpkin counters the common assumptions that romantic agrarian fables and imagery have little to do with actual agriculture practices and that small-scale farmers and small rural towns are anachronisms in the modern-day United States. Farmers and rural communities have relied on this old crop, and on the stories people have told about it, to become viable economic enterprises in the twenty-first century.

The establishment of most small-town pumpkin festivals seems to defy logic. The Circleville Pumpkin Show's reemergence was not a sign of an agricultural renaissance or the reopening of the local canning factory but a decision by a group of merchants to rejuvenate the town. When the local agricultural society abandoned the pumpkin show to establish an agricultural fair on grounds outside of town, nine businessmen formed the nonprofit organization Pumpkin Show, Inc., whose profits were to be distributed for the betterment of Circleville citizens. As the links between the town and local agriculture grew more distant, town residents used the pumpkin to maintain a connection to the land and the agrarian way of life.

Even though Eureka, Illinois, was a center of production for an array of vegetables and grains, the pumpkin became the town's mascot when local leaders decided to dedicate an annual celebration to it in 1939. The festival moved to nearby Morton in 1966, when pumpkin processing was transferred to the plant there. Holding a pumpkin festival at Morton might appear to make sense because of the factory's relocation, but the Caterpillar Tractor Company, the tractor and industrial equipment manufacturer, was actually the largest employer in town and by far overshadowed Libby's contribution to the local economy. Even today, the Nestlé-Libby's plant, the most productive one in the country, is not the largest business in Morton. The Libby's plant employs only around 30 full-time employees and 400 to 450 seasonal workers during packing season, from August to October. In contrast, Caterpillar has a permanent staff of 1,600 people.[7] Although the pumpkin is not the most significant business in town, it certainly surpasses tractors as the source of Morton residents' identity and inspiration. As Mike Badgerow, past executive director of the Morton Chamber of Commerce, told a Peoria, Illinois, newspaper, "The pumpkin has become an icon and visual calling card for Morton."[8] One has only to drive through the town to see the evidence—in local shop names, such as Pumpkin Patch Gift Shop and Pumpkin Packing and Shipping; in the town logo, a field pumpkin; and in the annual pumpkin festival, which recruits 1,500 local volunteers and hosts 60,000 to 80,000 visitors a year.[9]

Around Half Moon Bay, California, farmers have grown pumpkins since the nineteenth century. But it was not local farmers who began the town's Art and Pumpkin Festival in 1971; it was the town's Main Street Committee for Beautification. The committee initiated the festival to raise money for downtown restoration projects, such as planting trees and erecting streetlights along Main Street. Rather than local pumpkin production's fueling the town's economy, the festival generates the pumpkin business in and around Half Moon Bay with the tourists it brings in from nearby San Francisco.

Barnesville, Ohio; Keene, New Hampshire; and Spring Hope, North Carolina all stake a claim to being the pumpkin capital of the world, but with less historical legitimacy than Circleville, Morton, and Half Moon Bay.[10] Spring Hope (pop. 1,306) held the first "National Pumpkin Festival" in 1971, even though tobacco, cotton, sweet potatoes, and cucumbers were the local cash crops. Pumpkins do not grow well in the Spring Hope area because of its hot climate and loamy soil. The pumpkin, explained Vera Edwards, a resident since 1948, was never a central actor in the town's economy or history. Rather, the town initiated the festival as an excuse for local residents to get together and as a means of drawing visitors from the surrounding areas to boost the economy.[11] The plan worked—the pumpkin festival brings people in by the thousands.

Most pumpkin festivals are downtown street fairs with booths, games, and parades. The Morton Pumpkin Festival begins with the ceremonial cutting of a pumpkin vine.[12] The early years at Circleville—the oldest continuous festival, and one with a legitimate historical connection to pumpkins via the now-defunct canning factory—included horse shows, horse racing, high-wire acts, "girlie shows," and wild creatures.[13] Nowadays, the festivals offer much tamer family fun. At Circleville, the first morning kicks off with a ten-kilometer Pumpkin Run followed by a pumpkin-pancake breakfast. Giant pumpkin weigh-ins, pumpkin cooking contests, pumpkin tosses, pumpkin pie eating, and pumpkin carving contests all invite local participation and entertain onlookers. Emphasizing a sense of camaraderie among participants, one reviewer noted, "And when neighbors square off in the contests and competitions, you can bet it's pride—not prize money—that's at stake."[14]

In Spring Hope, the parade is the festival highlight. Local politicians, school classes, and civic groups wave from homemade floats, fire trucks, and sedans. Farmers on tractors used to be the most common entries, but businessmen in sports cars have replaced them over the years.[15] Miss Pumpkin Queen and Little Miss Pumpkin Queen, winners of the beauty pageants, usually receive the greatest fanfare along the parade route. The visual and thematic center of the Circleville festival is a tower of pumpkins weighing 250,000 pounds and measuring more than twenty feet high. Ten square blocks surrounding the tower are lined with booths offering almost every imaginable pumpkin-infused object and culinary delight. Visitors meander, often elbow to elbow, pausing to see the giant pumpkin pie or to taste pumpkin concoctions ranging from burgers to muffins and from ice cream to chili. Many go home clutching a festival t-shirt, a pumpkin basket, a painting, or a glass ornament from among the vast assortment of pumpkin-inspired souvenirs.

In some communities, front-yard decoration contests stretch the festivities into the surrounding neighborhoods. Spring Hope residents, for example, are encouraged to decorate their yards in order to make the town look prettier and more civic-minded.[16] In Morton, each yard must include at least one pumpkin, and residents appear to have no trouble complying with the decree. At the 2000 Spring Hope festival, the winner constructed a cornucopia the size of a child's clubhouse, with dozens of pumpkins and gourds pouring forth.

For sheer number of pumpkins per square foot of town space, no place compares to Keene, New Hampshire. From 1991 to 2005, the town held the *Guinness Book of World Records* title for the most jack-o'-lanterns assembled in one place.[17] The weekend before Halloween, residents and visitors

"Pumpkin Festival 2001," Keene, New Hampshire, festival brochure, 2001. Keene's festival features the display of thousands of jack-o'-lanterns carved and contributed by attendees. Photo: Al Braden.

register their carved pumpkins at an official booth. In the center of town, jack-o'-lanterns sit on dozens of shelves and platforms and on four 40-foot towers, and cover a good deal of open ground as well.

Although the Keene Pumpkin Festival offers a parade and plenty of food and crafts, the main attraction is strolling the streets and admiring the jack-o'-lanterns. Carvings range from the traditional triangle-eyed face to elaborate depictions of haunted Halloween scenes. One year, a man carved a marriage proposal into a set of pumpkins and set it on one of the pumpkin towers, to his girlfriend's surprise and, luckily, delight. Organizers counted 600 jack-o'-lanterns in 1991, the first year of the festival. By 2009 the number had reached 29,762.[18] (Boston beat Keene out of the world record with a display of 30,128 pumpkins in 2006.)[19] After dark, everywhere one looks is awash in glimmering, flickering jack-o'-lanterns. It is a picture of visual pageantry and community effort—all composed with fleshy pumpkins.

"Community is basically the raison d'être for the Pumpkin Festival," said one of the Half Moon Bay organizers succinctly.[20] In Keene, the level of community spirit can literally be measured in pumpkins, a fact that organizers are quick to acknowledge. "The magic of the Pumpkin Festival is in its participatory nature," stated the 2001 festival program. "It is an event everyone helps create by contributing their hand-carved master-pieces. Together—as friends, neighbors, Pumpkin Festival regulars and first-time visitors—we witness the power of community in the awe-inspir-ing sight of thousands of jack-o'-lanterns shimmering in the night. One cannot help but feel a sense of wonder stirred by the simple act of carving a pumpkin and adding it to so many others."[21] Keene and the other small towns have made decorating with pumpkins an overt act of community building.

By attracting visitors to small-town streets, pumpkin festivals have become economic boosters. Rural populations had experienced decline in the United States in the first half of the twentieth century. But the con-struction of interstate highways that bypassed main streets in the 1960s, postwar suburbanization, and the exodus of the farming population and tax base because of the 1980s farm crisis had many small rural towns barely limping into the last decades of the century.[22] Pumpkin festivals provided the towns with a renewed sense of vitality by improving their local economies and assisting local charities. "The Pumpkin Festival is our fund raiser. We use the money to help pay for sidewalks, restrooms at the park, Christmas decorations, and more," explained Carol James, acting president of the Spring Hope Chamber of Commerce in 2000.[23] In Half Moon Bay, money raised from the more than 250,000 annual visi-tors goes to urban improvement projects and local nonprofit organiza-tions. From its inception in 1970 until 2010, the festival raised more than $2 million.[24] "The Pumpkin Festival has done more for this city, by far, than any other thing in the city's history,'" said former city manager Fred Mortensen.[25] Furthermore, the Half Moon Bay festival permits other nonprofit organizations to operate concessions to raise money on their own. The Circleville Pumpkin Show's charter stipulates that the festival's revenue must be used for the town's benefit. As the festival sold more than 23,000 pumpkin pies and 100,000 pumpkin doughnuts in 1991, the pumpkin can be quite "fruitful" for the town's coffers.[26]

Besides solidifying a sense of community and financing local improvements, the festivals are a means of attracting tourists as well as new residents. Reporting on Pumpkintown, in northwestern South Carolina, one journalist observed, "You would completely miss it if it weren't for the blinking light and grocery store. [Because of its pumpkin festival] the community becomes famous one day each year."[27] More than thirty thousand people attend the annual festival, which turns this small crossroads into a regional hub.[28] Farther north, the "World Championship Punkin Chunkin" puts "slower lower Delaware" on center stage. There, tens of thousands of spectators have gathered every year since 1986 to watch competitors launch pumpkins from all sorts of hand-built, nonexplosive contraptions, including catapults, air cannons, and giant slings.[29] (The world record, set in 2008, was 4,483.51 feet, nearly a mile.) With a declining population base, Spring Hope organizers count on their pumpkin festival to lure people and money from the affluent nearby Raleigh-Durham area.[30]

But why not simply hold the "Spring Hope Festival" or the "Half Moon Bay Festival"? Why make it a *pumpkin* festival? In most cases, the reason has little to do with the town's economic history. Few small towns have any greater claim to pumpkindom than the urban centers from which visitors flock. Furthermore, the rise in pumpkin festivals in the late twentieth century coincided with a decline in the number of people working in agriculture. In 1935 there were 6.8 million farms in the United States; by 2002 the number had dropped to 2.1 million.[31] Since the creation of the National Pumpkin Festival in Spring Hope, "Agriculture in North Carolina has gone from mules to computers, from small family farms to agribusiness operations," wrote one journalist.[32] "We have a generation of people here now who do not know anything about agriculture," noted a candidate for North Carolina's commissioner of agriculture.[33] In Circleville, most of the surrounding county land is still farmland, but the trend is toward fewer and larger farms.[34] Even in Morton, parts manufacturing, not pumpkin processing, is the main industry. Although Nestlé-Libby's promotes and supports the festival, it is not the beige, oval, Libby's Select pumpkin that appears in the town's logo but the bright orange field pumpkin.

Morton, Illinois, Chamber
of Commerce logo, 2000.

For most of these towns, the pumpkin festival has become the largest event of the year, replacing the annual Fourth of July celebration and expressing many of the same patriotic ideas. "I like to think that the real reason for the growth and the glory of the Show is the fact that it is firmly rooted in American tradition and history," explained one Circleville promoter. "Harvest festivals go back into antiquity. Pumpkins, squash and corn were growing in this county long before the first settlements in Virginia and Massachusetts. The first families to settle on these farms and fields came here to cultivate the fertile soil. So it is only natural that we should celebrate the harvest and rejoice in the bounty that is ours."[35]

A newspaper article about the history of the Morton event tried to explain why the town chose the pumpkin from among the large array of crops grown and processed in the region and over the products of other prominent local industries: "Early settlers of this area brought with them seeds of the old 'Thanksgiving' pumpkin. Finding a favorable environment in the soil and climate of the community, this original strain of pumpkin prospered and has been grown here by families ever since."[36] The author fuses the natural and cultural history of the pumpkin to create the region's origin myth. He links the community to the pumpkin served at the first Thanksgiving, thereby connecting Morton to Plymouth Plantation and the Pilgrims, who are enshrined as paragons of American virtue and democratic values. The "original strain of pumpkin" represents not just a rootstock but a cultural stock. And the fact that the Pilgrims might not have served pumpkin at their immortalized Thanksgiving feast gets buried under deep layers of myth and wistful imaginings.

Like many other tourist attractions, pumpkin festivals are easy targets for cynicism and scrutiny.[37] One can claim that they are mere fabrications based on old clichés and have little to do with the past and present realities of rural America. One could argue that the pumpkin festival is just another pseudo-experience, an all-too-common example of crass commercialism that profits from sentimentality. Still, critics who deride such festivals as "Mickey Mouse history" should not ignore the renewed prosperity these events offer to small towns or dismiss the sense of community that a pumpkin festival engenders.[38] Many civil leaders established these festivals when their towns were teetering on extinction. In places like Circleville, as links between the town and local agriculture grew more distant, residents maintained a symbolic connection to the land and to the past agrarian way of life. What is remarkable is that they turned to the pumpkin to do so. For generations, Americans have invested deep meaning in a vegetable that is practically worthless in every quantifiable way. By using the pumpkin to maintain a sense of rural identity, small towns renewed their livelihoods and feelings of relevance and attracted many eager visitors in the process.

When driving out to these celebrations from nearby urban centers, we might commonly pass roadside stands and more elaborate pick-your-own farms. Since the 1980s, thousands of family farms have opened their gates to the public for the month of October and turned portions of their property into agrarian wonderlands where visitors reenact playful renditions of old-time harvest activities, including, especially, picking a pumpkin. The purpose of the farm festivals, however, is hardly to teach the practicalities of farm work. Echoing the sentiments of small-town pumpkin festival boosters, farm festival organizers imagine their pumpkin farms as places that offer a piece of American heritage and inculcate good agrarian values. "Farmer John" Muller, owner of Farmer John's Pumpkins and Daylight Nursery outside Half Moon Bay, told a reporter about his pumpkin crop, "It's not only something we grow to sell, but something we grow to bring happiness."[39]

In all their touristy and carnivalesque splendor, modern-day pumpkin patches are nevertheless places where many Americans experience traditions that tie them to the past, to nature, and to each other and thereby help sustain the very cornerstone of their longings—small family farms. The term *family farm* is deceiving and requires some explanation. Although the romantic image looks like a small place with a red barn, livestock, and diverse crops, even the largest farms in the country are usually family owned and operated. According to the USDA, a family farm is "any farm organized as a sole proprietorship, partnership, or family corporation. Family farms exclude farms organized as nonfamily corporations or cooperatives, as well as farms with hired managers."[40] In 2007, 98 percent of all

Cox Farms Pumpkin Festival, Centreville, Virginia, October 2000. The Cox family farm is one of thousands of small family farms that convert some of their land into pumpkin wonderlands every autumn. Photo: Cindy Ott.

American farms were family farms.[41] The issue today is that the largest farms (those earning more than $250,000 annually and usually measuring more than 500 acres) make up only 10 percent of farms yet generate 75 percent of the revenue. In turn, small to medium-size farms (those earning less than $250,000 annually and usually measuring 499 or fewer acres)— the ones that Americans celebrate—make up 90 percent of American farms but earn only 25 percent of the agricultural profits.[42] Because small operations cannot compete in output or efficiency, people who stay on the land seldom make a living solely from agriculture but instead have to rely on off-farm income to maintain their farming operations. They have also developed alternative markets as a means of survival.

Like the start of the Aratas' pumpkin farm market, the creation of Holsapple's Pumpkin Patch in Greenup, Illinois, in the early 1980s was spurred when passers-by were enticed by a pile of pumpkins. The stopping-and-shopping led to customers walking out to the fields and picking the produce themselves. "Although we planned to wholesale all the pumpkins to grocery stores, people came to the farm and asked if they could buy some. [That's how] the Pumpkin Patch was born," explained Sheila Holsapple, who, with her husband, Terry, owns the five-hundred-acre Illinois farm. A few carloads of people visiting the Holsapple farm in the 1980s grew to fifteen thousand visitors by the autumn of 1994.[43]

In the early eighties, the Holsapples and other small family farmers had strong motivations to seek out new economic opportunities. The same forces that encouraged many farmers to expand operations in the 1970s propelled their downfall in the next decade. Middling farms were hit hardest, although they, along with small farms (measuring 1 to 49 acres), had been declining in number for decades.[44] The early 1970s had been a time of great prosperity for American farmers because of changing international markets and domestic farm policies. Russia's decision to import grain from abroad created a huge new market for American farmers but also raised food prices at home. In order to fulfill the demand from abroad and to make food cheaper domestically, President Richard Nixon's secretary of agriculture, Earl Butz, replaced the checks-and-balances policy established under the New Deal, which sought to regulate prices through production and supply controls, with a policy of planting as much as possible, "from fencerow to fencerow." Federal farm subsidies for the top five commodity crops—corn, wheat, cotton, soybeans, and rice—were supposed to make up for any drop in prices due to increased production. Few farmers worried about falling prices at the time; most were more concerned about being able to expand fast enough. Many farmers, relying on the promise of soaring land values and commodity prices, borrowed money to increase their acreage and to buy the extra equipment needed to work it.

What happened instead was that the Russians turned to other sources for grain, and the bottom dropped out of the market, leaving many farmers with debts they could not repay. Increasing the acreage under production had lowered commodity prices for big buyers, and now put farmers in a constant struggle to make ends meet. Images of farmers auctioning off their land and equipment and stories of others who committed suicide filled the nightly news. The farmers' plight drew widespread popular sympathy, including from celebrities such as singer Willie Nelson, who organized Farm Aid concerts that drew hundreds of thousands of fans and supporters. The farm crisis exacerbated an existing problem, that of the long-decreasing viability of small to mid-size family farms in a world of expanding industrial agriculture.

Selling a sense of rural nostalgia as well as locally grown produce, many farmers, like the Holsapples, transformed portions of their farms into tourist destinations. By offering fun attractions along with quality fruits and vegetables, they encouraged customers to make the trip out to the country. As one farmer commented, "The direct farm retailer today has gone from 'growing the crop' to 'marketing the farm and the farm experience.'"[45] Al and Bart Bussell, differentiating their modest, 160-acre California fruit and vegetable farm from the corporate farms that surrounded it, referred to their mode of operation as "entertainment farming," because they were not only producing and selling goods but also providing recreation to their customers.[46] Noting the one area in agriculture in which small farms could best corporate farms, an agricultural specialist at the National Center for Appropriate Technology said, "Unlike the mega-hog facility or a corn/soybean operation producing bulk commodities, the small farm can recreate an earlier, simpler, human-scale vision of farming."[47]

Pick-your-own farms, as this form of farm direct marketing is known, developed a little later than roadside stands but from similar motivations.[48] One Illinois farmer who launched a PYO operation in the 1960s observed, "The pick your own method of retailing allows us to set our own price and to be independent of the wholesale market fluctuations, thus improving our profit margins after harvest and giving us an immediate return on our crops."[49] Between 1982 and 1992, the total number of farms selling directly to consumers rose by 40 percent, and at least half of them had annual incomes of less than $50,000, indicating that they were small-scale operations.[50] Describing the value of agri-tourism as a market niche for small-scale farmers, one analyst wrote, "Producers enjoy higher returns that have allowed them to stay in farming. Because it is initially less capital intensive, farm direct marketing provides opportunities for new farmers and smaller-scale producers with limited resources."[51] As Long Island farmer Edward Latham attested, "A lot of neighbors who didn't go retail ended up selling out to developers."[52]

Like roadside stands, pick-your-own operations rely heavily on large population centers for their customer base and usually need to be located within about an hour's drive of a city and its surrounding suburbs. Most

PYO operations began with strawberry picking, which remains extremely popular.[53] But although there is some logic to driving dozens of miles and enduring backbreaking work for succulently sweet, fresh-picked strawberries, why make similar efforts for a vegetable that you are probably not going to eat? The pumpkin, we know, provides intangible rewards that no other fruit or vegetable bestows. Strawberry farms might offer urbanites great fruit and the allure of a rural experience, but rows of strawberries hardly compare with the pomp and circumstance of the pumpkin patch.

In order to make the farm "an inviting place to relax, play, and enjoy," farmers revamp a portion of their property to create an idyllic, rustic farmscape, like a scene out of a Winslow Homer painting or a contemporary children's book.[54] "You can buy pumpkins at the store," explained a farmer, "but the farm atmosphere attracts people. We are trying to keep our farm as 'farmy' as possible and not commercialize it."[55] One farmer referred to his pumpkin stand as "a low tech theme park."[56] Several farmers noted that they planted corn merely for the added "ambiance" or "atmosphere."[57] Another referred to the requisite "farm critters" at the festivals as "added attractions," since their main function on the farm was for entertainment, not milk or meat.[58] The transformation of the Holsapples' place epitomizes the shift from traditional farming to entertainment enterprise. "To add 200 much-needed parking spaces," explained a reporter, "the Holsapples ripped up their hog feeding floor. 'Although they're equally hard to handle sometimes, the cars filled with customers make us more money in four weeks than year-round hogs,' stated Terry [Holsapple]."[59]

Presumably, the same financial motivation spurred Eric Cox and Gina Richard, co-owners of Cox Farms in Centreville, Virginia, on the outskirts of Washington, D.C., to convert some of their forty acres of fertile farmland into a parking lot. Their pumpkin festival began in 1983 and would soon become one of the most popular fall tourist attractions in the D.C. area. In the Philadelphia and Washington, D.C., metropolitan areas alone, seventy-one pumpkin festivals or roadside stands were open for business in October 2002. After enduring a lengthy traffic jam, each carload of visitors to Cox Farms in 2010 turned onto a dusty hillside on the property to park alongside hundreds of other vehicles. Paying $9 to $15 per person to enter the festival grounds, depending on whether they visited on a weekday or a weekend, visitors then sized up their options

Hand-painted wooden signs at the Cox Farms Pumpkin Festival, Centreville, Virginia, October 2000. The signs post all the festival events, from hayrides to pumpkin picking, which let visitors reenact playful renditions of old-time harvest activities. Photo: Cindy Ott.

from a long list of pumpkin farm activities hand-painted on a wooden sign board. Would it be a visit with "Farmer Jack"? Pet the milk cow? A horse-drawn wagon ride? A tour of the haystack maze? And of course all visitors had a chance to pick their own pumpkin from the pumpkin patch. The scene was "farmy" indeed, and more reminiscent of Currier and Ives scenes than of most modern agricultural operations.

About sixty miles away, David Heisler has raised pumpkins on fifteen acres of his family's land in Montgomery Country, Maryland, since 1988. His pumpkin stand is situated at a crossroads that leads to Sugarloaf Mountain, the closest mountain recreation area to Washington, D.C., which is thirty miles to the south. The property lies at the northern tip of the county, an area that was once a thriving agricultural community but has increasingly been divided up into housing developments and office parks. Like those who visit Cox Farms, most of Heisler's customers drive at least twenty miles to buy his pumpkins. For adult urban dwellers, the pilgrimage resonates with a sense of nostalgia for a past picturesque way of life as well as for similar past family outings. Heisler fulfills their fantasies by hanging bunches of Indian corn from the porch rafters and filling his yard with bundles of cornstalks and wooden crates of apples, squashes, and gourds. Hundreds of pumpkins cover the yard, front steps, and porch.

Rather than focus on the real-life drudgery of field labor, farmers create a "fun farm," where, for an entry fee, visitors can relax and enjoy games based loosely on farming chores.[60] These are chores, however, that one is more apt to see in turn-of-the-century romantic genre paintings than in current state agricultural extension reports. Whether at Chantilly Farms Pumpkinland in Virginia, Vala's Pumpkin Patch in Nebraska, Behmer's Pumpkin Fantasyland in Illinois, or any of the thousands of other pumpkin festivals held across the country in the early 2000s, one was likely to find a hayride, a pick-your-own pumpkin patch, nature displays, pony rides, country music, farm animals, haystacks, scarecrow building, and corn or hay-bale mazes.[61]

Tractors and wagons are the only vehicles allowed in the "Back Forty" at Vollmer Farm in North Carolina, a place where visitors tour "Grandpa's Animal Barnyard," "Grandma's Pond," and the "Punkin Patch Park" playground. At Vala's Pumpkin Patch, old farm equipment and buildings and an old schoolhouse on the property reinforce a sense of nostalgia for the "old days," when life was supposedly simpler and in closer rhythm with the natural world.[62] Piling into a wooden wagon pulled by horses or an old tractor provides both a ride out to a pumpkin field and a trip back in time. At Butler's Orchard in Germantown, Maryland, the trip takes riders over undulating hillsides and open fields and alongside picturesque hedgerows and tree lines that obscure nearby housing developments.

The goods offered for sale add to the natural, homespun character of the place. Pumpkin and Halloween crafts, honey, homemade fudge, preserves and jams, fresh apples and apple cider, homemade baked goods, Indian corn and gourds, and colorful varieties of squashes and pumpkins reinforce the site's old-fashioned, rural atmosphere. The lack of packaging, the hand-painted signs, and the farmer's relatives serving as checkout clerks make the place seem a world apart from everyday retail experiences. Farmer Deirdre Jones, owner of Windy Acres Pumpkin Patch near Alicel, Oregon, told a reporter, "People do not come out here just to buy a pumpkin, they come to share a family experience—one that cannot be found in a grocery store parking lot, digging through a bin."[63] Even though some of these goods are produced elsewhere, customers get a sense that they are supporting a local family farm and thereby preserving a beloved agrarian landscape, not just purchasing merchandise.

"Despite all the attractions," said Terry Holsapple, "the biggest draw is what fascinated onlookers years ago—pumpkins."[64] For most of America's past, picking a pumpkin meant little more than hefting a pitchfork out in the solitude of the back forty. It was a lot of work with few enumerable rewards. In the late twentieth century, it evolved into a form of family entertainment. Participants actually pay to pick the vegetable, and they hardly get their hands dirty. Pumpkins are spread over almost every surface of the festive landscapes, knee-deep in some places. The artifice at farm festivals is easy to spot, but it is also easy to ignore. Pumpkins are often cleaned, set upright, and arranged in pleasing displays. In pick-your-own patches, pumpkins are seldom even attached to a vine, much less still in the patch in which they actually grew. Customers nevertheless seem pleased to be able to cross a field to find a pumpkin.

Although growers try to construct the perfect fruit, variety is still important as each person searches for a distinctive look for his or her pumpkin. Pumpkins are sold by weight, by size, or, in the case of Renick's Farm outside Columbus, Ohio, by the number customers can carry in their arms. Bins of sugar pumpkins are available for those who actually want to cook pumpkin, but many visitors are just looking for one that represents an "old-fashioned" age, as a customer of Heisler's put it.[65] People come equipped with cameras more frequently than with recipes in mind. Several of Heisler's customers return year after year to take pictures of their children with the pumpkins. Returning to the same patch gives the trip a sense of personal nostalgia. Some customers at the Heisler stand have returned to buy their pumpkins there every year since it first opened in 1988.

Family trips to the country to pick a pumpkin are now a part of childhood lore. *Pumpkin Day, Pumpkin Night* (1999), by Anne Rockwell, is one of many children's tales about a family's annual excursion to the patch to pick a pumpkin for Halloween.[66] Departing from their suburban home, the family drives out to a pumpkin farm market in the country. The iconic images that illustrate the story include the scenic rural landscape, the rustic farm stand, and the piles of pumpkins. *Pumpkin Day, Pumpkin Night* is marketed as a "timeless story of a treasured childhood tradition," even

Renick's Family Pumpkin Patch, Ashville, Ohio, October 2000. The artifice at farm festivals like this one is easy to spot, but it is also easy to ignore. Photo: Cindy Ott.

though such annual excursions date back just a few generations. One Maryland farmer called going to the annual pumpkin festival "a rite of passage."[67]

Families with children are the target audience for farm festivals, which helps carry on the sense of tradition. Hay-bale slides and animal petting barns, along with more typical fair offerings such as face painting, are designed for the ten-and-under crowd. Small Oz and Jack-Be-Little pumpkins are for sale for children to hold and to paint. On weekdays, many farms offer tours to schoolchildren to show them how a farm operates. Along with lectures on planting and harvesting, some tours offer attractions such as a "Storybook Barn" and displays of antiquated farm tools.[68] The lessons have little practical application for these mostly urban and suburban children. Instead, they reinforce the cultural significance of the family farm in American history and consciousness. The focus is less on contemporary agricultural issues, such as chemical inputs, government subsidies, and genetic engineering, than on how farmers and nature work in harmony for the benefit of all.

"It's neat to know that I'm part of families' special memories," said Deirdre Jones. "People seem to need this place and the magic that happens here. I've never seen anyone get in an argument, I just see families having fun together."[69] The idea of finding harmony in a pumpkin patch perhaps reflects contemporary anxieties about the loss of a sense of community as the American population has become more transient, as well as feelings of dislocation from the natural world. For organizers and participants, the pumpkin patch is a place to regain those connections. Farmer Jim Vala commented, "We are happy that we are bringing families together. I think we are doing something good for the community."[70]

A rare controversy at northern Virginia's Cox Farms Pumpkin Festival in the autumn of 2000 offers a good example of the ways Americans instill the pumpkin patch with a sense of virtue. That year, some people attacked the farm for flying rainbow flags, insignias of gay pride, above its pumpkin patch. The owners said they had not intended for the flag to have political overtones. They flew it for fun, they said, but they did not mind the association with gay rights. Co-owner Gina Richard proclaimed, "This is a pumpkin patch. This is not a place where prejudice and bigoted actions take place. All families are welcome here."[71]

In the children's tale *Pumpkins* (1992), author Mary Lyn Ray infuses the pumpkin patch with similar moral values.[72] The pumpkin's age-old reputation as a noncommodity crop seems to have been the inspiration for this morality play, in which Ray portrays the pumpkin field as a bulwark against modernization and greed. An old man, his age signifying history and timeless values, wants to save a field from development. "The man talked to the field, and the field said that it would help," says the narrator. "They considered growing Christmas trees, which the man could sell in the city. But trees grow slowly. There wasn't time.... Then the man thought of pumpkins." A successful harvest of pumpkins provides the man with enough money to purchase the field and save it from the bulldozers. The story concludes: "The man might have planted more pumpkins. He had kept one back for seeds. Pumpkins would make him rich. But he had everything he needed. So he decided to give the seeds away. Because somewhere, someone might love another field [that] pumpkins could save."

Stories such as this one apply old sentiments about the humble yet virtuous pumpkin to modern anxieties about community, overdevelopment, and loss of open spaces. The author represents the pumpkin patch as an idyllic agrarian landscape that is a source of American values that can privilege community service over personal greed. Perhaps that is what John Muller meant when he said, "When the kids visit Farmer John, they learn what a farm is like. And what pumpkins are really all about."[73] So neatly have the stories about pumpkins and pumpkin farming intertwined with actual farms and farmers that some people find it difficult to draw a distinction between fact and fiction. "The idea of being outdoors, the animals, the nature—except for reading about it in storybooks or seeing pictures, this isn't something the kids would get to experience," said a mother of two who visited the Cottonwood Farms pumpkin festival outside Chicago in the fall of 2005.[74] Yet, ironically, these agrarian fairytale lands have now become as much fact as fantasy. In its own modest yet significant way, Americans' celebration of the pumpkin has in many places reconfigured the business of agriculture and the character of rural areas.

Pulling back the curtain, Wizard of Oz–style, on the hard economic and production realities behind these fanciful festivals reveals what the pumpkin—this iconic piece of American family farm heritage—has meant to actual American farmers. Central Illinois, where some of the largest pumpkin farms in the country are located in the early twenty-first century, is a good place to start. Dave Newhauser has been raising pumpkins for Libby's canning factory on his family farm near Eureka, Illinois, for about as long as he can remember.[75] He was born on the farm, which was deeded to his family under the Homestead Act in the late nineteenth century. He followed in the footsteps of his father and contracted with Libby's to grow about a hundred acres of pumpkins annually. In the 1960s he moved to Morton, Illinois, after the company hired him as field supervisor for neighboring farms that also produced pumpkins for the plant. Eventually, he became plant manager, although he continued to grow pumpkins on his own farm even after his retirement. Pumpkins are in Newhauser's blood, and images of them covered his office walls, desktop, and windowsills at the time I interviewed him in 2000.

Newhauser made a great spokesperson and symbol for all that pumpkin farm operations are supposed to be, and Libby's took full advantage of that. Nestlé, the parent company, cultivated the down-home image of the pumpkin by profiling Newhauser in its literature and by emphasizing his family's long connection to the vegetable. Rather than illustrating its

2000 annual report with the most advanced and up-to-date equipment used to harvest and process pumpkins, the cover featured Newhauser, who was wielding a small pocketknife in the middle of a pumpkin field. The company markets the crop as an old-fashioned business, even to its shareholders. And judging by Newhauser's family history, the company's glossy, picturesque illusions contain a fair bit of truth.

Although farmers in every state grow pumpkins, Illinois is the number one pumpkin producer, with 13,679 acres and nearly 219,000 tons harvested in 2007.[76] Farmers in the state produce 95 percent of all processing pumpkins (mainly Dickinson and Libby's Select) for canneries nationwide.[77] Almost all those farmers work for Libby's, but some also grow ornamental varieties for fresh market sales. In 1984, with prices falling for their staple crops—corn and soybeans—Newhauser's neighbors the Ackermans began to grow 33 acres (700 tons) of Libby's Select processing pumpkins for the factory and around 10 acres of ornamentals on their 300-acre farm. A few years later they started an annual pumpkin festival, complete with a petting zoo and a store selling goods produced in the state. In 2000, they were featured in a local newspaper article, "Ackerman Family Makes Pumpkins Full-Time Job."[78]

Another top pumpkin-producing state is Pennsylvania, which in 2007 had more farms that grew pumpkins than any other state—1,690 (Illinois listed 502 farms).[79] About one-quarter of the pumpkins produced in Pennsylvania are raised in Lancaster County, home of the modest-sized, 78-acre-average Amish and Mennonite family farms.[80] Each farm grew about four and a half acres of pumpkins, 95 percent of which were ornamentals grown for fresh market sales. The region that the USDA designates the Lower South is the smallest-producing region, with well under 50 farms and fewer than 200 acres planted in pumpkins in each of its six states.[81] Even here, though, the low production rate hardly equates with southerners' lack of interest in pumpkins. The region hosts hundreds of annual pumpkin festivals that rely on imported pumpkins to supplement what they can produce locally.

The yield for ornamental varieties is smaller than that for processing pumpkins because no blemished fruit can go to market. Although you cannot find records about it in the agricultural census, farmers have also established creative markets for these stragglers unfit for retail as animal feed. Cattle, hogs, and even some wild beasts get their fair share of leftovers after the top-grade pumpkins are picked over for human consumption. Robert Lewis, of Lewis Orchards in Dickerson, Maryland, averages an 85-percent yield for his ornamental pumpkin crop and sells the remaining 15 percent, which he considers seconds, to a local cattle farmer.[82] A New Mexico grower sells his damaged pumpkins to a neighboring rancher, whose cattle graze the pumpkin fields at a cost of $6 a head per month until all the fruit is consumed.[83] In New Jersey, hunters' demand for smashed, damaged, or half-rotten pumpkins to use as deer bait has created a steady new market for growers. Hunters may pay prices comparable to what festival-goers pay, leading some farmers to make as much money on culled pumpkins as from fresh market sales.[84] Even more exotic are the gorillas and elephants that get their share. For the last several years, farmers near Washington, D.C., have donated their remaining Halloween pumpkins to the National Zoo for the animals' eating and entertainment. According to zoo officials, the animals love to "kick, squash, and eat their fill of these seasonal treats."[85]

The day I visited Dave Newhauser in mid-October 2000, the Libby's plant operations were nearing their seasonal shutdown, having churned out one can of pumpkin after another, twenty-four hours a day, since mid-August. Within minutes of pulling out of the factory parking lot, with Newhauser as my tour guide, I was beyond the streets of Morton and surrounded by farmland. This was corporate agriculture, pumpkin style. In the world of pumpkin production, Libby's farms are some of the highest-tech operations, but it is difficult to recognize them as such. Fields of small to medium-size family farms, averaging 330 acres, such as Newhauser's, are separated by wooden houses perched amid protective groves of trees.[86] In the fall, when the vines have rotted, a sea of pumpkins is clearly visible in the fields. During most of the growing season they are hidden beneath a canopy of leaves. On the particular farm we visited, the pumpkins had already been windrowed into straight lines. The long, low piles of muddy beige vegetables stretched the length of a sixty-acre patch, ready to be picked up by a Libby's-invented pumpkin loader and taken to the factory ten miles away.

All the Libby's pumpkins are raised in fields that are in direct and close proximity to the plant. The company does not own the land itself but contracts acreage and labor from local farmers. Instead of constituting one megafarm, the pumpkin fields are dispersed on approximately 100-acre lots on these 300-acre family farms. (Statewide, the average field size for processing pumpkins is 105 acres, and for ornamentals, 9 acres, for a combined average of 31 acres.)[87] In the 2010 growing season, Libby's had 5,000 to 6,000 acres of pumpkins in production, which it doled out among dozens of growers in four counties near the Morton plant.[88] Libby's attempted to expand operations into southern Illinois in the late 1960s, and more recently tried growing and processing pumpkins in Gridley, California.[89] Neither expansion paid off, so the company returned to its original operations around Morton, thereby keeping its farming operations small-scale and local. A dismal 2009 harvest due to heavy rains has prompted the company again to consider planting farther afield.[90]

Illinois's 31-acre pumpkin farms are five times larger than the national average of 6.1 acres.[91] The total number of pumpkins harvested in the United States has jumped dramatically in the last forty years, but the average number of acres per farm has remained steady since the 1970s. (Some farms, of course, plant just a couple of acres, and others plant hundreds.) For most of the twentieth century, production was static, with approximately the same number of farms growing pumpkins in 1974 as in 1899.[92] In 1939, the low point in acreage since the government began keeping records, 2,194 farms grew just 5,975 acres, an average of 2.7 acres per farm.[93] The industry publication *The Packer: Produce Availability and Merchandizing Guide*, established in 1893, did not even include pumpkins in its yearly reports until 1986. By 1987, more than twice as many farms (6,921) raised almost double the acreage of pumpkins (40,652) than thirteen years before.[94] Between 1997 and 2007, the number of farms and acreage more than doubled again, to 15,088 farms harvesting 92,955 acres nationwide.[95]

Although nearly five times as many farms produce more than four times as many pumpkins than thirty-five years ago, one still has to put these numbers in perspective. In 2007, 432,077 farms harvested more than 92 million acres of corn, and 279,110 farms harvested almost 64 million acres of soybeans, which suggests that pumpkin production is minuscule by commercial agriculture standards.[96] Even the largest producers, such as Frey Farms of Keenes, Illinois, which plants 750 acres of pumpkins on its 1,200-acre farm, and the Torrey family farm in upstate New York, with 250-acre fields within a 10,000-acre operation, would be lost in the sea of corn fields that stretches across the Midwest.[97] In 2007, California, the state that produces by far the largest quantity of fresh fruits and vegetables and is the sixth largest pumpkin producer, registered 359 farms with a total of 5,106 acres under cultivation, an average of 14.2 acres of pumpkins per farm.[98]

In terms of overall vegetable production, the percentage of American farms that cultivate pumpkins is rather high, at 22 percent in 2007, yet the percentage of acreage devoted to pumpkins among all acreage harvested is a mere 0.02.[99] What all the statistics tells us is that pumpkin farms are not getting larger; instead, more and more small farmers are adding a few acres of pumpkins to their production. In other words, pumpkin farming, unlike the farming of many other crops, has not become concentrated in the hands of a few large producers over the last fifty years but is scattered among small operations like those around Morton.[100] Consequently, the pumpkin harvest festivals are not merely cultural fantasies but represent a significant economic strategy for small family farms.

Having gained a sense of what a pumpkin farm looks like, we can get down in the dirt and see how they operate. Production in Morton begins in mid-February, when the company contracts with local farmers. Libby's offers farmers bids based on price per ton. According to pumpkin farmer John Ackerman, the company usually sets a price a little higher than he could get for growing corn or soybeans.[101] In order to have the pumpkins ready by August, the crop is planted in late April, or perhaps in May in regions with colder climes or at farm operations geared toward October sales of ornamental pumpkins. Libby's provides the farmers with seeds. Elsewhere, most farmers purchase seeds from catalogs.

Farmers no longer plant pumpkins in hills of three to four seeds, as they did in the past. Instead, growers of both ornamental and processing pumpkins use a mechanized corn planter to drill holes and drop seeds, and then cover the holes. To compensate for the threat of frost and other dangers, Libby's farmers plant around nine thousand seeds per acre and then thin the plants to about four thousand seedlings after they are about six inches tall. The seeds are the cheapest component of production, which makes it easy and feasible to overplant. The farmers are responsible for managing the crop until harvest, including renting beehives to pollinate the flowers and applying pesticides and herbicides.[102] About half the fields are dry farmed, meaning that they are not irrigated. The standard policy among pumpkin farmers is to plant a particular field only one out of every four years to prevent weeds, disease, and nutrient deficiencies.

Because of the meandering nature of the vines, no mechanized hoeing equipment can be used on any patch of pumpkins after the early part of the season. To prevent weed growth, farmers must hand-hoe the ground, plant it with a cover crop, cover it with plastic, or spray herbicides on it. In the cover crop, or no-till, method, farmers cultivate a grass such as rye and then mow it down to create a straw or mat barrier against weeds. According to one Maryland farmer, the cover crop also improves the pumpkins' appearance by protecting them from "dirt splash," which bleaches out their orange color.[103]

The similarities between farming pumpkins for canning and farming pumpkins for jack-o'-lanterns end at harvest time. In Morton, to harvest processing pumpkins, the contracting growers step out of the operation, and Libby's hires other farmers to run the company-owned harvest equipment. The men who harvest the crop are mostly retired farmers who, according to the one I met, enjoy the part-time seasonal work. Libby's uses migrant labor only for factory work; agricultural production remains in the hands of locals. Harvesting is no longer backbreaking labor, because all aspects of processing pumpkins are now mechanized. Innovations were late in coming, however. Until 1955, farmers sliced pumpkins from the vine with handheld blades—a task now performed by two pieces of equipment. The first machine cuts the pumpkins from the vines and puts them in rows. This machine could not be used on ornamental pumpkins because it can inflict nicks, cuts, and other cosmetic problems.

The second piece of equipment is the Libby's-invented pumpkin loader, which looks like a tractor with a large conveyor belt up one side. The loader picks up the pumpkins and tosses them into an open trailer attached to the back of a semi-truck that drives alongside the loader in the field. The pace of the harvest is obviously much faster than when the task had to be performed by hand. Three pumpkin loaders working at once can load a ton of pumpkins in twenty minutes.[104] When the trailer is full, the truck driver takes the load down the road to Morton. There, an automated lift tilts the trailer up and pours the pumpkins onto conveyor belts that lead right into the factory, where the processing begins.

In contrast, harvesting ornamental pumpkins is very labor intensive and still almost completely unmechanized to ensure quality. It is backbreaking work. Each pumpkin is hand-cut from the vine with pruning loopers. After being left to cure in the field for a week or so to harden the skin and improve the color, they are piled manually, one by one, in rows for loading onto trucks or bins, or they are left in the field for pick-your-own operations.

Farmers sell pumpkins directly to consumers at their own markets or PYO operations; to retailers ranging from small local businesses and non-profit organizations that host harvest festivals to large-scale chains with national distribution; and to wholesale distributors or brokers. For sales to brokers and large retail chains, farmers usually hand-sort ornamental pumpkins by size and shape, because those customers want pumpkins to be uniform. Roadside sellers prefer a variety of shapes and sizes to accommodate buyers' individual preferences. Before workers hand-load ornamental pumpkins into cardboard bins or directly onto trucks, they either hose them down along a conveyor belt or, more likely, handwash them with a damp towel.[105] How picky farmers are about the appearance of their ornamental pumpkins and how delicately growers treat them greatly affect the yield per acre.[106]

Brokers either contract with farmers at the beginning of the season or purchase pumpkins directly from farmers or at auction houses when the season ends. Robert Lewis, a Maryland wholesale and retail grower, sells the vast majority of his pumpkins to local markets and neighboring farms with retail businesses, but he reported that a Chicago broker had bought pumpkins from him one year to sell in New England. Torrey Farms, in New York State, ships to Florida, where the climate prevents local farmers from fulfilling demand.[107] Frey Farms sells to Wal-Mart for national distribution, and the Arata Farm in California distributes pumpkins to Rite Aid stores.[108]

Jack-o'-lantern pumpkins are heavy, making transportation costs per unit almost prohibitive and cross-country shipments rare.[109] "No trucker in his right mind wants to haul pumpkins," said a Toledo, Ohio, broker.[110] Shipping them long distance is expensive and risky because of the high value placed on the vegetable's appearance. Transport greatly increases the likelihood of bruises and nicks, not to mention the loss of a stem—a death knell for any ornamental pumpkin. Don Nivens, who has a farm near Moore, South Carolina, stated that the best way to sell pumpkins is through PYO operations because the pumpkins he buys from other farmers often arrive neglected and rotten.[111] By and large, long-distance transactions occur only during shortages.[112] A website of pumpkin wholesalers and truckers lists only one company out of twenty-eight that transports pumpkins nationwide.[113] More common are regional sellers such as McCurdy's Pumpkin Patch, which ships pumpkins no more than seventy-five miles from its farm in Cass County, Iowa; farmers in Lancaster County, Pennsylvania, who draw buyers in the mid-Atlantic region to their local produce auction in Leola; and the Patterson Farm in Sunderland, Massachusetts, which has been supplying pumpkins to farm stands and stores in New England since 1983.[114]

While transportation is one practical explanation for why pumpkin farming is geared toward local and modest-size family farms, another is the vegetable's very short period of demand. Tomatoes, lettuce, and zucchini, not to mention apples and berries, are hot commodities throughout the year, but who wants a pumpkin in January, May, or August? According to *The Packer*, not many people. Charts of annual pumpkin shipments published by the guide are mostly blank, except for the slender columns of numbers in September, October, and November.[115]

Although producers and retailers attempt to expand the buying season into September, the sale of fresh pumpkins for jack-o'-lanterns is limited mainly to the four weeks of October. Sales for ornamental pumpkins, except for the few that go to feed animals, come to a screeching halt on October 31, Halloween, and sales of canned pumpkin plummet after Thanksgiving weekend. During the 2009 pumpkin shortage, one grocer remarked, "We [usually] order so much . . . that we can't get rid of it after the Thanksgiving season."[116] The narrow period of demand for pumpkins affirms the crop's symbolic import but also suggests constraints on its value as a commodity. Growers' sales are, in the words of Dave Newhauser, "lucrative but limited"—lucrative because of high demand but limited because they last for only a short period.[117] A Maryland farmer explained that he considered it too risky to expand his acreage because the "parameters of the market" were too inflexible.[118] If he did not find buyers or if the crop did not begin to turn orange by the end of September, then his investment was lost.

The size of the local market also limits the pumpkin business. A community or city can support only so many pumpkin farm markets, especially because of the crop's limited time of use. In the 1990s, many farmers got into the business, increasing supply and causing prices to drop in the early 2000s. Annual harvest variations due to climatic conditions also affect crop value and prices.[119] Because the 2009 season was an especially bad one, sellers across the country had to search far and wide and pay top dollar for pumpkins. The nature of the plant itself also contributes to the widespread propagation of pumpkins at small-scale farms across the country. Whereas the pumpkin's bulkiness is a liability for long-haul transport, its climatic versatility and ease of production enable growers to plant it just about anywhere, so many small farms are capable of fulfilling local demand. Farmers from Maine to Alabama and from Maryland to California can produce pumpkins at the time consumers desire them most.

When a northern Virginia pumpkin farmer told his grandmother he was growing pumpkins for sale, she questioned his sanity. "Who'd in their right mind pay for pumpkins?" she asked incredulously.[120] Lots of people, as it turns out. Pumpkin farmers might be quaint, but they are part of a multimillion dollar business. The dollar value of wholesale ornamental and processing pumpkins across the country was more than $250 million in 2007.[121] Maureen Torrey, of Torrey Farms, said with a chuckle and not a little bewilderment that "one big pumpkin is worth more than two thousand pounds of cabbage."[122]

For many growers, pumpkin farming started as a side business to supplement farm income and prolong the working season but then grew to be a major and pivotal source of revenue. "We got into pumpkin growing through the back door," said Don Nivens, owner of the forty-acre Nivens Apple Farm in northern South Carolina. The first year, Nivens planted a quarter acre of pumpkins. He then increased the acreage over the years to four acres, and by 1996 he had seven acres under cultivation. For Nivens, growing ornamental pumpkins was a means of protecting himself against the loss of his main crop, apples. The family hosts an annual pumpkin festival as well. He relies "on pumpkins to save his financial skin," explained a *Small Farm Today* reporter.[123] Tim and Jan Vala's pumpkin field on their farm near Gretna, Nebraska, began as a half-acre patch in 1983. Within ten years it had grown to 43 acres, and as of 2010 the couple was cultivating pumpkins on 55 acres of their 152-acre farm, where they also host an annual festival.[124]

Both the Holsapple family and the McAfee family—the latter fifth-generation farmers who operate County Line Orchard in Hoart, Illinois—estimate that half their annual farm income derives from pumpkins and their annual festival.[125] Many small farmers cannot survive on farming alone and depend on nonfarm income of some sort to allow them to keep their farm operations going. In general, farmers who grow processing pumpkins for factories have more acreage but reap smaller profits per acre than farmers who grow ornamentals for wholesale or local markets. For example, in 2005, farmers earned just 3 cents per pound for pumpkins in Illinois, which devoted 70 percent of production to processing pumpkins, whereas New Jersey and Virginia farmers, who devoted 100 percent and 96 percent of their production, respectively, to ornamental pumpkins, brought in 29 cents and 11 cents per pound at wholesale in 2009.[126] These averages do not take into account special business arrangements like the one Libby's set up with local farmers to pay them just over the price per acre for commodity crops of corn and soybeans.

When asked about the profitability of her enterprise, Diedre Jones said, "It is a little difficult to put a price on memories, fun and family togetherness."[127] Behind the romance, the hard facts are that pumpkins bring in thousands of dollars a year to farmers who grow them. "A significant minority of farmers are really cashing in on pumpkin crops. It is getting to be a fairly big business," stated the Massachusetts commissioner of food and agriculture in 1999.[128] The exact dollar value of pumpkins varies by federal reporting agency, state, weather, type of pumpkin harvested, yield, and the market. Yet all sources indicate their profitability for the small and medium-size farms that grow them.

According to the USDA, the value of the crop for the six highest producing states in 2007 was $123,519,000, which converts to an average of $2,691 per acre before production and harvest costs are deducted. The USDA estimates that these costs can run as high as $2,000 per acre, so farms net an average of $691 per acre.[129] For farmers in the top six states, who average 10 acres apiece in pumpkins, that amounts to a net profit of $6,910 annually, while farmers who grow the national average of 6.1 acres clear $4,215. These sums might be modest, but they make up a good portion of small-farm net income, which, according to the USDA, averages $25,000.[130]

The national totals reflect the most conservative profit estimates. State-by-state statistics paint an even more optimistic, though varied, picture. In Illinois in 2005, 12,900 pumpkin farmers earned a gross profit of $16,049,000, or an average of $37,320 per farm ($1,204 per acre).[131] In Texas in 2002, 38 farmers brought in $2,400,000, for an average of $27,360 per farm ($772 per acre).[132] New Hampshire farmers in 2007 grossed 40 cents per pound for wholesale ornamental pumpkins, or $10,353 total for each of the 225 farms, which harvested on average 2.81 acres of pumpkins ($3,685 per acre).[133] Another testament to the pumpkin's economic worth is the Maryland agricultural department's recommendation in the 1980s that farmers grow pumpkins to compensate for declining tobacco propagation in the southern part of the state.[134]

These production figures do not account for direct farm marketers who have fall harvest festivals and stands, which reap the highest profits. Besides earning up to $20 for an entry fee at some establishments, these farmers can charge retail prices of 35 to 50 cents per pound for jack-o'-lantern pumpkins, which amounts to $15 to $20 for a single pumpkin or a gross sum of $14,000 to $20,000 per acre.[135] The U.S. Agricultural Census does not record statistics for gourds and mini-pumpkins, such as Jack-Be-Littles, because the USDA considers them to be nonfood items—but they certainly add to farmers' sales.[136] According to Maureen Torrey, ninety acres of minis bring better returns than three hundred acres of peas.[137] Between 2006 and 2010, minis on average brought in 25 cents a pound to wholesalers and about $1 apiece to retailers.[138] These calculations omit as an income source all the ornamental and edible squashes that have gained popularity on the pumpkin's coattails, as well as the jams, ciders, apples, and other products sold at pumpkin patches and stands.

Dan Glickman, secretary of agriculture under President Bill Clinton, declared in 2000, "The rising popularity of urban pumpkin patches and fall festivals has helped spur demand for pumpkins and increased income for some farmers."[139] Paul Siegel's Cottonwood Farms, in Crest Hill, Illinois, near Chicago, started a pumpkin festival in 1990 that attracts more than 30,000 visitors every year and earns Siegel three times more than his 400 acres of corn, soybeans, and grains.[140] Jan and Tim Vala had more than 80,000 people purchase about 250 tons of pumpkins from their Pumpkin Patch in Nebraska in the fall of 1993, with average purchases of about $20 per family.[141] David Heisler's fall stand in suburban Washington, D.C., earns him more for pumpkins than he receives from local grocery stores for string beans, corn, and peppers.[142] These farmers take on additional costs of running the markets, such as insurance, labor, and toilet and parking facilities, but the financial benefits far outweigh the liabilities. Pumpkins allow farmers to continue farming, as opposed to doing something else.

The local food movement, driven by the desire to improve both the health of agricultural land and the food it produces, has inspired a whole new appreciation of the small farm at the turn of the twenty-first century.[143] With American agricultural policies that have increased farm production and government subsidies for commodity crops since the 1970s, more food is being manufactured from corn and soybeans. Ready-made entrees, fast food meals, sugary drinks, and savory treats are higher in calories yet less expensive than many whole foods, such as fresh fruits and vegetables, which are not supported by government subsidies. That is what makes products like jack-o'-lantern pumpkin cookie dough possible.

Concerned citizens worry about the environmental effects of large-scale production of mono-crops, including increased use of artificial inputs and petroleum-based products to produce, manufacture, and transport these foods to distant markets. They worry about the health consequences of Americans' ever-increasing waistlines, which have coincided with the greater availability of cheap, high-calorie foods. Activists such as Michael Pollan have encouraged consumers to avoid the inner aisles of grocery stores, where processed foods line the shelves, and instead to shop on the outer peripheries, where fresh meats and produce are on display. First Lady Michelle Obama planted an organic vegetable garden on the White House lawn and started the program "Let's Move" to help improve children's eating habits.[144] Farmers markets, food co-ops, urban gardens, and consumer-supported agriculture programs have proliferated alongside pumpkin stands with consumers' increased demand for local and organic foods and their desire to know the stories and people behind the food itself. Some of these initiatives were born out of Italian Carlo Petrini's slow food movement, founded in the 1980s. Yet in the global context, of equal concern is not just *what* to feed but *how* to feed the world's fast-multiplying population, which the United Nations expects to peak at 9.2 billion in 2075.[145]

The pumpkin fulfills many Americans' desire to maintain connections to the mythical family farm of lore, and it has rejuvenated many small farms in the process. It also plays into these current food challenges by reminding reformers that food is more than something to eat. Many reformers interpret the U.S. health crisis as a problem of diet and nutrition; however, imagining food as simply vitamins and calories misses the deep meanings that people invest in what they eat. As most of us know, proselytizing about the nutritional attributes of food has little chance of success in changing people's long-term eating habits. Almost anyone who has been on a diet is well aware of that. Eating is a complex cultural act, and appetites are stirred by many cultural factors beyond health and nutrition—including family, ethnic, regional, and national traditions—as well as by time and financial constraints. Changing food habits, whether getting people to eat more of one food or less of another, depends on understanding the cultural meanings that people invest in food. Modest American pumpkin farms will not solve the world's food problems, but their success proves that seemingly esoteric beliefs and romantic ideas about food are as important to people's food choices as health, nutrition, or even taste.

Not far from Heisler's pumpkin stand is the Pipe Creek Farm, now a national historic landmark. In the 1950s, this inconspicuous Maryland pumpkin patch was the scene of international intrigue after Whittaker Chambers hid a trove of microfilm in a hollowed-out pumpkin there. The film allegedly linked Alger Hiss to Soviet espionage.[146] The pumpkin patch, it seems, was considered one of the least likely places someone would look for evidence of high crimes against the American people. It was not only physically remote from the centers of power and culture but also ideologically removed. The pumpkin field, a place both unassuming and yet noble, was the last place anyone would expect to uncover evidence of treason. The story of the "pumpkin papers," as the incident came to be known, embodies both the prominence of the pumpkin in popular American culture and the evolution of the pumpkin's functions and meanings. Whereas the pumpkin patch was once considered a cultural backwater, over time its primitive status has made it a sacred place of American virtue.

Few people probably consider that the site of this famous episode in American international relations was anything very special, but a pumpkin patch is no ordinary place. Consider, too, a 1978 photograph by Joel Sternfeld of McLean's Farm Market in northern Virginia. At first glance, the center of drama might seem to be an old farmhouse's rooftop fire. The viewer's eye travels from a grassy foreground littered with smashed

Joel Sternfeld (American, b. 1944), "McLean's Farm Market, December 1978," digital C-print, 42 by 52 1/2 inches. In this photograph, Sternfeld captured a lone fireman intently selecting pumpkins from a farm market while his colleagues are occupied with the burning farmhouse behind him. Courtesy Joel Sternfeld and Luhring Augustine, New York.

and scattered orange pumpkins past an abandoned farm stand to the orange blaze erupting from the house in the distance. From a hook-and-ladder truck, firefighters battle the flames. The eye travels back down the picture frame to the pile of pumpkins nestled next to the rustic market building. Curiously, a lone firefighter intently selects some pumpkins while his colleagues are occupied with the house fire. The tension in the photograph emanates from the man's preoccupation with the pumpkins rather than the fire. What the photographer seems to be contemplating is Americans' "burning" fascination with the vegetable. The matching orange hues of the pumpkins, the blaze, and the fireman's uniform convey a synergy between the pumpkin and the man, and the intensity of the attraction. Like Whittaker Chambers's pumpkin patch, McLean's Farm Market is an unassuming landscape hiding a deep and compelling story. The man's simple act of picking a pumpkin from a pumpkin patch opens up a rich and complicated history about how Americans have found themselves in nature and, in the process, have changed both nature and themselves.

NOTES

1   A comprehensive survey of cucurbits (the pumpkin's botanical family, which also includes squashes, gourds, cucumbers, and melons) in literature—and a vital resource for me as I began my research—is Ralf Norrman and Jon Haarberg, *Nature and Language: A Semiotic Study of Cucurbits in Literature* (London: Routledge and Kegan Paul, 1980).

2   Mike Badgerow, executive director of the Morton Chamber of Commerce, interview by the author, Morton, Illinois, October 20, 2000.

3   In this book I rely on the ideas and methodologies of material culture studies. See Henry Glassie, *Material Culture* (Bloomington: Indiana University Press, 1999); Henry Glassie, "Artifacts: Folk, Popular, Imaginary and Real," in Marshall Fishwick and Ray B. Browne, eds., *Icons of Popular Culture* (Bowling Green, Ohio: Bowling Green University Press, 1970), 103–22; Jules David Prown, "Style as Evidence," *Winterthur Portfolio* 15, no. 3 (1980): 197–210; Jules David Prown, "Mind in Matter: An Introduction to Material Culture Theory and Method," *Winterthur Portfolio* 17, no. 1 (1982): 1–19; Siegfried Gideon, *Mechanization Takes Command: A Contribution to Anonymous History* (New York: W. W. Norton, 1948); Steven Lubar and W. David Kingery, eds., *History from Things: Essays on Material Culture* (Washington, D.C.: Smithsonian Institution Press, 1993); Thomas J. Schlereth, ed., *Material Culture Studies in America* (Nashville, Tenn.: American Association for State and Local History, 1982); Thomas J. Schlereth, ed., *Material Culture: A Research Guide* (Lawrence: University Press of Kansas, 1985); Robert Blair St. George, ed., *Material Life in America, 1600–1860* (Boston: Northeastern University Press, 1988); Marius Kwint, Christopher Breward, and Jeremy Aynsley, eds., *Material Memories: Design and Evocation* (New York: Berg, 1999); Ian M. G. Quimby, *Material Culture and the Study of American Life* (New York: W. W. Norton, 1978); Mihaly Csikszentmihalyi and Eugene Rochberg-Halton, *Meaning of Things: Domestic Symbols and the Self* (Cambridge: Cambridge University Press, 1981); Bill Brown, *A Sense of Things: The Object Matter of American Literature* (Chicago: University of Chicago Press, 2002); Bill Brown, ed., *Things* (Chicago: University of Chicago Press, 2004); Arjun Appadurai, ed., *The Social Life of Things: Commodities*

in Cultural Perspective (Cambridge: Cambridge University Press, 1986); Victor Buchli, ed., *Material Culture: Critical Concepts in the Social Sciences* (New York: Routledge, 2004); Daniel Miller, *The Comfort of Things* (Malden, Mass.: Polity, 2009); and Daniel Miller, *Stuff* (Malden, Mass.: Polity, 2010).

4 Raymond Williams, "The Idea of Nature," in *Problems in Materialism and Culture: Selected Essays* (London: Verso, 1980), 67–85; Hans Huth, *Nature and the American: Three Centuries of Changing Attitudes* (Berkeley: University of California Press, 1957); Roderick Nash, *Wilderness and the American Mind* (New Haven, Conn.: Yale University Press, 1967); Barbara Novak, *Nature and Culture: American Landscape and Painting, 1825–1875* (New York: Oxford University Press, 1980); Simon Schama, *Landscape and Memory* (New York: Knopf, 1995); Jennifer Price, *Flight Maps: Adventures with Nature in Modern America* (New York: Basic Books, 1999); Hans Bak and Walter Holbing, eds., *"Nature's Nation" Revisited: American Concepts of Nature from Wonder to Ecological Crisis* (Amsterdam: VU University, 2003).

5 Jules Prown recommended a close reading of objects as a way to get at their meanings and to reduce the influence of a researcher's preconceived notions of the objects. For an overview of his methodology, see Prown, "Style as Evidence" and "Mind in Matter." The idea that things have agency and one cannot conceive of a meaning of a word without the thing itself (snow, for example) is a particular argument of Bill Brown's "Thing Theory." See Brown, *A Sense of Things* and *Things*.

6 Works on specific plants and foods include Michael Pollan, *Botany of Desire: A Plant's Eye View of the World* (New York: Random House, 2001); Mark Kurlansky, *Salt: A World History* (New York: Walker, 2002); Redcliffe N. Salaman, *The History and Social Influence of the Potato* (Cambridge: Cambridge University Press, 1949); Larry Zuckerman, *The Potato: How the Humble Spud Rescued the Western World* (Boston: Faber and Faber, 1988); Sidney W. Mintz, *Sweetness and Power: The Place of Sugar in Modern History* (New York: Viking Penguin, 1985); Wendy A. Woloson, *Refined Tastes: Sugar, Confectionary, and Consumers in Nineteenth-Century America* (Baltimore, Md.: Johns Hopkins University Press, 2002); Virginia Scott Jenkins, *Bananas: An American History* (Washington, D.C.: Smithsonian Institution Press, 2000); and Dan Koeppel, *Banana: The Fate of the Fruit that Changed the World* (New York: Hudson Street Press, 2008). For use of plants to read cultural landscapes, see May Theilgaard Watts, *Reading the Landscape of America* (New York: Collier Books, 1975 [1957]), and Thomas J. Schlereth, "Vegetation as Historical Data: A Historian's Use of Plants and Natural Material Culture Evidence," in *Artifacts and the American Past* (Nashville, Tenn.: American Association for State and Local History, 1980), 147–59.

7 David Scofield Wilson and Angus K. Gillespie, eds., *Rooted in America: The Folklore of Popular Fruits and Vegetables* (Knoxville: University of Tennessee Press, 1999); Betty Fussell, *The Story of Corn* (New York: Farrar, Straus and Giroux, 1992); Anna Pavord, *The Tulip: The Story of a Flower that Has Made Men*

Mad (New York: Bloomsbury, 1999); John McPhee, *Oranges* (New York: Farrar, Straus and Giroux, 1967); Mark Pendergrast, *Uncommon Grounds: The History of Coffee and How It Transformed Our World* (New York: Basic Books, 1999); Mark Kurlansky, *Cod: A Biography of the Fish That Changed the World* (New York: Walker, 1997); Bernard Mergen, *Snow in America* (Washington, D.C.: Smithsonian Institution Press, 1997).

8   Eric Hobsbawm, "Introduction: Inventing Traditions," in *The Invention of Tradition,* eds. Eric Hobsbawm and Terrance Ranger (New York: Cambridge University Press, 1983), 1–14.

9   Works on the jack-o'-lantern include Nicolas Rogers, *Halloween: From Pagan Ritual to Party Night* (New York: Oxford University Press, 2002); David J. Skal, *Death Makes a Holiday: A Cultural History of Halloween* (New York: Bloomsbury, 2002); Jack Santino, *New Old Fashioned Ways: Holidays and Popular Culture* (Knoxville: University of Tennessee Press, 1996), 114–27; Jack Santino, ed., *Halloween and Other Festivals of Death and Life* (Knoxville: University of Tennessee Press, 1994); Jack Santino, *All Around the Year: Holidays and Celebrations in American Life* (Urbana: University of Illinois Press, 1994), 142–209; Jack Santino, "Halloween in America: Contemporary Customs and Performances," *Western Folklore* 42 (1983): 1–20; Jack Santino, "Night of the Wandering Souls," *Natural History* 92, no. 10 (1983): 42–51; Lesley Pratt Bannatyne, *Halloween: An American Holiday, an American History* (New York: Facts on File, 1990); and Ted Tuleja, "Pumpkins," in Wilson and Gillespie, *Rooted in America,* 142–65.

10   Henry Nash Smith, *Virgin Land: The American West as Symbol and Myth* (Cambridge, Mass.: Harvard University Press, 1950); Richard Hofstadter, *The Age of Reform* (New York: Knopf, 1955); Leo Marx, *Machine in the Garden: Technology and the Pastoral Ideal in America* (New York: Oxford University Press, 1964); Myra Jehlen, *American Incarnation: The Individual, the Nation, and the Continent* (Cambridge, Mass.: Harvard University Press, 1986); David Shi, *The Simple Life: Plain Living and High Thinking in American Culture* (New York: Oxford University Press, 1986); Raymond Williams, *The Country and the City* (New York: Oxford University Press, 1973); Michael Bunce, *The Countryside Ideal: Anglo-American Images of Landscape* (London: Routledge, 1994); Lawrence Buell, "American Pastoral Ideology Reappraised," *American Literary History* 1, no. 1 (1989): 1–29.

11   Roland Barthes, "Towards a Psychosociology of Contemporary Food Consumption," in *Food and Drink in History: Annales 5,* eds. Robert Forster and Orest Ranum (Baltimore, Md.: Johns Hopkins University Press, 1979), 166–73; Roland Barthes, "Wine and Milk," "Steak and Chips," and "Ornamental Cookery," in *Mythologies* (New York: Hill and Wang, 1957), 58–61, 62–64, and 78–80, respectively. The anthology *"We Gather Together"* provides many case studies of the ways Americans use food for symbolic purposes in ceremonies, festivals, and rituals. Theodore C. Humphrey and Lin T. Humphrey, *"We Gather Together": Food and Festival in American Life* (Logan: Utah State

University, 1988). See also Carole Counihan and Penny Van Esterik, eds., *Food and Culture: A Reader* (New York: Routledge, 1979); Deane W. Curtin and Lisa M. Heldke, *Cooking, Eating, Thinking: Transformative Philosophies of Food* (Bloomington: Indiana University Press, 1992); Jean-Louis Flandrin and Massimo Montanari, eds., *Food: A Culinary History* (New York: Columbia University Press, 1999); Paul Fieldhouse, *Food and Nutrition: Customs and Culture* (London: Croom Helm, 1986); Margaret L. Arnott, *Gastronomy: The Anthropology of Food and Food Habits* (The Hague: Mouton, 1975); Stephen Mennell et al., *The Sociology of Food: Eating, Dieting and Culture* (London: Sage, 1992); Ron Scapp and Brian Seitz, eds., *Eating Culture* (Albany: State University of New York Press, 1993); Charles Camp, *American Foodways: What, When, Why, and How We Eat in America* (Little Rock, Ark.: August House, 1989); Marvin Harris, *Good to Eat: Riddles of Food and Culture* (New York: Simon and Schuster, 1985); Alan Warde, *Consumption, Food and Taste: Culinary Antinomes and Commodity Culture* (London: Sage, 1997); and Mary Douglas, ed., *Food in the Social Order: Studies of Food and Festivities in Three American Communities* (New York: Russell Sage Foundation, 1984).

12   Combining cultural studies with economic and environmental history to argue that people experience and think about nature in a variety of ways at once might seem self-evident, but many environmental historians analyze their subject from a single avenue of inquiry, especially an economic avenue, without including the more complex cultural entanglements at play. For example, William Cronon's insightful analysis of Chicago's meatpacking industry in *Nature's Metropolis* might have revealed a more complicated story than simply alienation from nature if he had also considered Americans' feelings about pigs and their appetite for pork alongside the animal's commodification. William Cronon, *Nature's Metropolis: Chicago and the Great West* (New York: W. W. Norton, 1999). Other important works in environmental history that take a similar approach include William Cronon, *Changes in the Land: Indians, Colonists, and the Ecology of New England* (New York: Hill and Wang, 1983); Richard White, *Land Use, Environment, and Social Change: The Shaping of Island County, Washington* (Seattle: University of Washington Press, 1980); Donald Worster, *Dust Bowl: The Southern Plains in the 1930s* (New York: Oxford University Press, 1979); and Theodore Steinberg, *Down to Earth: Nature's Role in American History* (New York: Oxford University Press, 2002).

1. CORN, BEANS, AND JUST ANOTHER SQUASH: 10,000 BCE TO 1600

1   Edward Winslow, *Mourt's Relation, a Relation or Journal of the English Plantation Settled at Plymouth in New England, by Certain English Adventurers Both Merchants and Others*, ed. Dwight B. Heath (New York: Corinth Books, 1963 [1622]), 82.

2   Ibid.

3   William Bradford, "Some Observations of God's Merciful Dealing with Us in

the Wilderness," in *Collections of the Massachusetts Historical Society, for the Year 1794* (Boston: Apollo Press, 1794), as quoted in Sally Smith Booth, *Hung, Strung, and Potted: A History of Eating in Colonial America* (New York: Clarkson N. Potter, 1971), 140. Although Bradford mentioned only European crops in these lines, he included native American foodstuffs in other places in the rhyme.

4   Bruce D. Smith, *The Emergence of Agriculture* (New York: Scientific American Library, 1995), 166. Other sources for the archaeobotany of the pumpkin include Paul E. Minnis, ed., *People and Plants in Ancient Eastern North America* (Washington, D.C.: Smithsonian Books, 2003); Paul E. Minnis, ed., *People and Plants in Ancient Western North America* (Washington, D.C.: Smithsonian Books, 2004); R. W. Robinson and D. S. Decker-Walters, *Cucurbits* (New York: CAB International, 1997); Bruce D. Smith, *Rivers of Change: Essays on Early Agriculture in Eastern North America* (Washington, D.C.: Smithsonian Institution Press, 1992); R. Lira Saade and S. Montes Hernandez, "Cucurbits," http://www.hort.purdue.edu/newcrop/1492/cucurbits.html (accessed February 2, 2002); C. Margaret Scarry, ed., *Foraging and Farming in the Eastern Woodlands* (Gainesville: University Press of Florida, 1993); Hugh C. Cutler and Thomas W. Whitaker, "History and Distribution of the Cultivated Cucurbits in the Americas," *American Antiquity* 26, no. 4 (1961): 469–85; and A. Hyatt Verrill, *Foods America Gave the World* (Boston: L. C. Page, 1937).

5   Bruce D. Smith, "Origins of Agriculture: Enhanced. Between Foraging and Farming," *Science* 279 (March 13, 1998): 1651–52; Bruce D. Smith, "The Initial Domestication of *Cucurbita pepo* in the Americas 10,000 Years Ago," *Science* 276 (May 9, 1997): 932–34; Bruce D. Smith email exchange with the author, January 17, 2012.

6   Richard A. Yarnell, "The Importance of Native Crops during the Late Archaic and Woodlands Periods," in Scarry, *Foraging and Farming*, 17; Bruce D. Smith email exchange with the author, January 17, 2012.

7   Saade and Hernandez, "Cucurbits," 8; Smith, *Emergence of Agriculture*, 165.

8   Robinson and Decker-Walters, *Cucurbits*, 73. Native Americans domesticated the pear-shaped, green-striped cushaw (*Cucurbita argryosperma*) around seven thousand years ago, but the plant was never propagated outside the Americas, because, scientists have suggested, it bore low-quality fruit. Saade and Hernandez, "Cucurbits," 2.

9   For the most thorough botanical descriptions of pumpkins, see Robinson and Decker-Walters, *Cucurbits*; N. M Nayar and T. A. More, eds., *Cucurbits* (Enfield, N.H.: Science Publishers, 1998); Saade and Hernandez, "Cucurbits"; T. W Whitaker and I. C. Jagger, "Breeding and Improvement of Cucurbits," *Agricultural Yearbook, 1937* (Washington, D.C.: U.S. Department of Agriculture, 1937), 207–32; T. W. Whitaker and Glen N. Davis, *Cucurbits: Botany, Cultivation and Utilization* (New York: Interscience Publishers, 1962); and E. F. Castetter and A. T. Erwin, "A Systematic Study of the Squashes and Pumpkins," *Iowa Agricultural Station Bulletin* 244 (Ames: Iowa State College of Agriculture and

Mechanic Arts, 1927): 108–35. Another important source for horticultural data is *The Cucurbita Network News*. Since 1994, cucurbit scientists D. S. Decker-Williams, Thomas Andres, and Terrence Walters have published this biannual journal devoted to the research and dissemination of knowledge regarding cucurbits. See http://www.cucurbit.org (accessed July 13, 2010). See also the University of Illinois Extension website on pumpkins, http://urbanext.illinois .edu/pumpkins/ (accessed July 13, 2010). For the cucumber's and melon's botanical history, see Patrizia Sebastian, Hanno Schaefer, Ian R. H. Telford, and Susanne S. Renner, "Cucumber (*Cucumis sativus*) and melon (*C. melo*) have numerous wild relatives in Asia and Australia, and the sister species of melon is from Australia," *Proceedings of the National Academy of Sciences of the United States of America* 107, no. 32 (August 10, 2010): 14,269–73.

10 Robinson and Decker-Walters, *Cucurbits*, 24.

11 Smith, *Emergence of Agriculture*, 166.

12 Bruce D. Smith and C. Wesley Cowan, "Domesticated Crop Plants and the Evolution of Food Production Economies in Eastern North America," in Minnis, *People and Plants in Ancient Eastern North America*, 111.

13 Francis B. King, "Early Cultivated Cucurbits in Eastern North America," in *Prehistoric Food Production in North America*, ed. Richard I. Ford (Ann Arbor: Museum of Anthropology, University of Michigan, 1985), 77.

14 King, "Early Cultivated Cucurbits," 79; Smith and Cowan, "Domesticated Crop Plants," 109.

15 Archaeobotanist Bruce Smith provides a clear and concise overview of the processes of plant domestication in the Eastern Woodlands in Bruce D. Smith, "Prehistoric Plant Husbandry in Eastern North America," in *The Origins of Agriculture: An International Perspective*, eds. C. Wesley Cowan and Patty Jo Watson (Washington, D.C.: Smithsonian Institution Press, 1992), 101–14.

16 BCE stands for "before the common era," and CE, "common era."

17 Yarnell, "Importance of Native Crops," 16.

18 Esquire Johnson, interview with Mrs. Asher Wright, October 25, 1875, paraphrased in Arthur C. Parker, *Iroquois Uses of Maize and Other Food Plants*, New York State Museum Bulletin 144 (Albany, N.Y., 1910), 37.

19 Secondary sources rich in primary documentation of American Indians' production and use of pumpkins in the colonial period include Carolyn Raine, *A Woodland Feast: Native American Foodways of the Seventeenth and Eighteenth Centuries* (Hubert Heights, Ohio: Penobscot Press, 1997); U. P. Hedrick, *History of Horticulture in America to 1860* (New York: Oxford University Press, 1950); F. W. Waugh, *Iroquois Foods and Food Preparation* (Ottawa: Government Printing Bureau, 1916); Ann Leighton, *Early American Gardens: "For Meate or Medicine"* (Amherst: University of Massachusetts, 1970); Parker, *Iroquois Uses of Maize*, 90–92; and U. P. Hedrick, *Sturtevant's Notes on Edible Plants* (Albany, N.Y.: J. B. Lyon, 1919), 202–22.

20 Christopher Columbus, *Coleccion de los viajes y descubrimientos*, vol. 1, ed. Martin Fernandez de Navarrete (Madrid, 1825–37), 225, as quoted in A. Gray and J.

H. Trumbull, "Review of DeCandolle's Origin of Cultivated Plants," *American Journal of Science* 25 (1883): 371. Gray and Trumbull, as well as botanical historian Harry S. Paris, stated that they believed Columbus was referring to American pumpkins and squashes, not gourds, in his use of the term *calabash*, because he was more likely to have found the former something new to him and so worthy of observation. Harry S. Paris, "History of the Cultivar-Groups of *Cucurbita pepo*," *Horticultural Reviews* 25 (2001): 86.

21 Alvar Núñez Cabeza de Vaca, *Relation of Alvar Núñez Cabeza de Vaca*, trans. T. Buckingham Smith (Washington, D.C., 1851), as quoted in Gray and Trumbull, "Review of DeCandolle's Origin of Cultivated Plants," 374. Hernando de Soto remarked on seeing fields with pumpkins, beans, and corn planted together near Tampa Bay in 1539. Hernando de Soto, *Discovery and Conquest of Terra Florida* (1611), quoted in Gray and Trumbull, "Review of DeCandolle's Origin of Cultivated Plants," 374.

22 Father Claude Allouez, "Letter to the Reverend Father Superior," 1670, in *The Jesuit Relations and Allied Documents*, vol. 54, *Iroquois, Ottawas, Lower Canada, 1669–1671*, ed. Reuben Gold Thwaites (Cleveland, Ohio: Burrows Brothers, 1896–1901), 207. Captain John Smith recorded pumpkins and squashes growing in Virginia and New England in the early 1600s; Jacques Cartier noted their propagation in New France in 1535; and Thomas Hariot and William Strachey attested to their production in Virginia in 1586 and 1610, respectively. John Smith, *The Description of Virginia* (London, 1612), in *The Complete Works of Capt. John Smith*, vol. 1, ed. Philip L. Barbour (Chapel Hill: University of North Carolina Press, 1986), 158; Smith cited in John Pinkerton, *General Collection of the Best and Most Interesting Voyages and Travels in All Parts of the World*, vol. 13 (London, 1812), 33; John Smith, *A Description of New England* (1616): *An Online Electronic Text*, ed. Paul Royster, http://digitalcommons.unl.edu/cgi/viewcontent.cgi?article=1003&context=etas (accessed January 10, 2010), 40; Jacques Cartier cited in Peter Force, *Collection of . . . Voyages*, vol. 12 (London, 1812), 656; Thomas Hariot, *A Briefe and True Report of the New Found Land of Virginia . . .* (Charlottesville: University of Virginia Press, 2007 [1590]), 14; William Strachey, *The Historie of Travaile into Virginia Britannia* (London: Hakluyt Society, 1849), 72.

23 This issue is discussed in Jayme A. Sokolow, *The Great Encounter: Native Peoples and European Settlers in the Americas, 1492–1800* (Armonk, N.Y.: M. E. Sharpe, 2003), 3–8.

24 Paul Fieldhouse reiterated this point in Fieldhouse, *Food and Nutrition*, 45.

25 The crossbreed will not appear until the next year, when the seeds of the previous year's cross-pollinated fruit produce their offspring. The horticultural description was gleaned from contemporary guides and historic farm journals, including Castetter and Erwin, "Systematic Study of the Squashes and Pumpkins," and the Pumpkin Nook website, www.members.aol.com/ezpumpkin (accessed October 10, 1999).

26   For use of the term *isquoutersquash*, see William Wood, *New England's Prospect*
      (Amherst: University of Massachusetts Press, 1977 [1634]), 36, and for *askutas-
      quash*, see Roger Williams, *Key to the Language of the Indians* (Providence:
      Rhode Island Historical Society Collection, 1827 [1643]), 127, as quoted in
      Parker, *Iroquois Uses of Maize*, 90. The term also appears in John Josselyn, *New-
      England's Rarities Discovered in Birds, Beasts, Fishes, Serpents, and Plants of That
      Country* (Boston: William Veazie, 1865 [1627]), 109. Hedrick, *Sturtevant's Notes*,
      212, contains a list of primary colonial sources that made use of these terms.
      See also the entry for "squash" in *The Oxford English Dictionary* (New York:
      Oxford University Press, 1989).

27   Williams, *Key to the Language of the Indians*, 127, as quoted in Parker, *Iroquois
      Uses of Maize*, 90. In contrast to a pumpkin, for which he provided no physical
      description, Adriaen van der Donck noted in his 1649 *Description of the New
      Netherlands* that "the natives have another species of this vegetable peculiar to
      themselves, called by our people *quaasiens*, a name derived from the aborigi-
      nes, as the plant was not known to us before our intercourse with them. It is
      a delightful fruit, as well to the eye on account of its fine variety of colours,
      as to the mouth for its agreeable taste. . . . It is gathered early in summer, and
      when it is planted in the middle of April, the fruit is fit for eating by the first of
      June." Adriaen van der Donck, *Description of the New Netherlands* (New York:
      New York Historical Society, 1841), 186; online facsimile edition at http://www
      .americanjourneys.org/aj-032/ (accessed October 31, 2006).

28   Smith, *Description of Virginia*, 158; Robert Beverly, *The History and Present State
      of Virginia* (Chapel Hill: University of North Carolina Press, 1947 [1705]), 141.

29   Hariot, *Briefe and True Report*, 14. William Strachey's 1613 dictionary of the
      Virginia Indians' language defined *pumpeon* as *mahcawg*. John Harrington, ed.,
      "The Original Strachey Vocabulary of the Virginia Indian Language," *Bureau
      of Indian Affairs Bulletin 157* (Anthropology Papers 46): 189–202 (Washington,
      D.C.: Government Printing Office, 1955). The "pumpeon" citation is on sheet 12
      of the unpaginated dictionary reproduction inserted in the article.

30   C. C. James, "The Downfall of the Huron Nation," *Transactions of the Royal
      Society of Canada, Second Series*, 1906–1907, vol. 12, section 11 (Ottawa: J. Hope
      and Sons, 1906), 320.

31   The effects of foreign diseases on colonial Indians are discussed in Alfred W.
      Crosby Jr., *Ecological Imperialism: The Biological Expansion of Europe, 900–1900*
      (New York: Cambridge University Press, 1986), and Charles C. Mann, *1491:
      New Revelations of the Americas before Columbus* (New York: Vintage Books,
      2005), especially chapters 2 and 4.

32   For primary and secondary sources on precolonial and colonial American Indian
      societies and agricultural practices in the East, see Ronald Dale Kerr, ed., *Indian
      New England, 1524–1674: A Compendium of Eyewitness Accounts of Native American
      Life* (Pepperell, Mass.: Branch Line Press, 1999); James Axtell, *After Columbus:
      Essays in the Ethnohistory of Colonial North America* (New York: Oxford University

Press, 1988); Karen Ordahl Kupperman, *Indians and English: Facing Off in Early America* (Ithaca, N.Y.: Cornell University Press, 2000), especially 142–73; Mann, *1491*, 33–67; Peter Nabokov with Dean Snow, "Farmers of the Woodlands," and Clara Sue Kidwell, "Systems of Knowledge," both in Alvin M. Josephy Jr., ed., *America in 1492: The World of the Indian Peoples before the Arrival of Columbus* (New York: Knopf, 1992), 119–45 and 369–403, respectively; Howard S. Russell, *Indian New England before the Mayflower* (Hanover, N.H.: University Press of New England, 1980); R. Douglas Hurt, *Indian Agriculture in America* (Lawrence: University of Kansas Press, 1987), 27–41; Cronon, *Changes in the Land*, 34–53; Kathleen J. Bragdon, *Native People of Southern New England, 1500–1650* (Norman: University of Oklahoma Press, 1996); Charles C. Willoughby, "Houses and Gardens of New England Indians," *American Anthropologist* 8, no. 1 (1906): 115–32; and M. K. Bennett, "The Food Economy of the New England Indians, 1605–75," *Journal of Political Economy* 63, no. 5 (1955): 369–97.

33 Cronon, *Changes in the Land*, 34–53; Mann, *1491*, 54–65.

34 "De-o-ha-ko" is cited in Harriet M. Converse, *Myths and Legends of the New York Iroquois* (Albany: University of the State of New York, 1974 [1908]), 185. According to Converse, the source of the term was an 1875 interview with the Iroquois Esquire Johnson by Mrs. Asher Wright. "Dio'he-ko," the inseparable spirits of sustenance, is cited in Arthur C. Parker, *Seneca Myths and Folktales* (Buffalo, N.Y.: Buffalo Historical Society, 1923), 15–16. See also James Herrick, *Iroquois Medical Botany* (Syracuse, N.Y.: Syracuse University Press, 1995), 9. "Tune-ha'kwe" is cited in W. M. Beauchamp, "Onondaga Plant Names," *Journal of American Folklore* 57 (1902): 101.

35 Nicolas Perrot, *Indian Tribes of Upper Mississippi Valley and the Region of the Great Lakes, 1680–1718*, vol. 1 (Cleveland, Ohio: Arthur H. Clark, 1911 [1864]), 102.

36 Walter Ebeling, *Handbook of Indian Foods and Fibers of Arid America* (Berkeley: University of California Press, 1986), 710.

37 Samuel de Champlain, *Voyages of Samuel de Champlain*, ed. W. L. Grant (New York, 1907), 62, as quoted in Cronon, *Changes in the Land*, 43. Van der Donck also described the intercropping technique among Indians in New York. Van der Donck, *Descriptions of the New Netherlands*, 158. Thomas Hariot, who recorded the traditions of Virginia Indians, noted that there was "a yarde spare ground betweene every hole [where corn was planted]: where according to discretion here and there, they set as many Beanes and Peaze: in divers places also among the seedes of Macocqwer, Melden and Planta Solis." Hariot, *Briefe and True Report*, 14.

38 John White's drawing *Indian Village of Secotan, 1585–1586*, is at the British Museum. Theodore de Bry's engraving *The Tovvne of Secota* is published in Hariot, *Briefe and True Report*, 61.

39 Hariot stated that crops "are set or sowed, sometimes in groundes a part and severally by themselves; but for the most part together in one ground mixtly." Hariot, *Briefe and True Report*, 14.

40 Sources for colonial Indian food practices include Kupperman, *Indians and English*, especially 157–64; Barrie Kavasch, "Native Foods of New England," in *Enduring Traditions: The Native Peoples of New England*, ed. Laurie Weinstein (Westport, Conn.: Bergin and Garvey, 1994), 5–30; Richard I. Ford, *An Ethnobiology Source Book: The Uses of Plants and Animals by American Indians* (New York: Garland, 1986), which contains a collection of earlier publications on the subject; Parker, *Iroquois Uses of Maize*; Waugh, *Iroquois Foods*; Daniel Moerman, *Native American Ethnobotany* (Portland, Ore.: Timber Press, 1998); Daniel Moerman, *American Medical Ethnobotany: A Reference Dictionary* (New York: Garland 1977); Ebeling, *Indian Foods and Fibers*; and Raine, *Woodland Feast*.

41 Nutritional data from University of California-Davis, "Vegetable Research and Information Center: Home Vegetable Gardening: Pumpkin," http://www.aces .uiuc.edu/%7Enutrican/tables/pumpkin.html (accessed February 22, 2000); University of Iowa, "Nutrient Analysis for Pumpkin," pumpkin.html (accessed February 22, 2000); and Nicola Hill, *The Pumpkin Cookbook* (London: Reed International, 1996), 7.

42 Hierosme Lalemant, "On the Mission of Sainte Elizabeth among the Atontrataronnon Algonkians," in Thwaites, *Jesuit Relations*, vol. 27, *Hurons, Lower Canada (1642–1645)*, 65.

43 Gabriel Sagard, *Le Grand Voyage du Pays des Hurons*, 3rd ed. (Paris, 1865 [1632]), vol. 1, 96, as quoted in Parker, *Iroquois Uses of Maize*, 16. Daniel Gookin described a typical New England meal of "boiled maize . . . mixed with kidney-beans, or sometimes without. Also they frequently boil in this pottage fish and flesh of all sorts. . . . Also they mix with the said pottage several sorts of roots . . . and pompions and squashes." Daniel Gookin, "Historical Collections of the Indians in New England," in Massachusetts Historical Society, *Collections of . . . the Year 1792*, 1st series (Boston, 1792 [1674]), vol. 1, 150, as quoted in Bennett, "Food Economy of the New England Indians," 380.

44 Perrot, *Indian Tribes of the Upper Mississippi Valley*, 113.

45 Louis-Armand de Lom d'Arce Lahontan attested to this practice among the Iroquois in the 1680s. Louis-Armand de Lom d'Arce Lahontan, *New Voyages to North America* (London: Printed for H. Bonwicke et al., 1703), vol. 1, 369. The Jesuit missionary Jean de Brébeuf did as well among the Hurons in 1636. Jean de Brébeuf, "Journal des Pères Jesuites, en l'année 1648," in Thwaites, *Jesuit Relations*, vol. 32, *Gaspé, Hurons, Lower Canada (1647–1648)*, 101.

46 Lahontan, *New Voyages*, vol. 1, 369.

47 Harmen Meyndertsz van Bogaert, *Narrative of a Journey into the Mohawk and Oneida Country, 1634–1635* (Syracuse, N.Y.: Syracuse University Press, 1988), 12. Peter Kalm described the same process among Indians he visited in the Northeast in the 1730s. Peter Kalm, *Peter Kalm's Travels in North America*, ed. Adolph B. Benson (New York: Wilson-Erickson, 1937), 517–18. See also Waverly Root and Richard de Rochemont, *Eating in America: A History* (New York: Echo Press, 1976), 40.

48 Waugh, *Iroquois Foods*, 114–15.

49 Hariot, *Briefe and True Report*, 15.

50 For example, Jean de Brébeuf noted of the Huron village of Ihonatiria that "still less do we get meat, which is even more rarely seen here [than fish]." Brébeuf, "Journal des Pères Jesuites," 101. Sieur Aubry made similar observations from Quebec in 1723. Sieur Aubry, "Lettre à Monsieur son Frerè," in Thwaites, *Jesuit Relations*, vol. 67, *Lower Canada, Abenakis, Louisiana (1716–1727)*, 213.

51 Joseph Francois Lafitau, *Moeurs des Sauvages Ameriquains, Book II* (Paris, 1724), 47, as quoted in Russell, *Indian New England*, 177. Russell also cited Jonathan Carver, who stated that pumpkins stored for four to five months, and Paul LeJeune, who noted in the 1760s that the Hidatsa packed corn around squash in underground pits. Although these sources date from later than the early contact period, it seems probable that the customs were carried on from earlier traditions. Jonathan Carver, *Three Years' Travels through the Interior Parts of North America . . . 1766–1768* (Philadelphia: Key and Simpson, 1796), 349; Paul LeJeune, "The Conversion of the Savages Who Have Been Baptized in New France during This Year, 1610," in Thwaites, *Jesuit Relations*, vol. 1, 103, as quoted in Russell, *Indian New England*, 177.

52 Milo Milton Quaife, ed., *The Western Country in the Seventeenth Century: The Memoirs of Lamothe Cadillac and Pierre Liette* (Chicago: Lakeside Press, 1947), 125–26, as quoted in Hurt, *Indian Agriculture*, 35.

53 For practicality, Indians usually consumed only the infertile male flowers. Michael A. Weiner, *Earth Medicine—Earth Food: Plant Remedies, Drugs, and Natural Foods of the North American Indians* (New York: Fawcett Columbine, 1972), 205.

54 John Bartram, *Observations on the Inhabitants, Climate, Soil, Rivers, Productions, Animals, and Other Matters Worthy of Notice, made by John Bartram in His Travels from Pennsylvania to Onondaga, Oswego and the Lake Ontario, in Canada* (Ann Arbor: University Microfilms, 1966 [1751]), 60.

55 Moerman, *Native American Ethnobotany*, 187–88. These uses are also documented in Moerman, *American Medical Ethnobotany*, 333; Daniel E. Moerman, *Medicinal Plants of Native America* (Ann Arbor: University of Michigan Museum of Anthropology, 1986), 142; Herrick, *Iroquois Medical Botany*, 9 and 20; and James A. Duke, *Handbook of Northeastern Indian Medicinal Plants* (Lincoln, Mass.: Quarterman Publications, 1986), 44.

56 Jean de Brébeuf, "Important Advice for Those Whom It Shall Please God to Call to New France, and Especially to the Country of the Hurons," in Thwaites, *Jesuit Relations*, vol. 10, *Hurons (1636)*, 101. Henry Hudson reported in 1610 from the Catskill Mountains, "This morning the people came aboard and brought us eares of Ind corne, and Pompions, and Tobacco which we bought for trifles." Robert Juet, *The Third Voyage of Master Henry Hudson*, in J. Franklin James, ed., *Narratives of New Netherland, 1609–1664* (New York: Charles Scribner's Sons, 1909 [1610]), 21.

57   Daniel H. Usner Jr., "Food Marketing and Interethnic Exchange in the 18th-Century Lower Mississippi Valley," *Food and Foodways* 1 (1986): 284.

58   Kathleen Bragdon argued that the value of corn rose after colonization because of the increase in demand from the colonists. Bragdon, *Native People of Southern New England*, 100–101.

59   Parker, *Iroquois Uses of Maize*, 91–92. Publications on Indian mythology and cosmology that include references to squashes and pumpkins include Converse, *Myths and Legends*, 63–67 and 184–86; Terri Hardin, *Legends and Lore of the American Indians* (New York: Barnes and Noble Books, 1993), 44–45; and George Lankford, *Native American Legends* (Little Rock, Ark.: August House, 1987), 155–56.

60   Herrick, *Iroquois Medical Botany*, 9; Converse, *Myths and Legends*, 185–86.

61   Parker, *Seneca Myths and Folktales*, 64, as cited in Lankford, *Native American Legends*, 156.

62   Moerman, *Native American Ethnobotany*, 188.

63   Jacques Marquette, "Of the Mission of St. Ignace among the Tion-nontateron-nons," in Thwaites, *Jesuit Relations*, vol. 57, *Lower Canada, Iroquois, Ottawas, 1672–1673*, 251.

64   Bartram, *Observations on the Inhabitants*, 36–37.

65   See Hedrick, *Sturtevant's Notes*, 202–22, and *The Oxford English Dictionary* for the linguistic history of the terms *cucumber, melon, pumpkin,* and *gourd.*

66   Stephen Switzer, *Practical Kitchen Gardiner* (London: Thomas Woodward, 1727), 115.

67   Pliny the Elder, *The Natural History* (77 CE), eds. John Bostock and H. T. Riley, http://www.perseus.edu/cgi-bin/ptext?lookup=Plin.+Nat.+toc (accessed October 26, 2007). Ancient sources for the term *pumpkin* are also noted in many herbals, such as John Parkinson, *Theatrum Botanicum: The Theater of Plants of an Universiall and Complete Herball* (London: Thomas Cotes, 1640), 768–71. The introduction of the melon into Greece and Rome is discussed in Reay Tannahill, *Food in History* (New York: Three Rivers Press, 1988), 657.

68   Raymond Astbury, "The Apocolocyntosis," *Classical Review* 38, no. 1 (1988): 44–50; Norrman and Haarberg, *Nature and Language*, 54.

69   A. Palmer, "The Apocolocyntosis of Seneca," *Classical Review* 2, no. 6 (1888): 181.

70   On herbals, see Frank J. Anderson, *An Illustrated History of the Herbals* (New York: Columbia University Press, 1997); Agnes Arber, *Herbals: Their Origins and Evolution. A Chapter in the History of Botany, 1470–1670* (Cambridge: Cambridge University Press, 1938); Franz Schwartz, *The Origin of Cultivated Plants* (Cambridge, Mass.: Harvard University Press, 1966); Edward Lee Greene, *Landmarks of Botanical History: A Study of Certain Epochs in the Development of the Science of Botany* (Palo Alto, Calif.: Stanford University Press, 1983 [1909]); and Henry Lowood, "The New World and the European Catalog of Nature," in Karen O. Kupperman, ed., *America in the European Consciousness, 1493–1750* (Chapel Hill: University of North Carolina Press, 1995), 295–317.

71 Harry Paris et al., "First Known Image of *Cucurbita* in Europe, 1503–1508," *Annals of Botany* 98 (2006): 46.

72 Lowood, "New World," 305.

73 Jacques Cartier, *Brief recit & succinct narration de la navigation faicte es Ysles de Canada, Hochelage and Saguenay and autres* (Paris, 1545, 1863), 24 and 31, cited in Hedrick, *Sturtevant's Notes*, 216.

74 *Melopepo compressus* is in Jacobus Theodorus, *Eicones Plantarum* (Frankfurt am Main, 1590), 470–90, cited in Paris, "History of the Cultivar-Groups," 98. See also Joseph Tournefort, *The Compleat Herbal* (London, 1719–30), 34, for the term *melopepo*. *Pepo maximus oblongus* appears in Gerarde, *Herball*, 918–22. *Cucurbita indica rotundus* is used in Jacques Dalechamp, *Historia Generalis Plantarum*, vol. 1 (Lugdini: G. Rovillius, 1587), 616–26. *Cucurbita major* and *Cucurbita minor* appear in Gerarde, *Herball*, 909–25, and Rembert Dodoens, *A Niewe Herball or Historie of Plantes* (London, 1586), 586–93. "*Millions or Pompions*" is used in Parkinson, *Theatrum Botanicum*, 768–71. *Pepo maximus rotundus* is used in William Salmon, *The English Herbal; or History of Plants* (London: I. Dawes for H. Rhodes and J. Taylor, 1710), 698.

75 Herbal historians attest that the shape of the fruit and leaves in Fuchs's drawing indicated that he depicted an American pumpkin. See Paris, "History of the Cultivar-Groups," 88; Paris, "First Known Image of *Cucurbita*," 41; Anderson, *Illustrated History of the Herbals*, 141; and Arber, *Herbals*, 69.

76 Mark Graubard hypothesized that maize might have been called "turkie wheat" because it was introduced to Europe from America via Turkey. Mark Graubard, *Man's Food, Its Rhyme or Reason* (New York: Macmillan, 1943), 117. The botanist Harry Paris, however, stated that Europeans in this time period used the term more generically for any foreign product. Paris, "History of the Cultivar-Groups," 90.

77 Parkinson, *Theatrum Botanicum*, 770, as quoted in Gray and Trumbull, "DeCandolle's Origin of Cultivated Plants," 370.

78 Gerarde, *Herball*, 918.

79 See Keith Thomas, *Man and the Natural World: Changing Attitudes in England, 1500–1800* (New York: Oxford University Press, 1983), 65, and Leighton, *Early American Gardens*, 75.

80 Gerarde, *Herball*, 918.

81 As another example, summer squash were frequently called "vine apples" and a "lesser sort of pumpkin." See Beverly, *History and Present State of Virginia*, 141, and Josselyn, *New-England's Rarities*, 109, respectively. For a description of the culinary uses of summer squash, see John Worlidge, *Systema Horti-culture* (London, 1683), 184, and Hedrick, *Sturtevant's Notes*, 212.

82 Ken Albala, *Eating Right in the Renaissance* (Berkeley: University of California Press, 2002), 232–40; Tannahill, *Food in History*, 202–17.

83 Richard J. Hooker, *Food and Drink in America: A History* (Indianapolis, Ind.: Bobbs-Merrill, 1981), 5.

84 Dodoens, *Niewe Herball*, 681. Other herbalists verified Dodoens's account. See, for example, *The Great Herball* (London: Jhon Kynge, 1561), under the entry "*Cucurbita*."

85 Culinary histories of Europe in this time period include Jean-Louis Flandrin and Massimo Montanari, eds., *Food: A Culinary History* (New York: Columbia University Press, 1999); Phyllis Pray Bober, *Art, Culture, and Cuisine: Ancient and Medieval Gastronomy* (Chicago: University of Chicago Press, 1999); Philippa Pullar, *Consuming Passions: A History of English Food and Appetite* (London: Hamilton, 1970); Giovanni Rebora, *Culture of the Fork: A Brief History of Food in Europe* (New York: Columbia University Press, 2001); Melitta Weiss Adamson, *Food in Medieval Times* (Westport, Conn.: Greenwood Press, 2004); and Lynne Elliott, *Food and Feasts in the Middle Ages* (New York: Crabtree, 2004).

86 *The Great Herball*, entry "*Cucurbita*."

87 Harry S. Paris and Jules Janick, "Early Evidence for the Culinary Use of Squash Flowers in Italy," *Chronica Horticulturae* 45 (2005): 20–21.

88 Reindert Falkenburg, "Matters of Taste: Pieter Aertsen's Market Scenes, Eating Habits, and Pictorial Rhetoric in the Sixteenth Century," in *The Object as Subject: Studies in the Interpretation of Still Life*, ed. Anne W. Lowenthal (Princeton, N.J.: Princeton University Press, 1996), 16.

89 Albala, *Eating Right in the Renaissance*, 236.

90 Paris et al., "First Known Images of *Cucurbita*," 41–47. Evidence of the first American cucurbit of any sort is an illustration of a bottle-shaped wild squash (*Cucurbita pepo* subsp. *texana*) in *Grand Heures d'Anne de Bretagne*, a prayer book illustrated between 1503 and 1508 by Jean Bourdichon, the famous court painter to four French kings. Jules Janick and Harry S. Paris, "The Cucurbit Images (1515–1518) of the Villa Farnesina, Rome," *Annals of Botany* 97 (2006): 165–76.

91 "Giuseppe Arcimboldo," in Jane Turner, ed., *The Dictionary of Art* (London: Macmillan, 1996), 374. See also Andre Pieyre de Mand, *Arcimboldo the Marvelous* (New York: Abrams, 1978), and Pontus Hulten, ed., *The Arcimboldo Effect: Transformation of the Face from the Sixteenth Century to Twentieth Century* (New York: Abbeville, 1977).

92 William Shakespeare, *The Merry Wives of Windsor*, Act 3, iii, in *The Complete Works of William Shakespeare*, ed. William Aldis Wright (Garden City, N.Y.: Garden City Books, 1936), 800.

93 Works on Dutch life and genre painting in the sixteenth and seventeenth centuries include Simon Schama, *The Embarrassment of Riches: An Interpretation of Dutch Culture in the Golden Age* (Berkeley: University of California Press, 1988); Henry Nichols Blake Clark, "The Impact of Seventeenth-Century Dutch and Flemish Genre Painting on American Genre Painting, 1800–1865" (Ph.D. diss., University of Delaware, 1982); Peter C. Sutton, *Masters of Seventeenth-Century Dutch Genre Painting* (Philadelphia: University of Pennsylvania Press, 1984); Ildiko Ember, *Delights for the Senses: Dutch and Flemish Still-Life Paintings* (Budapest: Szepmuveszeti Muzeum/Museum of Fine Arts, Budapest, 1989); R.

L. Falkenburg, "Iconographical Connections between Antwerp Landscapes, Market Scenes and Kitchen Pieces, 1500–1580," *Oud Holland* 102 (1988): 114–26; Falkenburg, "Matters of Taste," 13–28; Sam Segal, *A Prosperous Past: The Sumptuous Still Life in the Netherlands, 1600–1700* (The Hague: SDU Publishers, 1988); Christopher Brown, *Images of a Golden Past: Dutch Genre Painting of the 17th Century* (New York: Abbeville, 1984); Donna R. Barnes and Peter G. Rose, *Matters of Taste: Food and Drink in Seventeenth-Century Dutch Art and Life* (Syracuse, N.Y.: Syracuse University Press, 2002); and Margaret A. Sullivan, "Aertsen's Kitchen and Market Scenes: Audience and Innovation in North Art," *Art Bulletin* 81, no. 2 (1999): 236–66.

94   Barnes and Rose, *Matters of Taste*, 9–10.

95   Brown, *Images of a Golden Past*, 42.

96   Sullivan, "Aertsen's Kitchen and Market Scenes," 240.

97   This observation was made in Ardis Grosjean, "Toward an Interpretation of Pieter Aertsen's Profane Iconography," *Konsthistorick Tidskrift* 43 (1974): 121.

98   Falkenberg, "Iconographic Connections," 19.

99   See Nanette Salomon, *Shifting Priorities: Gender and Genre in Seventeenth-Century Dutch Painting* (Stanford, Calif.: Stanford University Press, 2004); Sutton, *Masters of Seventeenth-Century Dutch Genre Painting*, 75; and Brown, *Images of a Golden Past*, 58.

100   Parkinson, *Theatrum Botanicum*, 768. For discussions of the pumpkin's sexual connotations, see Anderson, *Herbals*, 195–98; Leighton, *Early American Gardens*, 87; and many references under "cucurbitic connotations: sex" in the index to Norrman and Haarberg, *Nature and Culture*, 226.

101   Two classic works on the idea of wilderness in colonial America are Nash, *Wilderness and the American Mind*, and Huth, *Nature and the Americans*. Other significant works include John Stilgoe, *Common Landscape of America, 1580–1845* (New Haven, Conn.: Yale University Press, 1982); Thomas, *Man and the Natural World*; and Schama, *Landscape and Memory*, especially 517–38. Schama took an optimist's view of the health and security of the natural world, based on his belief in the preservation of Westerners' powerful nature myths. See also Michael Lewis, ed., *American Wilderness: A New History* (New York: Oxford University Press, 2007); Max Oelschlaeger, *The Idea of Wilderness: From Prehistory to the Age of Ecology* (New Haven, Conn.: Yale University Press, 1991); and Steinberg, *Down to Earth*.

102   Smith, *Description of New England, 1616*, 183.

103   George Withers quoted in Smith, *Description of New England*, 89.

104   Works about European images and ideas concerning America include Kupperman, *America in the European Consciousness*; John Huxtable Elliott, *The Old World and the New, 1492–1650* (New York: Oxford University Press, 1950); and Rachel Doggett, ed., *New World of Wonders: European Images of the Americas, 1492–1700* (Seattle: University of Washington Press, 1992).

105   Wood, *New England's Prospect*, 36.

106 De Soto, *Discovery and Conquest of Terra Florida*, 32, as quoted in Hedrick, *History of Horticulture*, 6.

107 Beverly, *History and Present State of Virginia*, 141.

108 Theodore de Bry, *Brevis Narratio Eorum Quae in Florida Americae* . . . (Frankfurt am Main, 1591).

109 Like other objects in the print, the artist's pumpkins might have been based on impressions gleaned from travelers' accounts or fanciful imaginings rather than firsthand observations. These pumpkin plants, in particular, are exact replicas of the drawing of *Cucumis turcicus* found in Leonhard Fuchs's 1542 *De historia Stirpium*, described earlier.

110 A reproduction and a description of the painting appear in Barnes and Rose, *Matters of Taste*, 116–17.

2. "THE TIMES WHEREIN OLD POMPION WAS A SAINT": FROM PUMPKIN BEER TO PUMPKIN PIE, 1600 TO 1799

1 John W. Bennett, "Food and Culture in Southern Illinois: A Preliminary Report," *American Sociological Review*, vol. 7, no. 5 (1942): 646, as quoted in Jay Allan Anderson, "'A Solid Sufficiency': An Ethnography of Yeoman Foodways in Stuart England" (Ph.D. diss., University of Pennsylvania, 1971), 277.

2 Edward Johnson, *Wonder-Working Providence of Sions Savior in New England* (Delmar, N.Y.: Scholar's Facsimiles and Reprints, 1974 [1654]), 84.

3 John Smith, *Description of Virginia* (Richmond, Va., 1819), 30, as quoted in Lucien Carr, "The Food of Certain American Indians and Their Methods of Preparing It," *Proceedings of the American Antiquarian Society*, April 24, 1895 (Worcester, Mass.: Charles Hamilton), 9.

4 Works on early encounters between Indians and settlers include Kupperman, *Indians and English*; Sokolow, *Great Encounter*; Ronald Wright, *Stolen Continents: The Americas through Indian Eyes since 1492* (Boston: Houghton Mifflin, 1992); Alden T. Vaughan, *New England Encounters: Indians and Euroamericans, ca. 1600–1850* (Boston: Northeastern University Press, 1999); James Axtell, *Beyond 1492: Encounters in Colonial North America* (New York: Oxford University Press, 1992); James Axtell, *The European and the Indian: Essays in the Ethnohistory of Colonial North America* (New York: Oxford University Press, 1981); James Axtell, *Natives and Newcomers: The Cultural Origins of North America* (New York: Oxford University Press, 2001); Peter C. Mancall and James H. Merrell, eds., *American Encounters: Natives and Newcomers from European Contact to Indian Removal, 1500–1850* (New York: Routledge, 2000); William W. Fitzhugh, ed., *Cultures in Contact: The Impact of European Contacts on Native American Cultural Institutions, A.D. 1000–1800* (Washington, D.C.: Smithsonian Institution Press, 1985); Daniel K. Richter, *Facing East from Indian Country: A Native History of Early America* (Cambridge, Mass.: Harvard University Press, 2001); and Peter Nabokov, ed., *Native American Testimony: An Anthology of*

Indian and White Relations, First Encounter to Dispossession (New York: Crowell, 1978).

5   Van Bogaert, *Narrative of a Journey into the Mohawk and Oneida Country*, 12, journal entry for December 30, 1634.

6   Winslow, *Mourt's Relation*, Section 1, n.p.

7   William Bradford, *History of Plymouth Plantation*, Massachusetts Historical Collection, vol. 3, 1912 [1606–46], 129, as quoted in Carr, "Food of Certain American Indians," 9.

8   Works on the history of the American Thanksgiving include James Deetz and Jay Anderson, "The Ethno-Gastronomy of Thanksgiving," *Saturday Review of Science*, November 25, 1972, 29–39; Diana Karter Appelbaum, *Thanksgiving: An American Holiday, an American History* (New York: Facts on File, 1984); Benjamin Botkin, ed., *A Treasury of New England Folklore: Stories, Ballads, and Traditions of Yankee Folk* (New York: American Legacy Press, 1989 [1965]); Hennig Cohen and Tristram Potter Coffin, eds., *The Folklore of American Holidays* (Detroit: Gale, 1999); Lucille Recht Penner, *The Thanksgiving Book* (New York: Hastings House, 1986); and printed materials in the vertical file in the Folklore Division of the Library of Congress. Two older but meticulously researched histories are W. DeLoss Love Jr., *The Fast and Thanksgiving Days of New England* (Boston: Houghton Mifflin, 1895), and Ralph Linton and Adelin Linton, *We Gather Together: The Story of Thanksgiving* (New York: Henry Schuman, 1949). Walter Tittle's *Colonial Holidays* (New York: Doubleday Page, 1910) contains many primary quotations and citations about the holiday.

9   John Parkinson, *Paradisi i Sole Paradisus Terrestris* (Norwood, N.J.: W. J. Johnson, 1975 [1629]), 526.

10 Hariot, *Briefe and True Report*, 14.

11 Gerarde, *Herball*, 918. Peter Kalm noted "the white color" of the pompion's pulp, though he was possibly referring to a zucchini. Kalm, *Travels in North America*, vol. 2, 518.

12 Tournefort, *Compleat Herbal*, 34.

13 Jean de La Quintinie, *The Compleat Gard'ner*, eds. George London and Henry Wise (London: M. Gillyflower, 1690), 190.

14 Lahontan, *New Voyages to North America*, 369.

15 La Quintinie, *Compleat Gard'ner*, 190.

16 Josselyn, *New-England's Rarities*, 109.

17 Ralph Hamor, *A True Discourse of the Present State of Virginia* (New York: Da Capo Press, 1971 [1615]), 21–22.

18 Philip Miller, "Cucurbita," in *The Gardener's Dictionary* (London: Printed by the author, 1735), n.p., http://www.archive.org/stream/gardenersdictioo3millgoog#page/n419/mode/2up (accessed March 18, 2011).

19 Edward Ward, *A Trip to New-England with a Character of the Country and People, both English and Indian* (New York: Burt Franklin, 1970 [1699]), 69–70. One of the best, most thoroughly researched works on colonial foodways is Sarah F.

McMahon, "A Comfortable Subsistence: The Changing Composition of Diet in Rural New England, 1620–1840," *William and Mary Quarterly* 42, no. 1 (1985): 26–65. McMahon used probate records to determine the foodways of residents of Middlesex County, Massachusetts. Jay Anderson's "A Solid Sufficiency" is another good source. For more general histories on food in America, see Root and Rochemont, *Eating in America*; Hooker, *Food and Drink in America*; Richard O. Cummings, *The American and His Food: A History of Food Habits in the United States* (Chicago: University of Chicago Press, 1940); Eleanor Noderer, ed., *The American Heritage Cookbook and Illustrated History of American Eating and Drinking* (New York: American Heritage, 1964); Booth, *Hung, Strung, and Potted*; Pullar, *Consuming Passions*; Tannahill, *Food in History*; Camp, *American Foodways*; Don Yoder, "Folk Cookery," in *Folklore and Folklife: An Introduction*, ed. Richard Dorson (Chicago: University of Chicago Press, 1972); and Elaine N. McIntosh, *American Food Habits in Historical Perspective* (Westport, Conn.: Praeger, 1995).

20   Francis Higginson, *New England's Plantation* (Salem, Mass.: Essex Book and Print Club, 1908 [1630]), 7.

21   Edward Winslow, *Good News from New England* (London: Printed I. D. John Dawson for W. Bladen and J. Bellamie, 1624), 204; "The Pumpkin in Poetry," *Daily Evening Bulletin* (San Francisco), November 28, 1891. The newspaper article states that the poem was written by a colonist in 1630. The poem has been reprinted in many sources; see, for example, Mary Caroline Crawford, *Social Life in Old New England* (Boston: Little, Brown, 1915), 472.

22   Anderson, "Solid Sufficiency," 220.

23   Josselyn, *New-England's Rarities*, 46.

24   Hamor, *True Discourse*, 21–22.

25   Parkinson, *Paradisi i Sole*, 526.

26   Ward, *Trip to New-England*, 50.

27   Historians Jack Greene and J. R. Pole referred to this initial period of settlement, before strong social and economic stratifications developed and while colonists were simply trying to survive in their new environment, as a time of "social simplification." See Jack Greene and J. R. Pole, "Reconstructing British-American Colonial History," in *Establishing Exceptionalism: Historiography and the Colonial Americas*, ed. Amy T. Bushnell (Aldershot, U.K.: Variorum, 1995), 1–17. See also Michael Zuckerman, "Identity in British America: Unease in Eden," in *Colonial Identity in the Atlantic World, 1500–1800*, eds. Nicholas Canny and Anthony Pagden (Princeton, N.J.: Princeton University Press, 1987), 115–57.

28   Winters quotation from James Phinney Baxter, "The Trelawny Papers," in *Documentary History of the State of Maine*, Collections of the Maine Historical Society, second series, vol. 3, 50, as quoted in Clarence A. Day, "A History of Maine Agriculture, 1604–1860," *University of Maine Bulletin* 56, no. 11 (1954): 10. For the history of corn, see Herman J. Viola and Carolyn Margolis, *Seeds of*

Change: A Quincentennial Commemoration (Washington, D.C.: Smithsonian Institution Press, 1991), 23–25, and Fussell, *Story of Corn*. General histories of colonial agriculture include R. Douglas Hurt, *American Agriculture: A Brief History* (Ames: Iowa State University Press, 1994), 35–77; Percy Wells Bidwell and John I. Falconer, *History of Agriculture in the Northern United States, 1620–1860* (Clifton, N.J.: A. M. Kelley, 1973), 5–145; Willard W. Cochrane, *The Development of American Agriculture: A Historical Analysis* (Minneapolis: University of Minnesota Press, 1979), 1–56; Hedrick, *History of Horticulture*, 1–175; Howard S. Russell, *A Long, Deep Furrow: Three Centuries of Farming in New England* (Hanover, N.H.: University Press of New England, 1976), 3–256; and John T. Schlebecker, *Whereby We Thrive: A History of American Farming, 1607–1972* (Ames: Iowa State University Press, 1975), 3–137.

29 Cochrane, *Development of American Agriculture*, 22.

30 For New England colonial economic conditions and town plans, see John Stilgoe, *Common Landscape of America*, 3–29 and 43–58; Cronon, *Changes in the Land*, 54–170; Cochrane, *Development of American Agriculture*, 13–27; John W. Reps, *Making of Urban America: A History of City Planning in the United States* (Princeton, N.J.: Princeton University Press, 1965), 115–46; and Michael Zuckerman, *Peaceable Kingdoms: New England Towns in the Eighteenth Century* (New York: Knopf, 1970). According to historian Edward Price, New Englanders also abandoned the nucleated town plan because the British Crown disavowed land titles that were granted by colonial towns. See Edward T. Price, *Dividing the Land: Early American Beginnings of Our Private Mosaic* (Chicago: University of Chicago Press, 1995), 65–85.

31 Colonial historians have debated the degree to which New England farmers should be considered capitalists. Cronon, in *Changes in the Land*, Stilgoe, in *Common Landscape*, and Hurt, in *American Agriculture*, argued that despite the small scale of operations in New England, the settlers were linked to a capitalist, for-profit economy. Others, such as James Henretta, in "Families and Farms: Mentalité in Pre-Industrial America," *William and Mary Quarterly* 35 (1979): 3–32, and Daniel Vickers, in "Competency and Competition: Economic Culture in Early America," *William and Mary Quarterly* 47 (1990): 3–29, concluded that settlers maintained subsistence levels of agriculture until the nineteenth century and therefore should not be considered capitalists. For an overview of the debate, see Allan Kulikoff, "The Transition to Capitalism in Rural America," *William and Mary Quarterly* 46 (1989): 13–33.

32 Johnson, *Wonder-Working Providence*, 175.

33 Faith Jaycox, *An Eyewitness History: The Colonial Era* (New York: Facts on File, 2002), 124.

34 Thomas L. Purvis, *Colonial America to 1763* (New York: Facts on File, 1999), 13.

35 Jack Greene, *The Pursuit of Happiness: The Social Development of Early Modern British Colonies and the Formation of American Culture* (Chapel Hill: University of North Carolina Press, 1988), 65–66.

36 Ward, *Trip to New-England*, 57.

37 "Manufacturer and Other Products Listed in the Rates on Imports and Exports Est'd by the House of Parliament," June 24, 1660, in George F. Dow, *Every Day Life in the Massachusetts Bay Colony* (New York: Benjamin Blom, 1935), Appendix E, 246–57.

38 Robert Johnson, *Nova Britannia: Offering Most Excellent Fruits by Planting in Virginia* (New York: Da Capo Press, 1969 [1609]), 24.

39 Johnson, *Wonder-Working Providence*, 84.

40 Gerarde, *Herball*, 918.

41 Parkinson, *Paradisi i Sole*, 526.

42 Ibid.

43 Nathaniel Ward, *Simple Cobler of Aggawam in America* (London: J. D. and R. I. for S. Bowtell, 1647), as quoted in Norrman and Haarberg, *Culture and Language*, 51. Alfred W. Crosby Jr. discussed the concept of American cultural inferiority in *The Columbian Exchange: Biological and Cultural Consequences of 1492* (Westport, Conn.: Greenwood Press, 1972), 20–21.

44 According to Samuel Peters, *General History of Connecticut* (New York: D. Appleton, 1877 [1781]), 153–54, the nickname "pumpkin-head" originated in colonial hairstyles. Without a hint of amusement, Peters explained, "New Haven is celebrated for having given the name of 'pumpkin-heads' to all the New Englanders. It originated from the 'Blue Laws,' which enjoined every male to have his hair cut round by a cap. When caps were not to be had, they substituted the hard shell of a pumpkin, which being put on the head every Saturday, the hair is cut by the shell all around the head."

45 Ward, *Trip to New-England*, 52.

46 Crawford, *Social Life in Old New England*, 472.

47 A reproduction and a brief essay on the painting appear in Marzia Cataldi Gallo et al., *Il Giardino de Flora: Natura e simbolo nell'immagine dei fiori* (Genoa: Sagep Editrice, 1986), 30–32 and plates 8 and 9.

48 See Erika Tietze-Conrat, *Dwarfs and Jesters in Art* (London: Phaidon Press, 1957), 81–82 and figure 86. The painting appears as plate 10 in Norrman and Haarberg, *Nature and Language*.

49 Bradford, *History of Plymouth Plantation*, 96, as quoted in Zuckerman, *Peaceable Kingdoms*, 28.

50 Nicholas Rogers, in *Halloween*, 11–22, offered a revisionist history of Halloween, arguing that Samhain's image as the lord of the dead is a popular misconception. See also Santino, "Night of the Wandering Souls," 43–50; Santino, "Introduction: Festivals of Life and Death," *Halloween and Other Festivals*, xiv–xix; Bannatyne, *Halloween*, 19–50; and Skal, *Death Makes a Holiday*, 36 and 62–66.

51 Bannatyne, *Halloween*, 14–16 and 39–40.

52 One of the most definitive works on the Salem witch trails is John Demos, *Entertaining Satan: Witchcraft and the Culture of Early New England* (New York:

Oxford University Press, 1982). Bannatyne, in *Halloween*, 23, noted the existence of laws against the use of magic.

53 Johnson, *Wonder-Working Providence*, 56.

54 Raymond Williams wrote, "And so we have this situation of the great interferers, some of the most effective interferers of all time, proclaiming the necessity of non-interference." Williams, "Idea of Nature," 79.

55 Benjamin Thompson, *New England's Crisis*, ed. James Frothingham Hunnewell (Boston: Club of Odd Volumes, 1894 [1673]), 5–6.

56 Jack Greene made this argument in *Pursuits of Happiness*.

57 Cronon, *Changes in the Land*, 108–26.

58 *Maryland Journal and Baltimore Daily Advertiser*, March 8, 1793, cited in Hedrick, *History of Horticulture*, 113.

59 Hedrick, *History of Horticulture*, 174.

60 Miller, "Cucurbita."

61 Carver, *Three Years' Travels*, 349.

62 Kalm, *Travels in North America*, vol. 2, 516.

63 For synopses of the development of the Linnaean system of classification, see Pamela Regis, *Describing Early America: Bartram, Jefferson, Crevecoeur, and the Rhetoric of Natural History* (DeKalb: Northern Illinois University, 1992), 8–14; David Quammen, *The Reluctant Mr. Darwin: An Intimate Portrait of Charles Darwin and the Making of His Theory of Evolution* (New York: Atlas Books/Norton, 2006), 98–99; Thomas, *Man and the Natural World*, 64–66; and Ann Leighton, *American Gardens in the Eighteenth Century: "For Use or for Delight"* (Amherst: University of Massachusetts Press, 1976), 94–99. Scientists today use a more varied, or "natural," classification system based on analyses of plant parts and characteristics.

64 Harry S. Paris, "Paintings (1769–1774) by A. N. Duchesne and the History of *Cucurbita pepo*," *Annals of Botany* 85 (2000): 815–16. Duchesne produced a major scientific study of the Cucurbitaceae, complete with detailed color illustrations. The well-known botanist Liberty Bailey was the first to classify all members of the genus *Cucurbita pepo* as pumpkins, which would technically define a zucchini as a pumpkin, a misnomer in common twentieth-century vegetable usage and terminology. Liberty Hyde Bailey, *Cyclopedia of American Horticulture* (New York: Macmillan, 1902), 409.

65 These physical characteristics that define the family are generalized from much more concise and detailed botanical definitions. See "Web site for the plant family Cucurbitaceae and home of the Cucurbit Network," http://www.cucurbit.org/family.html (accessed March 3, 2011).

66 Paris, "Paintings," 815–830.

67 Cotton Mather, letter, 1716, Royal Society Archives, as quoted in Conway Zirkle, "Plant Hybridization and Plant Breeding in Eighteenth-Century American Agriculture," *Agricultural History* 43 (January 1969): 29, as cited in Charles B. Heiser Jr., *The Gourd Book* (Norman: University of Oklahoma Press, 1979), 43.

68　Sarah Kemble Knight, *The Private Journal of a Journey from Boston to New York in the Year 1704* (Albany: Frank H. Little, 1865), 51, as quoted in Frances Phipps, *Colonial Kitchens, Their Furnishings and Their Gardens* (New York: Hawthorn Books, 1972), 113.

69　Thomas Anburey, Letter 55, May 20, 1787, in *Travels through the Interior Parts of America by an Officer*, vol. 2 (London: William Lane, 1789), 127, as quoted in Russell, *A Long, Deep Furrow*, 145. Anburey mistakenly stated that squash were brought from Europe instead of being native to the Americas.

70　Kalm, *Travels in North America*, vol. 2, 516.

71　Sieur Aubry, "Lettre à Monsieur son Frère," 213.

72　Journal of Major John Burrowes, August 27, 1779, as quoted in Parker, *Iroquois Uses of Maize*, 19.

73　Adelaide L. Fries, *Records of the Moravians of North Carolina* (Raleigh, N.C.: Edwards and Broughton, 1922), and Lewis Cecil Gray, *History of Agriculture in the Southern United States to 1860* (Washington, D.C.: Carnegie Institution of Washington, 1933), include many primary sources of people who witnessed the cultivation of pumpkins for domestic consumption. For example, a letter from Maurice Matthews to "Ashley," August 30, 1671, described seeing pumpkins propagated in South Carolina. The letter is in South Carolina Historical Society, *Collections*, vol. 5, 333, as quoted in Gray, *History of Agriculture*, 53. Another letter, from Thomas Jones to John Lyde, recorded the growing of pumpkins in Georgia. The letter is in Georgia Historical Society, *Collections*, vol. 1, 199, as quoted in Gray, *History of Agriculture*, 103. See also John Lawson, *The History of Carolina, Containing the Exact Description and Natural History of that Country . . .* (London, 1718), as quoted in Gray, *History of Agriculture*, 46.

74　John Lawson, *A New Voyage of Carolina* (London, 1709), 77, as quoted in Leighton, *American Gardens*, 62.

75　Thomas Nairne, *A Letter from South Carolina* (London, 1710), 53, as quoted in Gray, *History of Agriculture*, 327.

76　This rice plantation, which I visited in June 2000, is located in the South Carolina low country.

77　Histories of harvest celebrations are surprisingly few. Historians commonly trace the officially sanctioned holidays that led to the development of Thanksgiving as we know it, but more local, home-grown harvest festivals are poorly documented, especially for the South. Works that do exist are older ones that cover a broad range of time periods and cultures or are general surveys that provide little analysis of the events. See Penner, *The Thanksgiving Book*; the chapter on Thanksgiving in Cohen and Coffin, *Folklore of American Holidays*; Metropolitan Museum of Art, *Thanksgiving and Harvest Festivals* (New York, 1942); Laurence Whistler, *The English Festivals* (London: William Heinemann, 1947); E. O. James, *Seasonal Feasts and Festivals* (London: Thames and Hudson, 1961); and *Funk and Wagnalls Standard Dictionary of Folklore, Mythology and Legend* (New York: Funk and Wagnalls, 1949).

78   Francis Louis Michel, "Report of the Journey of Francis Louis Michel from Berne, Switzerland, to Virginia, October 2, 1701–December 1, 1702," *Virginia Magazine and Biography* 24 (1916): 32, as quoted in Mary N. Stanard, *Colonial Virginia: Its People and Customs* (Detroit: Singing Tree Press, 1970), 136.

79   The idea that Puritans were more accepting of forms of recreation that could be construed as having a practical purpose is one of the themes in Bruce Colin Daniels, *Puritans at Play: Leisure and Recreation in Colonial New England* (New York: St. Martin's, 1995).

80   Ward, *Trip to New-England*, 11, as quoted in Darrett B. Rutman, *Husbandmen of Plymouth: Farms and Villages in the Old Colony, 1620–1692* (Boston: Beacon Press, 1967), 53.

81   Joel Barlow, "Hasty Pudding" (Stockbridge, Mass.: Printed by Rosseter and Willard, 1797), as quoted in Metropolitan Museum of Art, *Thanksgiving and Harvest Festivals* (New York: Metropolitan Museum of Art, 1942), n.p.

82   Paul Dudley, "Observations on Some of the Plants in New England," *Philosophical Transactions of the Royal Society of London* (London, 1724), 197.

83   Carver, *Three Years' Travels*, 349. Robert Beverly concurred: "The cushaws and pumpkins they lay by, which will keep several months good after they are gathered." Beverly, *History and Present State of Virginia*, 181. La Quintinie, in *The Compleat Gard'ner*, 190, reported, "We keep them in our storehouses till about the middle of Lent, when they have been seasonably gather'd, and well defended from the cold." Peter Kalm also noted, "As soon as the cold weather comes, they remove all the pumpkins that remain on the stalk, whether ripe or not, and spread them on the floor in a part of the house, where the unripe ones grow perfectly ripe if they are not laid one upon the other. This is done round Montreal in the middle of September; but in Pennsylvania I have seen some in the field on the 19th of October." Kalm, *Travels in North America*, vol. 2, 517.

84   The best sources for the colonial culinary uses of pumpkins are travel accounts and personal journals, as cited throughout the chapter, which frequently note the kinds and quality of fare consumed. Some historians have also turned to probate records, wills, and inventories for clues to colonial consumption patterns of all sorts (e.g., McMahon, "Comfortable Sustenance"). These are less useful for foods such as pumpkins that had little monetary value. Even if a family consumed pumpkins, it did not necessarily list them in the family estate.

85   Kalm, *Travels in North America*, vol. 2, 517.

86   J. Heckewelder, *History, Manners, and Customs of the Indian Nations Who Once Inhabited Pennsylvania and the Neighboring States* (Philadelphia: Historical Society of Pennsylvania, 1876), 194, as quoted in Raine, *Woodland Feast*, 17.

87   Booth, *Hung, Strung, and Potted*, 131.

88   Carver, *Three Years' Travels*, 349. The use of pumpkin in bread was also noted in Ernest L. Bogart, *Peacham: The Story of a Vermont Hill Town* (Washington, D.C.: University Press of America, 1981 [1948]), 70.

89   Sarah Kemble Knight, *The Journal of Madam Knight* (Boston: Small, Maynard, 1825), 61, as quoted in Phipps, *Colonial Kitchens*, 113.

90   Richard J. Hooker, ed., *A Colonial Plantation Cookbook: The Receipt Book of Harriot Pinckey Harry, 1770* (Columbia: University of South Carolina Press, 1984), 22.

91   "The masons built an oven in the pumpkin house," noted the source, in order to dry the sliced pumpkins. Fries, *Records of the Moravians*, vol. 1, 80, as quoted in Kay Moss and Kathryn Hoffman, *Backcountry Wife: A Study of Eighteenth-Century Food* (Gastonia, N.C.: Schiele Museum, 1985), 88.

92   Kalm, *Travels in North America*, vol. 2, 518.

93   Pumpkin's use as a sweetener is noted in Phipps, *Colonial Kitchens*, 106; Gertrude Ida Thomas, *Food of Our Forefathers* (Philadelphia: F. A. Davis, 1941), 32; and Ellenore W. Doudiet, "Coastal Maine Cooking: Foods and Equipment from 1760," in *Gastronomy: The Anthropology of Food and Food Habits*, ed. Margaret L. Arnott (The Hague: Mouton, 1975), 219n12 and 220.

94   See Mintz, *Sweetness and Power*, and Steven R. Pendery, "The Archaeology of Urban Foodways in Portsmouth, New Hampshire," in Peter Benes, ed., *Foodways in the Northeast* (Boston: Boston University Press, 1984), 9–27.

95   Michael Coe and Sophie Coe, "Mid-Eighteenth-Century Food and Drink on the Massachusetts Frontier," in Benes, *Foodways in the Northeast*, 39–46. The Massachusetts Bay colony imported spices by 1629. See Hooker, *Food and Drink in America*, 34. See also Wolfgang Schivelbusch, *Tastes of Paradise: A Social History of Spices, Stimulants, and Intoxicants*, trans. David Jacobson (New York: Vintage Books, 1992), 12–14.

96   Andrew Barr, *Drink: A Social History of America* (New York: Carroll and Graf, 1999), 31–34.

97   Sloane Manuscripts 3338, British Museum, transcripts at the Library of Congress, ff. 33–36, as quoted in Gray, *History of Agriculture*, 327.

98   Beverly, *History and Present State of Virginia*, 141.

99   Unidentified rhyme quoted in Alice Morse Earle, *Customs and Fashions of Old New England* (Bowie, Md.: Heritage Books, 1992 [1893]), 174.

100   Van der Donck, *Description of the New Netherlands*, 68.

101   The recipe was signed by "Naso, Buckingham County, Virginia," and dated February 1771. Naso, recipe for "Pompion Ale," February 1771, American Philosophical Society, Manuscript Division, as quoted in Stanley Baron, *Brewed in America: A History of Beer and Ale in the United States* (Boston: Little, Brown, 1962), 98.

102   Ibid.

103   Landon Carter, *The Diary of Colonel Landon Carter of Sabine Hall, 1752–78*, ed. Jack P. Greene (Charlottesville: University Press of Virginia, 1965), 620 (diary entry for September 5, 1771) and 1149 (diary entry for September 1, 1778).

104   Kalm, *Travels in North America*, vol. 2, 518.

105   Anne G. Gardiner, *Mrs. Gardiner's Receipts from 1763* (Hallowell, Me.: White and Horne, 1938), 76.

106 George Washington called for the first national Thanksgiving holiday on Thursday, November 26, 1789, in recognition of the victory against England in the Revolutionary War. In this regard, the first national Thanksgiving was like the old, traditional form of the holiday, not the new, more familial one. Americans did not celebrate the holiday again on a national level until Lincoln revitalized it during the Civil War. Love, *Fast and Thanksgiving Days of New England*, 248.

107 Juliana Smith's diary quoted in Tittle, *Colonial Holidays*, 64.

108 Thomas, *Food of Our Forefathers*, 32. Some Carolina backcountry settlers considered stews of bear meat or venison, corn, beans, and pumpkin to be "wholesome and well tasted dishes." Joseph Doddridge, *Notes on Settlement . . . of the Western Parts of Virginia and Pennsylvania*, ed. Alfred J. Williams (Albany: Joel Munsell, 1876), 137–38, as quoted in Moss and Hoffman, *Backcountry Wife*, 96.

109 Amelia Simmons, *American Cookery* (New York: Eerdmans, 1965 [1796]). A great deal of scholarly discussion has been devoted to the authorship of this book and to the phrase "An American Orphan," which was included after Simmons's name. See, for example, Glynnis Ridley, "The First American Cookbook," *Eighteenth-Century Life* 23 (May 1999): 114–23. Ridley and food historian Janet Theophano have examined the cookbook as a political statement. See Janet Theophano, *Eat My Words: Reading Women's Lives through the Cookbooks They Wrote* (New York: Palgrave, 2002), 227–69.

110 James McWilliams made a similar point in *Revolution in Eating*. He argued that the importance Americans placed on being able to procure their own food freely is an overlooked yet significant cause of the American Revolution. James E. McWilliams, *Revolution in Eating: How the Quest for Food Shaped America* (New York: Columbia University Press, 2005).

111 Glynnis Ridley selected pumpkin pie as a representative recipe through which to examine Simmons's cookbook as a social and cultural document. She examined the pie's sugar and molasses content, the use of which she equated with the support of international and domestic markets, respectively. She basically ignored the pumpkin content in the pumpkin pie. Ridley, "First American Cookbook," 120–21.

112 Eliza Smith, *The Compleat Housewife* (London: Printed for S. Ware, R. Birt, et al., 1727); Susannah Carter, *The Frugal Colonial Housewife, or, Complete Woman Cook* (Philadelphia: Printed for Mathew Carey, 1802). See also Theophano, *Eat My Words*.

113 Theophano, *Eat My Words*, 235.

114 "Let us behave like dutiful children who have received unmerited blows from a beloved parent," advised a Philadelphia lawyer in response to acts of violence by England before the war. John Dickinson, *Letters from a Farmer in Pennsylvania*, ed. R. T. H. Halsey (New York: Outlook, 1903), 34, as quoted in John Mack Faragher et al., *Out of Many: A History of the American People* (Upper Saddle River, N.J.: Pearson Prentice Hall, 2002), 159.

115 Simmons, *American Cookery*, 34–35.

116 Kalm, *Travels in North America*, vol. 2, 481.

117 Thomas Jefferson, *Notes on the State of Virginia* (Richmond: J. W. Randolph, 1853 [1781–85]), 176.

118 Amy Kaplan made a similar argument about the political dimensions of work in the home in "Manifest Domesticity," *American Literature* 70, no. 3 (1998): 581–606.

3. THOREAU SITS ON A PUMPKIN:
THE MAKING OF A RURAL NEW ENGLAND ICON, 1800 TO 1860

1   *The Farmer and Gardener and Live-Stock Breeder and Manager* (Baltimore, Md.) 4, no. 6 (1837): 42.

2   John Lane to J. L. Boylston, January 5, 1829, *New England Farmer*, February 6, 1829. A farmer writing to Maine's *Kennebec Journal* in 1838 concurred: "Every farmer knows how easy it is, in a favorable season, to raise pumpkins, and that they are of much value in fattening cattle, feeding milch cows and feeding hogs.... For culinary purposes, however, they are very far ferior to squashes." Reprinted from the *Kennebec Journal* in "Pumpkins, Squashes, etc.," *American Farmer and Gardener*, December 18, 1838, 269.

3   Works on Jacksonian America include Daniel Walker Howe, *What Hath God Wrought: The Transformation of America, 1815–1848* (New York: Oxford University Press, 2007); Edward Pessen, *Jacksonian America: Society, Personality, and Politics* (Homewood, Ill.: Dorsey Press, 1978); David Freeman Hawke, *Everyday Life in Early America* (New York: Harper and Row, 1988); and Jack Larkin, *Reshaping of Everyday Life, 1790–1840* (New York: HarperPerennial, 1988). Historian Hal S. Barron argued that it was the inability of rural communities to attract new residents to replace those who died, not a mass exodus, that caused rural populations to decline. Hal S. Barron, "Staying Down on the Farm: Social Process of Settled Rural Life in the Nineteenth-Century North," in *The Countryside in the Age of Capitalist Transformation: Essays in the Social History of Rural America*, eds. Steven Hahn and Jonathan Prude (Chapel Hill: University of North Carolina Press, 1985), 333.

4   The most thorough surveys of squash and pumpkin varieties in the first half of the nineteenth century include Fearing Burr, *The Field and Garden Vegetables of America* (Boston: J. E. Tilton, 1865), 190–221; T. W. Harris, "Pumpkins and Squashes," *Southern Planter*, May 1855, 213–16; and David A. Wells, *The Year-Book of Agriculture: or, The Annual of Agricultural Progress and Discovery for 1855 and 1856* (Philadelphia: Childs and Peterson, 1856), 329–33. The seedsman J. J. H. Gregory, of Marblehead, Massachusetts, introduced the Hubbard squash in the 1850s. He supposedly acquired the seed from "an elderly man" from the Boston area around the turn of the century. Gregory also introduced the Marblehead squash, which is similar to the Hubbard. Burr, *Field and Garden Vegetables*, 210.

5   Harris, "Pumpkins and Squashes," 213.

6   *The Farmer's Cabinet; Devoted to Agriculture, Horticulture, and Rural Economy,*
     vol. 2 (Philadelphia: John, Libby, 1838), 252.

7   For the development of urban markets, see Helen Tangires, *Public Markets and
     Civic Culture in Nineteenth-Century America* (Baltimore, Md.: Johns Hopkins
     University Press, 2003).

8   Thomas F. De Voe, *The Market Assistant* (New York: Hurd and Houghton,
     1867), 321.

9   Scholarly works that describe and analyze American dietary habits of the
     nineteenth century include Calla Van Syckle, "Some Pictures of Food Con-
     sumption in the United States, Part I: 1630 to 1860," *Journal of the American
     Dietetic Association* 21 (1945): 508–12; Calla Van Syckle, "Some Pictures of Food
     Consumption in the United States, Part II: 1860 to 1941," *Journal of the Ameri-
     can Dietetic Association* 21 (1945): 690–95; Sarah F. McMahon, "Laying Foods
     By: Gender, Dietary Decisions, and the Technology of Food Preservation in
     New England Households, 1750–1850," in *Early American Technology: Making
     and Doing Things from the Colonial Era to 1850,* ed. Judith A. McGaw (Chapel
     Hill: University of North Carolina Press, 1994), 164–96; Sarah F. McMahon,
     "'All Things in Their Proper Season': Seasonal Rhythms of Diet in Nineteenth
     Century New England," *Agricultural History* 63, no. 2 (1989): 130–51; Sam B.
     Hilliard, "Hog Meat and Cornpone: Foodways in the Antebellum South,"
     in St. George, *Material Life in America,* 311–32; Kathryn Grover, ed., *Dining in
     America, 1850–1900* (Amherst: University of Massachusetts Press, 1987); and
     Harvey Levenstein, *Revolution at the Table: The Transformation of the American
     Diet* (New York: Oxford University Press, 1988). See also historical surveys
     of American foodways previously cited, including Hooker, *Food and Drink in
     America,* 127–283; Cummings, *The American and His Food,* 10–121; and Root and
     Rochemont, *Eating in America,* 104–81.

10   For the history of sugar consumption in the United States, see Mintz, *Sweetness
     and Power,* and Woloson, *Refined Tastes.*

11   The information about lager beers is from Noderer, *American Heritage Cook-
     book,* 270–71.

12   Miss Leslie, *Miss Leslie's Complete Cookery: Directions for Cookery in Its Various
     Branches* (Philadelphia, 1854), 191.

13   See Richard M. Dorson, *Jonathan Draws the Long Bow: New England Popular
     Tales and Legends* (New York: Russell and Russell, 1970 [1946]), and the chapter
     "Jonathan" in Sarah Burns, *Pastoral Inventions: Rural Life in Nineteenth-Century
     American Art and Culture* (Philadelphia: Temple University Press, 1989),
     149–67.

14   "Pumpkins," *New England Farmer,* May 11, 1831.

15   For the history of agriculture in the first half of the nineteenth century, see
     Bidwell, *History of Agriculture,* 147–473; Schlebecker, *Whereby We Thrive,* 113–37;
     Russell, *Long, Deep Furrow,* 257–416; and Hurt, *American Agriculture,* 78–164.

Scholarly works that focus on the changes and effects of industrialization on rural life include Hahn and Prude, *Countryside in the Age of Capitalist Transformation*; Hal S. Barron, *Those Who Stayed Behind: Rural Society in Nineteenth Century New England* (Cambridge: Cambridge University Press, 1984); David B. Danborn, *Born in the Country: A History of Rural America* (Baltimore, Md.: Johns Hopkins University Press, 1995); and Sally McMurry, *Transforming Rural Life: Dairying Families and Agricultural Change, 1820–1850* (Baltimore, Md.: Johns Hopkins University Press, 1995).

16 For the history of agricultural fairs, see Wayne Caldwell Neely, *The Agricultural Fair* (New York: Columbia University Press, 1935), and Robert S. Allen, "Early American Agricultural Societies and Organizations: Educational Activities and Numerical Growth at Key Periods until 1900," *Journal of Agricultural Food and Information* 8, no. 3 (2007): 17–31.

17 Susan Fenimore Cooper, *Rural Hours* (Atlanta: University of Georgia Press, 1998 [1850]), 193.

18 For a history of the Massachusetts Society for Promoting Agriculture, see Tamara Plakins Thornton, *Cultivating Gentlemen: The Meaning of Country Life among the Boston Elite, 1785–1860* (New Haven: Yale University Press, 1989).

19 Hedrick, *History of Horticulture*, 240.

20 Nathaniel Ingersoll, "Mr. Ingersoll's Piggery," *American Farmer*, October 1835, 205. In "Review of New York Retail Market," in the October 1848 issue of *American Agriculturist*, p. 325, pumpkins were listed as 50 to 75 cents a dozen, in comparison with squash at 75 cents to one dollar a dozen. These were probably culinary pumpkins rather than field pumpkins, which had little use in urban markets at this time.

21 Thomas Dunlap, *Catalogue of Garden, Flower, Shrub, Herb and Grass Seeds* (New York: Jared W. Bell, 1852), 8.

22 "Genesee County" and "St. Joseph County," in *Transactions of the State Agricultural Society of Michigan . . . for the Year 1856*, ed. J. C. Holmes (Lansing, Mich.: Hosmer and Kerr, 1857), 436 and 780, respectively.

23 C. S. Kafinesque, "Oil of Pumpkin Seed," *American Farmer*, April 9, 1819, 19.

24 Josiah White, "Pumpkin Seed Oil," letter to the president of the Hampshire, Franklin, and Hampden Agricultural Society, March 17, 1820, reprinted in *American Farmer*, April 4, 1823, 13.

25 Kafinesque, "Oil of Pumpkin Seed."

26 T. Bridgeman, "Pumpkin Bread," *American Farmer*, January 25, 1834, 367. The article was republished from *New York Farmer*.

27 "Pumpkins," *American Farmer*, May 8, 1838.

28 See, for example, "Pumpkins," *New England Farmer*, April 6, 1827, 294. Boiling was frequently recommended to make pumpkins more easily digestible. The seeds were of particular concern, and some farmers removed them before feeding pumpkin to animals. See "How to Select Pumpkin Seeds," *Southern Planter*, September 1854, 275.

29 Burr, *Field and Garden Vegetables*, 190.

30 John Douglas, *Catalog of Kitchen, Garden, Herb, Field and Grass Seeds* (Washington, D.C., 1843), 29.

31 "Pumpkins for Milch Cows," *American Agriculturalist*, March 1850, 81.

32 T. T. Lyon, "Fruit," in Holmes, *Transactions of the State Agricultural Society of Michigan*, 200.

33 "As every farmer and planter knows [pumpkins] can be grown in a corn-field without materially interfering with the production of the corn, or making an extra demand upon the labor of the farm," explained the *American Farmer* in 1838. "Pumpkins," *American Farmer*, May 8, 1838.

34 The earliest use of the term *pumpkin patch* that I found was in the April 28, 1841, issue of *American Farmer*. It connoted a small area of production for any crop, however, not just the pumpkin. "Pumpkins," *American Farmer*, April 28, 1841, 386.

35 "Pumpkins," *Farmer and Gardener*, June 6, 1837, 42.

36 "Extraordinary Produce," *American Farmer*, September 17, 1819, 200.

37 Douglas, *Catalog of Kitchen . . . Seeds*, 29.

38 For the use of the term *stolen crop*, see "Pumpkins as Stolen Crop," *Horticulturalist*, December 1870, 120, and "Pumpkins," *American Agriculturalist*, July 1882.

39 First quotation from "Productive Pumpkin Vine," *New England Farmer*, February 22, 1832, 253; second from Fred Rapp, letter to the editor, *American Farmer*, December 3, 1830, 304; third from "Big Pumpkins," *Western Farmer*, October 1840, 18.

40 "Great Pumpkin Story," *New England Farmer*, December 11, 1844, 192.

41 "Pumpkins," *Farmer and Gardener*, December 2, 1834, 242.

42 Michael Miller, "Pumpkins," *American Farmer*, December 21, 1827, 313.

43 "Enormous Product," *New England Farmer*, October 14, 1825, 95 (originally published in *Massachusetts Yeoman*).

44 David Landreth, *Descriptive Catalog of the Garden Seeds* (Philadelphia, 1844), 9.

45 Samuel Deane, *New England Farmer; or Geological Dictionary*, 3rd ed. (Boston: Wells and Lilly, 1822), 353. The origins of the mammoth pumpkin are discussed in W. S. Clark, "A Squash in Harness," *Horticulturalist*, July 1875, 13–14.

46 "A Mammoth Pumpkin," *New England Farmer*, January 11, 1828, 195; "A Mammoth Squash," *Farmer and Gardener*, October 27, 1835, 201; "Monster Pumpkin," *Horticulturalist*, February 1857, 96; N. E. F., "Largest Squash Yet," *New England Farmer*, November 24, 1841.

47 "Mammoth Squash."

48 *The Commercial Advertiser*, as quoted in De Voe, *Market Assistant*, 346.

49 "Mammoth Pumpkin." Similar announcements appeared in *American Farmer*, November 24, 1826; *Farmer and Gardener*, October 27, 1835, 201; and *Western Farmer* (Cincinnati, Ohio), October 1840, 18.

50 Both specimens were described in "Mammoth Fruits, etc.," *New England Farmer*, October 9, 1829, 91.

51   Comstock, Ferre and Company, *The Gardener's Almanac* (Wethersfield, Conn., 1856), 42, and "Editor's Table," *Horticulturalist*, February 1857, 96.

52   "Extravangances of Nature," *Boston Gazette*, October 27, 1819, as quoted in De Voe, *Market Assistant*, 346.

53   Comstock, Ferre and Company, *Gardener's Almanac*, 42.

54   James Jackson Jarves, *Parisian Sights and French Principles Seen through American Spectacles* (New York: Harper and Brothers, 1852), 30.

55   "A Great Pumpkin Story," *New England Farmer*, December 11, 1844, 192. For indexes to folktales, see Ernest W. Baughman, *Type and Motif Index of Folktales of England* (The Hague: Mouton, 1966); Ernest W. Baughman, "A Complete Study of the Folktales of England and North America" (Ph.D. diss., Indiana University, 1954); Botkin, *Treasury of American Folklore*; and Stith Thompson, *Motif Index of Folk Literature* (Bloomington: Indiana University Press, 1989 [1932]). See also Susan Stewart, *On Longing: Narratives of the Miniature, the Gigantic, the Souvenir, the Collection* (Baltimore, Md.: Johns Hopkins University Press, 1984), 96–101, in which she discusses the tall tale genre.

56   "A Great Pumpkin Story," *Spirit of the Times* 14 (January 25, 1845): 568, as quoted in Dorson, *Jonathan Draws the Long Bow*, 130. Another tall tale describes a pumpkin vine that grew "at a pace faster than a galloping horse." "A Bit of a Punkin," *Yankee Blade* 4 (December 4, 1847), as quoted in Dorson, *Jonathan Draws the Long Bow*, 132.

57   "Great Pumpkin Story," *New England Farmer*.

58   "A Bit of a Punkin," as quoted in Dorson, *Jonathan Draws the Long Bow*, 131.

59   *Hoosier Tall Stories* 26, Federal Writers Project of Indiana, WPA, 1937, cited in Baughman, *Motif Index*, no. X1402.1. A similar tale describes a pumpkin chasing a man on horseback across a field. The man climbs up on a leaf and calls for help. Botkin, *America Folklore*, 601.

60   "Great Pumpkin Story," *New England Farmer*.

61   Harris, "Pumpkins and Squashes."

62   Wells, *Year-Book of Agriculture*, 332.

63   Jacob Fowler, *The Journal of Jacob Fowler . . . , 1821–22*, ed. Elliott Coues (New York: Francis P. Harper, 1898), 15; Lewis H. Garrard, *Wah-To-Yah and the Taos Trail* (Palo Alto, Calif.: American West Publishing, 1968 [1850]), 64; Benjamin F. Taylor, *January and June* (New York: Oakley and Mason, 1853), 252, as quoted in William Craigie, *A Dictionary of American English on Historical Principles* (Chicago: University of Chicago Press, 1942), 1858.

64   *Western Reserve* 1 (1819): 185, and John A. Hart and Charles Goodnight et al., *Pioneer Days in the Southwest from 1850 to 1879* (Guthrie, Okla.: State Capital Company, 1909), 252, both as quoted in Craigie, *Dictionary of American English*, 1858.

65   Isaac Lippincott, "Pioneer Industry in the West," *Journal of Political Economy* 18 (1910): 274–78, as quoted in Van Syckle, "Some Pictures of Food Consumption in the United States, Part I," 512.

66   The exact quotation is that pumpkin bread was "as common Kentucky food like pie in New England." *Western Reserve* 1 (1819): 185, as quoted under the heading "pumpkin bread" in *The Oxford English Dictionary* and in Craigie, *Dictionary of American English*, 1858.

67   William Kenrick, *The New American Orchardist: Or, an Account of the Most Valuable Varieties of Fruit, Adapted to Cultivation in the Climate of the United States. . .* (Boston: Otis, Broaders and Company, 1848), 369. Other sources that advocated pumpkin as a source of sugar include Levi Woodbury, "Pumpkin Sugar," *Daily Commercial Bulletin and Missouri Literary Register*, October 28, 1837, and "Pumpkin Sugar," *The North American* (Philadelphia, Pa.), August 3, 1939.

68   Franc Adams, *Pioneer History of Ingham County* (Lansing, Mich.: Wynkoop, Hallenbeck, Crawford Company, 1923), 358, as quoted in *A Dictionary of Americanisms on Historical Principles*, ed. Mitford M. Mathews (Chicago: University of Chicago Press, 1951), 1328.

69   Johnson, *Wonder-Working Providence*, 56.

70   Accounts of pumpkin production in the South include *Southern Planter*, January 1843, 17; "A Pumpkin . . . ," *Raleigh Register, and North-Carolina Gazette*, November 29, 1822, issue 1210, col. E; "A Pumpkin . . . ," *Maryland Gazette and Political Intelligencer*, November 6, 1823, issue 45, col. B, which reports pumpkins being raised in Virginia; and "The editor of the New Orleans Bulletin acknowledges the receipts of a pumpkin raised in Texas . . . ," *Charleston Mercury*, September 17, 1859, col. G. Examples of pumpkin recipes printed in southern publications include Mary Randolph, *The Virginia House-Wife* (Washington, D.C.: Davis and Force (1838 [1824]), 108, which offers a savory pumpkin recipe; Lettice Bryan, *Kentucky Housewife* (Cincinnati: Stereotyped by Shepard and Steams, 1839), 215–16, 238, 270, 314, and 324; Sarah Rutledge, *Carolina Housewife; or, House and Home* (Charleston, S.C.: S.S.S. Publishers, 1963 [1847]), 165; and "Pumpkin Soup," *Mississippi Free Trader and Natchez Gazette*, January 10, 1849, issue 160, col. E. The place names are listed in Richard Swainson Fisher, *A New and Complete Statistical Gazetteer of the United States of America* (New York: J. H. Colton, 1853), accessed July 10, 2009, at the website "Making of America," http://quod.lib.umich.edu/cgi/t/text/text-idx?c=moaandcc=moaan dtype=simpleandrgn=full+textandq1=Pumpkinandcite1=fisher%2C+richardan dcite1restrict=authorandcite2=andcite2restrict=authorandfirstpubl1=1800andfi rstpubl2=1865andSubmit=Search.

71   George White, *Historical Collections of Georgia* (New York: Pudney and Russell, 1854), 443.

72   A.B.C., "Pumpkin Pies," *American Farmer*, January 11, 1833, 350.

73   J. Parton, "The Life of Horace Greeley, Editor New York Tribune," in *Tales and Sketches for the Fireside by the Best American Authors; Selected from Putnam's Magazine* (New York: A. Dowling, 1857), 76.

74   John Palmer, *Journal of Travels in the United States . . . in the year 1817* (London: Sherwood, Nealy and Jones, 1818), 241.

75 "All the Squashes," *American Farmer*, November 18, 1834, 231.

76 Cooper, *Rural Hours*, 201.

77 Williams, "The Idea of Nature," 67–85; Shi, *Simple Life*; John Sears, *Sacred Places: American Tourist Attractions in the Nineteenth Century* (New York: Oxford University Press, 1989).

78 Angela L. Miller, *Empire of the Eye: Landscape Representation and American Cultural Politics, 1825–1875* (Ithaca, N.Y.: Cornell University Press, 1993); Novak, *Nature and Culture.*

79 The idea that expanding commodity networks increasingly concealed the actual ties between urban and rural places is William Cronon's thesis in *Nature's Metropolis.*

80 Henry David Thoreau, *Walden or, Life in the Woods* (New York: New American Library, 1960 [1854]), 30.

81 Henry David Thoreau, *A Week on the Concord and Merrimac Rivers*, ed. Odell Shepard (New York: Charles Scribner's Sons, 1921), 37, as quoted in John B. Jackson, "Jefferson, Thoreau and After," in *Landscapes: Selected Writings of J. B. Jackson* (Amherst: University of Massachusetts Press, 1970), 3.

82 Sarah Burns discussed these ambivalent attitudes in *Pastoral Inventions: Rural Life in Nineteenth-Century Life and Culture* (Philadelphia: Temple University Press, 1989).

83 Ralph Waldo Emerson, "Nature," in *The Portable Emerson*, ed. Carl Bode (New York: Penguin, 1981), 43.

84 Ralph Waldo Emerson, "Farming," in Bode, *Portable Emerson*, 559–60.

85 Ibid., 568. See also Douglas C. Stenerson, "Emerson and the Agrarian Tradition," *Journal of the History of Ideas* 4 (January 1953): 95–115.

86 Nathaniel Hawthorne, *The Scarlet Letter: An Authoritative Text, Background and Sources, Criticism*, eds. Scully Bradley et al. (New York: Norton, 1978), 79. This passage was also analyzed in Norrman and Haarberg, *Nature and Language*, 46–47.

87 Albert H. Hovey, *Albert H. Hovey's Catalog of Seeds* (Chicago: A. H. Hovey, 1865), 92.

88 *American Farmer*, May 1854, 350.

89 "Pumpkins," *New England Farmer*, April 6, 1827, 294.

90 "Tales for Youth: The Jack O'Lantern," *South Carolina Temperance Advocate and Register of Agriculture and General Literature* (Columbia, S.C.), May 7, 1846, 176.

91 See Alan Dundes, ed., *Cinderella: A Casebook* (New York: Wildman Press, 1983); and Anna Birgitta Rooth, *The Cinderella Cycle* (Lund, Sweden: CWK Gleerup, 1951).

92 Charles Perrault, *Memoirs of My Life* (Columbia: University of Missouri Press, 1989), 18.

93 Charles Perrault, *Cinderella; or the Little Glass Slipper* (Albany, N.Y.: E. and E. Hosford, 1811), 12.

94   Ibid.

95   See Jane Yolen, "America's Cinderella," *Children's Literature in Education* 8 (1977): 21–29.

96   According to Opie and Opie, the rhyme first appeared in *Mother Goose's Quarto; or Melodies Complete* (Boston, 1825). Iona Opie and Peter Opie, *The Oxford Dictionary of Nursery Rhymes* (Oxford University Press, 1951), 333–34. The website "Nursery Rhymes: Lyrics and Origins" also states that the rhyme is of American origin. http://www.rhymes.org.uk/peter_peter_pumpkin_eater.htm (accessed August 8, 2008).

97   The term is cited in many dictionaries of American phrases, including Harold Wentworth and Stuart B. Flexner, *Dictionary of American Slang* (New York: Thomas Y. Crowell, 1975), 410, and C. Edward Wall, *Words and Phrases Index,* vol. 3 (Ann Arbor, Mich.: Pierian Press, 1970), 225.

98   "Finger Ring," at *The Mudcat Café*, an online magazine "dedicated to blues and folk music," http://www.mudcat.org (accessed December 29, 2000).

99   Carolyn Merchant, *Death of Nature: Women, Ecology, and the Scientific Revolution* (New York: Harper and Row, 1989 [1980]). See also Sherry B. Ortner, "Is Female to Male as Nature Is to Culture?" in *Women, Culture and Society*, eds. Michelle Zimbalist Rosaldo and Louise Lamphere (Palo Alto, Calif.: Stanford University Press, 1974), 67–87.

100   Sydney Whiting, *Memoirs of a Stomach, Written by Himself, That All Who Eat May Read. Edited by a Minister of the Interior* (London: Chapman and Hall, 1855).

101   Many examples of pumpkin numbskull tales are listed in Thompson, *Motif Index*, vol. 4, 145, motif J172.1. Other pumpkin folklore references are under the heading "pumpkin" in the index to Thompson, *Motif Index*, vol. 6, 617. See also Baughman, *Folktales*, 540–41, and D. L. Ashliman, *A Guide to Folktales in the English Language* (New York: Greenwood Press, 1987), 230.

102   W. A. Clouston, *The Book of Noodles* (London, 1888), 7, as quoted in Thompson, *Motif Index*, vol. 4, 168–69, motif J2013.3.

103   Samuel Warren, *Ten Thousand a Year* (Philadelphia: Jesper Harding, 1851), 126 and 398; J. H., "Iconoclastes: A Domestic Story," in *The Train: A First-Class Magazine*, January–June, 1857, 116–17.

104   Washington Irving, "The Legend of Sleepy Hollow," in *Sketchbook* (New York: G. P. Putnam's Sons, 1848), 416–56.

105   A painting by George Washington Allston Jenkins, titled *Headless Horseman of Sleepy Hollow* (1840–1865), illustrates the tale. Vera Conover Collection, Monmouth County Historical Society, Freehold, N.J.

106   This variation of the tale is from Bannatyne, *Halloween*, 78, and Carin Dewhirst and Joan Dewhirst, *My Tricks and Treats: Halloween Stories, Songs, Poems, Recipes, Crafts, and Fun for Kids* (New York: Smithmark, 1993), 35–36.

107   The connections between the jack-o'-lantern and the will-o'-the-wisp are discussed in Wayland D. Hand, "Will-o'-Wisps, Jack-o'-Lanterns and Their Congeners: A Consideration of the Fiery and Luminous Creatures of Lower

Mythology," *Fabula* 18, nos. 3–4 (1977): 226–33. See also Bannatyne, *Halloween*, 78, 90–91; Tuleja, "Pumpkins," 151–52; and Santino, *All Around the Year*, 157. On the jack-ma-lantern, see "Jack-Ma-Lantern," in *The Book of Negro Folklore*, eds. Langston Hughes and Arna Bontemps (New York: Dodd, Mead, 1958), 166–67; Newbell Niles Puckett, *Folk Beliefs of the Southern Negro* (New York: Dover, 1969), 134; Virginia Hale, "Jack-Ma-Lanterns," in *The Silver Bullet and Other American Witch Stories*, ed. Hubert Davis (Middle Village, N.Y.: Jonathan David, 1975), 48; and F. Roy Johnson, *Legends and Myths of North Carolina Roanoke-Chawan Area* (Murfreesboro, N.C.: Johnson Publishing, 1971), 80.

108   "Jack o' Lantern," *Daily National Intelligencer* (Washington, D.C.), October 12, 1830.

109   Puckett, *Folk Beliefs of the Southern Negro*, 134, as quoted in Bannatyne, *Halloween*, 78.

110   "Tales for Youth," 176.

111   Nathaniel Hawthorne, "Feathertop: A Moralized Legend," in *Twice-Told Tales* (Columbus: Ohio State University Press, 1974 [1837]), 124–48.

112   Hawthorne, "Feathertop," 126.

113   Ibid., 128.

114   Ibid., 129.

115   Cultural histories of New England regional identity include Dona Brown, *Inventing New England: Regional Tourism in the Nineteenth Century* (Washington, D.C.: Smithsonian Institution Press, 1999), and William H. Truettner and Roger B. Stein, *Picturing Old New England: Image and Memory* (New Haven, Conn.: Yale University Press, 1999).

116   The earliest date for the poem's publication that I could locate was 1846. John Greenleaf Whittier, "The Pumpkin," *New Hampshire Statesman and State Journal*, December 18, 1846.

117   *American Farmer*, October 9, 1833.

118   "A Thanksgiving Dinner," *Village Register* (Dedham, Mass.), November 24, 1825, 3, at "Historic American Thanksgiving Dinner Menus," http://www.food-timeline.org/foothanksgiving.html (accessed January 10, 2009).

119   "New Bedford," *New-Bedford Mercury*, December 1, 1836, 2, at "Historic American Thanksgiving Dinner Menus," http://www.foodtimeline.org/foothanks-giving.html (accessed January 10, 2009).

120   Lydia Maria Child, "A Boy's Thanksgiving Day," in Helen Ferris, *Favorite Poems Old and New* (Garden City, N.Y.: Doubleday, 1957), 84.

121   Works about Hale include Ruth E. Finley, *The Lady of Godey's: Sarah Josepha Hale* (New York: Arno Press, 1974), and Sarah Robbins, "'The Future Good and Great of Our Land': Republican Mothers, Female Authors, and Domesticated Literacy in Antebellum New England," *New England Quarterly* 75, no. 4 (2002): 562–91.

122   Sarah Josepha Hale, *Northwood; or Life North and South, Showing the True Color of Both* (New York: H. Long and Brother, 1852), 7–8. The original edition is

Sarah Josepha Hale, *A Tale of New England* (Boston: Bowles and Dearborn, 1827).

123 Hale, *Northwood* (1852 ed.), 8.

124 Ibid., 89 and 90, respectively.

125 "Pumpkin Pies," *Omaha Nebraskan*, November 11, 1857.

126 "Thanksgiving Days," *Niles' National Register*, November 26, 1842, 199.

127 Charles A. Jarvis, "Admission to Abolition: The Case of John Greenleaf Whittier," *Journal of the Early Republic* 4, no. 2 (1984): 161–76; Whitman Bennett, *Whittier: Bard of Freedom* (Port Washington, N.Y.: Kennikat Press, 1972).

128 Beth A. Salerno, *Sister Societies: Women's Antislavery Societies in Antebellum America* (DeKalb: Northern Illinois University Press, 2005).

129 Hale, *Northwood* (1852 ed.), 157. Finley's biography *Lady of Godey's* barely mentions her antislavery stance.

130 Alfred R. Ferguson, "The Abolition of Blacks in Abolitionist Fiction, 1830–1860," *Journal of Black Studies* 5, no. 2 (1974): 141–45.

131 Emerson, "Farming," 560–61.

132 Hale, *Northwood* (1827 ed.), 158.

133 Classic works on the American agrarian myth in the nineteenth century include Smith, *Virgin Land*; Hofstadter, *Age of Reform*; and Marx, *Machine in the Garden*. See also Joyce Appleby, "Commercial Farming and the 'Agrarian Myth' in the Early Republic," *Journal of American History* 68, no. 4 (1982), 833–49, and Buell, "American Pastoral Ideology Reappraised."

134 William R. Taylor, *Cavalier and Yankee: The Old South and American National Character* (New York: George Braziller, 1961).

135 Lady Emmeline Stuart-Worley, *Travels in the U.S., etc.; During 1849 and 1850* (New York: Harper and Brothers, 1851), 357.

136 Appelbaum, *Thanksgiving*, 134. The author provided no citation for the original quotation.

137 Hale, Child, and Whittier rarely mentioned the Pilgrims in their holiday verses. Louis C. Schaedler, "Whittier's Attitude toward Colonial Puritanism," *New England Quarterly* 21, no. 3 (1948): 354.

4. "WONDERFULLY GRAND AND COLOSSAL": THE PUMPKIN AND THE NATION, 1861 TO 1899

1 See Hurt, *American Agriculture*, 165–216. For an overview of the industrialization of agriculture in the nineteenth century, see also Schlebecker, *Whereby We Thrive*, 138–205; Russell, *Long, Deep Furrow*, 417–76; Cochrane, *Development of American Agriculture*; and Alan Trachtenberg, *The Incorporation of America: Culture and Society in the Gilded Age* (New York: Hill and Wang, 1982), 52–53.

2 Works on the settlement of the Great Plains include Smith, *Virgin Land*; Walter Prescott Webb, *Great Plains* (Lincoln: University of Nebraska Press, 1959); and Cronon, *Nature's Metropolis*.

3   "Pumpkins as Stolen Crop."

4   U.S. Department of Agriculture, "Sheep, Hogs and Horses in the Pacific
    Northwest," *Farmers Bulletin* 117 (1900): 22. The value of rice is from *The Value
    of a Dollar, 1860–1999* (Amenia, N.Y.: Grey House Publishing, 1999), as cited in
    "U.S. Diplomatic Mission to Germany," http://www.usa.usembassy.de/etexts/
    his/e_prices1.htm (accessed August 10, 2008).

5   "Pumpkins," *American Agriculturalist*, July 1882.

6   Biggs and Brothers, *Illustrated Catalogue of Flower and Vegetable Seeds, 1870–71.*

7   See, for example, "Badger Pumpkin Shows," *Milwaukee Sentinel*, October 6,
    1883, col. F, and "Oshkosh Pumpkin Fair: Bouck Says It's a Thing of the Past,"
    Milwaukee Sentinel, December 10, 1896, 8.

8   "True Potiron or Genuine Mammoth," *Burpee's Farm Annual* (Philadelphia: W.
    Atlee Burpee and Company, 1899).

9   "King of the Mammoths," in *H. W. Buckbee Seed and Plant Guide* (Rockland, Ill.,
    1899), 53.

10 "The Pumpkin in Kansas," *Rocky Mountain News*, October 18, 1879, 4.

11 Samuel Wilson, *12th Annual Price List and Catalog* (Mechanicsville, Pa., 1888).

12 Clark, "A Squash in Harness."

13 "The Pumpkin Cut: Wallenstein, of the Boston Store, Distinguishes Himself,"
    Atkinson (Kansas) Champion, November 30, 1890, 4.

14 "Some Pumpkins: The Pumpkin Festival Given by the 'St. Paul. One Price' a
    Grand Success," *Bismarck Daily Tribune*, October 7, 1886.

15 Scholarly works on the image of country life in popular culture include Wil-
    liams, *The Country and the City*; Bunce, *Countryside Ideal*; Marx, *Machine in the
    Garden*; Shi, *Simple Life*; and Peter J. Schmidt, *Back to Nature: The Arcadian
    Myth in Urban America* (New York: Oxford University Press, 1969).

16 See Brown, *Inventing New England*; Cindy S. Aron, *Working at Play: A History
    of Vacations in the United States* (New York: Oxford University Press, 1999); and
    Shi, *Simple Life*.

17 See Frederick Jackson Turner, "The Significance of the Frontier in American
    History" (1894), in Turner, *The Frontier in American History* (New York: Holt,
    Rinehart and Winston, 1962), 1–38. For analyses of Turner, the frontier thesis,
    and agrarianism, see Smith, *Virgin Land*; Marx, *Machine in the Garden*, 116–44;
    Wayne C. Rohrer and Louis H. Douglas, *The Agrarian Transition in America:
    Dualism and Change* (Indianapolis, Ind.: Bobbs-Merrill, 1969); Jehlen, *American
    Incarnation*; Patricia Nelson Limerick, *Legacy of Conquest: The Unbroken Past
    of the American West* (New York: W. W. Norton, 1987); and Cronon, *Nature's
    Metropolis*.

18 Percy Fielding and Anna Margaret Price, "Halloween Romps and Frolics by
    Two Experienced Entertainers," *Ladies' Home Journal*, October 1897, 25.

19 In *Halloween*, Bannatyne mentions a source from the early 1800s who described
    the pumpkin's use as a lighted vessel. In a complaint about the demise of Guy
    Fawkes Day, the source stated, "The observances have dwindled to horn

blowing, and the carrying about of pumpkin lanterns by the boys. The origin of the celebration is quite forgotten." Bannatyne, *Halloween*, 30. I could not find the original source for this quotation.

20   "A Pumpkin Effigy," *Harper's Weekly,* November 23, 1867, 1.

21   "The Story of the Harvard Students . . .," *Boston Daily Advertiser*, October 29, 1887, 4; "Electrical News," *St. Louis Globe-Democrat*, November 18, 1887, 4.

22   For studies of Halloween in the nineteenth century, see Rogers, *Halloween*, 49–77; Bannatyne, *Halloween*, 99–120; Skal, *Death Makes a Holiday*, 31–37; and Sarah Ban Breathnach, *Victorian Family Celebrations* (New York: Simon and Schuster, 1990), 174–85. Besides women's magazines, some of the most useful sources on the holiday at the turn of the century are Halloween collectibles books. These colorful volumes contain endless illustrations of old Halloween artifacts, from postcards and decorations to toys and other party favors. See Stuart Schneider, *Halloween in America: A Collector's Guide with Prices* (Atglen, Pa.: Schiffer, 1995); Pamela E. Apkarian-Russell, *Collectible Halloween* (Atglen, Pa.: Schiffer, 1997); Pamela E. Apkarian-Russell, *More Halloween Collectibles* (Atglen, Pa.: Schiffer, 1998); and Pamela E. Apkarian-Russell, *Halloween: Collectible Decorations and Games* (Atglen, Pa.: Schiffer, 2000).

23   Fielding and Price, "Halloween Romps," 25. Other primary sources on late nineteenth-century Halloween activities include "Hallow-een," *Scribner's Monthly,* November 1871, 119; A. G. Lewis, "All Hallow Eve," *Ladies Home Journal*, October 1889, 3; and "Merry Moments for Halloween," *Ladies' Home Journal*, October 1899, 38.

24   A useful resource for Halloween symbols is a children's book: Edna Barth, *Witches, Pumpkins, and Grinning Ghosts: The Story of Halloween Symbols* (New York: Clarion Books, 1972).

25   "The Magic Halloween" and "Halloween Pumpkins" appear on Winsch postcards (1913) in Schneider, *Halloween in America*, 69 and 71, respectively. Articles such as "A Suckling Squash," which described how a farmer fed milk to a mammoth pumpkin plant, as if it were a baby animal, by cutting off a vine and setting it in a pan, enhanced the vegetable's spirited identity. "A Suckling Squash," *American Agriculturalist,* December 1875.

26   Anna Margaret Price, "Merry Halloween Games," *Ladies' Home Journal*, October 1897, 25.

27   Ibid.

28   Ibid.

29   "The Old Yellow Pumpkin," *American Farm News*, reprinted in *Western Garden and Poultry Journal* (Des Moines, Iowa), October, 1891, 17.

30   "Gone Forever: No More Do We See the Pumpkin Pies of Old," *St. Louis Globe-Democrat*, December 1, 1885, 10.

31   James Whitcomb Riley, "When the Frost Is on the Punkin," *North American*, November 15, 1887, column B. This is the earliest citation for the poem that I could locate. See also James Whitcomb Riley, "When the Frost Is on the

Punkin," in *The Complete Poetic Works of James Whitcomb Riley* (Garden City, N. Y.: Garden City Publishing, 1945), 254–55.

32   Winslow Homer, *Pumpkins among the Corn*, 1878, illustration for Rowland Robinson, "Glimpses of New England Farm Life," *Century/Scribner's Monthly*, October 1878, 520. Paintings similar to J. Francis Murphy's *The Pumpkin Field*, n.d., include Murphy's *Upland Cornfield*, n.d.; William Henry Howe's *The Pumpkin Harvest*, n.d.; and W. M. Cary's *Harvest Time*, which was reproduced in *Harper's Weekly*, August 30, 1879.

33   Homer's *The Last Days of the Harvest* was reproduced as an engraving in *Harper's Weekly*, December 6, 1873.

34   "Pumpkins," *New Eclectic Magazine*, January–June 1869, 472.

35   "The State Elections," *Harper's Weekly*, October 31, 1863, 704.

36   Frederick Burr Opper, "The Supreme Court, as It May Hereafter Be Constituted," *Puck*, September 9, 1896.

37   Henry Ward Beecher, *Eyes and Ears* (Boston: Ticknor and Fields, 1862), 348.

38   The painting was reproduced in Sotheby's auction catalog, *American 18th Century, 19th Century and Western Paintings, Drawings, Watercolors and Sculpture* (April 23, 1981), plate 76.

39   Olivia Lovell Wilson, *Luck of the Golden Pumpkin* (New York: Readex Microprint, 1968 [1887]).

40   William Dean Howells, "The Pumpkin Glory," in *Christmas Everyday and Other Stories* (New York: Harper and Brothers, 1892), 71–107.

41   "Genuine Pumpkin Pie," *Kansas City Journal*, reprinted in the *Macon (Georgia) Telegraph*, October 23, 1897, 3.

42   For a history of canning, see Ruth Schwartz Cowan, *A Social History of American Technology* (New York: Oxford University Press, 1997), 165–71, and Jack Goody, "Industrial Food: Towards the Development of a World Cuisine," in *Food and Culture: A Reader*, eds. Carole Counihan and Penny Van Esterik (New York: Routledge, 1997), 338–56. Until recently, most histories of American technology focused on agricultural innovations instead of culinary developments—that is, the production rather than the consumption of food. Harvey Levenstein, *Paradox of Plenty: A Social History of Eating in America* (New York: Oxford University Press, 1993), is one example of a contemporary work that does focus on consumption.

43   Sarah Josepha Hale, "Our National Thanksgiving—A Domestic Festival," *Godey's Lady's Book*, November 1864, 440.

44   May C. Hanks, "Pumpkin Is Queen," in *Local and National Poets of America 1891*, ed. Thomas Herringshaw (Chicago: American Publishers Association, 1890), 485.

45   Levenstein, *Revolution at the Table*, 176.

46   Abraham Lincoln, "Proclamation for Thanksgiving, October 3, 1863, by the President of the United States of America," in *Complete Works of Abraham Lincoln*, vol. 9, eds. John G. Nicolay and John Hay (New York: Francis D. Tandy, c. 1905), 151.

47 Timothy Horton Ball, "A Thanksgiving Discourse at Crown Point, November 24, 1898," in *The Home of the Redeemed: and Other Discourses* (Crown Point, Ind.: Register Print, 1899), 179.

48 "The Annual Thanksgiving," *Scribner's Monthly Magazine*, November 1869, 212.

49 Elizabeth Share, "Preparation for Thanksgiving," *Primary Education*, November 1899, 399.

50 Hale is quoted in Breathnach, *Victorian Family Celebrations*, 194.

51 "Pumpkin Pies," *Good Housekeeping*, November 9, 1899, 29.

52 "Annual Thanksgiving."

53 Elizabeth Parker, "Bill of Fare for Thanksgiving," *Ladies' Home Journal*, November 1888, 11.

54 "Puritan Costume Party for Thanksgiving," *Rocky Mountain News*, November 14, 1897, 17. See also Andrew P. Haley, *Turning the Tables: Restaurants and the Rise of the American Middle Class, 1880–1920* (Chapel Hill: University of North Carolina Press, 2011).

55 Charles Dudley Warner, "The Season of Pumpkin Pie," *Chautauquan*, November 1891, 252.

56 Hanks, "Pumpkin Is Queen," 485.

57 "The American Pumpkin," *St. Louis Globe-Dispatch*, November 7, 1884, 4.

58 William E. Barton, *The Story of Pumpkin Pie* (Boston: Pilgrim Press, 1898), 43.

59 In addition to the sources already cited, a sampling includes "Grandma's Pumpkin Pies," *Morning Oregonian*, December 8, 1889, 10; "The Making of Pumpkin Pies Is Becoming a Lost Art," *Atchison Daily Globe*, October 3, 1893; and "Pumpkin-Pies," *Lowell Daily Citizen*, March 2, 1877.

60 "Peppery Pumpkin Pies: A Thanksgiving Story," *Chicago Daily Inter Ocean*, November 27, 1879, 6.

61 "Pumpkin Pie," *Werner's Magazine*, October 1896, 10.

62 "He Longs for Pie: Away with Foreign Cooks Who Won't Serve Mince and Pumpkin," *Emporia (Kansas) Daily Gazette*, May 1, 1895, col. D.

63 Margaret E. Sangster, "Thanksgiving Pumpkin Pies," *Ladies' Home Journal*, November 1889, 7.

64 Mary E. Wilkins, "The Pumpkin Giant," in *The Pot of Gold and Other Stories* (Boston: Lothrop, Lee and Shepard, 1892), 98–114. As with most fairy tales, it is difficult to cite an exact date of origin.

65 Ibid., 113.

66 Sarah Josepha Hale, "Domestic," *Godey's Lady's Book*, November 1864, 1.

67 C. G. Bush, "Thanksgiving Sketches—*Preparation*," *Harper's Weekly*, December 8, 1866; "Pumpkin Pie," *Werner's Magazine*, October 1898, 121. Norrman and Haarberg, throughout their *Nature and Language*, discuss the sexual associations of cucurbits based on the plants' fertility.

68 Beecher, *Eyes and Ears*, 349.

69 Congregational Home Missionary Society, "Encouraging from Texas," *Home*

Missionary: For the Year Ending April 1884 (New York: American Home Missionary Society, 1884), 395.

70 "Daily Dispatch," *Richmond Daily Dispatch*, February 15, 1865, http://imls.richmond.edu:80/d/ddr/ (accessed November 12, 2008).

71 Sources regarding Thanksgiving in the South, in addition to those cited in subsequent notes, are "Editor's Study," *Harper's New Monthly Magazine*, December 1889–May 1890, 156, and Atticus Haygood, *The New South: Gratitude, Amendment, Hope. A Thanksgiving Sermon for November 25, 1880* (Oxford, Ga.: 1880).

72 George Campbell, *White and Black: The Outcome of a Visit to the United States* (London: Chatto and Windus, Piccadilly, 1879), 403.

73 Hampton Institute, "Hampton School Record," *Southern Workman*, December 1892, 184.

74 First quotation from E. Shippen, "Among Our Contemporaries," *The United Service: A Monthly Review of Military and Naval Affairs* 11 (1894): 475; second quotation from W. E. B. DuBois, *The Philadelphia Negro: A Social Study* (Philadelphia: University of Pennsylvania, 1899), 196.

75 Miss K. Le Grange, "Thanksgiving at All Healing, N.C.," *American Missionary* 46, no. 1 (1892): 93.

76 "Black Letters; or Uncle Tom-Foolery in Literature," *Graham's Magazine*, January 1853, 214.

77 "Thanksgiving Morning in the Johnson Family," *Harper's Weekly*, 1887, at "Slavery in America: Teacher Resources," http://www.slaveryinamerica.org (accessed November 25, 2008).

78 A. I. Root, "The Pumpkin Business: Pumpkin Pies by the Carload," *Gleanings in Bee Culture*, January 15, 1891, 469.

79 Bureau of the Census, Department of Commerce, "Miscellaneous Vegetables Raised for Sale . . . 1899–1919," table 97 in *Fourteenth Census of the United States Taken in the Year 1920*, vol. 5, *Agriculture* (Washington, D.C.: Government Printing Office, 1922), 820.

80 Root, "Pumpkin Business."

81 *Rocky Mountain News*, March 30, 1896, 3.

5. JACK-O'-LANTERN SMILES: AMERICANS CELEBRATE THE FALL HARVEST WITH PUMPKINS, 1900 TO 1945

1 Arata quoted in Stacy Trevenon, "A Growing Tradition: Who Really Grows Pumpkins on the Coast," *Review* (Half Moon Bay, Calif.), October 2000, 23.

2 According to the 1920 census, 54.2 percent of the American population fell into the "rural" category in 1910, and 48.6 percent in 1920. U.S. Department of Commerce, *Fourteenth Census of the United States Taken in the Year 1920* (Washington, D.C.: Government Printing Office, 1922), 23.

3 Franklin D. Roosevelt, "Special Message to the Congress on Farm Security,"

in *Selected Speeches*, ed. Basil Rauch (New York: Holt, Rinehart and Winston, 1957), 170, as quoted in James Guimond, *American Photography and the American Dream* (Chapel Hill: University of North Carolina Press, 1991), 134.

4   Sources on American agriculture in the first half of the twentieth century include Hurt, *American Agriculture*, 221–330; Danborn, *Born in the Country*, 161–232; and Bruce L. Gardner, *American Agriculture in the Twentieth Century: How It Flourished and What It Cost* (Cambridge, Mass.: Harvard University Press, 2002).

5   "Mourn the Lack of Pumpkin Pies," *New York Times*, October 6, 1901, 19.

6   U.S. Department of Agriculture, "Animal Production," *Experiment Station Record* 38 (January–June 1918) (Washington, D.C.: Government Printing Office): 571.

7   U.S. Department of Agriculture, *1920 Census of Agriculture*, vol. 5 (Washington, D.C.: Government Printing Office, 1922), table 97, "Miscellaneous Vegetables Raised for Sale . . .," 820, and table 1, "Population, Farms and Farm Property in the United States 1920 and 1910," 24.

8   "Pumpkin Pie Has Arrived," *New York Times*, September 21, 1902, 27.

9   "Pumpkins Very Scarce This Year," *New York Times*, November 16, 1902, 33.

10   Lee Cleveland Corbett, *Garden Farming* (Boston: Ginn and Company, 1913), 390.

11   Information about the history of Libby's was gleaned from my interview with Dave Newhauser, Libby's plant manager and a pumpkin farmer, Morton, Illinois, October 19, 2000, and from the Libby's Company Archives at the Morton plant.

12   Federal Writers Project, *Iowa: A Guide to the Hawkeye State* (New York: Hastings House, 1959 [1938]), 496.

13   U.S. Department of Commerce, *Fifteenth Census of the United States: 1930—Population 1: Number and Distribution of Inhabitants* (Washington, D.C.: Government Printing Office, 1931), table 3, "Rural and Urban Populations of the United States: 1880 to 1930," 8. In the 1920 census, an urban area was defined as one with 2,500 or more inhabitants. In the 1930 census, an urban area was one with a population density of more than 1,000 inhabitants per square mile and a total population of 10,000 or more within a township or "other political subdivision." Ibid., 7.

14   Donald Worster, *Dust Bowl: The Southern Plains in the 1930s* (New York: Oxford University Press, 1979). See also Deborah Fitzgerald, *Every Farm a Factory: The Industrial Ideal in American Agriculture* (New Haven, Conn.: Yale University Press, 2003).

15   See, for example, U.S. Department of Agriculture, *Yearbook in Agriculture 1938: Soil and Men* (Washington, D.C.: Government Printing Office, 1938).

16   U.S. Department of Agriculture, *1950 Census of Agriculture*, vol. 2 (Washington, D.C.: Government Printing Office, 1952), table 3, "Specified Vegetables: Farms Reporting and Acreage . . .," 520 and 520n5. By 1949, despite the near

doubling of acreage, the number of farms growing pumpkins (2,194) was still below the 1899 total of 3,194. And for an unknown reason, 1939 saw an anomalous peak season of production at 13,182 acres, although the number of farms remained the same, leading me to believe that the 1939 statistic might be a census error. Ibid. Another point to note is a change in statistical record-keeping. The 1920 agricultural census reported that the number of farms growing pumpkins had dropped from 3,194 in 1899 to 321 in 1909, but unlike in previous censuses, beginning in 1909 only farms that had at least one acre planted in pumpkins were recorded. U.S. Department of Agriculture, *1920 Census of Agriculture*, vol. 5, table 97, 820.

17   The percentages of acreage devoted to feed and processing pumpkins were derived from U.S. Department of Agriculture, *1950 Census of Agriculture*, vol. 2, table 3, 520, and table 92, "Root and Grain Crops Hogged or Grazed . . . and Pumpkins for Feed," 654. To arrive at the percentages, I divided the total acreage (5,975) by the acreage devoted to feed pumpkins (1,904).

18   Federal Writers Project, *Iowa*, 496. The U.S. Agricultural Census did not paint as bright a picture of the crop's value in 1939. That year, it valued the crop at $24.34 per acre, less than the value of any other vegetable. U.S. Department of Agriculture, *1940 Census of Agriculture*, vol. 3, table 5, "Farms Reporting, Acreage Harvested, Production, and Value of Specified Vegetables," 706. Although a discrepancy exists between this figure and the more positive commentary in agricultural publications, it does not affect the basic overall trend of the pumpkin's increasing value to farmers.

19   The 2.7 average acreage per farm was derived by dividing the total pumpkin acreage of 5,975 acres by the 2,194 farms that grew pumpkins in 1939. The annual income statistic is from the website The People History, http://www .thepeoplehistory.com/1940s.html (accessed August 15, 2011).

20   The geographical distribution information for 1949 is from U.S. Department of Agriculture, *1950 Census of Agriculture*, vol. 2, table 96, "Specified Vegetables Harvested for Sale . . .," 665. The East North Central region reported 802 farms and 2,840 acres. The Mid-Atlantic reported 529 farms and 1,298 acres. New England reported 176 farms and 134 acres.

21   Surveys of this period in American food history include Levenstein, *Revolution at the Table*; Laura Shapiro, *Perfection Salad: Women and Cooking at the Turn of the Century* (New York: Farrar, Straus and Giroux, 1986); and Alice L. McLean, *Cooking in America, 1840–1945* (Westport, Conn.: Greenville Press, 2006).

22   William Cronon, "Annihilating Space: Meat," in *Nature's Metropolis*, 207–47. See also Siegfred Gideon, "Mechanization and Organic Substance: Bread," in *Mechanization Takes Command: A Contribution to Anonymous History* (New York: W. W. Norton, 1970 [1948]), 169–208.

23   John L. Cowan, "The Golden Pumpkin Pie," *Pacific Monthly*, November 1906, 570.

24   Upton Sinclair, *The Jungle* (New York: Doubleday, 1906).

25   The Natural Food Company ad appeared in *The Delineator*, November 1906, 854.

26   John Guernsey, "Food Retailing," in U.S. Department of Commerce, *Fifteenth Census of the United States: Census of Distribution, Retail Distribution: Food Retailing* (Washington, D.C.: Government Printing Office, 1934), 1.

27   Edward Henry Philippi, "A Variety of Halloween Window Plans," in *The Grocer's Window Book: A Compilation of Practical Plans for Displays in the Grocer's Window* (Chicago: R. R. Donnelly and Sons, 1914), 97.

28   Guernsey, "Food Retailing," 1.

29   Quotation from "Streamlined Thanksgiving Dinner: Modern Kitchen Technique Applied to American Menu," *New York Times*, November 21, 1937, 152.

30   Catherine MacKenzie, "Our Thanksgiving Feast," *New York Times*, November 24, 1935, SM17.

31   "A New Pumpkin Pie Mix," *New York Times*, September 29, 1945, 18.

32   The Connecticut Pie Company ad appeared in the *Washington (D.C.) Times*, October 15, 1910, last edition, 5.

33   Cowan, "Golden Pumpkin Pie," 570.

34   "Pumpkin Pie Has Arrived."

35   Harvey Wiley, *Foods and Their Adulteration: Origin, Manufacture and Composition of Food Products* . . . (Philadelphia: P. Blakiston's Son, 1917), 283.

36   "Wave Your Magic Wand over Pumpkins," *Ladies' Home Journal*, November 1946, 73; following quotation from Arvill Wayne Bitting, *The Canning of Foods* (Washington, D.C.: Government Printing Office, 1913), 55.

37   B. M. Davis, "Organization of Nature-Study in the Primary Grades," *Nature Study Review* 4 (1908): 108.

38   "Fall Church Sociables for Grown Folks," *Ladies' Home Journal*, October 1903, 50.

39   Cowan, "Golden Pumpkin Pie," 570.

40   Appelbaum, *Thanksgiving*, 230–31.

41   Cowan, "Golden Pumpkin Pie," 570.

42   "Extra Special Pumpkin Pie," *Ladies' Home Journal*, November 1943, 75.

43   Carolyn Sherwin Bailey, *What to Do for Uncle Sam: A First Book of Citizenship* (Chicago: A. Flanagan, 1918), 76.

44   In 1942, the photograph division of FSA shifted over to the Office of War Information (OWI). Scholarly works on the subject include Carl Fleischhauer and Beverly W. Brannan, eds., *Documenting America, 1935–1943* (Berkeley: University of California Press, 1988), especially the essay by Lawrence Levine, "The Historian and the Icon: Photography and the History of the American People in the 1930s and 1940s," and Alan Trachtenberg's introduction to the volume. See also Guimond, *American Photography*, and Timothy Davis, "Beyond the Sacred and Profane: Cultural Landscape Photography in America, 1930–1990," in *Mapping American Culture*, eds. Wayne Franklin and Michael Steiner (Iowa City: University of Iowa Press, 1992), 191–230.

45 See Karal Ann Marling, *Wall to Wall America: Post Office Murals in the Great Depression* (Minneapolis: University of Minnesota Press, 1982).

46 An image of the mural is located at "New Deal/WPA Art in Chilton, Wisconsin," http://www.wpamurals.com/ChiltonW.htm (accessed June 13, 2009).

47 John Steinbeck, *The Grapes of Wrath* (New York: Viking Press, 1939); James Agee and Walker Evans, *Let Us Now Praise Famous Men* (Boston: Houghton Mifflin, 1939).

48 James M. Dennis, *Renegade Regionalists: The Modern Independence of Grant Wood, Thomas Hart Benton, and John Steuart Curry* (Madison: University of Wisconsin Press, 1998); Wanda Corn, *Grant Wood: The Regionalist Vision* (New Haven, Conn.: Yale University Press, 1983); Joseph S. Czestochowski, *John Steuart Curry and Grant Wood: A Portrait of Rural America* (Columbia: University of Missouri Press, 1981); Deborah Bricker Balken, *After Many Springs: Regionalism, Modernism, and the Midwest* (Des Moines, Iowa: Des Moines Art Center, 2009). Some of the paintings of the three artists, especially Curry's, portray the ominous threats of modern machinery and industry to family farms. In *Tornado over Kansas* (1929), Curry depicted a farm family escaping into its root cellar as its modest wooden farm buildings and house stand to be ruined by an approaching cyclone, a symbolic rendering of threats from the modern world. Other artists offered idyllic and inviting pictures of an unchanging way of life. In *Renegade Regionalists*, Dennis argued that the artists had modern, not nostalgic, sensibilities.

49 For example, see a November 1942 photograph by Howard R. Hollem (Farm Security Administration, Office of War Information Photograph Collection, Library of Congress, Digital ID fsa 8b04621).

50 For example, "Pie 'Like Mother's' to Cheer Soldiers Here; Obtained by Woman Who Baked in 1st A.E.F.," *New York Times*, November 26, 1942; "Soldiers to Be Hosts: 700 at Fort Dix to Share Thanksgiving with Kin," *New York Times*, November 16, 1941, 42; "Extra Special Pumpkin Pie."

51 "Tricks or Treats," *Chicago Daily Tribune*, October 31, 1944, 10. Scholarly works on the development of trick-or-treating include Bannatyne, *Halloween*, 135, 141–43; Rogers, *Halloween*, 86–92; Skal, *Death Makes a Holiday*, 53–56; Santino, *All Around the Year*, 150–53, in which he associates it with other mumming traditions; and Tad Tuleja, "Trick or Treat: Pre-texts and Contexts," in *Halloween and Other Festivals of Death and Life*, ed. Jack Santino (Knoxville: University of Tennessee Press, 1994), 82–102.

52 Sources documenting Halloween violence include "1000 Windows in Queens Broken on Halloween," *New York Times*, November 1, 1939, 12, and "'No Halloween Rough Stuff,' Mayor Warns; He Urges Children to Shun 'Hoodlumism,'" *New York Times*, October 31, 1942, 17. See also Rogers, *Halloween*, 78–88.

53 Grace L. Weeks, "Merry Hallowe'en Larks," *Ladies' Home Journal*, October 1903, 48.

54 Ruby Ross Goodnow, "A Halloween Housewarming," *The Delineator*, October 1911.

55 Jack Pumpkinhead appeared in L. Frank Baum, *The Marvelous Land of Oz* (Chicago: Reilly and Britton, 1904); L. Frank Baum, *The Road to Oz* (Chicago: Reilly and Britton, 1909); L. Frank Baum, *Jack Pumpkinhead and the Sawhorse* (Chicago: Reilly and Britton, 1913); and L. Frank Baum, *The Visitors of Oz* (Chicago: Reilly and Lee, 1960). He was also a part of the Oz series written by Ruth P. Thompson, including *Jack Pumpkinhead of Oz* (Chicago: Reilly and Lee, 1929). He appeared in the comic strip series and board games based on the Oz stories as well.

56 These descriptions are based on thousands of Halloween postcards produced at the turn of the twentieth century. For collectors' guidebooks that illustrate many of them, see Schneider, *Halloween in America*; Apkarian-Russell, *Collectible Halloween*; Apkarian-Russell, *More Halloween Collectibles*; and Apkarian-Russell, *Halloween: Collectible Decorations and Games*.

57 Glen MacDonough, "The Jack O'Lantern Girl" (New York: M. Witmark and Sons, 1905), music supplement, *Chicago Sunday American*, March 12, 1905, 5–8.

58 The dramatic increase in the number of women in the workforce is discussed in V. F. Nieva and B. A. Gutek, *Women and Work: A Psychological Perspective* (New York: Praeger, 1981), as cited in Desirae M. Domenico and Karen H. Jones, "Career Aspirations of Women in the 20th Century," *Journal of Career and Technical Education* 22 (Fall 2006): 2.

59 Hannah Ayer, "The Pumpkin," *American Kitchen Magazine: A Domestic Science Monthly* 18 (October 1902–March 1903): 24.

60 John Kirkpatrick, *The Light of the Pumpkin: A Comedy in One Act* (New York: Samuel French, 1934).

61 MacKenzie, "Our Thanksgiving Feast," SM17.

62 Frank W. Sinks, "A Poem on Cow-Pumpkins and the 'Land of the Pumpkin Pie': Something to Make Your Mouth Water, Michigan's Greatest Bid for Fame," *Gateway: A Magazine of Literature, Commerce and Development*, November 1904, 31–32.

63 See, for example, Jane Eckert, "Farm Direct Marketing from a Producer's Perspective," *Agricultural Outlook Forum 1999*, February 22, 1999, http://www.usda.gov/agency/oce/waob/outlook99/speeches/023/eckert.txt (accessed April 18, 2001); Monika Roth, "Overview of Farm Direct Marketing Industry Trends," *Agricultural Outlook Forum 1999*, February 22, 1999, http://www.usda.gov/agency/oce/waob/outlook99/speeches/023/roth.txt (accessed April 18, 2001); "USDA Progress and Achievements on Small Farms Report no. 1: Market Development," 2001, http://www.usda.gov/oce/smallfarm/reports/rpt1md.htm (accessed June 24, 2009); and "Agricultural Marketing Service Farmers Markets—Facts," 2001, http://www.ams.usda.gov/farmersmarkets/facts (accessed June 24, 2009).

64 In 1900, only a few thousand people owned cars; by 1920, more than 2 million automobiles a year rolled off the assembly lines; and by 1930 there were an estimated 26.5 million cars in the United States. Sean Dennis Cashman, *America*

in the Twenties and Thirties (New York: New York University Press, 1989), 8–9; Danborn, Born in the Country, 166.

65 James Agee, "The Great American Roadside," Fortune, October 1934, 53–63, 172, 174, and 177, provides an excellent contemporary overview of the early period of auto tourism. The most recent scholarly works on the subject, especially in regard to pilgrimages to national parks and monuments, are Marguerite S. Shaffer, See America First: Tourism and National Identity, 1880–1940 (Washington, D.C.: Smithsonian Institution Press, 2001); Paul Sutter, Driven Wild: How the Fight against Automobiles Launched the Modern Wilderness Movement (Seattle: University of Washington Press, 2002); and Hal K. Rothman, Devil's Bargain: Tourism in the Twentieth-Century American West (Lawrence: University Press of Kansas, 1998). For works on the relationship between road design and national identity, see Warren James Belasco, Americans on the Road: From Autocamp to Motel, 1910–1945 (Cambridge, Mass.: MIT Press, 1979); John A. Jakle, The Tourist: Travel in Twentieth-Century North America (Lincoln: University of Nebraska Press, 1985); John A. Jakle, "Landscapes Redesigned for the Automobile," in The Making of the American Landscape, ed. Michael P. Conven (New York: Routledge, 1990); Jan Jennings, ed., Roadside America: The Automobile in Design and Culture (Ames: Iowa State University Press, 1990); and Karal Ann Marling, The Colossus of Roads: Myth and Symbol along the American Highway (Minneapolis: University of Minnesota Press, 1984). Few of these works discuss local tourism, the focus of my chapter. Instead, they look at national tourist sites and cross-country road trips.

For works on the way American tourists have explored the natural world through consumption, see Rothman, Devil's Bargain; Shaffer, See America First; Sutter, Driven Wild, especially chapter 5, "Knowing Nature through Leisure: Outdoor Recreation during the Inter-war Years"; and White, Land Use, Environment, and Social Change. Works on nature and consumption of goods include Susan G. Davis, Spectacular Nature: Corporate Culture and the Sea World Experience (Berkeley: University of California Press, 1997), and Price, Flight Maps.

66 Robert S. Lynd and Helen M. Lynd, Middletown in Transition: A Study in Cultural Conflicts (New York: Harcourt, Brace, 1937), 256–66.

67 Robert S. Lynd and Helen M. Lynd, Middletown: A Story in American Culture (New York: Harcourt, Brace, 1929), 254 and 262–63.

68 This was the argument made in Rothman, Devil's Bargain, 149; Shaffer, See America First, 1–6; and Sutter, Driven Wild, 19–53. Rothman and Shaffer argued that after the 1920s, tourists were, in Rothman's words, less concerned with "enlightenment and the cultural message" than with recreation. The history of pumpkin stands contradicts their findings. The stands reveal how tourism, in the form of small-scale, locally run operations, have benefited rural communities.

69 Agee, "Great American Roadside," 53.

70 University of Connecticut, Economic Digest for Connecticut Agriculture, 1929, 95.

71   Lee Haystead, *Meet the Farmer: A Personal Introduction to Thirty Million Americans* (New York: Putnam, 1944), 62.

72   See, for example, Fred Emerson Clark and Louis D. H. Wield, eds., *Marketing Agricultural Products in the United States* (New York: Macmillan, 1932), 54.

73   "Improvements in Roadside Marketing," *American Cookery*, August-September 1929, 101.

74   Maryland Agricultural Experiment Station, *Bulletin of the Maryland Agricultural Experiment Station*, 1925, 197; Elmer Otterbein Fippin, *First Principles of Cooperation in Buying and Selling in Agriculture* (Richmond, Va.: Garrett and Massie, 1934). *Economic Geography* was published by Clark University.

75   David B. Greenberg and Charles Corbin, *So You're Going to Buy a Farm* (New York: Greenberg, 1944), 46.

76   Robert Frost, "A Roadside Stand," in *Collected Poems of Robert Frost* (Cutchogue, N.Y.: Buccaneer Books, 1986), 370–71. According to *The Robert Frost Encyclopedia*, the poem was first published in the June 1936 issue of *Atlantic Monthly* and also in the collection *A Further Range* (1936), where it had the subtitle "On Being Put Out of Our Misery." Nancy Lewis Tuten and John Zubizarreta, eds., *The Robert Frost Encyclopedia* (Westport, Conn.: Greenwood Press, 2001), 306.

77   Florence Bourgeois, *Peter, Peter, Pumpkin Grower* (Garden City, N.Y.: Doubleday, Doran, 1937).

78   Roy E. Stryker and Nancy Wood, *In This Proud Land: America 1935–1943 as Seen in the FSA Photographs* (Greenwich, Conn.: New York Graphic Society, 1973), 38, as quoted in Levine, "The Historian and the Icon," 16.

79   The photographs date from 1939 to 1941 and depict stands outside small towns in Massachusetts and Connecticut.

80   John Collier, untitled, between 1935 and 1942, Library of Congress Prints and Photograph Division, FSA Photo no. 34–081646-D.

81   John Collier, "Sales Promotion at a Wayside Harvest Market, Greenfield (vicinity), Mass," October 1941, Library of Congress Prints and Photograph Division, LC-USF34–080845-D.

82   John Collier, "Pumpkins for Sale from a Farm Wagon, Mohawk Trail, in the Berkshires Hills, Massachusetts," October 1941, Library of Congress Prints and Photograph Division, LC-USF34–081636-D.

83   The expression "pig and pumpkin show" is quoted from Isaac Brandt, "The State Fair: Past and Present," *The Mid-western* (Midwestern Association of University Student Employment Directors) 1 (September 1906): 71. *Annual Report, Nebraska State Board of Agriculture 1910* (Lincoln: Jacob North, 1910), 117, stated, "They had a crackling good pumpkin show and everything was filled with fun."

84   For a history of town festivals at the turn of the twentieth century, see David Glassberg, *American Historical Pageantry: The Uses of Tradition in the Early Twentieth Century* (Chapel Hill: University of North Carolina Press, 1990). A

good historical source for these events is Constance Cary Harrison, "American Rural Festivals," *Century* 1, no. 3 (1895): 323–33. For the history of the Circleville Pumpkin Show in particular, refer to the Circleville Pumpkin Show hanging files, Pickaway Historical Society collections, Circleville, Ohio.

85   Quoted from Circleville Pumpkin Festival, Inc., "Fantastic Facts about the Circleville Pumpkin Festival," Pickaway Historical Society collections, Circleville, Ohio.

86   The rate charged to visit the Arata Pumpkin Farm is provided on the farm's website, http://www.aratapumpkinfarm.com/?pid=home (accessed August 17, 2011).

6. ATLANTIC GIANTS TO JACK-BE-LITTLES: THE CHANGING NATURE OF PUMPKINS, 1946 TO THE PRESENT

1   W. Atlee Burpee Company, *Burpee Seeds and Everything for the Garden* (Warminster, Pa., 1975), 21.

2   I calculated the totals using a 12-ton average yield per acre, multiplied by the number of acres harvested in the United States each year, although the yield per acre in 1959 was probably lower than that in 2007. In 2007, 92,955 acres of pumpkins were harvested, which results in an estimate of 1,115,460 tons. In 1959, 16,275 acres of pumpkins were harvested, for 195,300 tons. In 1949, 5,975 were harvested, for 71,700 tons. U.S. Department of Agriculture, *2007 Census of Agriculture*, vol. 1 (Washington, D.C.: Government Printing Office, 2009), table 30, "Vegetables, Potatoes, and Melons Harvested for Sale: 2007 and 2002," 532; U.S. Department of Agriculture, *1959 Census of Agriculture*, vol. 2 (Washington, D.C.: Government Printing Office, 1961), table 126, "Specified Vegetables Harvested for Sale—Farms Reporting," 874; U.S. Department of Agriculture, *1950 Census of Agriculture*, vol. 2, table 3, 519. I estimated yield per acre from various sources, including Jonathan R. Schultheis, "Growing Pumpkins and Squash" (North Carolina Cooperative Extension Service, revised January 1995, reviewed January 1998), http://www.ces.ncsu.edu/depts/hort/hil/hil-24.html (accessed May 24, 2010). Schultheis stated that smaller varieties yielded 5 to 7 tons, or 2,000 to 4,000 fruits per acre, and large types for fresh market yielded 10 to 30 tons, or 1,000 to 2,000 fruits per acre. For Texas's average of 20 to 30 tons per acre, see "Crop Profile for Pumpkin in Texas," June 2002, http://www.ipmcenters.org/cropprofiles/docs/TXpumpkin.pdf (accessed June 23, 2010). For Kansas's average of 20 to 30 tons per acre, see Charles Mar, Terry Schaplowsky, and Ted Carey, "Pumpkins," Kansas State University Agricultural Experiment Station and Cooperative Extension Service, Horticultural Report MF-2030, November 2004, 2. For Virginia's average of 15 to 25 tons per acre, see Anthony Bratsch, "Specialty Crop Profile: Pumpkins," Virginia Cooperative Extension, May 1, 2009, http://pubs.ext.vt.edu/438/438-100/438-100.html (accessed June 23, 2010). For Oregon's average of 10 to 20 tons per acre, see "Pumpkin and

Winter Squash," Commercial Vegetable Production Guides, North Willamette Research and Extension Center, Oregon State University, August 2004, 12, http://nwrec.hort.oregonstate.edu/pumpkin.html. Gary Lucier, an agriculturalist economist at the USDA specializing in vegetable production, suggested 12 tons as a good estimate of the average yield per acre. Gary Lucier telephone interview by the author, April 21, 2010. See also Gary Lucier and Rachael Dettman, "Vegetable and Melons Outlook: Commodity Highlight: Pumpkins," U.S. Department of Agriculture, Economic Research Service Report VGS-323, October 25, 2007, 23.

3   U.S. Department of Agriculture, 1964 Census of Agriculture, vol. 2 (Washington, D.C.: Government Printing Office, 1967), 332.

4   Polk Laffoon, "Pump-kin," TWA Ambassador, October 1979, 64.

5   Works on Halloween traditions from the 1950s to the present include Bannatyne, Halloween, 121–60; Rogers, Halloween, 78–172; Skal, Death Makes a Holiday; Santino, Halloween and Other Festivals; Santino, "Halloween in America"; Santino, "Night of the Wandering Souls"; Santino, All Around the Year; and Tuleja, "Pumpkins," 142–65.

6   Works on the twentieth-century environmental movement include William Cronon, ed., Uncommon Ground: Toward Reinventing Nature (New York: W. W. Norton, 1995); Michael Lewis, ed., American Wilderness: A New History (New York: Oxford University Press, 2007), 167–272; Steinberg, Down to Earth, 206–81; John R. McNeill, Something under the Sun: An Environmental History of the Twentieth-Century World (New York: W. W. Norton, 2000); Samuel P. Hays, A History of Environmental Politics since 1945 (Pittsburgh: University of Pittsburgh Press, 2000); and Carolyn Merchant, Major Problems in Environmental History: Documents and Essays (Boston: Houghton Mifflin, 2005), 484–568.

7   Jack Santino examined Halloween displays as celebrations of the season, rural life, and community in "The Folk Assemblage of Autumn: Tradition and Creativity in Halloween Folk Art," in John Vlach and Simon J. Bronner, eds., Folk Art and Art Worlds (Logan: Utah State University Press, 1992), 151–69; Santino, "Halloween in America"; and Santino, All Around the Year, 34–41.

8   Scholarly works on lawns and yard displays include Virginia Scott Jenkins, The Lawn: A History of an American Obsession (Washington, D.C.: Smithsonian Institution Press, 1994); Georges Teyssot, The American Lawn (New York: Princeton Architectural Press, 1999); Kenneth T. Jackson, Crabgrass Frontier: The Suburbanization of the United States (New York: Oxford University Press, 1985); Jennifer Price, "A Brief History of the Plastic Pink Flamingo," in Flight Maps, 111–66; Helen Bradley Griebel, "Worldview on the Landscape: A Regional Yard Art Study," Pennsylvania Folklife 36, no. 1 (1986): 39–48; Colleen Josephine Sheehy, "The Flamingo in the Garden: Artifice, Aesthetics, and Popular Taste in American Yard Art" (Ph.D. diss., University of Minnesota, 1991); and Ted Steinberg, American Green: The American Obsessive Quest for the Perfect Lawn (New York: W. W. Norton, 2007).

9   Eve Merriam, "Jack o'Lantern," in *Halloween ABC: Poems by Eve Merriam* (New York: Macmillan, 1987), n.p.

10 N. M. Bodecker, "Pumpkin, Pumpkin, Pumpkin Bright," http://www.bconnex .net/-mbuchana/realms/halloween/pumpkin.html (accessed November 12, 1999).

11 Publishers such as Celestial Arts, which produces many New Age books, also publish stories about kind-hearted jack-o'-lanterns. See, for example, Deborah Turney Zagwyn, *The Pumpkin Blanket* (Berkeley, Calif.: Celestial Arts, 1990).

12 David Ray, *Pumpkin Light* (New York: Philomel Books, 1993), 1 and 19, respectively.

13 *It's the Great Pumpkin, Charlie Brown* (Paramount Pictures, 1966). The character and storyline also appear in Charles M. Schulz, *How Long, Great Pumpkin, How Long?* (New York: Holt, Rinehart and Winston, 1977). See also David Michaelis, *Schulz and Peanuts: A Biography* (New York: Harper Perennial, 2008).

14 Eloise Franco, "The Ugly Pumpkin," in *Little Stories* (North Quincy, Mass.: Christopher Publishing, 1970); John Ott, *Peter Pumpkin* (Garden City, N.Y.: Doubleday, 1963). See also Michael Chabon, "Along the Frontage Road," *New Yorker*, November 19, 2001, 74–77. Chabon's story is not children's literature, but it sentimentalizes the connection between a child and the vegetable. It is about a young boy who visits a pumpkin patch and finds solace in a baby pumpkin after the death of his little sister.

15 Likewise, many growers anthropomorphize their pumpkins as children. Pumpkin Nook, one of the major giant pumpkin grower websites, has a section called "Naming Your Baby," which lightheartedly suggests, "Ah!! The blessed moment has finally arrived!! You have carefully pollinated your female pumpkin and a tiny baby fruit is beginning to grow! If you haven't done so already, you should now select a name for your baby. Selection of a name . . . is a healthy part of the bonding." Pumpkin Nook, http://members.aol.com/ ezpumpkin/ names.htm (accessed June 22, 1999). Scholars from Claude Lévi-Strauss to Keith Thomas have considered the naming of nonhuman forms to be a way of bringing them into the human social circle. See Claude Lévi-Strauss, *The Savage Mind* (Chicago: University of Chicago Press, 1966), 204–7, and Thomas, *Man and the Natural World*, 110–13.

16 The Libby's advertisement appeared in *Parade* magazine, November 12, 1995, 11. Anne Geddes is the photographer.

17 This idea, along with analyses of Halloween pranks, is addressed in Bill Ellis, "'Safe' Spooks: New Halloween Traditions in Response to Sadism Legends," in Santino, *Halloween*, 24–44, and Steve Siporin, "Halloween Pranks: 'Just a Little Inconvenience,'" in Santino, *Halloween*, 45–61.

18 See Ellis, "'Safe' Spooks," and Joel Best and Gerald T. Horiuchi, "The Razor Blade in the Apple: The Social Construction of Urban Legends," *Social Problems* 32 (June 1985): 488–99.

19 *Sleepy Hollow*, directed by Tim Burton (Los Angeles: Paramount Pictures, 1999).

Another Burton-directed movie featuring pumpkins is *Nightmare before Christmas* (Los Angeles: Walt Disney Pictures, 1993).

20 James Wyeth, *Pumpkinhead—Self Portrait* (1977), reproduced in Susan Larsen et al., *Wondrous Strange: The Wyeth Tradition* (Boston: Little, Brown, 1998), 76. The book was published in conjunction with an exhibition of the same title at the Farnsworth Museum in Rockland, Maine. Other James Wyeth paintings featuring pumpkins include *Halloween* (1964) and *Smashing Pumpkins* (2007). The artist's famous father, Andrew Wyeth, also painted pumpkins; see, for example, *Jack Be Nimble* (1976). For a reproduction, see Larsen, *Wondrous Strange*, 94. Men with pumpkin heads make many appearances in *New Yorker* cartoons. See *New Yorker* cartoon bank, http://www.cartoonbank.com (accessed June 21, 2010).

21 *Pulp Fiction*, directed by Quentin Tarantino (Los Angeles: Miramax Films, 1994). A pumpkin horror movie is *Pumpkinhead*, directed by Stan Winston (Los Angeles: United Artists, 1988).

22 Bill Pronzini, "Pumpkin," in *Halloween Horrors*, ed. Alan Ryan (Garden City, N.Y.: Doubleday, 1986), 141–48.

23 Eric A. Kimmel's book *Pumpkinhead* uses the pumpkin in a morality tale about narrow-mindedness, ignorance, and bigotry. In it, a pumpkinhead is a metaphor for ignorant people who appreciate only their own kind and are blind to different ways of life beyond what is familiar to them. Eric A. Kimmel, *Pumpkinhead* (Delray Beach, Fla.: Winslow Press, 2001).

24 Jeff MacNelly, "The Great Debate," *Washington Post*, October 30, 1999 (originally for the *Chicago Tribune*), A25. See also a *New Yorker* article that refers to millionaire Republican candidate Steve Forbes as "a geeky, hopelessly awkward plutocrat" and is illustrated with a drawing of Forbes standing with outstretched arms and his body metamorphosed into a pile of pumpkins, implying the "pumpkinification" of the businessman on the campaign stump. Elizabeth Kolbert, "It's Only Money," *New Yorker*, November 8, 1999, 50.

25 "Top 10 Aphrodisiacs," Science Channel, http://science.discovery.com/top-ten/2009/aphrodisiacs-09.html (accessed April 16, 2010).

26 Philip Roth, *Portnoy's Complaint* (London: Jonathan Cape, 1969), cited in Norrman and Haarberg, *Language of Nature*, 67. Tad Tuleja developed a gender analysis of pumpkin carving in "Pumpkins," in *Rooted in America*, 142–65. He described pumpkin carving as a male activity because, he contended, it is usually performed by the father and is related to the world outside the home. He perceived pumpkin pie-making to be women's domain because it involves domestic activities. The problem with this construction is that it is based on antiquated gender divisions, which fall apart under more precise evaluation, especially for customs in the late twentieth century.

27 Penelope Mortimer, *The Pumpkin Eater* (New York: McGraw Hill, 1963); Harold Pinter, "The Pumpkin Eater," in *Five Screenplays* (New York: Grove Press, 1973). The screenplay was made into the movie *The Pumpkin Eater*, directed by Jack

Clayton and starring Anne Bancroft (London: Royal Films International, 1964). Susanna Hofmann McShea, *The Pumpkin-Shell Wife: A Hometown Heroes Mystery* (New York: St. Martin's, 1992).

28   Advertisement sent in a mailer of Valu-Pak coupons to the author's house in Washington, D.C., October 1999.

29   William Booth and Sharon Waxman, "The Colorful Cast on the Red Carpet," *Washington Post*, March 26, 2001, C9.

30   Glenn Peake, "By Pumpkin Light," *Martha Stewart Living*, October 1998, 194.

31   See Santino, *All Around the Year*, 161. Tuleja writes that smashing pumpkins represents both the destruction of property—and therefore an encroachment on the domestic realm—and the "closing of the circle" of Halloween festivities, because the act disposes of the now useless jack-o'-lantern. Tuleja, "Pumpkins," 155. I refer to the rock band The Smashing Pumpkins.

32   Don Nivens, quoted in Bill Weekes, "Pumpkins for the Holidays," *Small Farm Today*, December 1996, 34.

33   "Handsome" described the Big Max variety in Gurney's Seed and Nursery Company, 2010 *Catalog*, http://gurneys.com/product.asp_o_pn_E_66293 (accessed February 5, 2010). "Very uniform and attractive" described the Ghost Rider variety in Agway, Inc., 1992 *Agway Commercial Grower Vegetable Seed Catalog* (Elizabethtown, Pa.: Agway, Inc., 1992), 29. "Well-colored and classy" described the Jack o'Lantern variety in Harris Seeds, 1992–93 *Harris Seeds: Professional Vegetable and Bedding Plant Growers' Catalog* (Rochester, N.Y.: Harris Seeds, 1992), 40.

34   Holmes Seed Company, 1990 *Wholesale Price List for Commercial Growers* (Canton, Ohio, 1990).

35   The definition of a hybrid is from Raymond J. Samulis, county department head, Cooperative Extension of Burlington County, New Jersey Agricultural Extension Station, email to the author, July 6, 2010.

36   Charles W. Marr, *Commercial Vegetable Production: Pumpkins* (Manhattan, Kans.: Co-operative Extension Service, Kansas State University, 1995), 2.

37   As I discuss in more detail in the next chapter, some farmers sell their pumpkins to cattle owners, zoos, and hunters, who use them as deer feed or bait. Information about the hunters courtesy of Ray Samulis.

38   Harris Moran Seed Company, 1986 *HM Community Vegetable Growers Seed Guide* (Rochester, N.Y., 1986), 61.

39   Harris Seeds, 1992–93 *Harris Seeds Home Garden Catalog* (Rochester, N.Y.: Harris Seeds, 1992), 39.

40   Joanne Thuente and John W. Francis, *Seed Savers 2001 Yearbook* (Decorah, Iowa: Seed Savers Exchange, 2001), 281.

41   Gurney's Seed and Nursery Company, 1999 *Spring Catalog* (Yankton, S.D.), 21.

42   Gurney's Seed and Nursery Company, 1998 *Spring Catalog* (Yankton, S.D.), 19.

43   W. Atlee Burpee and Company, *Seeds and Everything for the Garden*, 25.

44   The key chain was advertised in Tiffany and Company, *Fall Selections 2001*, 20.

I have named only a few of the hundreds of types of objects for sale every fall. Besides exploring the aisles and displays of the stores previously mentioned, I scanned dozens of catalogs, including those of Celebration Fantastic, Camella and Main, Indian Summer, Pottery Barn, Martha by Mail, Panache, and Faith Mountain Company, and newspaper advertising supplements from CVS, Rite Aid, Caldor's, and K-Mart.

45 The Cotton Gin, fall 2001 catalog, 54. For an analysis of American consumerism and nature, see Jennifer Price, "Looking for Nature at the Mall: A Field Guide to the Nature Company," in Cronon, *Uncommon Ground*, 187–202.

46 Another giant variety is Burpee's Prizewinner, but it cannot compete with the Atlantic Giant for size.

47 Al Kingsbury, *The Pumpkin King: Four-Time World Champion Howard Dill and the Atlantic Giant* (Hantsport, Nova Scotia: Lancelot Press, 1992). Dill died in 2008.

48 Pumpkin Nook website, http://www.pumpkinnook.com/giants/giantpumpkins .htm (accessed February 10, 2010).

49 Ray Vicker, "Pumpkins, Plywood, Squash, and Balloon: A Tale of Five Cities," *Wall Street Journal*, October 5, 1981.

50 Steve Bender, "Champion Vegetables," *Southern Living*, October, 1995, 96.

51 Don Langevin, *How-to-Grow World Class Giant Pumpkins, II* (Norton, Mass.: Annedawn Press, 1998), 45.

52 Ibid., 50–51.

53 Lyle Rockwell, letter to the listserve pumpkins@mallorn.com, April 16, 2001.

54 Julia Scott, "The Race to Grow the One-Ton Pumpkin," *New York Times*, October 5, 2011. Quotation from Katy Kelly, "Growing Great Pumpkins, an All-Consuming Passion," *USA Today*, October 4, 1996, D-1 and D-2. An example of an online seed auction is at the website BigPumpkins.com, http://www.bigpumpkins.com/MsgBoard/ViewBoard.asp?b=26 (accessed February 11, 2010).

55 For guides to growing giant pumpkins, see Langevin, *How-to-Grow World Class Giant Pumpkins* (Norton, Mass.: Annedawn Publishing, 1993); Langevin, *How-to-Grow World Class Giant Pumpkins, II*; Don Langevin, *How-to-Grow World Class Giant Pumpkins, III* (Norton, Mass.: Annedawn Publishing, 2003); Don Langevin, *How-to-Grow World Class Giant Pumpkins the All Organic Way* (Norton, Mass.: Annedawn Publishing, 2009); Michael Evans, "Big: The Pumpkin. A Tale of International Intrigue Takes Shape as Three Towns Named Shelburne Plot to Grow the Biggest Pumpkin," *National Gardening*, October 1988, 18–21; Catherine Yronwode, "Here's How to Grow Giant Vegetables!" *Organic Gardening*, December 1994, 22–29; and Paul Dunphy, "The Great Pumpkin: Breeders Continue to Improve the Easy-to-Grow Jack-o'-Lantern," *Horticulture*, October 1992, 40–44.

56 Block was featured in Michael Vitez, "The Great Orange Hope," *Philadelphia Inquirer Magazine*, October 29, 1995, 12–17 and 21.

57 Alan Sternberg, "A Growing Concern: Rivals in Big E Pumpkin Contest

Throwing Their Weight Around," *Hartford Courant*, September 28, 1984, B-1.

58 The growers were Richard and Lloyd Koch, who competed in the Circleville Pumpkin Show weigh-off in 1998. See Mary Bridgman, "Pumped Up," *Columbus Dispatch*, October 16, 1998, C-1.

59 "Largest pumpkin world record set by Christy Harp," World Records Academy website, http://www.worldrecordsacademy.org/nature/largest_pumpkin-world_record_set_by_Christy_Harp_90368.htm (accessed August 10, 2010).

60 Pumpkin Nook website, http://members.aol.com/ezpumpkin/hitters.htm (accessed October 8, 1999).

61 Statistics from H. C. Wein, "The Cucurbits: Cucumbers, Melons, Squash and Pumpkins," in *The Physiology of Vegetable Crops* (New York: CAB International, 1997), 364, and Robinson and Decker-Walters, *Cucurbits*, 19, respectively. Robinson and Decker-Walters cited an 1894 study in which a scientist weighed a pumpkin hourly to determine its growth rate.

62 Langevin, *How-to-Grow World Class Giant Pumpkins*, 71.

63 Mission statement, Giant Urban Pumpkin Growers of America website, http://www.gupga.com (accessed February 21, 2001).

64 The email address for the message board is www.bigpumpkins.com/msgboard/Viewboard.asp?b=26 (accessed during the 2010 growing season).

65 Howard Dill, quoted in Yronwode, "Here's How to Grow Giant Vegetables!" 22.

66 World Records Academy website, http://www.worldrecordsacademy.org/nature/largest_pumpkin-world_record_set_by_Chris_Stevens_101905.html (accessed April 30, 2011).

67 "Pumpkins" listserve at pumpkins@mallorn (accessed 2001).

68 Big Pumpkins.com, http://www.bigpumpkins.com (accessed May 20, 2010).

69 Christy Harp, video interview, World's Record Academy website, www.worldrecordsacademy.org/nature/largest_pumpkin-world_record_set_by_Christy_Harp_90368.htm (accessed August 8, 2010).

70 Howard Dill, giant pumpkin seed brochure, 1995.

71 Langevin, *How-to-Grow World Class Giant Pumpkins*, 6.

72 Dave Stelts quoted in Michael Inbar, "Pumpkin Sets New World Record: 1,725 pounds," *Today*, http://today.msnbc.msn.com/id/33379464/ns/today-today_halloween_guide (accessed August 24, 2010).

73 Langevin, *How-to-Grow World Class Giant Pumpkins*, 1. The Great Pumpkin Commonwealth stipulates that the fruit must be 75 percent orange to yellow. Safeway World Champion Pumpkin Weigh-Off, http://www.miramarevents.com/weighoff/facts.html (accessed May 20, 2010).

74 Langevin, *How-to-Grow World Class Giant Pumpkins*, 1.

75 Ibid., 20.

76 Information on the woman who grows pumpkins at her Los Angeles apartment building is from the Pumpkin Nook website, http://www.pumpkinnook.com (accessed April 10, 2001). The person who grows pumpkins in the urban

neighborhood is Joe Mills, a photographer working at Dumbarton Oaks House Museum in the Georgetown neighborhood of Washington, D.C. Mills raised the largest pumpkin in the district on the House Museum property. Joe Mills, interview by the author, Washington, D.C., February 1998.

77 Sternberg, "Growing Concern."

78 In *On Longing*, 135, Susan Stewart called a souvenir "an object arising out of the necessarily insatiable demands of nostalgia." On consumerism, see Richard Butsch, *For Fun and Profit: The Transformation of Leisure into Consumption* (Philadelphia: Temple University Press, 1990); Susan Strasser, *Satisfaction Guaranteed: The Making of the American Mass Market* (Washington, D.C.: Smithsonian Institution Press, 1989); Susan Strasser, Charles McGovern, and Matthias Judt, eds., *Getting and Spending: European and American Consumer Societies in the Twentieth Century* (Cambridge: Cambridge University Press, 1998); and Lizabeth Cohen, *A Consumer's Republic: The Politics of Mass Consumption in Post-war America* (New York: Vintage, 2003).

79 Vitez, "Great Orange Hope," 16.

80 Santino, in *New Old-Fashioned Ways*, 30, called holiday-inspired foods "manifestations" because they are expressions of the holiday celebration.

81 I purchased molds for Jell-O's Halloween Creepy Jigglers at a Safeway grocery store in Germantown, Maryland, in October 1999. I obtained the pumpkin truffle ingredients during a telephone interview with a Godiva representative, May 26, 2010. Linus' Great Pumpkin Cookies were on sale at a Safeway grocery store in Washington, D.C., in October 2000.

82 Dave Newhauser, Libby's plant manager, interview by the author, Morton, Illinois, October 19, 2000.

83 "Spoon Fed," *Cooking Light,* October 2000, 38. The sauce costs $6.00 a bottle. For an analysis of food as sign and symbol, see Barthes, "Towards a Psychosociology of Contemporary Food Consumption." Humphrey and Humphrey, *"We Gather Together,"* also provides many case studies of the ways Americans use food for symbolic purposes in ceremonies, festivals, and rituals.

84 Georgeanne Brennan, *Holiday Pumpkins* (New York: Smithmark, 1998). For another example, a photograph of piles of pumpkins before a turn-of-the-century farmhouse accompanies a set of pumpkin recipes in "The Great Pumpkin: Why Stop at Pie?" *Woman's Day,* October 6, 1998.

85 I purchased Bark and Bradley's "Pumpkin Spice Cookies" in October 1999.

86 Pumpkin Seed Health Food Store, http://www.pumpkinseed.com (accessed October 2001). Producers tout pumpkin as a low-fat, low-calorie addition to the daily diet. See Libby's pumpkin website, http://www.verybestbaking.com/products/libbys/pumpkin.aspx (accessed April 23, 2010). Pricey pumpkin seed oil is sold at health food stores and gourmet groceries such as the Dean and Deluca chain, which in October 2001 offered it for sale for a hefty $17.50 for 8.5 ounces. Americans' appetite for whole and organic foods is part of the health food revival born out of the 1960s quest for alternative lifestyles, defiance

against corporate culture, and increased environmental awareness. For an analysis of contemporary Americans' attitudes toward food and how they trace back to the food reformers Sylvester Graham and William Kellogg, who advocated for the health benefits of whole versus processed grains, see Michelle Stacey, *Consumed: Why Americans Love, Hate, and Fear Food* (New York: Simon and Schuster, 1994), and Warren Belasco, *Appetite for Change: How the Counterculture Took on the Food Industry* (Ithaca, N.Y.: Pantheon, 1993 [1989]). See also Michael Pollan, *The Omnivore's Dilemma: A Natural History of Four Meals* (New York: Penguin Press, 2006).

87 The recipe for the pumpkin ale produced by Buffalo Bill's Brewery in Hayward, California, called for "a 40 pound pumpkin and a blend of other spices, [including] cinnamon, nutmeg, and pumpkin spices." Quoted from Buffalo Bill's Brewery flyer for pumpkin ale, received at a liquor store in Washington, D.C., in the fall of 2001. According to the Blue Moon Harvest Pumpkin Ale label, which depicts a lush field of pumpkins under the light of a blue moon, the ale "combines the flavor of vine-ripened pumpkin with traditional crystal malt." Label from ale purchased in Washington, D.C., in the fall of 2000. Blue Moon Harvest Pumpkin Ale is brewed by Blue Moon Brewing Company, Denver, Colorado.

88 Label from Post Road Pumpkin Ale purchased in Washington, D.C., in the fall of 2000. The ale is brewed and bottled by Post Road Brewing Company, Utica, New York.

89 Jonathan Hayes, "Pumpkin Pie 101," *Martha Stewart Living,* November 2000, 98. The *Washington Post* food section on November 1995 stated, "Even with all the variety, most Americans have a hard time even thinking of pumpkin without sugar and a healthy sprinkling of what some people call pumpkin-pie spice." Andrew Schloss, "Smashing Pumpkins," *Washington Post,* October 25, 1995, E10.

90 "The Desserts," *Bon Appétit,* November 2001, 224. Jack Santino would argue that these new versions are not examples of a falling away of tradition but, to the contrary, expressions of its strength and continuity, because they show the tradition's adaptation rather than stagnation, which in turn promotes its survival. Santino, *New Old-Fashioned Ways,* 27–37.

91 Quotation from a flyer distributed by the Marvelous Market retail store in Friendship Heights, Maryland, November 2001.

92 The ingredients listed are for "Grandma's Delicious Double Layer Pumpkin Pie," from a Jell-O advertisement in *Better Homes and Gardens,* November 1995.

93 "Kivanta" posted her comment to "Trader Joe's vs. Libby's Canned Pumpkin—The Results Are In," Chowhound website, November 13, 2005, http://chowhound.chow.com/topics/28093 (accessed May 23, 2010).

94 I arrived at the sum of 222,000 tons by multiplying a yield of 18 tons per acre by the 12,306 acres of processing pumpkins harvested in 2007. Processing pumpkins have a larger yield than ornamental varieties because the ornamentals must be blemish free, which reduces the number per acre that can go to market.

U.S. Department of Agriculture, *2007 Census of Agriculture*, vol. 1, table 30, 532. Yield estimate is from Schultheis, "Growing Pumpkins and Squash." Libby's also produces a canned pumpkin pie mix that contains pumpkin and spices, allowing the home baker simply to add condensed milk and eggs. Other popular canned pumpkin brands include One Pie and Farmer's Market Organic.

The statistic about Libby's having 85 percent of the market share is from Geisler, "Pumpkins." In 2000, Libby's had 80 percent of the market share, according to my interview with plant manager Dave Newhauser. Data are reiterated in materials in the vertical file at the Libby's plant archives, including "Pumpkin Harvest Rolls On," *Journal Star* (October 17, 2000).

95   Roz O'Hearn, a Libby's spokeswoman, stated, "If we had picked every pumpkin on all our acres and it was all canned and all turned into pies, it would make 90 million pumpkin pies." Quoted in Georgina Gustin, "Fields Are Awash in Pumpkins, but the Crop Is Stuck in Muck; As a Result, Pumpkin Pie Will Be a Little Hard to Come By," *St. Louis Today*, November 20, 2009, http://www.stltoday.com/news/article_612a2ead-b119–5c89-afba-fb2168e99840 .html?print=1 (accessed May 9, 2011).

96   Libby's website, http://www.verybestbaking.com/products/pumpkin (accessed August 21, 2000).

97   The packaging used in October 2001 called the pie "an old-fashioned, full-bodied pumpkin filling cradled in our famous Mrs. Smith's tender and flaky crust." For another example of the use of the old-fashioned theme, see the cookbook *Old Fashioned Pumpkin Recipes* (Nashville, Ind.: Bear Wallow Books, 1979).

98   *Time*, November 19, 2001.

99   Barbara Fairchild, "Notes from the Editor," *Bon Appétit*, November 2001, 32.

100   Food historian Sallie Tisdale evoked a sense of loss when describing the Americanization of tacos and other processed foods in *The Best Thing I Ever Tasted: The Secret of Food* (New York: Riverhead Books, 2000). For other works on processed food, see Erika Endrijonas, "Processed Foods from Scratch: Cooking for a Family in the 1950s," in *Kitchen Culture in America: Popular Representations of Food, Gender, and Race*, ed. Sherrie A. Inness (Philadelphia: University of Pennsylvania Press, 2001), 157–74; and Levenstein, *Paradox of Plenty*, 101–18.

101   This is a central analytical point in Cronon, *Nature's Metropolis*.

7. PULLING UP A PIG STY TO PUT IN A PUMPKIN PATCH: THE CHANGING NATURE OF AMERICAN RURAL ECONOMIES, 1946 TO THE PRESENT

1   Unless otherwise noted, population statistics are from the U.S. Census Bureau population finder, located on its home page, http:/www.census.gov (accessed May 8, 2011).

2   Half Moon Bay Art and Pumpkin Festival website, http://www.miramaevents .com/pumpkinfest/facts.html (accessed February 2, 2001).

3   San Mateo County Farm Bureau Pumpkin Patch Guide, http://sanmateo.cfbf
.com/pdf/PumpkinPatchGuide.pdf (accessed January 2, 2010).

4   John C. Kuehner, "Odd Their Gourds, or Real Fear?" *Cleveland Plain Dealer*,
December 9, 1999. Population as of July 2008, Chagrin Falls, Ohio, city data,
http://www.city-data.com/city/Chagrin-Falls-Ohio.html (accessed June 20,
2010).

5   Marsh quoted in Stacy Trevenon, "A Growing Tradition," *Review* (Half Moon
Bay, Calif.), October 2000, 25.

6   "The Keene Pumpkin Festival, October 27–28, 2000," Keene Pumpkin Festival
website, http://www.pumpkinfestival.com (accessed September 6, 2000).

7   Mike Badgerow, former executive director of the Morton Chamber of Commerce, interview by the author, October 20, 2000.

8   "Pumpkin Harvest Rolls On," *Journal Star* (Peoria, Ill.), October 17, 2000.

9   Mike Badgerow interview.

10   A survey on the Internet in April 2010 uncovered at least twenty towns across
the country that hold annual pumpkin festivals, most of them having started
after World War II. This number does not include the thousands of farm and
harvest festivals.

11   Vera Edwards, interview by the author, Spring Hope, North Carolina, October
7, 2000. Special thanks to Pete Daniel for introducing me to her.

12   This ritual is documented in photographs in the Libby's Company Archives,
Morton, Illinois.

13   Johnda T. Davis, ed., "'I Remember—': Personal Recollections of the Pumpkin
Show through the Years," *Pickaway Quarterly* 23, no. 3 (1981): 10–19.

14   "Harvest Festivals: Ohio's Pumpkin Show," *Better Homes and Gardens*, October
1980, 191.

15   Vera Edwards interview.

16   Ken Ripley, "SH Festival Set to Begin This Friday," *Spring Hope Enterprise*,
October 5, 2000, 1; Vera Edwards interview.

17   The festival organizers offer pumpkins for sale for those who neglect to bring
one.

18   Lehman and Wilkinson, accountants for the *Guinness Book of World Records*,
counted the pumpkins. See Jennifer Jordan, "1999: 50,000 People and 18,349
Jack-o'-Lanterns Crowd Downtown Keene," Keene Pumpkin Festival website,
http://pumpkinfestival.com (accessed September 6, 2000). The annual count is
recorded at www.pumpkinfestival.org/index.html (accessed April 25, 2010).

19   "The Keene, New Hampshire Pumpkin Festival," Keene Pumpkin Festival
website, http://www.pumpkinfestival.com/future10-17-2010d.asp (accessed
May 7, 2011).

20   Anastasia Burke, "It's a Community Thing," *Review* (Half Moon Bay, Calif.),
October 2000, 15.

21   "Pumpkin Festival History," Keene Pumpkin Festival 2001 program, 3.

22   Sources on the economic woes of small rural towns include Richard Davies,

Main Street Blues (Columbus: Ohio State University Press, 1999); Carole Rifkind, Main Street: A Face of Urban America (New York: HarperCollins, 1977);
and Alison Isenberg, Downtown America: A History of the Place and the People
Who Made It (Chicago: University of Chicago Press, 2005), 42–77.

23 Carol James quoted in Ken Murchison, "SH Stressing Vendor Fees for Festival," Spring Hope Enterprise, September 28, 2000, 1.

24 "Great Pumpkins," Half Moon Bay Chamber of Commerce website, http://
www.halfmoonbaychamber.org/visiting_hmb/greatpumpkins.html (accessed
April 25, 2010).

25 "History," Half Moon Bay Festival website, http://www.miramarevents.com/
pumpkinfest/history.html (accessed April 25, 2010).

26 "Fantastic Facts about the Circleville Pumpkin Show," document given to me
by Ned Harden, longtime show organizer, June 1999.

27 Green Giraffe, "Reviewing the Annual Pumpkin Festival in Pumpkintown, South Carolina," April 18, 2007, http://www.associatedcontent.com/
article/206077/reviewing_the_annual_pumpkin_festival.html?cat=16 (accessed
April 25, 2010).

28 Ibid.

29 "Slower Lower," the name for the rural parts of Delaware, is quoted from Darragh Johnson, "The Great Pumpkin Flinger," Washington Post, November 3,
2001, B1.

30 Vera Edwards interview; advertisements in the Spring Hope festival program,
2000.

31 Robert A. Hoppe et al., Structure and Finances of U.S. Farms: Family Farm Report,
2007 Edition, U.S. Department of Agriculture, Economic Information Bulletin
EIB-24, June 2007, chapter titled "U.S. Farms: Numbers, Size and Ownership,"
1, http://www.ers.usda.gov/Publications/EIB24 (accessed June 21, 2010).

32 Dennis Patterson, "Agriculture Comes Long Way since Graham Entered
Office," Spring Hope Enterprise, October 19, 2000, 1.

33 Steve Toxler, candidate for state commissioner of agriculture, quoted in Patterson, "Agriculture Comes Long Way," 1.

34 Circleville-Pickaway Area Chamber of Commerce, "Where We're Going:
Agriculture," in Pickaway County at a Glance (Circleville, Ohio: Crown Printing, 1999), 18.

35 Davis, "I Remember—," 19.

36 "Pumpkin Festival Has Nurtured Many Memories," Pumpkin Festival clipping
file, Morton Chamber of Commerce, Morton, Illinois.

37 Some works critical of modern tourism are by Daniel Boorstein and Dean Mac-
Cannell. In The Image: A Guide to Pseudo-events in America, 25th anniversary
edition (New York: Vintage Books, 1987), Boorstein described modern tourism
as superficial, artificial, and uninspired, because tourists are more interested in
seeing familiar images and attractions (such as stores) and because, he argued,
tourist sites usually offer flattened, stereotypical interpretations of their

subjects. MacCannell, in *The Tourist: A New Theory of the Leisure Class* (New York: Schocken Books, 1976), criticized Boorstein for being elitist because he distinguished between people like himself, the wise "traveler," and the ignorant tourist. MacCannell also argued that tourists seek authenticity in communities they visit, but that this is nearly unattainable because it is impossible, as well as undesirable, to intrude into the everyday lives of the people they travel to see. As a result, he said, people at tourist sites fabricate inauthentic modes of interaction. For a revision of these ideas, see David M. Wrobel and Patrick T. Long, eds., *Seeing and Being Seen: Tourism in the American West* (Lawrence: University Press of Kansas, 2001), especially Wrobel's chapter, "Introduction: Tourists, Tourism, and the Toured Upon." In contrast to the earlier scholars, Wrobel defended modern tourists by arguing that the social dynamics among tourists and between tourists and tourist sites are more complex than a simple binary opposition, and he argued for some of the positive effects of the tourist trade, especially when it is under local control. His arguments are more in line with my own findings. See also John Urry, *The Tourist Gaze: Leisure and Travel in Contemporary Societies* (London: Sage, 1990). Urry's introductory historiographical essay is especially useful. In it, he defines different modes of tourism over time and across cultures, their effects on the places tourists visit, and responses from people the tourists come to see. See also John D. Dorst, *Looking West* (Philadelphia: University of Pennsylvania Press, 1999); Jakle, *The Tourist*; and Lucy R. Lippard, *On the Beaten Track: Tourism, Art, and Place* (New York: New Press, 1999).

38   "Mickey Mouse history" is quoted from Mike Wallace, *Mickey Mouse History and Other Essays on American Memory* (Philadelphia: Temple University Press, 1996). For a critical analysis of small-town festivals, see John D. Dorst, *The Written Suburb: An American Site, an Ethnographic Dilemma* (Philadelphia: University of Pennsylvania Press, 1989). In his critique of the Chadds Ford, Pennsylvania, festival as a celebration of pseudo-tradition and made-up history, the author fails to analyze the way residents' nostalgic ideas shape the area in positive, not just negative, ways. Works on history and memory and on heritage tourism include David Lowenthal, *The Past Is a Foreign Country* (New York: Cambridge University Press, 1985); David Lowenthal, *Possessed by the Past: The Heritage Crusade and the Spoils of History* (New York: Cambridge University Press, 1998); Mary Hufford, ed., *Conserving Culture: A New Discourse on Heritage* (Urbana: University of Illinois Press, 1994); John E. Bodnar, *Remaking America: Public Memory, Commemoration and Patriotism in the Twentieth Century* (Princeton, N.J.: Princeton University Press, 1992); Marita Sturken, *Tourists of History: Memory, Kitsch, and Consumerism from Oklahoma City to Ground Zero* (Durham, N.C.: Duke University Press, 2007); Paul Shackel, ed., *Myth, Memory, and the Making of the American Landscape* (Gainesville: University Press of Florida, 2001); Stephanie Yuhl, *The Golden Haze of Memory: The Making of Historic Charleston* (Chapel Hill: University of North Carolina Press, 2002); Maurice

Halbwachs, ed., *On Collective Memory* (Chicago: University of Chicago Press, 1992); Michael Kammen, *The Mystic Chords of Memory: The Transformation of Tradition in American Culture* (New York: Vintage, 1993); Roy Rosenzweig and David Thelen, *The Presence of the Past: Popular Uses of History in American Life* (New York: Columbia University Press, 1998); and David Thelen, ed., *Memory and American History* (Bloomington: Indiana University Press, 1990).

39 John Muller, quoted in Stacy Trevenon, "Pumpkins with a Heart," *Review* (Half Moon Bay, Calif.), October 2000, 13.

40 Hoppe et al., *Structure and Finances of U.S. Farms, 2007 Edition*, 2. See also U.S. Department of Agriculture, National Institute of Food and Agriculture, Family Farm Report website, w.csrees.usda.gov/nea/ag_systems/in_focus/family-farm_if_overview.html (accessed June 21, 2010).

41 Robert A. Hoppe et al., *America's Diverse Family Farms, 2007 edition*, U.S. Department of Agriculture, Economic Information Bulletin EIB-26, June 2007, 1, http://www.ers.usda.gov/publications/EIB26 (accessed June 28, 2010).

42 Hoppe et al., *Structure and Finances of U.S. Farms, 2007 Edition*, 1. According to these authors, farm size is generally measured by revenue instead of physical size, because the amount of acreage needed to sustain production varies across different environments around the country. The physical farm size categories are from Jason Manning, "The Midwest Farm Crisis of the 1980s," http://eightiesclub.tripod.com/id395.htm (accessed May 29, 2010).

43 Bob Hofstetter, "Pumpkin Power: Halloween Hoopla Treats This Farm to Half Its Yearly Profits," *New Farm Magazine of Regenerative Agriculture*, September–October 1994, 43 and 44.

44 Manning, "Midwest Farm Crisis." Other works on the farm crisis include Gilbert Fite, "The 1980s Farm Crisis," *Montana: The Magazine of Western History*, Winter 1986, 69–71; Robert D. Atkinson, "Reversing Rural America's Economic Decline: The Case for a National Balanced Growth Strategy," Progressive Policy Institute, Policy Report, February 2004, http://www.ppionline.org/documents/rural_economy_0204.pdf (accessed May 29, 2010); Danborn, *Born in the Country*, 233–70; Hurt, *American Agriculture*, 287–378; William P. Browne, *The Failure of National Rural Policy: Institutions and Interests* (Washington, D.C.: Georgetown University Press, 2001); Kathryn Marie Dudley, *Debt and Dispossession: Farm Loss in America's Heartland* (Chicago: University of Chicago Press, 2002); and Pollan, *Omnivore's Dilemma*, 15–64.

45 Jane Eckert, "Farm Direct Marketing from a Producer's Perspective," Agricultural Outlook Forum, 1999, 2, http://www.usda.gov/agency/oce/waob/outlook99/speeches/023/eckert.txt (accessed April 18, 2001). Eckert is the vice president of Eckert's Country Store and Farms, Belleville, Illinois.

46 Vance Merrill-Corum, "California Farmers Apply Fun and Quality in Direct Marketing," *Rural Enterprise*, Fall 1987, 28–30. Works on rural tourism include William Galston, *Rural Development in the United States* (Washington, D.C.: Island Press), 173–96; Dennis W. Brown, "Rural Tourism: An Annotated

Bibliography," U.S. Department of Agriculture, Economic Research Service, July 2008, 1–29, http://nal.usda.gov/ric/ricpubs/rural_tourism.html (accessed June 28, 2009); Dennis S. Brown and Richard J. Reeder, "Farm-Based Recreation: A Statistical Profile," U.S. Department of Agriculture, Economic Research Service, Report 53, December 2007, 1–22; Glen C. Pulver and Glenn R. Rogers, "Changes in Income Sources in Rural America," *American Journal of Agricultural Economics* 68, no. 5 (1986): 1181–87; Samuel N. Stokes, A. Elizabeth Watson, and Shelley S. Mastran, *Saving America's Countryside: A Guide to Rural Conservation* (Baltimore, Md.: Johns Hopkins University Press, 1989), 255–300; and Derek Hall, Irene Kirkpatrick, and Morag Mitchel, eds., *Rural Tourism and Sustainable Business (Aspects of Tourism)* (Buffalo, N.Y.: Channel View Publications, 2005).

47   Katherine L. Adam, "Entertainment Farming and Agri-Tourism: Business Management Guide," National Center for Appropriate Technology Business Management Guide, September 2004, 2, http://attar.ncat.org/attar-pub/PDF/entertn.pdf (accessed June 19, 2009).

48   Sources on pick-your-own farms date their origin from the 1930s to the 1960s. One author makes a link between their proliferation in the sixties and seventies to the search for alternative lifestyles, including healthier and more natural ways of living, and to a renewed reverence for nature in that time period. See Roth, "Overview of Farm Direct Marketing Industry Trends," and Eckert, "Farm Direct Marketing," 1–3.

49   Eckert, "Farm Direct Marketing," 1.

50   Roth, "Overview," 2.

51   Ibid., 4.

52   Latham quoted in Molly O'Neill, "A Nation Hungers for Farm Stands and a Harvest without Cellophane," *New York Times*, August 21, 1991.

53   C. M. Sabota and J. W. Courter, "An Analysis of the Potential for Pick-Your-Own Marketing in a Rural Area," *USDATE 79: Research Report of the Dixon Springs Agricultural Center* (University of Illinois, January 1979), 241.

54   Karen Tannehill, "Field of Pumpkins," *Small Farm Today*, October 1997, 23.

55   Tim Vala, quoted in Marlene Novotny, "Vala's Pumpkin Patch," *Small Farm Today*, October 1994, 37.

56   Eric Cox, in "About Us," Cox Farms website, http://www.coxfarms.com (accessed September 22, 2000). For analyses of the representation of nature in large-scale American theme parks, see Alexander Wilson, *The Nature of Culture: North American Landscape from Disney to Exxon Valdez* (Cambridge, Mass.: Blackwell, 1992), and Davis, *Spectacular Nature*. Other works on the history of theme parks include Michael Sorkin, ed., *Variations on a Theme Park: The New American City and the End of Public Space* (New York: Hill and Wang, 1992), and David Nasaw, *Going Out: The Rise and Fall of Public Amusements* (New York: Basic Books, 1993).

57   "About Us," Cox Farms website; Trevenon, "Growing Tradition," 27.

58   Lewis Small, "Ideas for Marketing Your Fall Ornaments," *Countryside and Small Stock Journal*, September–October, 1997, 32.

59   Hofstetter, "Pumpkin Power," 23.

60   For scholarly works on symbolic landscapes, see Keith H. Basso, *Wisdom Sits in Places: Landscape and Language among the Western Apache* (Albuquerque: University of New Mexico Press, 1996); Bunce, *Countryside Ideal*; Denis E. Cosgrove, *Social Formation and Symbolic Landscape* (Madison: University of Wisconsin Press, 1996 [1984]); Steven Feld and Keith H. Basso, eds., *Senses of Place* (Santa Fe, N.M.: School of American Research Press, 1996); Schama, *Landscape and Memory*; George F. Thompson, ed., *Landscape in America* (Austin: University of Texas Press, 1995); and Yi-Fu Tuan, *Topophilia: A Study of Environmental Perception, Attitudes, and Values* (New York: Columbia University Press, 1974). Schama's work is especially pertinent because he investigates Western myths about natural places over a broad time span. He criticizes environmental historians for being too narrowly focused on the worst-case scenarios of nature exploitation. Critics claim that his work is too optimistic regarding the ability of nature myths to save or sustain natural landscapes. The North American cases he presents are mostly wild places rather than the agrarian ones I explore, though some of his arguments support my thesis that ideas about nature, even romantic ones, reshape the material world.

61   For an index of thousands of annual pumpkin festivals by state, see the Pumpkin Patches and More website, http://www.pumpkinpatchesandmore.org/index.php#states (accessed June 22, 2010).

62   Novotny, "Vala's Pumpkin Patch," 36.

63   Jones quoted in Tannehill, "Field of Pumpkins," 22.

64   Holsapple quoted in Hofstetter, "Pumpkin Power," 44.

65   These observations were made while I worked at the Heisler farm stand from 1994 to 1999. The quotation is from a customer there in the fall of 1995.

66   Anne Rockwell, *Pumpkin Day, Pumpkin Night* (New York: Walker, 1999). Another example is James Reid, *Peter, Peter Pumpkin Eater* (Philadelphia: Fortress Press, 1970), which describes a family's trip from their suburban home out to "Bumpkin's Pumpkin Farm." See also Nancy J. Skarmeas, *Jack-o'-Lantern* (Nashville, Tenn.: Candy Cane Press, 2001), which describes a boy going to his grandparent's farm to get a pumpkin to bring to his suburban home to carve for Halloween.

67   Todd Butler, interview with the author, Germantown, Maryland, June 27, 2001.

68   The two features noted are from Vala's Pumpkin Patch, but others like them exist at most other patches. Novotny, "Vala's Pumpkin Patch," 36–38.

69   Jones quoted in Tannehill, "Field of Pumpkins," 23.

70   Vala quoted in Novotny, "Vala's Pumpkin Patch," 38.

71   Richard quoted in Leef Smith, "Politics of Pumpkin Picking," *Washington Post*, October 12, 2000, B1.

72   Mary Lyn Ray, *Pumpkins* (San Diego: Harcourt Brace, 1992).

73   Muller quoted in Trevenon, "Pumpkins with a Heart," 13.

74   "That's Agritainment!" *Time*, October 24, 2005.

75   Dave Newhauser interview, October 19, 2000.

76   The actual estimate, 218,864 tons, is derived by multiplying the total number of acres of pumpkins harvested in Illinois in 2007 (13,679) by 16 tons, which is slightly less than Schultheis's estimate of an average yield of 18 tons per acre for processing pumpkins, because the Illinois acreage total is based on the state's total production, which in 2007 was two-thirds for processing pumpkins (9,749 out of 13,679) and one-third for ornamentals (3,930 out of 13,679). Ornamentals yield less per acre than processing pumpkins. Schultheis, "Growing Pumpkins and Squash." State statistics are from U.S. Department of Agriculture, *2007 Census of Agriculture*, vol. 1, table 30, 532.

77   Lucier and Dettman, "Vegetable and Melons Outlook," 23.

78   The statistics of 33 acres and 700 tons are from Gustin, "Fields Are Awash in Pumpkins." Information also obtained from John Ackerman, telephone interview by the author, July 2, 2001. See also the farm website, http://www .ackermanfarms.com (accessed June 21, 2010). For further information on the Ackermans' farm, see Angie Spitzer, "Ackerman Family Makes Pumpkins Full-time Job," *34th Annual Morton Pumpkin Festival Guide* (Times Newspapers, 2000).

79   U.S. Department of Agriculture, *2007 Census of Agriculture*, vol. 1, table 30, 532. The other top producing states, in order, are Ohio, New York, Michigan, and California.

80   Lucier and Dettman, "Vegetables and Melons Outlook," 23. For average size of farm and other agricultural statistics about Lancaster County, Pennsylvania, see "2007 Census of Agriculture County Profile: Lancaster County, Pennsylvania," at http://www.agcensus.usda.gov/Publications/2007/Online_ Highlights/County_Profiles/Pennsylvania/cp42071.pdf (accessed May 9, 2011).

81   States included in the Lower South region are Alabama, Florida, Georgia, Louisiana, Mississippi, and South Carolina.

82   Robert Lewis, owner and operator of Lewis Orchards in Dickerson, Maryland, telephone interview by the author, June 27, 2001.

83   The farmer is Craig Thorp, in Deming, New Mexico, as described in George W. Dickerson, "Pumpkins Can Be a Plus in Seasonal Pocketbooks," *AgVentures*, December 1997–January 1998, 54.

84   Raymond J. Samulis, e-mail to the author, July 6, 2010.

85   Smithsonian National Zoological Park, press advisory for "Elephant Pumpkin Stomp," November 5, 1999. The event was featured in "Smashing Pumpkins," *Washington Times*, November 14, 1997, A1, and "And Step On It," *Washington Post*, November 11, 1998, B3.

86   U.S. Department of Agriculture, *2007 Census of Agriculture*, "County Profile: Tazewell County, Illinois," http://www.agcensus.usda.gov/Publications/2002/ County_Profiles/Illinois/cp17179.pdf (accessed June 22, 2010).

87   U.S. Department of Agriculture, *2007 Census of Agriculture*, vol. 1, table 30, 532.

88   Gustin, "Fields Are Awash in Pumpkins." Nestlé-Libby's declined to provide me with the exact number of farmers with whom they contracted to grow Libby's Select pumpkins.

89   Statistics are from U.S. Department of Agriculture, *2007 Census of Agriculture*, "County Profile: Tazewell County, Illinois," 1–2. Information about Libby's is from "Pumpkins: Libby's Leads the Way," *Scanner*, June–August, 1968, 6–10 (Libby's Company Archives, Morton, Illinois).

90   Roz O'Hearn, Libby's spokeswoman, telephone interview by the author, May 24, 2010.

91   In the 2007 agricultural census, 15,088 farms reported harvesting 92,955 acres of pumpkins nationwide, which averages to 6.1 acres per farm. U.S. Department of Agriculture, *2007 Census of Agriculture*, vol. 1, U.S. Data, table 34, "Vegetables, Potatoes, and Melons Harvested for Sale: 2007 and 2002," 35.

92   In 1899, 3,194 farms cultivated 3,341 acres of pumpkins, or an average of 1.04 acres per farm. In 1974, 3,309 farms harvested 21,516 acres of pumpkins, or 6.5 acres per farm. U.S. Department of Agriculture, *1920 Census of Agriculture*, vol. 5, 820; U.S. Department of Agriculture, *1974 Census of Agriculture*, vol. 11 (Washington, D.C.: Government Printing Office, 1976), table 10, "Vegetables Harvested for Sale," 26–27.

93   U.S. Department of Agriculture, *1940 Census of Agriculture*, vol. 3, 698.

94   U.S. Department of Agriculture, *1987 Census of Agriculture* (Washington, D.C.: Government Printing Office, 1989), vol. 1, part 51, "United States Summary and State Data," table 27, "Vegetables . . .", 370.

95   U.S. Department of Agriculture, *1997 Census of Agriculture* (Washington, D.C.: Government Printing Office, 1999), vol. 1, part 51, "United States Summary and State Data," table 29, "Vegetables . . .", 480–81; U.S. Department of Agriculture, *2007 Census of Agriculture*, vol. 1, U.S. Data, table 34, "Vegetables, Potatoes, and Melons Harvested for Sale: 2007 and 2002," 35.

96   U.S. Department of Agriculture, *2007 Census of Agriculture*, vol. 1, U.S. Data, table 33, "Specified Crops by Acres Harvested," 27 and 29.

97   Information about Frey Farms is from Illinois Department of Agriculture, press release, "Illinois Leads Nation in Pumpkin Production," October 22, 2004, http://www.agr.state.il.us/newsrels/r1022041.html (accessed June 23, 2010). Information about the Torrey farm is from Maureen Torrey, interview with the author, July 18, 2001.

98   U.S. Department of Agriculture, *2007 Census of Agriculture*, vol. 1, State Data, table 30, 532. See also Mark Gaskell, "Pumpkin Production in California," Vegetable Production Series, Publication 7222 (undated), Vegetable Research and Information Center, University of California, Division of Agriculture and Natural Resources. In the *2007 Census of Agriculture*, the average tomato field in California was 188 acres, and the average strawberry field, 45 acres. U.S. Department of Agriculture, *2007 Census of Agriculture*, vol. 1, table 30, 35, and vol. 1, State Data, table 34, "Berries: 2007 and 2002," 564.

99   I derived the percentages by comparing the total number of vegetable farms and their acreage with the total number of farms that grow pumpkins and their acreage, as reported in U.S. Department of Agriculture, *2007 Census of Agriculture*, vol. 1, U.S. Data, tables 33, 34, and 35, 27–42.

100 For scholarly works on the benefit of small-scale agriculture, see Wendell Berry, *Home Economics: Fourteen Essays* (San Francisco: North Point Press, 1987); Wendell Berry, *Art of the Common Place: The Agrarian Essays of Wendell Berry*, ed. Norman Wirzba (Washington, D.C.: Counterpoint, 2002); and Wes Jackson, *New Roots of Agriculture* (Lincoln: University of Nebraska Press, 1985). See also Eric T. Freyfogle, *The New Agrarianism: Land, Culture and the Community of Life* (Washington, D.C.: Island Press, 2001). One aberration in the trend toward fewer but larger farms is the introduction of hobby farms, or farmettes.

101 John Ackerman, telephone interview with the author, July 21, 2001.

102 According to Dave Newhauser, the farmers spray herbicides and pesticides on the plants but have not used them on the fruits since 1990, because squash bugs, the greatest threat to the fruits, were killed off in the area. Newhauser interview, October 19, 2000.

103 David Heisler, interview by the author, Comus, Maryland, June 2, 2001. As another testament to the growing symbiotic relationship between pumpkin farms and urban areas, researchers at the Department of Plant Biology and Pathology at the Rutgers, New Jersey, Agricultural Experiment Station found a way to help both pumpkin farmers and cities through the recycling of fall leaves as a ground cover on ornamental pumpkin fields to protect against such blemishes. Municipalities have a cheap, environmentally friendly outlet for their leaves, and local farmers are financially compensated for mulch that improves the health of the soil and the appearance of the crop. "A Win-Win: U-Pick Pumpkin Farms Recycle Urban Leaves," *ScienceDaily*, January 14, 2009, http://www.sciencedaily.com/releases/2008/12/081229104654.htm (accessed January 14, 2009). Thanks to Michael Pollan for this reference.

104 Dave Newhauser interview, October 19, 2000.

105 This information is based on my conversations with farmers and my own experience working on Heisler's pumpkin farm. See also Dickerson, "Pumpkins Can Be a Plus."

106 According to Heisler, he has to throw away about a third of a truckload of the pumpkins he gets from one wholesaler, versus less than 10 percent from a farmer who does more careful culling before shipment. On his own fields, he prefers to grow hybrids because, he says, they produce a greater number of top-grade pumpkins relative to non-hybrids, many of which have to be left behind in the fields for roving wildlife. Heisler interview, June 2, 2001.

107 Maureen Torrey telephone interview, July 18, 2001.

108 Illinois Department of Agriculture, press release, "Illinois Leads Nation in Pumpkin Production"; "About Us," Arata Pumpkin Farm website, http://www.aratapumpkinfarm.com/about_us.html (accessed June 22, 2010).

109 Lucier and Dettman, "Vegetable and Melons Outlook," 24.

110 Laffoon, "Pump-kin," 62.

111 Nivens quoted in Weekes, "Pumpkins for the Holidays," 34.

112 In the summer of 2000, which was a poor pumpkin-growing season in the Southeast, Vollmer Farms in Burn, North Carolina, purchased pumpkins from Texas. Vollmer employee, interview by the author, Burn, North Carolina, October 8, 2000.

113 A list of whole pumpkin farmers and truckers nationwide is at the website Pumpkin Patches and More, http://www.pumpkinpatchesandmore.org/fundraisers.php (accessed June 22, 2010).

114 Patterson Farm website, http://www.pattersonfarmllc.com (accessed June 22, 2010).

115 "Availabilities: 1995 to 1999 Averages of Arrivals from Providing Areas" (chart), *The Packer: 2000 Produce Availability and Price Guide* 107, no. 53 (2000): 285.

116 Adam Kuban, "Nationwide Shortage of Canned Pumpkin Threatens Thanksgiving Pie," September 28, 2009, www.seriouseats.com/2009/09/nationwide-shortage-of-caned-pumpkin-threatens-Thanksgiving-pies.html (accessed April 23, 2010).

117 Dave Newhauser interview, October 19, 2000.

118 Robert Lewis interview.

119 Lucier and Dettman mention price fluctuations in "Vegetable and Melon Outlook," 24. Local market restraints are noted in "Pumpkin," University of Kentucky Cooperative Extension Service report (April 2010), 1.

120 David Nalls, owner of Nalls Farm Stand in Berryville, Virginia, telephone interview with the author, October 10, 2000.

121 The figure of $250 million is based on dividing the crop's value for the top six pumpkin-producing states ($123,519,000) by the total number of acres in those states (45,900) for 2007, which gives a value per acre of $2,691. Then I multiplied $2,691 times the 92,955 total acres harvested in 2007. Lucier and Dettman, "Vegetable and Melons Outlook," 22.

122 Maureen Torrey, telephone interview by the author, October 10, 2000.

123 Weekes, "Pumpkins for the Holidays," 35.

124 Novotny, "Vala's Pumpkin Patch," 36. For the 2010 statistics, see the farm's website at http://www.valaspumpkinpatch.com/meet_the_valas (accessed June 16, 2010).

125 Hofstetter, "Pumpkin Power," 43; Geisler, "Pumpkins," 2. Walters' Pumpkin Patch, in Burns, Kansas, started operation in 1998 and now brings in around twenty thousand visitors a season. See also Pumpkins and More, the University of Illinois Extension website for pumpkins, http://urbanext.illinois.edu/pumpkins (accessed June 22, 2010), and Pumpkin Patches and More, http://www.pumpkinpatchesandmore.org/index.php#states (accessed June 22, 2010).

126 Illinois statistics at Illinois Department of Agriculture, Bureau of Marketing and Promotions, "October Marketing Perspectives: Pumpkins," http://www.agr.state

.il.us/marketing/news/October_2006/October2006MarketingPerspectives.html (accessed April 25, 2010). To get the price per pound, I divided the number of pounds (496,000,000) by the cash receipts ($16,049,000). The New Jersey data are from U.S. Department of Agriculture, National Agricultural Statistics Service, New Jersey Field Office, "2009 New Jersey Annual Vegetable Report," including table, "Annual Summary, 2008–2009," January 2010, http://www.nass .usda.gov/Statistics_by_State/New_Jersey/Current_Releases/2009njannualvegbro chure.pdf (accessed June 10, 2010). Virginia data are from Virginia Market News Service, "2009 Virginia Potato and Vegetable Review," 19, http://www.vdacs .virginia.gov/marketnews/pdffiles/pvr.pdf (accessed June 23, 2010).

127 After the first year of operation of Diedre Jones's Oregon pumpkin farm festival in 1992, she grossed $700. Five years later, her total rose to $20,000 for the same five-week period. Tannehill, "Field of Pumpkins," 22–23.

128 Commissioner quoted in Roberta Holland, "Pumpkin Farmers Hit Profitable Patch with Bumper Pumpkin Crop," *Boston Business Journal*, September 27, 1999.

129 The total profit ($123,519,000) and acreage (45,900) for the top six producing states in 2007 is provided in U.S. Department of Agriculture, National Agricultural Statistics Service, "Vegetables 2009 Summary: Pumpkins for Fresh Market and Processing . . ., 2007–2009," January 2010, 29, http://usda.mannlib .cornell.edu/usda/current/VegeSumm/VegeSumm-01-27-2010.pdf (accessed April 28, 2010). Lucier and Dettman, in "Vegetable and Melons Outlook," 25, estimated fixed and variable production costs to be approximately $2,000 per acre. The sum of $2,691 per acre is based on dividing the crop's value for the top six pumpkin-producing states ($123,519,000) by the total number of acres planted in pumpkins in those states (45,900) for 2007. Every source on the pumpkin's dollar value differs from the others, so it is difficult to state concisely how much the crop is worth at any given time.

130 Robert A. Hoppe and David E. Banker, *Structure and Finances of U.S. Farms: Family Farm Report, 2010 Edition,* U.S. Department of Agriculture, Economic Information Bulletin EIB-66, July 2010, chapter titled "Farm Income and Financial Performance," 27.

131 Illinois Department of Agriculture, Bureau of Marketing and Promotions, "October Marketing Perspectives: Pumpkins."

132 Integrated Pest Management Centers, "Crop Profile for Pumpkin in Texas," June 2002, http://www.ipmcenters.org/cropprofiles/docs/TXpumpkin.pdf (accessed May 12, 2011).

133 To arrive at these figures I used the figure of 40 cents per pound and the yield per acre of 9,200 pumpkins reported for 2007 in "New England Fruits and Vegetables 2009 Crop," May 18, 2010, 11, http://www.nass.usda.gov/Statistics_by_State/New_England_includes/Publications/05frtveg.pdf (accessed June 23, 2010).

134 Wallace T. Garrett, "Growing Pumpkins," Fact Sheet: Enterprise Guide for

Southern Maryland (University of Maryland, Cooperative Extension Service, 1987–88), 1.

135   Entry fees charged at Cox Farms and the Arata Pumpkin Farm are from their respective websites, http://www.cerr.com/2011-fall-festival (accessed August 20, 2011), and http://www.aratapumpkinfarm.com/?pid=prices (accessed August 20, 2011). Retail prices are from Raymond J. Samulis, e-mail, July 6, 2010.

136   In 2007 the state of Iowa added a 6 percent sales tax for field pumpkins because it judged them to be decorations, not food. Bob Kautz, owner of Buffalo Pumpkin Patch near Davenport, Iowa, complained, "It gets unfeasible for people to have small businesses." The tax was overturned by 2010. "New Iowa Pumpkin Tax Puts Damper on Grower's Halloween Spirit," Foxnews.com (October 31, 2007), http://www.foxnews.com/story/0,2933,306636,00.html (accessed June 23, 2010).

137   Maureen Torrey telephone interview, July 18, 2001.

138   Price per pound noted in Lucier and Dettman, "Vegetables and Melons Outlook," 24, and price per piece based on author's survey of pumpkin-stand prices.

139   Glickman quoted in Ben White, "Flora and Fauna: Pumpkin Politics," *Washington Post*, October 31, 2000, A21.

140   "That's Agritainment!"

141   Novotny, "Vala's Pumpkin Patch," 36.

142   David Heisler, interview with the author, October 2004.

143   Works on food politics include Karl Weber, ed., *A Participant Guide: How Industrial Food Is Making Us Sicker, Fatter, and Poorer—And What You Can Do About It* (New York: PublicAffairs, 2009); Marion Nestle, *Food Politics: How the Food Industry Influences Nutrition and Health* (Berkeley: University of California, 2002); Warren Belasco and Roger Horowitz, eds., *Food Chains: From Farmyard to Shopping Cart* (Philadelphia: University of Pennsylvania Press, 2010); Raj Patel, *Stuffed and Starved: The Hidden Battle of the World Food System* (Brooklyn, N.Y.: Melville House, 2008); Vandana Shiva, *Stolen Harvest: The Hijacking of the Global Food Supply* (Cambridge, Mass.: South End Press, 2000); and Robert Gottlieb and Anupama Joshi, eds., *Food Justice* (Cambridge, Mass.: MIT Press, 2010).

144   Michael Pollan, *Food Rules: An Eater's Manual* (New York: Penguin Books, 2009), and Michael Pollan, *In Defense of Food: An Eater's Manifesto* (New York: Penguin Press, 2008). Information about the mission and programs of Let's Move is available at its website, http://letsmove.org (accessed May 9, 2011).

145   United Nations, Economic and Social Affairs, "World Population to 2300," 1, http://www.un.org/esa/population/publications/longrange2/WorldPop2300final.pdf (accessed May 9, 2011). Sources on the slow food movement include Carlo Petrini, *Slow Food Nation: The Creation of a New Gastronomy* (New York: Rizzoli Ex Libris, 2007).

146 Whittaker Chambers Farm, also known as Pipe Creek Farm, is located near Westminster, Maryland. It was designated a National Historic Landmark in 1988. Chambers's son, John, still raises pumpkins on the property. For source material on the site, including links to the national register nomination, go to http://www.whittakerchambers.org/pipecreekfarm.html (accessed May 12, 2011).

BIBLIOGRAPHY

A.B.C. "Pumpkin Pies." *American Farmer*, January 11, 1833, 350.

Adam, Katherine L. "Entertainment Farming and Agri-tourism: Business Management Guide." National Center for Appropriate Technology, Business Management Guide, September 2004, 1–16. http://attar.ncat.org/attar-pub/PDF/entertn .pdf (accessed June 19, 2009).

Adamson, Melitta Weiss. *Food in Medieval Times*. Westport, Conn.: Greenwood Press, 2004.

Agee, James. "The Great American Roadside." *Fortune*, October 1934, 53–63, 172, 174, and 177.

Agee, John, and Walker Evans. *Let Us Now Praise Famous Men*. Boston: Houghton Mifflin, 1939.

"Agricultural Marketing Service Farmers Markets—Facts." 2001. http://www.ams .usda.gov/farmersmarkets/facts (accessed June 24, 2009).

Agway, Inc. 1992 *Agway Commercial Grower Vegetable Seed Catalog*. Elizabethtown, Pa.: Agway, Inc., 1992.

Albala, Ken. *Eating Right in the Renaissance*. Berkeley: University of California Press, 2002.

Allen, Robert S. "Early American Agricultural Societies and Organizations: Educational Activities and Numerical Growth at Key Periods until 1900." *Journal of Agricultural Food and Information* 8, no. 3 (2007): 17–31.

Allouez, Father Claude. "Letter to the Reverend Father Superior." In *Jesuit Relations and Allied Documents: Travels and Explorations of the Jesuit Missionaries in New France, 1610–1791*, vol. 54, *Iroquois, Ottawas, Lower Canada, 1669–1671*, edited by Reuben Gold Thwaites, 207. Cleveland, Ohio: Burrows Brothers, 1896–1901.

"All the Squashes." *American Farmer*, November 18, 1834, 231.

"The American Pumpkin." *St. Louis Globe-Dispatch*, November 7, 1884, 4.

Anderson, Frank J. *An Illustrated History of the Herbals*. New York: Columbia University Press, 1997.

Anderson, Jay Allan. "'A Solid Sufficiency': An Ethnography of Yeoman Foodways in Stuart England." PhD dissertation, University of Pennsylvania, 1971.

"And Step on It." *Washington Post*, November 11, 1998, B3.

"The Annual Thanksgiving." *Scribner's Monthly Magazine*, November 1869, 212.

Apkarian-Russell, Pamela E. *Collectible Halloween.* Atglen, Pa.: Schiffer, 1997.

———. *Halloween: Collectible Decorations and Games.* Atglen, Pa.: Schiffer, 2000.

———. *More Halloween Collectibles.* Atglen, Pa.: Schiffer, 1998.

Appadurai, Arjun, ed. *The Social Life of Things: Commodities in Cultural Perspective.* Cambridge: Cambridge University Press, 1986.

Appelbaum, Diana Karter. *Thanksgiving: An American Holiday, an American History.* New York: Facts on File, 1984.

Appleby, Joyce. "Commercial Farming and the 'Agrarian Myth' in the Early Republic." *Journal of American History* 68, no. 4 (1982): 833–49.

Arber, Agnes. *Herbals: Their Origins and Evolution: A Chapter in the History of Botany, 1470–1670.* Cambridge: Cambridge University Press, 1938.

Arnott, Margaret L. *Gastronomy: The Anthropology of Food and Food Habits.* The Hague: Mouton, 1975.

Aron, Cindy S. *Working at Play: A History of Vacations in the United States.* New York: Oxford University Press, 1999.

Ashliman, D. L. *A Guide to Folktales in the English Language.* New York: Greenwood Press, 1987.

Astbury, Raymond. "The Apocolocyntosis." *Classical Review* 38, no. 1 (1988): 44–50.

Atkinson, Robert D. "Reversing Rural America's Economic Decline: The Case for a National Balanced Growth Strategy." Progressive Policy Institute, Policy Report, February 2004. http://www.ppionline.org/documents/rural_economy_0204.pdf (accessed May 29, 2010).

Aubry, Sieur. "Lettre a Monsieur son Frére." In *The Jesuit Relations and Related Documents: Travels and Explorations of the Jesuit Missionaries in New France, 1610–1791,* vol. 67, *Lower Canada, Abenakis, Louisiana,* edited by Reuben Gold Thwaites, 132–229. Cleveland: Burrows Brothers, 1896–1901.

"Availabilities: 1995 to 1999 Averages of Arrivals from Providing Areas." *The Packer: 2000 Produce Availability and Price Guide* 107, no. 53 (2000): 285.

Axtell, James. *After Columbus: Essays in the Ethnohistory of Colonial North America.* New York: Oxford University Press, 1988.

———. *Beyond 1492: Encounters in Colonial North America.* New York: Oxford University Press, 1992.

———. *The European and the Indian: Essays in the Ethnohistory of Colonial North America.* New York: Oxford University Press, 1981.

———. *Natives and Newcomers: The Cultural Origins of North America.* New York: Oxford University Press, 2001.

Ayer, Hannah. "The Pumpkin." *American Kitchen: A Domestic Science Monthly* 18 (October 1902–March 1903): 24.

"Badger Pumpkin Shows." *Milwaukee Sentinel,* October 6, 1883.

Bailey, Carolyn Sherwin. *What to Do for Uncle Sam: A First Book of Citizenship.* Chicago: A. Flanagan, 1918.

Bak, Hans, and Walter Holbing, eds. *"Nature's Nation" Revisited: American Concepts of Nature from Wonder to Ecological Crisis.* Amsterdam: Vu University, 2003.

Balken, Deborah Bricker. *After Many Springs: Regionalism, Modernism, and the Midwest*. Des Moines, Iowa: Des Moines Art Center, 2009.

Ball, Timothy Horton. "A Thanksgiving Discourse at Crown Point, November 24, 1898." In *The Home of the Redeemed, and Other Discourses*, 179. Crown Point, Ind.: Register Print, 1899.

Bannatyne, Lesley Pratt. *Halloween: An American Holiday, an American History*. New York: Facts on File, 1990. Reprint, Gretna, La.: Pelican Publishing, 1998.

Barnes, Donna R., and Peter G. Rose. *Matters of Taste: Food and Drink in Seventeenth-Century Dutch Art and Life*. Syracuse, N.Y.: Syracuse University Press, 2002.

Baron, Stanley. *Brewed in America: A History of Beer and Ale in the United States*. Boston: Little, Brown, 1962.

Barr, Andrew. *Drink: A Social History of America*. New York: Carroll and Graf, 1999.

Barron, Hal S. "Staying Down on the Farm: Social Process of Settled Rural Life in the Nineteenth-Century North." In *The Countryside in the Age of Capitalist Transformation: Essays in the Social History of Rural America*, edited by Steven Hahn and Jonathan Prude, 327–44. Chapel Hill: University of North Carolina Press, 1985.

———. *Those Who Stayed Behind: Rural Society in Nineteenth Century New England*. Cambridge: Cambridge University Press, 1984.

Barth, Edna. *Witches, Pumpkins, and Grinning Ghosts: The Story of Halloween Symbols*. New York: Clarion, 1972.

Barthes, Roland. *Mythologies*. New York: Hill and Wang, 1957.

———. "Towards a Psychosociology of Contemporary Food Consumption." In *Food and Drink in History*, edited by Robert Forster and Orest Ranum, 166–73. Baltimore, Md.: Johns Hopkins University Press, 1979.

Barton, William E. *The Story of Pumpkin Pie*. Boston: Pilgrim Press, 1898.

Bartram, John. *Observations on the Inhabitants, Climate, Soil, Rivers, Productions, Animals, and Other Matters Worthy of Notice, made by John Bartram in His Travels from Pennsylvania to Onondaga, Oswego and the Lake Ontario, in Canada*. London: J. Whiston and B. White, 1751. Reprint, Ann Arbor, Mich.: University Microfilms, 1966.

Basso, Keith H. *Wisdom Sits in Places: Landscape and Language among the Western Apache*. Albuquerque: University of New Mexico Press, 1996.

Baughman, Ernest W. "A Complete Study of the Folktales of England and North America." Ph.D. dissertation, Indiana University, 1954.

———. *Type and Motif Index of Folktales of England*. The Hague: Mouton, 1966.

Baum, L. Frank. *Jack Pumpkinhead and the Sawhorse*. Chicago: Reilly and Britton, 1913.

———. *The Marvelous Land of Oz*. Chicago: Reilly and Britton, 1904.

———. *The Road to Oz*. Chicago: Reilly and Britton, 1909.

———. *The Visitors of Oz*. Chicago: Reilly and Lee, 1960.

Beauchamp, W. M. "Onondaga Plant Names." *Journal of American Folklore* 57 (1902): 101.

Beecher, Henry Ward. *Eyes and Ears*. Boston: Ticknor and Fields, 1862.

Belasco, Warren James. *Americans on the Road: From Autocamp to Motel, 1910–1945.* Cambridge, Mass.: MIT Press, 1979.

———. *Appetite for Change: How the Counterculture Took on the Food Industry.* Ithaca, N.Y.: Pantheon, 1993 [1989].

———, and Roger Horowitz, eds. *Food Chains: From Farmyard to Shopping Cart.* Philadelphia: University of Pennsylvania Press, 2010.

Bender, Steve. "Champion Vegetables." *Southern Living,* October 1995, 96.

Bennett, M. K. "The Food Economy of the New England Indians, 1605–75." *Journal of Political Economy* 63, no. 5 (1955): 369–97.

Bennett, Whitman. *Whittier: Bard of Freedom.* Port Washington, N.Y.: Kennikat Press, 1972.

Berry, Wendell. *Art of the Common Place: The Agrarian Essays of Wendell Berry.* Edited by Norman Wirzba. Washington, D.C.: Counterpoint, 2002.

———. *Home Economics: Fourteen Essays.* San Francisco: North Point Press, 1987.

Best, Joel, and Gerald T. Horiuchi. "The Razor Blade in the Apple: The Social Construction of Urban Legends." *Social Problems* 32 (June 1985): 488–99.

Beverly, Robert. *The History and Present State of Virginia.* London: R. Parker at Unicorn, 1705. Reprint, Chapel Hill: University of North Carolina Press, 1947.

Bidwell, Percy Wells, and John I. Falconer. *History of Agriculture in the Northern United States, 1620–1860.* Clifton, N.J.: A. M. Kelley, 1973.

"Big Pumpkins." *Western Farmer* (Cincinnati, Ohio), October 1840, 18.

Bitting, Arvill Wayne. *The Canning of Foods.* Washington, D.C.: Government Printing Office, 1913.

"Black Letters; or Uncle Tom-Foolery in Literature." *Graham's Magazine,* January 1853, 214.

Bober, Phyllis Pray. *Art, Culture, and Cuisine: Ancient and Medieval Gastronomy.* Chicago: University of Chicago Press, 1999.

Bodecker, N. M. "Pumpkin, Pumpkin, Pumpkin Bright." http://www.bconnex .net/~mbuchana/realms/halloween/pumpkin.html (accessed November 12, 1999).

Bodnar, John E. *Remaking America: Public Memory, Commemoration and Patriotism in the Twentieth Century.* Princeton: Princeton University Press, 1992.

Bogart, Ernest L. *Peacham: The Story of a Vermont Hill Town.* Vermont Historical Society, 1948. Reprint, Washington, D.C.: University Press of America, 1981.

Boorstein, Daniel, and Dean MacCannell. *The Image: A Guide to Pseudo-Events in America.* 25th anniversary edition. New York: Vintage Books, 1987.

Booth, Sally Smith. *Hung, Strung, and Potted: A History of Eating in Colonial America.* New York: Clarkson N. Potter, 1971.

Booth, William, and Sharon Waxman. "The Colorful Cast on the Red Carpet." *Washington Post,* March 26, 2001, C9.

Botkin, Benjamin, ed. *A Treasury of New England Folklore: Stories, Ballads, and Traditions of Yankee Folk.* New York: American Legacy Press, 1989 [1965].

Bourgeois, Florence. *Peter, Peter, Pumpkin Grower.* Garden City, N.Y.: Doubleday, Doran, 1937.

Bradford, William. *History of Plymouth Plantation, 1620–1647.* Boston: The Massachusetts Historical Society, 1912.

Bragdon, Kathleen J. *Native People of Southern New England, 1500–1650.* Norman: University of Oklahoma Press, 1996.

Bratsch, Anthony. "Specialty Crop Profile: Pumpkins." Virginia Cooperative Extension, May 1, 2009. http://pubs.ext.vt.edu/438/438-100/438-100.html (accessed June 23, 2010).

Breathnach, Sarah Ban. *Victorian Family Celebrations.* New York: Simon and Schuster, 1990.

Brébeuf, Jean de. "Important Advice for Those Whom It Shall Please God to Call to New France, and Especially to the Country of the Hurons." In *The Jesuit Relations and Related Documents: Travels and Explorations of the Jesuit Missionaries in New France, 1610–1791,* vol. 10, *Hurons, 1636,* edited by Reuben Gold Thwaites. Cleveland: Burrows Brothers, 1896–1901.

———. "Journal des Peres Jesuites, en l'annee 1648." In *The Jesuit Relations and Related Documents: Travels and Explorations of the Jesuit Missionaries in New France, 1610–1791,* vol. 32, *Gaspe, Hurons, Lower Canada,* edited by Reuben Gold Thwaites, 66–110. Cleveland: Burrows Brothers, 1896–1901.

Breck, Joseph, and Company. *Annual Catalog of the New England Agricultural Warehouse and Seed Store.* Boston, 1838.

Brennan, Georgeanne. *Holiday Pumpkins.* New York: Smithmark, 1998.

Bridgeman, T. "Pumpkin Bread." *American Farmer,* January 25, 1834, 367.

Bridgman, Mary. "Pumped Up." *Columbus Dispatch,* October 16, 1998, C-1.

Briggs and Brothers. *Illustrated Catalogue of Flower and Vegetable Seeds,* 1870–71.

Brown, Bill. *A Sense of Things: The Object Matter of American Literature.* Chicago: University of Chicago Press, 2002.

———, ed. *Things.* Chicago: University of Chicago Press, 2004.

Brown, Christopher. *Images of a Golden Past: Dutch Genre Painting of the 17th Century.* New York: Abbeville, 1984.

Brown, Dennis S., and Richard J. Reeder. "Farm-Based Recreation: A Statistical Profile." U.S. Department of Agriculture, Economic Research Service, Report 53, December 2007, 1–22. Washington, D.C.

Brown, Dennis W. "Rural Tourism: An Annotated Bibliography." U.S. Department of Agriculture, Economic Research Service, July 2008, 1–29. http://nal.usda.gov/ric/ricpubs/rural_tourism.html (accessed June 28, 2009).

Brown, Dona. *Inventing New England: Regional Tourism in the Nineteenth Century.* Washington, D.C.: Smithsonian Institution Press, 1999.

Browne, William P. *The Failure of National Rural Policy: Institutions and Interests.* Washington, D.C.: Georgetown University Press, 2001.

Bryan, Lettice. *Kentucky Housewife.* Cincinnati, Ohio: Stereotyped by Shepard and Steams, 1839.

Buchli, Victor, ed. *Material Culture: Critical Concepts in the Social Sciences.* 5 vols. New York: Routledge, 2004.

Buell, Lawrence. "American Pastoral Ideology Reappraised." *American Literary History* 1, no. 1 (1989): 1–29.

Bunce, Michael. *The Countryside Ideal: Anglo-American Images of Landscape*. London: Routledge, 1994.

Bureau of the Census, U.S. Department of Commerce. "Miscellaneous Vegetables Raised for Sale . . . 1899–1919." Table 97 in *Fourteenth Census of the United States Taken in the Year 1920*, vol. 5, *Agriculture*. Washington, D.C.: Government Printing Office, 1922.

Burgess Seed and Plant Company. *Spring 1975*. Galesburg, Mich., 1975.

Burke, Anastasia. "It's a Community Thing." *Review*, October 2000, 15.

Burns, Sarah. *Pastoral Inventions: Rural Life in Nineteenth-Century American Art and Culture*. Philadelphia: Temple University Press, 1989.

Burr, Fearing. *The Field and Garden Vegetables of America*. Boston: J. E. Tilton, 1865.

Bush, C. G. "Thanksgiving Sketches—Preparation." *Harper's Weekly*, December 8, 1866.

Butsch, Richard. *For Fun and Profit: The Transformation of Leisure into Consumption*. Philadelphia: Temple University Press, 1990.

Camp, Charles. *American Foodways: What, When, Why, and How We Eat in America*. Little Rock, Ark.: August House, 1989.

Campbell, George. *White and Black: The Outcome of a Visit to the United States*. London: Chatto and Windus, Piccadilly, 1879.

Carr, Lucien. "The Food of Certain American Indians and Their Methods of Preparing It." *Proceedings of the American Antiquarian Society*, April 24, 1895. Worcester, Mass.: Charles Hamilton, 1895.

Carter, Landon. *The Diary of Colonel Landon Carter of Sabine Hall, 1752–78*. Edited by Jack P. Greene. Charlottesville: University Press of Virginia, 1965.

Carter, Susannah. *The Frugal Colonial Housewife, or, Complete Woman Cook*. Philadelphia: Printed for Mathew Carey, 1802.

Cartier, Jacques. *Brief recit & succincte narration de la navigation faicte es Ysles de Canada, Hochelage and Saguenay and autres*. Paris, 1545. Reprint, 1863.

Carver, Jonathan. *Three Years' Travels through the Interior Parts of North America . . . 1766–1768*. Philadelphia: Key and Simpson, 1796.

Cashman, Dennis. *America in the Twenties and Thirties*. New York: New York University Press, 1989.

Castetter, E. F., and A. T. Erwin. "A Systematic Study of the Squashes and Pumpkins." *Iowa Agricultural Station Bulletin* 244. Ames: Iowa State College of Agriculture and Mechanic Arts, 1927.

Chabon, Michael. "Along the Frontage Road." *New Yorker*, November 19, 2001, 74–77.

Child, Lydia Maria. "A Boy's Thanksgiving Day." In *Favorite Poems Old and New*, by Helen Ferris. Garden City, N.Y.: Doubleday, 1957.

Circleville-Pickaway Area Chamber of Commerce. "Where We're Going: Agriculture." In *Pickaway County at a Glance*, 18. Circleville, Ohio: Crown Printing, 1999.

Circleville Pumpkin Festival, Inc. "Fantastic Facts about the Circleville Pumpkin Festival." Pickaway Historical Society collections, Circleville, Ohio.

Clark, Fred Emerson, and Louis D. H. Wield, eds. *Marketing Agricultural Products in the United States.* New York: Macmillan, 1932.

Clark, Henry Nichols Blake. "The Impact of Seventeenth-Century Dutch and Flemish Genre Painting on American Genre Painting, 1800–1865." Ph.D. dissertation, University of Delaware, 1982.

Clark, W. S. "A Squash in Harness." *Horticulturalist,* July 1875, 13–14.

Clements, William M., and Frances M. Malpezzi. *Native American Folklore, 1879–1979: An Annotated Bibliography.* Athens, Ohio: Swallow Press, 1984.

Cochrane, Willard. *The Development of American Agriculture: A Historical Analysis.* Minneapolis: University of Minnesota Press, 1979.

Coe, Michael, and Sophie Coe. "Mid-Eighteenth-Century Food and Drink on the Massachusetts Frontier." In *Foodways in the Northeast,* edited by Peter Benes, 39–46. Boston: Boston University Press, 1984.

Cohen, Hennig, and Tristram Potter Coffin, eds. *The Folklore of American Holidays.* Detroit: Gale, 1999.

Cohen, Lizabeth. *A Consumer's Republic: The Politics of Mass Consumption in Post-War America.* New York: Vintage, 2003.

Comstock, Ferre and Company. *The Gardener's Almanac.* Wethersfield, Conn., 1856.

Congregational Home Missionary Society. "Encouraging from Texas." *Home Missionary: For the Year Ending April 1884.* New York: American Home Missionary Society, 1884.

Converse, Harriet M. *Myths and Legends of the New York Iroquois.* New York State Museum Bulletin 125, no. 437 (1908). Reprint, Albany: University of the State of New York, 1974.

Cooper, Susan Fenimore. *Rural Hours.* New York: G. P. Putnam, 1850. Reprint, edited by Rochelle Johnson and Daniel Patterson, Atlanta: University of Georgia Press, 1998.

Corbett, Lee Cleveland. *Garden Farming.* Boston: Ginn and Company, 1913.

Corn, Wanda. *Grant Wood: The Regionalist Vision.* New Haven, Conn.: Yale University Press, 1983.

Cosgrove, Denis E. *Social Formation and Symbolic Landscape.* London: Croom Helm, 1984. Reprint, Madison: University of Wisconsin Press, 1996.

Counihan, Carole, and Penny Van Esterik, eds. *Food and Culture: A Reader.* New York: Routledge, 1979.

Cowan, John L. "The Golden Pumpkin Pie." *Pacific Monthly,* November 1906, 570.

Cowan, Ruth Schwartz. *A Social History of American Technology.* New York: Oxford University Press, 1997.

Crawford, Mary Caroline. *Social Life in Old New England.* Boston: Little, Brown, 1915.

Cronon, William. *Changes in the Land: Indians, Colonists, and the Ecology of New England.* New York: Hill and Wang, 1983.

———. *Nature's Metropolis: Chicago and the Great West.* New York: W. W. Norton, 1999.

————, ed. *Uncommon Ground: Toward Reinventing Nature*. New York: W. W. Norton, 1995.

Crosby, Alfred W., Jr. *The Columbian Exchange: Biological and Cultural Consequences of 1492*. Westport, Conn.: Greenwood Press, 1972.

————. *Ecological Imperialism: The Biological Expansion of Europe, 900–1900*. New York: Cambridge University Press, 1986.

Csikszentmihalyi, Mihaly, and Eugene Rochberg-Halton. *Meaning of Things: Domestic Symbols and the Self*. Cambridge: Cambridge University Press, 1981.

Cummings, Richard O. *The American and His Food: A History of Food Habits in the United States*. Chicago: University of Chicago Press, 1940.

Curtin, Deane W., and Lisa M. Heldke. *Cooking, Eating, Thinking: Transformative Philosophies of Food*. Bloomington: Indiana University Press, 1992.

Cutler, Hugh C., and Thomas W. Whitaker. "History and Distribution of the Cultivated Cucurbits in the Americas." *American Antiquity* 26, no. 4 (1961): 469–85.

Czestochowski, Joseph S. *John Steuart Curry and Grant Wood: A Portrait of Rural America*. Columbia: University of Missouri Press, 1981.

Dalechamp, Jacques. *Historia Generalis Plantarum*, vol. 1. Lugdini: G. Rovillius, 1597.

Danborn, David B. *Born in the Country: A History of Rural America*. Baltimore, Md.: Johns Hopkins University Press, 1995.

Daniels, Bruce Colin. *Puritans at Play: Leisure and Recreation in Colonial New England*. New York: St. Martin's, 1995.

Davies, Richard. *Main Street Blues*. Columbus: Ohio State University Press, 1999.

Davis, B. M. "Organization of Nature-Study in the Primary Grades." *Nature Study Review* 4 (1908): 108.

Davis, Johnda T., ed. "'I Remember—': Personal Recollections of the Pumpkin Show through the Years." *Pickaway Quarterly* 23, no. 3 (1981): 10–19.

Davis, Susan G. *Spectacular Nature: Corporate Culture and the Sea World Experience*. Berkeley: University of California Press, 1997.

Davis, Timothy. "Beyond the Sacred and Profane: Cultural Landscape Photography in America, 1930–1990." In *Mapping American Culture*, edited by Wayne Franklin and Michael Steiner, 191–230. Iowa City: University of Iowa Press, 1992.

Day, Clarence A. "A History of Maine Agriculture, 1604–1860." *University of Maine Bulletin* 56, no. 11 (1954).

Deane, Samuel. *New England Farmer; or Geological Dictionary*. 3d ed. Boston: Wells and Lilly, 1822.

de Bry, Theodore. *Brevis Narratio Eorum Quae in Florida Americae. . . .* Frankfort am Main, 1591.

Deetz, James, and Jay Anderson. "The Ethno-Gastronomy of Thanksgiving." *Saturday Review of Science*, November 25, 1972, 29–39.

Demos, John. *Entertaining Satan: Witchcraft and the Culture of Early New England*. New York: Oxford University Press, 1982.

Dennis, James M. *Renegade Regionalists: The Modern Independence of Grant Wood, Thomas Hart Benton and John Steuart Curry*. Madison: University of Wisconsin

Press, 1998.

"The Desserts." *Bon Appetit*, November 2001, 224.

De Voe, Thomas F. *The Market Assistant*. New York: Hurd and Houghton, 1867.

Dewhirst, Carin, and Joan Dewhirst. *My Tricks and Treats: Halloween Stories, Songs, Poems, Recipes, Crafts, and Fun for Kids*. New York: Smithmark, 1993.

Dickerson, George W. "Pumpkins Can Be a Plus in Seasonal Pocketbooks." *AgVentures*, December 1997–January 1998, 53–56.

Dodoens, Rembert. *A Niewe Herball or Historie of Plantes*. London, 1578.

Doggett, Rachel, ed. *New World of Wonders: European Images of the Americas, 1492–1700*. Seattle: University of Washington Press, 1992.

Domenico, Desirae M., and Karen H. Jones. "Career Aspirations of Women in the 20th Century." *Journal of Career and Technical Education* 22 (Fall 2006): 2.

Dorson, Richard M. *Jonathan Draws the Long Bow: New England Popular Tales and Legends*. Boston: Harvard College, 1946. Reprint, New York: Russell and Russell, 1970.

Dorst, John D. *Looking West*. Philadelphia: University of Pennsylvania Press, 1999.

———. *The Written Suburb: An American Site, an Ethnographic Dilemma*. Philadelphia: University of Pennsylvania Press, 1989.

Doudiet, Ellenore W. "Coastal Maine Cooking: Foods and Equipment from 1760." In *Gastronomy: The Anthropology of Food and Food Habits*, edited by Margaret L. Arnott, 215–32. The Hague: Mouton, 1975.

Douglas, John. *Catalog of Kitchen, Garden, Herb, Field and Grass Seeds*. Washington, D.C., 1843.

Douglas, Mary, ed. *Food in the Social Order: Studies of Food and Festivities in Three American Communities*. New York: Russell Sage Foundation, 1984.

Dow, George F. *Every Day Life in the Massachusetts Bay Colony*. New York: Benjamin Blom, 1935.

DuBois, W. E. B. *The Philadelphia Negro: A Social Study*. Philadelphia: University of Pennsylvania, 1899.

Dudley, Kathryn Marie. *Debt and Dispossession: Farm Loss in America's Heartland*. Chicago: University of Chicago Press, 2002.

Duke, James A. *Handbook of Northeastern Indian Medicinal Plants*. Lincoln, Mass.: Quarterman Publications, 1986.

Dundes, Alan, ed. *Cinderella: A Casebook*. New York: Wildman Press, 1983.

Dunlap, Thomas. *Catalogue of Garden, Flower, Shrub, Herb and Grass Seeds*. New York: Jared W. Bell, 1852.

Dunphy, Paul. "The Great Pumpkin: Breeders Continue to Improve the Easy-to-Grow Jack-o'-Lantern." *Horticulture*, October 1992, 40–44.

Earle, Alice Morse. *Customs and Fashions of Old New England* (1893). Bowie, Md.: Heritage Books, 1992.

Ebeling, Walter. *Handbook of Indian Foods and Fibers of Arid America*. Berkeley: University of California Press, 1986.

Eckert, Jane. "Farm Direct Marketing from a Producer's Perspective." Agricultural

Outlook Forum 1999, February 22, 1999. http://www.usda.gov/agency/oce/waob/ outlook99/speeches/023/eckert.txt (accessed April 18, 2001).

"The editor of the New Orleans Bulletin acknowledges the receipts of a pumpkin raised in Texas. . . ." *Charleston Mercury*, September 17, 1859.

"Editor's Study." *Harper's New Monthly Magazine*, December 1889-May 1890, 156.

"Editor's Table." *Horticulturalist*, February 1857.

"Electrical News." *St. Louis Globe-Democrat*, November 18, 1887, 4.

Elliott, John Huxtable. *The Old World and the New, 1492–1650*. New York: Oxford University Press, 1950.

Elliott, Lynne. *Food and Feasts in the Middle Ages*. New York: Crabtree, 2004.

Ellis, Bill. "'Safe' Spooks: New Halloween Traditions in Response to Sadism Legends." In *Halloween and Other Festivals of Death and Life*, edited by Jack Santino, 24–44. Knoxville: University of Tennessee Press, 1994.

Ember, Ildiko. *Delights for the Senses: Dutch and Flemish Still-Life Paintings*. Budapest: Szepmuveszeti Muzeum/Museum of Fine Arts, 1989.

Emerson, Ralph Waldo. "Nature." In *The Portable Emerson*, edited by Carl Bode, 7–50. New York: Penguin, 1981.

———. "Farming." In *The Portable Emerson*, edited by Carl Bode, 559–61. New York: Penguin, 1981.

Endrijonas, Erika. "Processed Foods from Scratch: Cooking for a Family in the 1950s." In *Kitchen Culture in America: Popular Representations of Food, Gender, and Race*, edited by Sherrie A. Inness, 157–74. Philadelphia: University of Pennsylvania Press, 2001.

"Enormous Product." *New England Farmer*, October 14, 1825, 95.

Evans, Michael. "Big: The Pumpkin. A Tale of International Intrigue Takes Shape as Three Towns Named Shelburne Plot to Grow the Biggest Pumpkin." *National Gardening*, October 1988, 18–21.

"Extraordinary Produce." *American Farmer*, September 17, 1819, 200.

"Extra Special Pumpkin Pie." *Ladies' Home Journal*, November 1943, 75.

Fairchild, Barbara. "Notes from the Editor." *Bon Appetit*, November 2001, 32.

Falkenburg, Reindert L. "Iconographical Connections between Antwerp Landscapes, Market Scenes and Kitchen Pieces, 1500–1580." *Oud Holland* 102 (1988): 114–26.

———. "Matters of Taste: Pieter Aertsen's Market Scenes, Eating Habits, and Pictorial Rhetoric in the Sixteenth Century." In *The Object as Subject: Studies in the Interpretation of Still Life*, edited by Anne W. Lowenthal. Princeton, N.J.: Princeton University Press, 1996.

"Fall Church Sociables for Grown Folks." *Ladies' Home Journal*, October 1903, 50.

Faragher, John Mack, Mary Jo Buhle, Daniel Czitrom, and Susan H. Armitage. *Out of Many: A History of the American People*. Upper Saddle River, N.J.: Pearson Prentice Hall, 2002.

Federal Writers Project, Works Progress Administration of Iowa. *Iowa: A Guide to the Hawkeye State*. New York: Hastings House, 1959 [1938].

Feld, Steven, and Keith H. Basso, eds. *Senses of Place*. Santa Fe, N.M.: School of American Research Press, 1996.

Ferguson, Alfred R. "The Abolition of Blacks in Abolitionist Fiction, 1830–1860." *Journal of Black Studies* 5, no. 2 (1974): 134–56.

Fieldhouse, Paul. *Food and Nutrition: Customs and Culture*. London: Croom Helm, 1986.

Fielding, Percy, and Anna Margaret Price. "Halloween Romps and Frolics by Two Experienced Entertainers." *Ladies' Home Journal*, October 1897, 25.

Finley, Ruth E. *The Lady of Godey's: Sarah Josepha Hale*. New York: Arno Press, 1974.

Fippin, Elmer Otterbein. *First Principles of Cooperation in Buying and Selling in Agriculture*. Richmond, Va.: Garrett and Massie, 1934.

Fisher, Richard Swainson. *A New and Complete Statistical Gazetteer of the United States of America*. New York: J. H. Colton, 1853.

Fite, Gilbert. "The 1980s Farm Crisis." *Montana: The Magazine of Western History*, Winter 1986, 69–71.

Fitzgerald, Deborah. *Every Farm a Factory: The Industrial Ideal in American Agriculture*. New Haven, Conn.: Yale University Press, 2003.

Fitzhugh, William W., ed. *Cultures in Contact: The Impact of European Contacts on Native American Cultural Institutions, A.D. 1000–1800*. Washington, D.C.: Smithsonian Institution Press, 1985.

Flandrin, Jean-Louis, and Massimo Montanari, eds. *Food: A Culinary History*. New York: Columbia University Press, 1999.

Fleischhauer, Carl, and Beverly W. Brannan, eds. *Documenting America, 1935–1943*. Berkeley: University of California Press, 1988.

Force, Peter. *Collection of . . . Voyages*, vol. 12. London, 1812.

———. *Tracts and Other Papers, Relating Principally to the Origin, Settlement and Progress of the Colonies in North America*, vol. 2. Washington, D.C.: Force, 1838.

Ford, Richard I. *An Ethnobiology Source Book: The Uses of Plants and Animals by American Indians*. New York: Garland, 1986.

Fowler, Jacob. *The Journal of Jacob Fowler . . . , 1821–22*. Edited by Elliott Coues. New York: Francis P. Harper, 1898.

Franco, Eloise. "Ugly Pumpkin." In *Little Stories*. North Quincy, Mass.: Christopher Publishing, 1970.

Freyfogle, Eric T. *The New Agrarianism: Land, Culture and the Community of Life*. Washington, D.C.: Island Press, 2001.

Fries, Adelaide L. *Records of the Moravians of North Carolina*. 8 vols. Raleigh: Edwards and Broughton, 1922.

Frost, Robert. "A Roadside Stand." In *Collected Poems of Robert Frost*, 370–71. Cutchogue, N.Y.: Buccaneer Books, 1986.

Fuchs, Leonard. *De historia Stirpium*. Basel, Switzerland, 1542.

Funk and Wagnalls Standard Dictionary of Folklore, Mythology and Legend. New York: Funk and Wagnalls, 1949.

Fussell, Betty. *The Story of Corn*. New York: Farrar, Straus and Giroux, 1992.

Gallo, Marzia Cataldi, Farida Simonetti, Piero Boccardo, and Luigi Viacava. *Il*

Giardino de Flora: Natura e simbolo nell'immagine dei fiori. Genoa: Sagep Editrice, 1986.

Galston, William. *Rural Development in the United States.* Washington, D.C.: Island Press, 1995.

Gardiner, Anne G. *Mrs. Gardiner's Receipts from 1763.* Hallowell, Me.: White and Horne, 1938.

Gardner, Bruce L. *American Agriculture in the Twentieth Century: How It Flourished and What It Cost.* Cambridge, Mass.: Harvard University Press, 2002.

Garrard, Lewis H. *Wah-To-Yah and the Taos Trail.* New York: A. S. Barnes, 1850. Reprint, Palo Alto, Calif.: American West Publishing, 1968.

Garrett, Wallace T. "Growing Pumpkins." Fact Sheet: Enterprise Guide for Southern Maryland. University of Maryland, Cooperative Extension Service, 1987–88.

Gaskell, Mark. "Pumpkin Production in California." Vegetable Production Series, Publication 7222. Vegetable Research and Information Center, University of California, Division of Agriculture and Natural Resources, undated.

Geisler, Malinda. "Pumpkins." AgMRC: A National Information Resource for Value-Added Agriculture, August 2009. http://www.agmrc.org/commodities_products/vegetables/pumpkins.cfm (accessed April 25, 2010).

"Genuine Pumpkin Pie." *Kansas City Journal*, reprinted in the *Macon (Georgia) Telegraph*, October 23, 1897, 3.

Gerarde, John. *The Herball, or Generall Historie of Plantes.* London: J. Norton and R. Whitakers, 1633.

Gideon, Siegfred. *Mechanization Takes Command: A Contribution to Anonymous History.* New York: W. W. Norton, 1970 [1948].

Glassberg, David. *American Historical Pageantry: The Uses of Tradition in the Early Twentieth Century.* Chapel Hill: University of North Carolina Press, 1990.

Glassie, Henry. "Artifacts: Folk, Popular, Imaginary and Real." In *Icons of Popular Culture*, edited by Marshall Fishwick and Ray B. Browne, 103–22. Bowling Green, Ohio: Bowling Green University Press, 1970.

———. *Material Culture.* Bloomington: Indiana University Press, 1999.

"Gone Forever: No More Do We See the Pumpkin Pies of Old." *St. Louis Globe-Democrat*, December 1, 1885, 10.

Goodnow, Ruby Ross. "A Halloween Housewarming." *Delineator*, October 1911.

Goody, Jack. "Industrial Food: Towards the Development of a World Cuisine." In *Food and Culture: A Reader*, edited by Carole Counihan and Penny Van Esterik, 338–56. New York: Routledge, 1997.

Gottlieb, Robert, and Anupama Joshi, eds. *Food Justice.* Cambridge, Mass.: MIT Press, 2010.

"Grandma's Pumpkin Pies." *Morning Oregonian*, December 8, 1889, 10.

Graubard, Mark. *Man's Food, Its Rhyme or Reason.* New York: Macmillan, 1943.

Gray, A., and J. H. Trumbull. "Review of DeCandolle's Origin of Cultivated Plants." *American Journal of Science* 25 (1883): 370–79.

Gray, Lewis Cecil. *History of Agriculture in the Southern United States to 1860.* Washington, D.C.: Carnegie Institution of Washington, 1933.

The Great Herball. London: Jhon Kynge, 1561.

"The Great Pumpkin: Why Stop at Pie?" *Woman's Day*, October 6, 1998.

"A Great Pumpkin Story." *New England Farmer*, December 11, 1844, 192.

Greenberg, David B., and Charles Corbin. *So You're Going to Buy a Farm.* New York: Greenberg, 1944.

Greene, Edward Lee. *Landmarks of Botanical History: A Study of Certain Epochs in the Development of the Science of Botany.* Washington, D.C.: Smithsonian Institution, 1909. Reprint, Palo Alto, Calif.: Stanford University Press, 1983.

Greene, Jack. *The Pursuit of Happiness: The Social Development of Early Modern British Colonies and the Formation of American Culture.* Chapel Hill: University of North Carolina Press, 1988.

———, and J. R. Pole. "Reconstructing British-American Colonial History." In *Establishing Exceptionalism: Historiography and the Colonial Americas*, edited by Amy T. Bushnell, 1–17. Aldershot, U.K.: Variorum, 1995.

Green Giraffe. "Reviewing the Annual Pumpkin Festival in Pumpkintown, South Carolina." April 18, 2007. http://www.associatedcontent.com/article/206077/reviewing_the_annual_pumpkin_festival.html?cat=16 (accessed April 25, 2010).

Griebel, Helen Bradley. "Worldview on the Landscape: A Regional Yard Art Study." *Pennsylvania Folklife* 36, no. 1 (1986): 39–48.

Grosjean, Ardis. "Toward an Interpretation of Pieter Aertsen's Profane Iconography." *Konsthistorick Tidskrift* 43 (1974): 121–43.

Grover, Kathryn, ed. *Dining in America, 1850–1900.* Amherst: University of Massachusetts Press, 1987.

Guernsey, John. "Food Retailing." In *U.S. Department of Commerce, Fifteenth Census of the United States: Census of Distribution, Retail Distribution: Food Retailing.* Washington, D.C.: Government Printing Office, 1934.

Guimond, James. *American Photography and the American Dream.* Chapel Hill: University of North Carolina Press, 1991.

"Giuseppe Arcimboldo." In *The Dictionary of Art*, edited by Jane Turner, 374. London: Macmillan, 1996.

Gurney's Seed and Nursery Company. *1998 Spring Catalog.* Yankton, S.D., 1998.

———. *1999 Spring Catalog.* Yankton, S.D., 1999.

———. *2010 Catalog.* http://gurneys.com/product.asp_o_pn_E_66293 (accessed February 5, 2010).

Gustin, Georgina. "Fields Are Awash in Pumpkins, but the Crop Is Stuck in Muck; as a Result, Pumpkin Pie Will Be a Little Hard to Come By." *St. Louis Today*, November 20, 2009. http://www.stltoday.com/news/article_612a2ead-b119-5c89-afba-fb2168e99840.html?print=1 (accessed May 9, 2011).

Hahn, Steven, and Jonathan Prude, eds. *The Countryside in the Age of Capitalist Transformation: Essays in the Social History of Rural America.* Chapel Hill: University of North Carolina Press, 1985.

Halbwachs, Maurice, ed. *On Collective Memory*. Chicago: University of Chicago Press, 1992.

Hale, Sarah Josepha. "Domestic." *Godey's Lady's Book*, November 1864, 1.

———. *Northwood; or Life North and South: Showing the True Color of Both*. New York: H. Long and Brother, 1852.

———. "Our National Thanksgiving—A Domestic Festival." *Godey's Lady's Book*, November 1864, 440.

Hale, Virginia. "Jack-Ma-Lanterns." In *The Silver Bullet and Other American Witch Stories*, edited by Hubert Davis, 48. Middle Village, N.Y.: Jonathan David, 1975.

Hall, Derek, Irene Kirkpatrick, and Morag Mitchel, eds. *Rural Tourism and Sustainable Business (Aspects of Tourism)*. Buffalo, N.Y.: Channel View Publications, 2005.

"Hallow-een." *Scribner's Monthly*, November 1871, 119.

Hamor, Ralph. *A True Discourse of the Present State of Virginia*. London, 1615. Reprint, New York: Da Capo Press, 1971.

Hampton Institute. "Hampton School Record." *Southern Workman*, December 1892.

Hand, Wayland D. "Will-o'-Wisps, Jack-o'-Lanterns and Their Congeners: A Consideration of the Fiery and Luminous Creatures of Lower Mythology." *Fabula* 18, nos. 3–4 (1977): 226–33.

Hanks, May C. "Pumpkin Is Queen." In *Local and National Poets of America 1891*, edited by Thomas Herringshaw, 485. Chicago: American Publishers Association, 1890.

Hardin, Terri. *Legends and Lore of the American Indians*. New York: Barnes and Noble, 1993.

Hariot, Thomas. *A Briefe and True Report of the New Found Land of Virginia. . . .* Frankfurt: Theodore de Bry, 1590. Reprint, Charlottesville: University of Virginia Press, 2007.

Harrington, John, ed. "The Original Strachey Vocabulary of the Virginia Indian Language." *Bureau of Indian Affairs Bulletin* 157 (Anthropology Papers 46), 189–202. Washington, D.C.: Government Printing Office, 1955.

Harris, Marvin. *Good to Eat: Riddles of Food and Culture*. New York: Simon and Schuster, 1985.

Harris, T. W. "Pumpkins and Squashes." *Southern Planter*, May 1855, 213–16.

Harris Moran Seed Company. *1986 HM Community Vegetable Growers Seed Guide*. Rochester, N.Y., 1986.

Harrison, Constance Cary. "American Rural Festivals." *Century* 1, no. 3 (1895): 323–33.

Harris Seeds. *1992–93 Harris Seeds: Professional Vegetable and Bedding Plant Growers' Catalog*. Rochester, N.Y., 1992.

"Harvest Festivals: Ohio's Pumpkin Show." *Better Homes and Gardens*, October 1980, 191.

Hawke, David Freeman. *Everyday Life in Early America*. New York: Harper and Row, 1988.

Hawthorne, Nathaniel. "Feathertop: A Moralized Legend." In *Twice-Told Tales*. Boston: American Stationers' Company, 1837. Reprint, Columbus: Ohio State University Press, 1974.

————. *The Scarlet Letter: An Authoritative Text, Background and Sources, Criticism.* Edited by Scully Bradley, Richmond Croom Beatty, and Hudson E. Long. New York: W. W. Norton, 1978.

Hayes, Jonathan. "Pumpkin Pie 101." *Martha Stewart Living*, November 2000, 98.

Haygood, Atticus. *The New South: Gratitude, Amendment, Hope. A Thanksgiving Sermon for November 25, 1880.* Oxford, Ga., 1880.

Hays, Samuel P. *A History of Environmental Politics since 1945.* Pittsburgh: University of Pittsburgh Press, 2000.

Haystead, Lee. *Meet the Farmer: A Personal Introduction to Thirty Million Americans.* New York: Putnam, 1944.

Hedrick, U. P. *History of Horticulture in America to 1860.* New York: Oxford University Press, 1950.

————. *Sturtevant's Notes on Edible Plants.* Albany, N.Y.: J. B. Lyon Company, State Printers, 1919.

Heiser, Charles B., Jr. *The Gourd Book.* Norman: University of Oklahoma Press, 1979.

"He Longs for Pie: Away with Foreign Cooks Who Won't Serve Mince and Pumpkin." *Emporia (Kansas) Daily Gazette*, May 1, 1895, col. D.

Henretta, James. "Families and Farms: *Mentalité* in Pre-industrial America." *William and Mary Quarterly* 35 (1979).

Herrick, James. *Iroquois Medical Botany.* Syracuse, N.Y.: Syracuse University Press, 1995.

Higginson, Francis. *New England's Plantation.* Salem, Mass.: Essex Book and Print Club, 1908 [1630].

Hilliard, Sam B. "Hog Meat and Cornpone: Foodways in the Antebellum South." In *Material Life in America, 1600–1860*, edited by Robert Blair St. George, 311–32. Boston: Northeastern University Press, 1988.

Hobsbawm, Eric. "Introduction: Inventing Traditions." In *The Invention of Tradition*, edited by Eric Hobsbawm and Terrance Ranger, 1–14. New York: Cambridge University Press, 1983.

Hofstadter, Richard. *The Age of Reform.* New York: Knopf, 1955.

Hofstetter, Bob. "Pumpkin Power: Halloween Hoopla Treats This Farm to Half Its Yearly Profits." *New Farm Magazine of Regenerative Agriculture*, September–October 1994, 43–45.

Holland, Roberta. "Pumpkin Farmers Hit Profitable Patch with Bumper Pumpkin Crop." *Boston Business Journal*, September 27, 1999.

Holmes, J. C., ed. *Transactions of the State Agricultural Society of Michigan . . . for the Year 1856.* Lansing, Mich.: Hosmer and Kerr, 1857.

Holmes Seed Company. *1990 Wholesale Price List for Commercial Growers.* Canton, Ohio, 1990.

Hooker, Richard J., ed. *A Colonial Plantation Cookbook: The Receipt Book of Harriot Pinckey Harry, 1770.* Columbia: University of South Carolina Press, 1984.

————. *Food and Drink in America: A History.* Indianapolis, Ind.: Bobbs-Merrill, 1981.

Hoppe, Robert A., and David E. Banker. *Structure and Finances of U.S. Farms: Family*

Farm Report, 2010 Edition. U.S. Department of Agriculture, Economic Information Bulletin EIB-66, July 2010.

——, David E. Banker, Penni Korb, Erik O'Donoghue, and James MacDonald. *America's Diverse Family Farms, 2007 Edition.* U.S. Department of Agriculture, Economic Information Bulletin EIB-26, June 2007. http://www.ers.usda.gov/publications/EIB26 (accessed June 28, 2010).

——, Penni Korb, Erik J. O'Donoghue, and David E. Banker. *Structure and Finances of U.S. Farms: Family Farm Report, 2007 Edition.* U.S. Department of Agriculture, Economic Information Bulletin EIB-24, June 2007. www.ers.usda.gov/publications/eib24/eib24a.pdf (accessed June 21, 2010).

Hovey, Albert H. *Albert H. Hovey's Catalog of Seeds.* Chicago, 1865.

Howe, Daniel Walker. *What Hath God Wrought: The Transformation of America, 1815–1848.* New York: Oxford University Press, 2007.

Howells, William Dean. "The Pumpkin Glory." In *Christmas Everyday and Other Stories,* 71–107. New York: Harper and Brothers, 1892.

"How to Select Pumpkin Seeds." *Southern Planter,* September 1854, 275.

Hufford, Mary, ed. *Conserving Culture: A New Discourse on Heritage.* Urbana: University of Illinois Press, 1994.

Hulten, Pontus, ed. *The Arcimboldo Effect: Transformation of the Face from the Sixteenth Century to Twentieth Century.* New York: Abbeville, 1977.

Humphrey, Theodore C., and Lin T. Humphrey. *"We Gather Together": Food and Festival in American Life.* Logan: Utah State University, 1988.

Hurt, R. Douglas. *American Agriculture: A Brief History.* Ames: Iowa State University Press, 1994.

——. *Indian Agriculture in America.* Lawrence: University of Kansas Press, 1987.

Huth, Hans. *Nature and the Americans: Three Generations of Changing Attitudes.* Berkeley: University of California Press, 1957.

Illinois Department of Agriculture, Bureau of Marketing and Promotions. "October Marketing Perspectives: Pumpkins." http://www.agr.state.il.us/marketing/news/October_2006/October2006MarketingPerspectives.html (accessed April 25, 2010).

"Improvements in Roadside Marketing." *American Cookery,* August–September 1929, 101.

Inbar, Michael. "Pumpkin Sets New World Record: 1,725 Pounds." *Today,* http://today.msnbc.msn.com/id/33379464/ns/today-today_halloween_guide (accessed August 24, 2010).

Ingersoll, Nathaniel. "Mr. Ingersoll's Piggery." *American Farmer,* October 1835, 205.

Integrated Pest Management Centers. "Crop Profile for Pumpkin in Texas." June 2002. http://www.ipmcenters.org/cropprofiles/docs/TXpumpkin.pdf (accessed June 23, 2010).

Irving, Washington. "The Legend of Sleepy Hollow." In *Sketchbook,* 416–56. New York: G. P. Putnam's Sons, 1848.

Isenberg, Alison. *Downtown America: A History of the Place and the People Who Made It.* Chicago: University of Chicago Press, 2005.

"Jack-Ma-Lantern." In *The Book of Negro Folklore*, edited by Langston Hughes and Arna Bontemps, 166. New York: Dodd, Mead, 1958.

"Jack o' Lantern." *Daily National Intelligencer* (Washington, D.C.), October 12, 1830.

Jackson, John B. "Jefferson, Thoreau and After." In *Landscapes: Selected Writings of J. B. Jackson*, 1–9. Amherst: University of Massachusetts Press, 1970.

Jackson, Kenneth T. *Crabgrass Frontier: The Suburbanization of the United States*. New York: Oxford University Press, 1985.

Jackson, Wes. *New Roots of Agriculture*. Lincoln: University of Nebraska Press, 1985.

Jakle, John A. "Landscapes Redesigned for the Automobile." In *The Making of the American Landscape*, edited by Michael P. Conven, 293–310. New York: Routledge, 1990.

———. *The Tourist: Travel in Twentieth-Century North America*. Lincoln: University of Nebraska Press, 1985.

James, C. C. "The Downfall of the Huron Nation." *Transactions of the Royal Society of Canada, Second Series, 1906–1907*, vol. 12, section 11. Ottawa: J. Hope and Sons, 1906.

James, E. O. *Seasonal Feasts and Festivals*. London: Thames and Hudson, 1961.

Janick, Jules, and Harry S. Paris. "The Cucurbit Images (1515–1518) of the Villa Farnesina, Rome." *Annals of Botany* 97 (2006): 165–76.

Jarves, James Jackson. *Parisian Sights and French Principles, Seen through American Spectacles*. New York: Harper and Brothers, 1852.

Jarvis, Charles A. "Admission to Abolition: The Case of John Greenleaf Whittier." *Journal of the Early Republic* 4, no. 2 (1984): 161–76.

Jaycox, Faith. *An Eyewitness History: The Colonial Era*. New York: Facts on File, 2002.

Jefferson, Thomas. *Notes on the State of Virginia*. Richmond, Va.: J. W. Randolph, 1853 [1781–85].

Jehlen, Myra. *American Incarnation: The Individual, the Nation, and the Continent*. Cambridge, Mass.: Harvard University Press, 1986.

Jenkins, Virginia Scott. *Bananas: An American History*. Washington, D.C.: Smithsonian Institution Press, 2000.

———. *The Lawn: A History of an American Obsession*. Washington, D.C.: Smithsonian Institution Press, 1994.

Jennings, Jan, ed. *Roadside America: The Automobile in Design and Culture*. Ames: Iowa State University Press, 1990.

Johnson, Darragh. "The Great Pumpkin Flinger." *Washington Post*, November 3, 2001, B1.

Johnson, Edward. *Wonder-Working Providence of Sions Savior in New England* (1654). Reprint, with introduction by Edward Gallagher, Delmar, N.Y.: Scholar's Facsimiles and Reprints, 1974.

Johnson, F. Roy. *Legends and Myths of North Carolina Roanoke-Chawan Area*. Murfreesboro, N.C.: Johnson Publishing, 1971.

Johnson, Robert. *Nova Britannia: Offering Most Excellent Fruites by Planting in Virginia*. London, 1609. Reprint, New York: Da Capo Press, 1969.

Jordan, Jennifer. "1999: 50,000 People and 18,349 Jack-o'-Lanterns Crowd Downtown Keene." *New Hampshire Sentinel Source*, n.d., at the Keene Pumpkin Festival website, http://pumpkinfestival.com (accessed September 6, 2000).

Josselyn, John. *New-England's Rarities Discovered in Birds, Beasts, Fishes, Serpents, and Plants of That Country.* London, 1627. Reprint, Boston: William Veazie, 1865.

Juet, Robert. *The Third Voyage of Master Henry Hudson* (1610). In *Narratives of New Netherland, 1609–1664*, edited by J. Franklin James. New York: Charles Scribner's Sons, 1909.

Kafinesque, C. S. "Oil of Pumpkin Seed." *American Farmer*, April 9, 1819, 19.

Kalm, Peter. *Peter Kalm's Travels in North America.* 2 vols. Edited by Adolph B. Benson. New York: Wilson-Erickson, 1937.

Kammen, Michael. *The Mystic Chords of Memory: The Transformation of Tradition in American Culture.* New York: Vintage, 1993.

Kaplan, Amy. "Manifest Domesticity." *American Literature* 70, no. 3 (1998): 581–606.

Kavasch, Barrie. "Native Foods of New England." In *Enduring Traditions: The Native Peoples of New England*, edited by Laurie Weinstein, 5–30. Westport, Conn.: Bergin and Garvey, 1994.

Kelly, Katy. "Growing Great Pumpkins, an All-Consuming Passion." *USA Today*, October 4, 1996, D-1 and D-2.

Kenrick, William. *The New American Orchardist: Or, an Account of the Most Valuable Varieties of Fruit, Adapted to Cultivation in the Climate of the United States. . . .* 8th ed. Boston: Otis, Broaders and Company, 1848.

Kerr, Ronald Dale, ed. *Indian New England, 1524–1674: A Compendium of Eyewitness Accounts of Native American Life.* Pepperell, Mass.: Branch Line Press, 1999.

Kidwell, Clara Sue. "Systems of Knowledge." In *America in 1492: The World of the Indian Peoples before the Arrival of Columbus*, edited by Alvin M. Josephy Jr. New York: Knopf, 1992.

Kimmel, Eric A. *Pumpkinhead.* Delray Beach, Fla.: Winslow Press, 2001.

King, Francis B. "Early Cultivated Cucurbits in Eastern North America." In *Prehistoric Food Production in North America*, edited by Richard I. Ford. Ann Arbor: Museum of Anthropology, University of Michigan, 1985, 1992.

"King of the Mammoths." In *H. W. Buckbee Seed and Plant Guide.* Rockland, Ill., 1895.

Kingsbury, Al. *The Pumpkin King: Four-Time World Champion Howard Dill and the Atlantic Giant.* Hantsport, Nova Scotia: Lancelot Press, 1992.

Kirkpatrick, John. *The Light of the Pumpkin: A Comedy in One Act.* New York: Samuel French, 1934.

Koeppel, Dan. *Banana: The Fate of the Fruit that Changed the World.* New York: Hudson Street Press, 2008.

Kolbert, Elizabeth. "It's Only Money." *New Yorker*, November 8, 1999, 50.

Kuban, Adam. "Nationwide Shortage of Canned Pumpkin Threatens Thanksgiving Pie." September 28, 2009. www.seriouseats.com/2009/09/nationwide-shortage-of-canned-pumpkin-threatens-Thanksgiving-pies.html (accessed

June 23, 2010).

Kuehner, John C. "Off Their Gourds, or Real Fear?" *Cleveland Plain Dealer*, December 9, 1999.

Kulikoff, Allan. "The Transition to Capitalism in Rural America." *William and Mary Quarterly* 46 (1989): 13–33.

Kupperman, Karen Ordahl, ed. *America in the European Consciousness, 1493–1750.* Chapel Hill: University of North Carolina Press, 1995.

———. *Indians and English: Facing Off in Early America.* Ithaca, N.Y.: Cornell University Press, 2000.

———. *Settling with the Indians: The Meeting of English and Indian Cultures in America, 1580–1640.* Totowa, N.J.: Rowman and Littlefield, 1980.

Kurlansky, Mark. *Cod: A Biography of the Fish That Changed the World.* New York: Walker, 1997.

———. *Salt: A World History.* New York: Walker, 2002.

Kwint, Marius, Christopher Breward, and Jeremy Aynsley, eds. *Material Memories: Design and Evocation.* New York: Berg, 1999.

Laffoon, Polk. "Pump-kin." *TWA Ambassador*, October 1979, 64.

Lahontan, Louis-Armand de Lom d'Arce. *New Voyages to North America.* London: Printed for H. Bonwicke et al., 1703.

Lalemant, Hierosme. "On the Mission of Sainte Elizabeth among the *Atontrataron-non* Algonkians." In *The Jesuit Relations and Related Documents: Travels and Explorations of the Jesuit Missionaries in New France, 1610–1791*, vol. 27, *Hurons, Lower Canada, (1642–1645)*, edited by Reuben Gold Thwaites, 19–72. Cleveland: Burrows Brothers, 1896–1901.

Landreth, David. *Descriptive Catalog of the Garden Seeds.* Philadelphia, 1844.

Lane, John. Letter to J. L. Boylston, January 5, 1829. *New England Farmer*, February 6, 1829.

Langevin, Don. *How-To-Grow World Class Giant Pumpkins.* Norton, Mass.: Annedawn Publishing, 1993.

———. *How-To-Grow World Class Giant Pumpkins, II.* Norton, Mass.: Annedawn Publishing, 1998.

———. *How-To-Grow World Class Giant Pumpkins, III.* Norton, Mass.: Annedawn Publishing, 2003.

———. *How-To-Grow World Class Giant Pumpkins the All Organic Way.* Norton, Mass.: Annedawn Publishing, 2009.

Lankford, George. *Native American Legends.* Little Rock, Ark.: August House, 1987.

la Quintinie, Jean de. *The Compleat Gard'ner.* Edited by George London and Henry Wise. London: M. Gillyflower, 1690.

Larkin, Jack. *The Reshaping of Everyday Life, 1790–1840.* New York: Harper Perennial, 1988.

Larsen, Susan, David Michaelis, Stephen T. Bruni, Betsey James Wyeth, Theodore E. Wolff, and Christopher Crosman. *Wondrous Strange: The Wyeth Tradition.* Boston: Little, Brown, 1998.

Leighton, Ann. *American Gardens in the Eighteenth Century: "For Use or for Delight."* Amherst: University of Massachusetts Press, 1976.

———. *Early American Gardens: "For Meate or Medicine."* Amherst: University of Massachusetts Press, 1970.

Leslie, Eliza. *Miss Leslie's Complete Cookery: Directions for Cookery in Its Various Branches.* Philadelphia, 1854.

Levenstein, Harvey. *Paradox of Plenty: A Social History of Eating in America.* New York: Oxford University Press, 1993.

———. *Revolution at the Table: The Transformation of the American Diet.* New York: Oxford University Press, 1988.

Levine, Lawrence. "The Historian and the Icon: Photography and the History of the American People in the 1930s and 1940s." In *Documenting America, 1935–1943,* edited by Beverly W. Brannan, 14–42. Berkeley: University of California Press, 1988.

Lévi-Strauss, Claude. *The Savage Mind.* Chicago: University of Chicago Press, 1966.

Lewis, A. G. "All Hallow Eve." *Ladies Home Journal,* October 1889, 3.

Lewis, Michael, ed. *American Wilderness: A New History.* New York: Oxford University Press, 2007.

Limerick, Patricia Nelson. *Legacy of Conquest: The Unbroken Past of the American West.* New York: W. W. Norton, 1987.

Lincoln, Abraham. "Proclamation for Thanksgiving, October 3, 1863, by the President of the United States of America." In *Complete Works of Abraham Lincoln,* edited by John G. Nicolay and John Hay, 151. New York: Francis D. Tandy, c. 1905.

Linton, Ralph, and Adelin Linton. *We Gather Together: The Story of Thanksgiving.* New York: Henry Schuman, 1949. Reprint, Detroit: Omnigraphics, 1990.

Lippard, Lucy R. *On the Beaten Track: Tourism, Art, and Place.* New York: New Press, 1999.

Love, W. DeLoss, Jr. *The Fast and Thanksgiving Days of New England.* Boston: Houghton Mifflin, 1895.

Lowenthal, David. *The Past Is a Foreign Country.* New York: Cambridge University Press, 1985.

———. *Possessed by the Past: The Heritage Crusade and the Spoils of History.* New York: Cambridge University Press, 1998.

Lowood, Henry. "The New World and the European Catalog of Nature." In *America in the European Consciousness, 1493–1750,* edited by Karen O. Kupperman, 295–317. Chapel Hill: University of North Carolina Press, 1995.

Lubar, Steven, and W. David Kingery, eds. *History from Things: Essays on Material Culture.* Washington, D.C.: Smithsonian Institution Press, 1993.

Lucier, Gary, and Rachael Dettman. "Vegetable and Melons Outlook: Commodity Highlight: Pumpkins." U.S. Department of Agriculture, Economic Research Service Report VGS-323, October 25, 2007.

Lynd, Robert S., and Helen M. Lynd. *Middletown: A Story in American Culture.* New York: Harcourt, Brace, 1929.

———. *Middletown in Transition: A Study in Cultural Conflicts.* New York: Harcourt, Brace, 1937.

MacCannell, Dean. *The Tourist: A New Theory of the Leisure Class.* New York: Schocken Books, 1976.

MacDonough, Glen. "The Jack O'Lantern Girl." New York: M. Witmark and Sons, 1905.

MacKenzie, Catherine. "Our Thanksgiving Feast." *New York Times*, November 24, 1935, SM17.

MacNelly, Jeff. "The Great Debate." *Washington Post*, October 30, 1999, A25.

"The Making of Pumpkin Pies Is Becoming a Lost Art." *Atchison Daily Globe*, October 3, 1893.

"Mammoth Fruits, etc." *New England Farmer*, October 9, 1829.

"A Mammoth Pumpkin." *New England Farmer*, January 11, 1828.

"A Mammoth Squash." *Farmer and Gardener*, October 27, 1835.

Mancall, Peter C., and James H. Merrell, eds. *American Encounters: Natives and Newcomers from European Contact to Indian Removal, 1500–1850.* New York: Routledge, 2000.

Mann, Charles C. *1491: New Revelations of the Americas before Columbus.* New York: Vintage Books, 2005.

Manning, Jason. "The Midwest Farm Crisis of the 1980s." http://wightiesclub.tripod.com/id395.htm (accessed May 29, 2010).

Mar, Charles, Terry Schaplowsky, and Ted Carey. "Pumpkins." Horticultural Report MF-2030, Agricultural Experiment Station and Cooperative Extension Service, Kansas State University, November 2004.

Marling, Karal Ann. *The Colossus of Roads: Myth and Symbol along the American Highway.* Minneapolis: University of Minnesota Press, 1984.

———. *Wall to Wall America: Post Office Murals in the Great Depression.* Minneapolis: University of Minnesota Press, 1982.

Marquette, Jacques. "Of the Mission of St. Ignace among the Tion-nontateronnons." In *The Jesuit Relations and Related Documents: Travels and Explorations of the Jesuit Missionaries in New France, 1610–1791*, vol. 57, *Lower Canada, Iroquois, Ottawas, 1672–1673*, edited by Reuben Gold Thwaites, 247–63. Cleveland: Burrows Brothers, 1896–1901.

Marr, Charles W. *Commercial Vegetable Production: Pumpkins.* Manhattan, Kans.: Cooperative Extension Service, Kansas State University, 1995.

Marx, Leo. *The Machine in the Garden: Technology and the Pastoral Ideal in America.* New York: Oxford University Press, 1964.

Maryland Agricultural Experiment Station. *Bulletin of the Maryland Agricultural Experiment Station*, 1925.

Mathews, Mitford M., ed. *A Dictionary of Americanisms on Historical Principles.* Chicago: University of Chicago Press, 1951.

McIntosh, Elaine N. *American Food Habits in Historical Perspective.* Westport, Conn.: Praeger, 1995.

McLean, Alice L. *Cooking in America, 1840–1945*. Westport, Conn.: Greenville Press, 2006.

McMahon, Sarah F. "'All Things in Their Proper Season': Seasonal Rhythms of Diet in Nineteenth Century New England." *Agricultural History* 63, no. 2 (1989): 130–51.

———. "A Comfortable Subsistence: The Changing Composition of Diet in Rural New England, 1620–1840." *William and Mary Quarterly* 42, no. 1 (1985): 26–65.

———. "Laying Foods By: Gender, Dietary Decisions, and the Technology of Food Preservation in New England Households, 1750–1850." In *Early American Technology: Making and Doing Things from the Colonial Era to 1850*, edited by Judith A. McGaw. Chapel Hill: University of North Carolina Press, 1994.

McMurry, Sally. *Transforming Rural Life: Dairying Families and Agricultural Change, 1820–1850*. Baltimore, Md.: Johns Hopkins University Press, 1995.

McNeill, John R. *Something under the Sun: An Environmental History of the Twentieth-Century World*. New York: W. W. Norton, 2000.

McPhee, John. *Oranges*. New York: Farrar, Straus and Giroux, 1967.

McShea, Susanna Hofmann. *The Pumpkin-Shell Wife: A Hometown Heroes Mystery*. New York: St. Martin's, 1992.

McWilliams, James E. *Revolution in Eating: How the Quest for Food Shaped America*. New York: Columbia University Press, 2005.

Mennell, Stephen, Anne Murcott, and Anneke H. van Otterloo. *The Sociology of Food: Eating, Dieting and Culture*. London: Sage, 1992.

Merchant, Carolyn. *Death of Nature: Women, Ecology, and the Scientific Revolution*. New York: Harper and Row, 1989.

———. *Major Problems in Environmental History: Documents and Essays*. Boston: Houghton Mifflin, 2005.

Mergen, Bernard. *Snow in America*. Washington, D.C.: Smithsonian Institution Press, 1997.

Merriam, Eve. "Jack o'Lantern." In *Halloween ABC: Poems by Eve Merriam*. New York: Macmillan, 1987.

Merrill-Corum, Vance. "California Farmers Apply Fun and Quality in Direct Marketing." *Rural Enterprise*, Fall 1987, 28–30.

"Merry Moments for Halloween." *Ladies' Home Journal*, October 1899, 38.

Metropolitan Museum of Art. *Thanksgiving and Harvest Festivals*. New York: Metropolitan Museum of Art, 1942.

Michaelis, David. *Schulz and Peanuts: A Biography*. New York: Harper Perennial, 2008.

Miller, Angela L. *Empire of the Eye: Landscape Representation and American Cultural Politics, 1825–1875*. Ithaca, N.Y.: Cornell University Press, 1993.

Miller, Daniel. *The Comfort of Things*. Malden, Mass.: Polity, 2009.

———. *Stuff*. Malden, Mass.: Polity, 2010.

Miller, Michael. "Pumpkins." *American Farmer*, December 21, 1827, 313.

Miller, Philip. *The Gardeners Dictionary*. London, 1735.

Minnis, Paul E., ed. *People and Plants in Ancient Eastern North America*. Washington, D.C.: Smithsonian Books, 2003.

————, ed. *People and Plants in Ancient Western North America.* Washington, D.C.: Smithsonian Books, 2004.

Mintz, Sidney W. *Sweetness and Power: The Place of Sugar in Modern History.* New York: Viking Penguin, 1985.

Moerman, Daniel. *American Medical Ethnobotany: A Reference Dictionary.* New York: Garland, 1977.

————. *Medicinal Plants of Native America.* Ann Arbor: University of Michigan Museum of Anthropology, 1986.

————. *Native American Ethnobotany.* Portland, Ore.: Timber Press, 1998.

"Monster Pumpkin." *Horticulturalist,* February 1857, 96.

"Morning Session." *Annual Report, Nebraska State Board of Agriculture 1910.* Lincoln: Jacob North, 1910.

Mortimer, Penelope. *The Pumpkin Eater.* New York: McGraw Hill, 1963.

Moss, Kay, and Kathryn Hoffman. *Backcountry Wife: A Study of Eighteenth-Century Food.* Gastonia, N.C.: Schiele Museum, 1985.

"Mourn the Lack of Pumpkin Pies." *New York Times,* October 6, 1901, 19.

Murchison , Ken. "SH Stressing Vendor Fees for Festival." *Spring Hope Enterprise,* September 28, 2000, 1.

Nabokov, Peter, ed. *Native American Testimony: An Anthology of Indian and White Relations, First Encounter to Dispossession.* New York: Crowell, 1978.

————, with Dean Snow. "Farmers of the Woodlands." In *America in 1492: The World of the Indian Peoples before the Arrival of Columbus,* edited by Alvin M. Josephy Jr., 119–45. New York: Knopf, 1992.

"Naming Your Baby." Pumpkin Nook. http://members.aol.com/ ezpumpkin/names. htm (accessed June 22, 1999).

Nasaw, David. *Going Out: The Rise and Fall of Public Amusements.* New York: Basic Books, 1993.

Nash, Roderick. *Wilderness and the American Mind.* New Haven, Conn.: Yale University Press, 1967.

Nayar, N. M., and T. A. More, eds. *Cucurbits.* Enfield, N.H.: Science Publishers, 1998.

Neely, Wayne Caldwell. *The Agricultural Fair.* New York: Columbia University Press, 1935.

N. E. F. "Largest Squash Yet." *New England Farmer,* November 24, 1841.

Nestle, Marion. *Food Politics: How the Food Industry Influences Nutrition and Health.* Berkeley: University of California, 2002.

"New Bedford." *New-Bedford Mercury,* December 1, 1836.

New England Agricultural Statistics. "New England Fruits and Vegetables, 2009 Crop." May 18, 2010. http://www.nass.usda.gov/Statistics_by_State/New_England_includes/Publications/05frtveg.pdf (accessed June 23, 2010).

"New Iowa Pumpkin Tax Puts Damper on Grower's Halloween Spirit." FoxNews.com, October 31, 2007. http://www.foxnews.com/printer_friendly_story/0,3566,306636,00.htl (accessed June 23, 2010).

"A New Pumpkin Pie Mix." *New York Times*, September 29, 1945, 18.

Noderer, Eleanor, ed. *The American Heritage Cookbook and Illustrated History of American Eating and Drinking*. New York: American Heritage, 1964.

"'No Halloween Rough Stuff,' Mayor Warns; He Urges Children to Shun 'Hoodlumism.'" *New York Times*, October 31, 1942, 17.

Norrman, Ralf, and Jon Haarberg. *Nature and Language: A Semiotic Study of Cucurbits in Literature*. London: Routledge and Kegan Paul, 1980.

Novak, Barbara. *Nature and Culture: American Landscape and Painting, 1825–1875*. New York: Oxford University Press, 1980.

Novotny, Marlene. "Vala's Pumpkin Patch." *Small Farm Today*, October 1994, 37.

Oelschlaeger, Max. *The Idea of Wilderness: From Prehistory to the Age of Ecology*. New Haven, Conn.: Yale University Press, 1991.

Old Fashioned Pumpkin Recipes. Nashville, Ind.: Bear Wallow Books, 1979.

"The Old Yellow Pumpkin." *American Farm News*, in *Western Garden and Poultry Journal* (Des Moines, Iowa), October 1891, 17.

O'Neill, Molly. "A Nation Hungers for Farm Stands and a Harvest without Cellophane." *New York Times*, August 21, 1991.

"1000 Windows in Queens Broken on Halloween." *New York Times*, November 1, 1939, 12.

Opie, Iona, and Peter Opie. *The Oxford Dictionary of Nursery Rhymes*. Oxford: Oxford University Press, 1951.

Opper, Frederick Burr. "The Supreme Court, as It May Hereafter Be Constituted." *Puck*, September 9, 1896.

Ortner, Sherry B. "Is Female to Male as Nature Is to Culture?" In *Women, Culture and Society*, edited by Michelle Zimbalist Rosaldo and Louise Lamphere, 67–87. Stanford, Calif.: Stanford University Press, 1974.

"Oshkosh Pumpkin Fair: Bouck Says It's a Thing of the Past." *Milwaukee Sentinel*, December 10, 1896, 8.

Ott, John. *Peter Pumpkin*. Garden City, N.Y.: Doubleday, 1963.

Palmer, A. "The Apocolocyntosis of Seneca." *Classical Review* 2, no. 6 (1888): 181.

Palmer, John. *Journal of Travels in the United States . . . in the year 1817*. London: Sherwood, Nealy and Jones, 1818.

Paris, Harry S. "History of the Cultivar-Groups of *Cucurbita pepo*." *Horticultural Reviews* 25 (2001): 71–170.

———. "Paintings (1769–1774) by A. N. Duchesne and the History of *Cucurbita pepo*." *Annals of Botany* 85 (2000): 815–16.

———, Marie-Christine Daunay, Michel Pitrat, and Jules Janick. "First Known Image of *Cucurbita* in Europe, 1503–1508." *Annals of Botany* 98 (2006): 46.

———, and Jules Janick. "Early Evidence for the Culinary Use of Squash Flowers in Italy." *Chronica Horticulturae* 45 (2005): 20–21.

Parker, Arthur C. *Iroquois Uses of Maize and Other Food Plants*. New York State Museum Bulletin 144. Albany, N.Y., 1910.

———. *Seneca Myths and Folktales*. Buffalo, N.Y.: Buffalo Historical Society, 1923.

Parker, Elizabeth. "Bill of Fare for Thanksgiving." *Ladies' Home Journal,* November 1888, 11.

Parkinson, John. *Paradisi i Sole Paradisus Terrestris.* London: H. Lownes and R. Young, 1629. Reprint, Norwood, N.J.: W. J. Johnson, 1975.

———. *Theatrum Botanicum.* London: Thomas Cotes, 1640.

Parton, J. "The Life of Horace Greeley, Editor New York Tribune." In *Tales and Sketches for the Fireside by the Best American Authors; Selected from Putnam's Magazine,* 76–90. New York: A. Dowling, 1857.

Patel, Raj. *Stuffed and Starved: The Hidden Battle of the World Food System.* Brooklyn, N.Y.: Melville House, 2008.

Patterson, Dennis. "Agriculture Comes Long Way since Graham Entered Office." *Spring Hope Enterprise,* October 19, 2000, 1.

Pavord, Anna. *The Tulip: The Story of a Flower That Has Made Men Mad.* New York: Bloomsbury, 1999.

Peake, Glenn. "By Pumpkin Light." *Martha Stewart Living,* October 1998, 194.

Pendergrast, Mark. *Uncommon Grounds: The History of Coffee and How It Transformed Our World.* New York: Basic Books, 1999.

Pendery, Steven R. "The Archaeology of Urban Foodways in Portsmouth, New Hampshire." In *Foodways in the Northeast,* edited by Peter Benes, 9–27. Boston: Boston University Press, 1984.

Penner, Lucille Recht. *The Thanksgiving Book.* New York: Hastings House, 1986.

"Peppery Pumpkin Pies: A Thanksgiving Story." *Chicago Daily Inter Ocean,* November 27, 1879, 6.

Perrault, Charles. *Cinderella; or the Little Glass Slipper.* Albany, N.Y.: E. and E. Hosford, 1811.

———. *Memoirs of My Life.* Columbia: University of Missouri Press, 1989.

Perrot, Nicolas. *Indian Tribes of the Upper Mississippi Valley and the Region of the Great Lakes, 1680–1718.* Leipzig: Jules Tailhan, 1864. Reprint, Cleveland, Ohio: Arthur H. Clark, 1911.

Pessen, Edward. *Jacksonian America: Society, Personality, and Politics.* Homewood, Ill.: Dorsey Press, 1978.

Peters, Samuel. *General History of Connecticut.* New York: D. Appleton, 1877.

Petrini, Carlo. *Slow Food Nation: The Creation of a New Gastronomy.* New York: Rizzoli Ex Libris, 2007.

Philippi, Edward Henry. "A Variety of Halloween Window Plans." In *The Grocer's Window Book: A Compilation of Practical Plans for Displays in the Grocer's Window.* Chicago: R. R. Donnelly and Sons, 1914.

Phipps, Frances. *Colonial Kitchens, Their Furnishings and Their Gardens.* New York: Hawthorn Books, 1972.

"Pie 'Like Mother's' to Cheer Soldiers Here; Obtained by Woman Who Baked in 1st A.E.F." *New York Times,* November 26, 1942.

Pieyre de Mand, Andre. *Arcimboldo the Marvelous.* New York: Abrams, 1978.

"Pig and Pumpkin Show." Published in "The State Fair—Past and Present," by

Isaac Brandt, *The Mid-western* (Midwestern Association of University Student Employment Directors), September 1906, 71.

Pinkerton, John. *General Collection of the Best and Most Interesting Voyages and Travels in All Parts of the World*, vol. 13. London, 1812.

Pinter, Harold. "The Pumpkin Eater." In *Five Screenplays*. New York: Grove Press, 1973.

Pliny the Elder. *The Natural History* (77 a.d.). Edited by John Bostock and H. T. Riley. http://www.perseus.edu/cgi-bin/ptext?lookup=Plin.+Nat.+toc (accessed October 26, 2007).

Pollan, Michael. *Botany of Desire: A Plant's Eye View of the World*. New York: Random House, 2001.

———. *Food Rules: An Eater's Manual*. New York: Penguin, 2009.

———. *In Defense of Food: An Eater's Manifesto*. New York: Penguin, 2008.

———. *The Omnivore's Dilemma: A Natural History of Four Meals*. New York: Penguin, 2006.

Price, Anna Margaret. "Merry Halloween Games." *Ladies' Home Journal*, October 1897, 25.

Price, Edward T. *Dividing the Land: Early American Beginnings of Our Private Mosaic*. Chicago: University of Chicago Press, 1995.

Price, Jennifer. *Flight Maps: Adventures with Nature in Modern America*. New York: Basic Books, 2000.

———. "Looking for Nature at the Mall: A Field Guide to the Nature Company." In *Uncommon Ground: Toward Reinventing Nature*, edited by William Cronon, 187–202. New York: W. W. Norton, 1995.

"Productive Pumpkin Vine." *New England Farmer*, February 22, 1832, 253.

Pronzini, Bill. "Pumpkin." In *Halloween Horrors*, edited by Alan Ryan, 141–48. Garden City, N.Y.: Doubleday, 1986.

Prown, Jules David. "Mind in Matter: An Introduction to Material Culture Theory and Method." *Winterthur Portfolio* 17, no. 1 (1982): 1–19.

———. "Style as Evidence." *Winterthur Portfolio* 15, no. 3 (1980): 197–210.

Puckett, Newbell Niles. *Folk Beliefs of the Southern Negro*. New York: Dover, 1969.

Pullar, Philippa. *Consuming Passions: A History of English Food and Appetite*. London: Hamilton, 1970.

Pulver, Glen C., and Glenn R. Rogers. "Changes in Income Sources in Rural America." *American Journal of Agricultural Economics* 68, no. 5 (1986): 1181–87.

"A Pumpkin. . . ." *Maryland Gazette and Political Intelligencer*, November 6, 1823.

"A Pumpkin. . . ." *Raleigh Register, and North-Carolina Gazette*, November 29, 1822.

"Pumpkin and Winter Squash." Commercial Vegetable Production Guides, North Willamette Research and Extension Center, Oregon State University, August 2004. http://nwrec.hort.oregonstate.edu/pumpkin.html.

"The Pumpkin Cut: Wallenstein, of the Boston Store, Distinguishes Himself." *Atkinson (Kansas) Champion*, November 30, 1890, 4.

"A Pumpkin Effigy." *Harper's Weekly*, November 23, 1867, 1.

"Pumpkin Harvest Rolls On." *Journal Star* (Peoria, Ill.), October 17, 2000.

"The Pumpkin in Kansas." *Rocky Mountain News*, October 18, 1879, 4.

"Pumpkin Pie." *Werner's Magazine*, October 1896, 10.

"Pumpkin Pie." *Werner's Magazine*, October 1898, 121.

"Pumpkin Pie Has Arrived." *New York Times*, September 21, 1902, 27.

"Pumpkin Pies." *Good Housekeeping*, November 9, 1899, 29.

"Pumpkin-Pies." *Lowell Daily Citizen*, March 2, 1877.

"Pumpkin Pies." *Omaha Nebraskan*, November 11, 1857.

"Pumpkin Soup." *Mississippi Free Trader and Natchez Gazette*, January 10, 1849.

"Pumpkin Sugar." *The North American* (Philadelphia, Pa.), August 3, 1939.

"Pumpkins." *American Agriculturalist*, July 1882.

"Pumpkins." *American Farmer*, May 8, 1838.

"Pumpkins." *American Farmer*, April 28, 1841, 386.

"Pumpkins." *Farmer and Gardener*, December 2, 1834, 242.

"Pumpkins." *Farmer and Gardener*, June 6, 1837, 42.

"Pumpkins." *New Eclectic Magazine*, January–June 1869, 472.

"Pumpkins." *New England Farmer*, April 6, 1827, 294.

"Pumpkins." *New England Farmer*, May 11, 1831.

"Pumpkins: Libby's Leads the Way." *Scanner*, June–August 1968, 6–10. Libby's Company Archives, Morton, Illinois.

"Pumpkins as Stolen Crop." *Horticulturalist*, December 1870, 120.

"Pumpkins for Milch Cows." *American Agriculturalist*, March 1850, 81.

"Pumpkins, Squashes, etc." *American Farmer and Gardener*, December 18, 1838, 269.

"Pumpkins Very Scarce This Year." *New York Times*, November 16, 1902, 33.

"Puritan Costume Party for Thanksgiving." *Rocky Mountain News*, November 14, 1897, 17.

Purvis, Thomas L. *Colonial America to 1763*. New York: Facts on File, 1999.

Quammen, David. *The Reluctant Mr. Darwin: An Intimate Portrait of Charles Darwin and the Making of His Theory of Evolution*. New York: Atlas Books/Norton, 2006.

Quimby, Ian M. G. *Material Culture and the Study of American Life*. New York: W. W. Norton, 1978.

Raine, Carolyn. *A Woodland Feast: Native American Foodways of the Seventeenth and Eighteenth Centuries*. Hubert Heights, Ohio: Penobscot Press, 1997.

Randolph, Mary. *The Virginia House-Wife*. Washington, D.C.: Davis and Force, 1838 [1824].

Rapp, Fred. Letter to the Editor. *American Farmer*, December 3, 1830, 304.

Ray, David. *Pumpkin Light*. New York: Putnam and Grosset, 1993.

Ray, Mary Lyn. *Pumpkins*. San Diego: Harcourt Brace, 1992.

Rebora, Giovanni. *Culture of the Fork: A Brief History of Food in Europe*. Translated by Albert Sonnenfeld. New York: Columbia University Press, 2001.

"Recitation and Declamation." *Werner's Magazine*, October 1898, 121.

Regis, Pamela. *Describing Early America: Bartram, Jefferson, Crevecoeur, and the Rhetoric of Natural History*. DeKalb: Northern Illinois University, 1992.

Reid, James. *Peter, Peter Pumpkin Eater*. Philadelphia: Fortress Press, 1970.

Reps, John W. *Making of Urban America: A History of City Planning in the United States.* Princeton, N.J.: Princeton University Press, 1965.

Richter, Daniel K. *Facing East from Indian Country: A Native History of Early America.* Cambridge, Mass.: Harvard University Press, 2001.

Ridley, Glynnis. "The First American Cookbook." *Eighteenth-Century Life* 23 (May 1999): 114–23.

Rifkind, Carole. *Main Street: A Face of Urban America.* New York: HarperCollins, 1977.

Riley, James Whitcomb. "When the Frost Is on the Punkin." In *The Complete Poetic Works of James Whitcomb Riley*, 254–55. Garden City, N.Y.: Garden City Publishing, 1945.

Ripley, Ken. "SH Festival Set to Begin This Friday." *Spring Hope Enterprise*, October 5, 2000, 1.

Robbins, Sarah. "'The Future Good and Great of Our Land': Republican Mothers, Female Authors, and Domesticated Literacy in Antebellum New England." *New England Quarterly* 75, no. 4 (2002): 562–91.

Robinson, R. W., and D. S. Decker-Walters. *Cucurbits.* New York: CAB International, 1997.

Robinson, Rowland. "Glimpses of New England Farm Life." *Century/Scribner's Monthly*, October 1878, 520.

Rockwell, Anne. *Pumpkin Day, Pumpkin Night.* New York: Walker, 1999.

Rogers, Nicolas. *Halloween: From Pagan Ritual to Party Night.* New York: Oxford University Press, 2002.

Rohrer, Wayne C., and Louis H. Douglas. *The Agrarian Transition in America: Dualism and Change.* Indianapolis, Ind.: Bobbs-Merrill, 1969.

Root, A. I. "The Pumpkin Business: Pumpkin Pies by the Carload." *Gleanings in Bee Culture*, January 15, 1891, 469.

Root, Waverly, and Richard de Rochemont. *Eating in America: A History.* New York: Echo Press, 1976.

Rooth, Anna Birgitta. *The Cinderella Cycle.* Lund, Sweden: CWK Gleerup, 1951.

Rosenzweig, Roy, and David Thelen. *The Presence of the Past: Popular Uses of History in American Life.* New York: Columbia University Press, 1998.

Roth, Monika. "Overview of Farm Direct Marketing Industry Trends." Agricultural Outlook Forum 1999, February 22, 1999, http://www.usda.gov/agency/oce/waob/outlook99/speeches/023/roth.txt (accessed April 18, 2001).

Rothman, Hal K. *Devil's Bargain: Tourism in the Twentieth-Century American West.* Lawrence: University Press of Kansas, 1998.

Russell, Howard S. *Indian New England before the Mayflower.* Hanover, N.H.: University Press of New England, 1980.

———. *A Long, Deep Furrow: Three Centuries of Farming in New England.* Hanover, N.H.: University Press of New England, 1976.

Rutledge, Sarah. *Carolina Housewife; or, House and Home.* Charleston, S.C.: W. R. Babcock, 1847. Reprint, Charleston, S.C.: S. S. S. Publishers, 1963.

Rutman, Darrett B. *Husbandmen of Plymouth: Farms and Villages in the Old Colony,*

1620–1692. Boston: Beacon Press, 1967.

Saade, R. Lira, and S. Montes Hernandez. "Cucurbits." http://www.hort.purdue
.edu/newcrop/1492/cucurbits.html (accessed February 2, 2002).

Sabota, C. M., and J. W. Courter. "An Analysis of the Potential for Pick-Your-Own
Marketing in a Rural Area." *USDATE 79: Research Report of the Dixon Springs
Agricultural Center*. University of Illinois, January 1979.

Salaman, Redcliffe N. *The History and Social Influence of the Potato*. Cambridge: Cambridge University Press, 1949.

Salerno, Beth A. *Sister Societies: Women's Antislavery Societies in Antebellum America*.
DeKalb: Northern Illinois University Press, 2005.

Salmon, William. *The English Herbal; or History of Plants*. London: I. Dawes for H.
Rhodes and J. Taylor, 1710.

Salomon, Nanette. *Shifting Priorities: Gender and Genre in Seventeenth-Century Dutch
Painting*. Stanford, Calif.: Stanford University Press, 2004.

Sangster, Margaret E. "Thanksgiving Pumpkin Pies." *Ladies' Home Journal*, November 1889, 7.

Santino, Jack. *All Around the Year: Holidays and Celebrations in American Life*. Urbana:
University of Illinois Press, 1994.

———. "The Folk Assemblage of Autumn: Tradition and Creativity in Halloween
Folk Art." In John Vlach and Simon J. Bronner, eds. *Folk Art and Art Worlds*,
151–69. Logan: Utah State University, 1992.

———, ed. *Halloween and Other Festivals of Death and Life*. Knoxville: University of
Tennessee Press, 1994.

———. "Halloween in America: Contemporary Customs and Performances." *Western Folklore* 42 (1983): 1–20.

———. *New Old Fashioned Ways: Holidays and Popular Culture*. Knoxville, Tenn.:
University of Tennessee Press, 1996.

———. "Night of the Wandering Souls." *Natural History* 92, no. 10 (1983): 42–51

Scapp, Ron, and Brian Seitz, eds. *Eating Culture*. Albany: State University of New
York Press, 1993.

Scarry, C. Margaret, ed. *Foraging and Farming in the Eastern Woodlands*. Gainesville:
University Press of Florida, 1993.

Schaedler, Louis C. "Whittier's Attitude toward Colonial Puritanism." *New England
Quarterly* 21, no. 3 (1948): 350–67.

Schama, Simon. *The Embarrassment of Riches: An Interpretation of Dutch Culture in the
Golden Age*. Berkeley: University of California Press, 1988.

———. *Landscape and Memory*. New York: Knopf, 1995.

Schivelbusch, Wolfgang. *Tastes of Paradise: A Social History of Spices, Stimulants, and
Intoxicants*. Translated by David Jacobson. New York: Vintage Books, 1992.

Schlebecker, John T. *Whereby We Thrive: A History of American Farming, 1607–1972*.
Ames: Iowa State University Press, 1975.

Schlereth, Thomas J., ed. *Material Culture: A Research Guide*. Lawrence: University
Press of Kansas, 1985.

————, ed. *Material Culture Studies in America*. Nashville, Tenn.: American Association for State and Local History, 1982.

————. "Vegetation as Historical Data: A Historian's Use of Plants and Natural
Material Culture Evidence." In *Artifacts and the American Past*, by Thomas J.
Schlereth, 147–59. Nashville, Tenn.: American Association for State and Local
History, 1980.

Schloss, Andrew. "Smashing Pumpkins." *Washington Post*, October 25, 1995, E10.

Schmidt, Peter J. *Back to Nature: The Arcadian Myth in Urban America*. New York:
Oxford University Press, 1969.

Schneider, Stuart. *Halloween in America: A Collector's Guide with Prices*. Atglen, Pa.:
Schiffer, 1995.

Schultheis, Jonathan R. "Growing Pumpkins and Squash." North Carolina Cooperative Extension Service, revised January 1995; reviewed January 1998. http://
www.ces.ncsu.edu/depts/hort/hil/hil-24.html (accessed May 24, 2010).

Schultz, Charles M. *How Long, Great Pumpkin, How Long?* New York: Holt, Rinehart
and Winston, 1977.

Schwartz, Franz. *The Origin of Cultivated Plants*. Cambridge, Mass.: Harvard University Press, 1966.

Sears, John. *Sacred Places: American Tourist Attractions in the Nineteenth Century*. New
York: Oxford University Press, 1989.

Sebastian, Patrizia, Hanno Schaefer, Ian R. H. Telford and Susanne S. Renner.
"Cucumber (*Cucumis sativus*) and melon (*C. melo*) have numerous wild relatives
in Asia and Australia, and the Sister Species of Melon Is from Australia." *Proceedings of the National Academy of Sciences of the United States of America* 107, no.
32 (August 10, 2010): 14,269–73.

Segal, Sam. *A Prosperous Past: The Sumptuous Still Life in the Netherlands, 1600–1700*.
The Hague: SDU Publishers, 1988.

Shackel, Paul, ed. *Myth, Memory, and the Making of the American Landscape*. Gainesville: University Press of Florida, 2001.

Shaffer, Marguerite S. *See America First: Tourism and National Identity, 1880–1940*.
Washington, D.C.: Smithsonian Institution Press, 2001.

Shakespeare, William. "The Merry Wives of Windsor." In *The Complete Works of
William Shakespeare*, edited by William Aldis Wright. Garden City, N.Y.: Garden
City Books, 1936.

Shapiro, Laura. *Perfection Salad: Women and Cooking at the Turn of the Century*. New
York: Farrar, Straus and Giroux, 1986.

Share, Elizabeth. "Preparation for Thanksgiving." *Primary Education*, November
1899, 399.

Sheehy, Colleen Josephine. "The Flamingo in the Garden: Artifice, Aesthetics, and
Popular Taste in American Yard Art." Ph.D. dissertation, University of Minnesota, 1991.

Shi, David. *The Simple Life: Plain Living and High Thinking in American Culture*. New
York: Oxford University Press, 1986.

Shippen, E. "Among Our Contemporaries." *The United Service: A Monthly Review of Military and Naval Affairs* 11 (1894): 475.

Shiva, Vandana. *Stolen Harvest: The Hijacking of the Global Food Supply.* Cambridge, Mass.: South End Press, 2000.

Simmons, Amelia. *American Cookery.* Hartford, Conn.: Hudson & Goodwin, 1796. Reprint, New York: Eerdmans, 1965.

Sinclair, Upton. *The Jungle.* New York: Doubleday, 1906.

Sinks, Frank W. "A Poem on Cow-Pumpkins and the 'Land of the Pumpkin Pie': Something to Make Your Mouth Water, Michigan's Greatest Bid for Fame." *Gateway: A Magazine of Literature, Commerce and Development,* November 1904, 31–32.

Siporin, Steve. "Halloween Pranks: 'Just a Little Inconvenience.'" In *Halloween and Other Festivals of Death and Life,* edited by Jack Santino, 45–61. Knoxville: University of Tennessee Press, 1994.

Skal, David J. *Death Makes a Holiday: A Cultural History of Halloween.* New York: Bloomsbury, 2002.

Skarmeas, Nancy J. *Jack-o'-Lantern.* Nashville, Tenn.: Candy Cane Press, 2001.

Small, Lewis. "Ideas for Marketing Your Fall Ornamentals." *Countryside and Small Stock Journal,* September–October 1997, 32.

"Smashing Pumpkins." *Washington Times,* November 14, 1997, A1.

Smith, Bruce D. *The Emergence of Agriculture.* New York: Scientific American Library, 1995.

———. "The Initial Domestication of *Cucurbita pepo* in the Americas 10,000 Years Ago." *Science* 276 (May 9, 1997): 932–34.

———. "Origins of Agriculture: Enhanced. Between Foraging and Farming." *Science* 279 (March 13, 1998): 1651–52.

———. "Prehistoric Plant Husbandry in Eastern North America." In *The Origins of Agriculture: An International Perspective,* edited by C. Wesley Cowan and Patty Jo Watson, 101–14. Washington, D.C.: Smithsonian Institution Press, 1992.

———. *Rivers of Change: Essays on Early Agriculture in Eastern North America.* Washington, D.C.: Smithsonian Institution Press, 1992.

———, and C. Wesley Cowan. "Domesticated Crop Plants and the Evolution of Food Production Economies in Eastern North America." In *People and Plants in Ancient Eastern North America,* edited by Paul E. Minnis, 105–25. Washington, D.C.: Smithsonian Books, 2004.

Smith, Eliza. *The Compleat Housewife.* London: Printed for S. Ware, R. Birt, et al., 1727.

Smith, Henry Nash. *Virgin Land: The American West as Symbol and Myth.* Cambridge, Mass.: Harvard University Press, 1950.

Smith, John. *The Description of Virginia* (1612). In *The Complete Works of Capt. John Smith,* vol. 1, edited by Philip L. Barbour. Chapel Hill: University of North Carolina Press, 1986.

———. *A Description of New England* (1616): *An Electronic Text.* Edited by Paul Royster. http://digitalcommons.unl.edu/cgi/viewcontent.cgi?article=1003&context=etas (accessed January 10, 2010).

Smith, Leef. "Politics of Pumpkin Picking." *Washington Post*, October 12, 2000, B1.

Sokolow, Jayme A. *The Great Encounter: Native Peoples and European Settlers in the Americas, 1492–1800*. Armonk, N.Y.: M. E. Sharpe, 2003.

"Soldiers to Be Hosts: 700 at Fort Dix to Share Thanksgiving with Kin." *New York Times*, November 16, 1941, 42.

"Some Pumpkins: The Pumpkin Festival Given by the 'St. Paul. One Price' a Grand Success." *Bismarck Daily Tribune*, October 7, 1886.

Sorkin, Michael, ed. *Variations on a Theme Park: The New American City and the End of Public Space*. New York: Hill and Wang, 1992.

Spitzer, Angie. "Ackerman Family Makes Pumpkins Full-Time Job." *34th Annual Morton Pumpkin Festival Guide*. Times Newspapers, 2000.

"Spoon Fed." *Cooking Light*, October 2000, 38.

Stacey, Michelle. *Consumed: Why Americans Love, Hate, and Fear Food*. New York: Simon and Schuster, 1994.

Stanard, Mary N. *Colonial Virginia: Its People and Customs*. Detroit: Singing Tree Press, 1970.

"The State Elections." *Harper's Weekly*, October 31, 1863, 704.

St. George, Robert Blair, ed. *Material Life in America, 1600–1860*. Boston: Northeastern University Press, 1988.

"St. Joseph County." In *Transactions of the State Agricultural Society of Michigan . . . for the Year 1856*, edited by J. C. Holmes, 780. Lansing, Mich.: Hosmer and Kerr, 1857.

Steinbeck, John. *The Grapes of Wrath*. New York: Viking Press, 1939.

Steinberg, Theodore. *American Green: The American Obsessive Quest for the Perfect Lawn*. New York: W. W. Norton, 2007.

———. *Down to Earth: Nature's Role in American History*. New York: Oxford University Press, 2002.

Stenerson, Douglas C. "Emerson and the Agrarian Tradition." *Journal of the History of Ideas* 4 (January 1953): 95–115.

Sternberg, Alan. "A Growing Concern: Rivals in Big E Pumpkin Contest Throwing Their Weight Around." *Hartford Courant*, September 28, 1984, B-1.

Stewart, Susan. *On Longing: Narratives of the Miniature, the Gigantic, the Souvenir, the Collection*. Baltimore, Md.: Johns Hopkins University Press, 1984. Reprint, Durham, N.C.: Duke University Press, 1993.

Stilgoe, John. *Common Landscape of America, 1580–1845*. New Haven, Conn.: Yale University Press, 1982.

Stokes, Samuel N., A. Elizabeth Watson, and Shelley S. Mastran. *Saving America's Countryside: A Guide to Rural Conservation*. Baltimore, Md.: Johns Hopkins University Press, 1989.

"The Story of the Harvard Students. . . ." *Boston Daily Advertiser*, October 29, 1887, 4.

Strachey, William. *The Historie of Travaile into Virginia Britannia*. London: Hakluyt Society, 1849.

Strasser, Susan. *Satisfaction Guaranteed: The Making of the American Mass Market*. Washington, D.C.: Smithsonian Institution Press, 1989.

———, Charles McGovern, and Matthias Judt, eds. *Getting and Spending: European and American Consumer Societies in the Twentieth Century*. Cambridge: Cambridge University Press, 1998.

"Streamlined Thanksgiving Dinner: Modern Kitchen Technique Applied to American Menu." *New York Times*, November 21, 1937.

Stuart-Worley, Lady Emmeline. *Travels in the U.S., etc.; during 1849 and 1850*. New York: Harper and Brothers, 1851.

Sturken, Marita. *Tourists of History: Memory, Kitsch, and Consumerism from Oklahoma City to Ground Zero*. Durham, N.C.: Duke University Press, 2007.

"A Suckling Squash." *American Agriculturalist*, December 1875.

Sullivan, Margaret A. "Aertsen's Kitchen and Market Scenes: Audience and Innovation in North Art." *Art Bulletin* 81, no. 2 (1999): 236–66.

Sutter, Paul. *Driven Wild: How the Fight against Automobiles Launched the Modern Wilderness Movement*. Seattle: University of Washington Press, 2002.

Sutton, Peter C. *Masters of Seventeenth-Century Dutch Genre Painting*. Philadelphia: University of Pennsylvania Press, 1984.

Switzer, Stephen. *Practical Kitchen Gardiner*. London: Thomas Woodward, 1727.

"Tales for Youth: The Jack o'Lantern." *South Carolina Temperance Advocate and Register of Agriculture and General Literature* (Columbia, S.C.), May 7, 1846, 176.

Tangires, Helen. *Public Markets and Civic Culture in Nineteenth-Century America*. Baltimore, Md.: Johns Hopkins University Press, 2003.

Tannahill, Reay. *Food in History*. New York: Three Rivers Press, 1988.

Tannehill, Karen. "Field of Pumpkins." *Small Farm Today*, October 1997, 22–23.

Taylor, William R. *Cavalier and Yankee: The Old South and American National Character*. New York: George Braziller, 1961.

Teyssot, Georges. *The American Lawn*. New York: Princeton Architectural Press, 1999.

"Thanksgiving Days." *Niles' National Register*, November 26, 1842, 199.

"A Thanksgiving Dinner." *Village Register* (Dedham, Mass.), November 24, 1825.

"Thanksgiving Morning in the Johnson Family." *Harper's Weekly*, 1887.

"That's Agritainment!" *Time*, October 24, 2005.

Thelen, David, ed. *Memory and American History*. Bloomington: University of Indiana Press, 1990.

Theodorus, Jacobus. *Eicones Plantarum*. Frankfurt-on-Main, 1590.

Theophano, Janet. *Eat My Words: Reading Women's Lives through the Cookbooks They Wrote*. New York: Palgrave, 2002.

Thomas, Gertrude Ida. *Food of Our Forefathers*. Philadelphia: F. A. Davis, 1941.

Thomas, Keith. *Man and the Natural World: Changing Attitudes in England, 1500–1800*. New York: Oxford University Press, 1983.

Thompson, Benjamin. *New England's Crisis* [1673]. Edited by James Frothingham Hunnewell. Boston: Club of Odd Volumes, 1894.

Thompson, George F., ed. *Landscape in America*. Austin: University of Texas Press, 1995.

Thompson, Ruth P. *Jack Pumpkinhead of Oz*. Chicago: Reilly and Lee, 1929.

Thompson, Stith. *Motif Index of Folk Literature: A Classification of Narrative Elements in Folktales, Ballads, Myths, Fables, Mediaeval Romances, Exempla, Fabliaux, Jest-Books, and Local Legends*. 5 vols. Bloomington: Indiana University Press, 1989 [1932].

Thoreau, Henry David. *Walden, or, Life in the Woods*. Boston: Ticknor and Fields, 1854. Reprint, New York: New American Library, 1960.

Thornton, Tamara Plakins. *Cultivating Gentlemen: The Meaning of Country Life among the Boston Elite, 1785–1860*. New Haven, Conn.: Yale University Press, 1989.

Thuente, Joanne, and John W. Francis. *Seed Savers 2001 Yearbook*. Decorah, Iowa: Seed Savers Exchange, 2001.

Tietze-Conrat, Erika. *Dwarfs and Jesters in Art*. London: Phaidon Press, 1957.

Tisdale, Sallie. *The Best Thing I Ever Tasted: The Secret of Food*. New York: Riverhead Books, 2000.

Tittle, Walter. *Colonial Holidays*. New York: Doubleday Page, 1910.

"To Preserving Garden Vegetables." *American Farmer*, November 22, 1833, 294.

"To the Editor of the New England Farmer." *New England Farmer*, January 28, 1825, 209.

Tournefort, Joseph. *The Compleat Herbal*. London, 1719–30.

Trachtenberg, Alan. *Incorporation of America: Culture and Society in the Gilded Age*. New York: Hill and Wang, 1982.

"Trader Joe's vs. Libby's Canned Pumpkin—The Results Are In." Chowhound, November 13, 2005. http://chowhound.chow.com/topics/28093 (accessed May 23, 2010).

Trevenon, Stacy. "A Growing Tradition: Who Really Grows Pumpkins on the Coast." *Review* (Half Moon Bay, Calif.), October 2000, 23–25.

———. "Pumpkins with a Heart." *Review* (Half Moon Bay, Calif.), October 2000, 13.

"Tricks or Treats." *Chicago Daily Tribune*, October 31, 1944, 10.

"True Potiron or Genuine Mammoth." *Burpee's Farm Annual*. Philadelphia: W. Atlee Burpee and Company, 1899.

Truettner, William H., and Roger B. Stein. *Picturing Old New England: Image and Memory*. New Haven, Conn.: Yale University Press, 1999.

Tuan, Yi-Fu. *Topophilia: A Study of Environmental Perception, Attitudes, and Values*. New York: Columbia University Press, 1974.

Tuleja, Ted. "Pumpkins." In *Rooted in America: Foodlore of Popular Fruits and Vegetables*, edited by David Scofield Wilson and Angus K. Gillespie, 142–65. Knoxville: University of Tennessee Press, 1999.

———. "Trick or Treat: Pre-Texts and Contexts." In *Halloween and Other Festivals of Death and Life*, edited by Jack Santino, 82–102. Knoxville: University of Tennessee Press, 1994.

Turner, Frederick Jackson. "The Significance of the Frontier in American History (1894)." In *The Frontier in American History*, by Frederick Jackson Turner, with a foreword by Ray Allen Billington, 1–38. New York: Holt, Rinehart and Winston, 1962.

Turney Zagwyn, Deborah. *The Pumpkin Blanket*. Berkeley, Calif.: Celestial Arts, 1990.

Tuten, Nancy Lewis, and John Zubizarreta, eds. *The Robert Frost Encyclopedia*. Westport, Conn.: Greenwood Press, 2001.

University of Connecticut. *Economic Digest for Connecticut Agriculture*, 1929.

Urry, John. *The Tourist Gaze: Leisure and Travel in Contemporary Societies*. London: Sage, 1990.

"USDA Progress and Achievements on Small Farms Report no. 1: Market Development." 2001. http://www.usda.gov/oce/smallfarm/reports/rpt1md.htm (accessed June 24, 2009).

U.S. Department of Agriculture. "Animal Production." *Experiment Station Record* 38 (January–June 1918): 571.

———. *1920 Census of Agriculture*, vol. 5. Washington, D.C.: Government Printing Office, 1922.

———. *1940 Census of Agriculture*, vol. 3. Washington, D.C.: Government Printing Office, 1943.

———. *1950 Census of Agriculture*, vols. 2 and 3. Washington, D.C.: Government Printing Office, 1952.

———. *1959 Census of Agriculture*, vol. 2. Washington, D.C.: Government Printing Office, 1961.

———. *1964 Census of Agriculture*, vol. 2. Washington, D.C.: Government Printing Office, 1967.

———. *1974 Census of Agriculture*, vol. 11. Washington, D.C.: Government Printing Office, 1976.

———. *1987 Census of Agriculture*, vol. 1. Washington, D.C.: Government Printing Office, 1989.

———. *1997 Census of Agriculture*, vol. 1. Washington, D.C.: Government Printing Office, 1999.

———. *2007 Census of Agriculture*, vols. 1 and 3. Washington, D.C.: Government Printing Office, 2009.

———. "Sheep, Hogs and Horses in the Pacific Northwest." *Farmers Bulletin* 117 (1900): 22.

———. *Yearbook in Agriculture 1938: Soil and Men*. Washington, D.C.: Government Printing Office, 1938.

U.S. Department of Agriculture, National Agricultural Statistics Service. "Vegetables 2009 Summary: Pumpkins for Fresh Market and Processing . . . , 2007–2009." January 2010. http://usda.mannlib.cornell.edu/usda/current/VegeSumm/VegeSumm-01-27-2010.pdf (accessed April 28, 2010).

U.S. Department of Agriculture, National Agricultural Statistics Service, New Jersey Field Office. "2009 New Jersey Annual Vegetable Report." http://www.nass.usda.gov/Statistics_by_State/New_Jersey/Current_Releases/2009njannualvegbrochure.pdf.

———. "Annual Summary, 2008–2009." January 2010. http://www.nass.usda.gov/Statistics_by_State/New_Jersey/Current_Releases/.

U.S. Department of Commerce. *Fourteenth Census of the United States, Taken in the Year 1920.* Washington, D.C.: Government Printing Office, 1922.

———. *Fifteenth Census of the United States: 1930—Population 1: Number and Distribution of Inhabitants.* Washington, D.C.: Government Printing Office, 1931.

Usner, Daniel H., Jr. "Food Marketing and Interethnic Exchange in the 18th-Century Lower Mississippi Valley." *Food and Foodways* 1 (1986): 279–310.

"Value of a Dollar 1860–1999." Grey House Publishing, 1999. In "U.S. Diplomatic Mission to Germany," http://www.usa.usembassy.de/etexts/his/e_prices1.htm (accessed August 10, 2008).

van Bogaert, Harmen Meyndertsz. *Narrative of a Journey into the Mohawk and Oneida Country, 1634–1635.* Syracuse, N.Y.: Syracuse University Press, 1988.

van der Donck, Adriaen. *Description of the New Netherlands.* 1655. New York: New York Historical Society, 1841. Online facsimile edition at http://www.americanjourneys.org/aj-032/ (accessed October 31, 2006).

Van Syckle, Calla. "Some Pictures of Food Consumption in the United States, Part I: 1630 to 1860." *Journal of the American Dietetic Association* 21 (1945): 508–12.

———. "Some Pictures of Food Consumption in the United States, Part II: 1860 to 1941." *Journal of the American Dietetic Association* 21 (1945): 690–95.

Vaughan, Alden T. *New England Encounters: Indians and Euroamericans, ca. 1600–1850.* Boston: Northeastern University Press, 1999.

Verrill, A. Hyatt. *Foods America Gave the World.* Boston: L. C. Page, 1937.

Vicker, Ray. "Pumpkins, Plywood, Squash and Balloon: A Tale of Five Cities." *Wall Street Journal*, October 5, 1981.

Vickers, Daniel. "Competency and Competition: Economic Culture in Early America." *William and Mary Quarterly* 47 (1990), 3–29.

Viola, Herman J., and Carolyn Margolis. *Seeds of Change: A Quincentennial Commemoration.* Washington, D.C.: Smithsonian Institution Press, 1991.

Virginia Market News Service. "2009 Virginia Potato and Vegetable Review." http://www.vdacs.virginia.gov/marketnews/pdffiles/pvr.pdf (accessed June 23, 2010).

Vitez, Michael. "The Great Orange Hope." *Philadelphia Inquirer Magazine*, October 29, 1995, 12–17, 21.

Wall, C. Edward. *Words and Phrases Index*, vol. 3. Ann Arbor, Mich.: Pierian Press, 1970.

Wallace, Mike. *Mickey Mouse History and Other Essays on American Memory.* Philadelphia: Temple University Press, 1996.

Ward, Edward. *A Trip to New-England with a Character of the Country and People, both English and Indian* (London, 1699). In *Boston in 1682 and 1699*, edited by George Parker Winship. Providence, R.I.: George Parker Winship, 1905. Reprint, New York: Burt Franklin, 1970.

Warde, Alan. *Consumption, Food and Taste: Culinary Antinomes and Commodity Culture.* London: Sage, 1997.

Warner, Charles Dudley. "The Season of Pumpkin Pie." *Chautauquan*, November 1891, 252.

Warren, Samuel. *Ten Thousand a Year*. Philadelphia: Jesper Harding, 1851.

W. Atlee Burpee and Company. *Seeds and Everything for the Garden*. Warminster, Pa., 1975.

Watts, May Theilgaard. *Reading the Landscape of America*. New York: Macmillan, 1957. Reprint, New York: Collier Books, 1975.

Waugh, F. W. *Iroquois Foods and Food Preparation*. Canada Department of Mines, Geological Survey Memoir 86, no. 12: Anthropology Series. Ottawa: Government Printing Bureau, 1916.

"Wave Your Magic Wand over Pumpkins." *Ladies' Home Journal*, November 1946, 73.

Webb, Walter Prescott. *The Great Plains*. Lincoln: University of Nebraska Press, 1959.

Weber, Karl, ed. *A Participant Guide: How Industrial Food Is Making Us Sicker, Fatter, and Poorer—And What You Can Do About It*. New York: PublicAffairs, 2009.

Webster, Thomas, Williams Parkes, and Frances Byerley Parkes. *An Encyclopedia of Domestic Economy*. London: Longman, Brown, Green, and Longmans, 1852.

Weekes, Bill. "Pumpkins for the Holidays." *Small Farm Today*, December 1996, 34.

Weeks, Grace L. "Merry Hallowe'en Larks." *Ladies' Home Journal*, October 1903, 48.

Wein, H. C. "The Cucurbits: Cucumbers, Melons, Squash and Pumpkins." In *The Physiology of Vegetable Crops*, edited by H. C. Wein. New York: CAB International, 1997.

Weiner, Michael A. *Earth Medicine—Earth Food: Plant Remedies, Drugs, and Natural Foods of the North American Indians*. New York: Fawcett Columbine, 1972.

Wentworth, Harold, and Stuart B. Flexner. *Dictionary of American Slang*. New York: Thomas Y. Crowell, 1975.

Whistler, Laurence. *The English Festivals*. London: William Heinemann, 1947.

Whitaker, T. W., and Glen N. Davis. *Cucurbits: Botany, Cultivation and Utilization*. New York: Interscience Publishers, 1962.

——, and I. C. Jagger. "Breeding and Improvement of Cucurbits." *Agricultural Yearbook, 1937*. Washington, D.C.: U.S. Department of Agriculture, 1937, 207–32.

White, Ben. "Flora and Fauna: Pumpkin Politics." *Washington Post*, October 31, 2000, A21.

White, George. *Historical Collections of Georgia*. New York: Pudney and Russell, 1854.

White, Josiah. "Pumpkin Seed Oil." Letter to the president of the Hampshire, Franklin, and Hampden Agricultural Society, March 17, 1820. Reprinted in *American Farmer*, April 4, 1823, 13.

White, Richard. *Land Use, Environment, and Social Change: The Shaping of Island County, Washington*. Seattle: University of Washington Press, 1980.

Whiting, Sydney. *Memoirs of a Stomach, Written by Himself, That All Who Eat May Read. Edited by a Minister of the Interior*. London: Chapman and Hall, 1855.

Whittier, John Greenleaf. "The Pumpkin." *New Hampshire Statesman and State Journal*, December 18, 1846. Reprinted in Whittier, *Complete Poetical Works*, Boston: Houghton Mifflin, 1910.

Wiley, Harvey. *Foods and Their Adulteration: Origin, Manufacture and Composition of Food Products.* . . . Philadelphia: P. Blakiston's Son, 1917.

Wilkins, Mary E. "The Pumpkin Giant." In *The Pot of Gold and Other Stories*, 98–114. Boston: Lothrop, Lee and Shepard, 1892.

Williams, Raymond. *The Country and the City.* New York: Oxford University Press, 1973.

———. "The Idea of Nature." In *Problems in Materialism and Culture: Selected Essays.* London: Verso, 1980.

Willoughby, Charles C. "Houses and Gardens of New England Indians." *American Anthropologist* 8, no. 1 (1906): 115–32.

Wilson, Alexander. *The Nature of Culture: North American Landscape from Disney to Exxon Valdez.* Cambridge, Mass.: Blackwell, 1992.

Wilson, David Scofield, and Angus K. Gillespie, eds. *Rooted in America: The Folklore of Popular Fruits and Vegetables.* Knoxville: University of Tennessee Press, 1999.

Wilson, Olivia Lovell. *Luck of the Golden Pumpkin.* 1887. Reprint, New York: Readex Microprint, 1968.

Wilson, Samuel. *12th Annual Price List and Catalog.* Mechanicsville, Pa., 1888.

Winslow, Edward. *Good News from New England.* London: Printed I. D. John Dawson for W. Bladen and J. Bellamie, 1624.

———. *Mourt's Relation, a Relation or Journal of the English Plantation Settled at Plymouth in New England, by Certain English Adventurers Both Merchants and Others* (1622). Edited by Dwight B. Heath. New York: Corinth Books, 1963.

"A Win-Win: U-Pick Pumpkin Farms Recycle Urban Leaves." *Science Daily*, January 14, 2009. http://www.sciencedaily.com/releases/2008/12/081229104654.htm.

Woloson, Wendy. *Refined Tastes: Sugar, Confectionery, and Consumers in Nineteenth-Century America.* Baltimore, Md.: Johns Hopkins University Press, 2002.

Wood, William. *New England's Prospect.* London, 1634. Reprint, Amherst, Mass.: University of Massachusetts Press, 1977.

Woodbury, Levi. "Pumpkin Sugar." *Daily Commercial Bulletin and Missouri Literary Register*, October 28, 1837.

Worlidge, John. *Systema Horti-culture.* London, 1683.

Worster, Donald. *Dust Bowl: The Southern Plains in the 1930s.* New York: Oxford University Press, 1979.

Wright, Ronald. *Stolen Continents: The Americas through Indian Eyes since 1492.* Boston: Houghton Mifflin, 1992.

Wrobel, David M., and Patrick T. Long, eds. *Seeing and Being Seen: Tourism in the American West.* Lawrence: University Press of Kansas, 2001.

Yarnell, Richard A. "The Importance of Native Crops during the Late Archaic and Woodlands Periods." In *Foraging and Farming in the Eastern Woodlands*, edited by C. Margaret Scarry, 13–26. Gainesville: University Press of Florida, 1993.

Yoder, Don. "Folk Cookery." In *Folklore and Folklife: An Introduction*, edited by Richard Dorson. Chicago: University of Chicago Press, 1972.

Yolen, Jane. "America's Cinderella." *Children's Literature in Education* 8 (1977): 21–29.

Yronwode, Catherine. "Here's How to Grow Giant Vegetables!" *Organic Gardening,* December 1994, 22–29.

Yuhl, Stephanie. *The Golden Haze of Memory: The Making of Historic Charleston.* Chapel Hill: University of North Carolina Press, 2002.

Zuckerman, Larry. *The Potato: How the Humble Spud Rescued the Western World.* Boston: Faber and Faber, 1988.

Zuckerman, Michael. "Identity in British America: Unease in Eden." In *Colonial Identity in the Atlantic World, 1500–1800,* edited by Nicholas Canny and Anthony Pagden, 115–57. Princeton, N.J.: Princeton University Press, 1987.

———. *Peaceable Kingdoms: New England Towns in the Eighteenth Century.* New York: Knopf, 1970.

INDEX

Illustrations are indicated in italic type.

A

abolitionism, 80, 82–83
Ackermann Farms (IL), 185, 188
Aertsen, Pieter, 27
African Americans: caricatures of, 109;
  jack-o'-lanterns (jack-ma-lantern), 77,
  82; slaves, 44, 86; sweet potato pies,
  109; Thanksgiving, 108, 109
Agee, James, 113, 123, 132
agrarianism: and abolitionism, 82–83;
  and capitalism, 7, 120, 138; farm stands,
  133–34, 174, 180–81, 184; and farming,
  167, 184; festivals, town, 136, 167, 174;
  FSA photographs, 122; genre paintings, American, 93, 94–95, 95, 96, 97;
  giant pumpkins, 151, 156; homesteading, 67; Jefferson, Thomas, 55, 90; in
  literature, 42–43, 93–94; New England
  colonists, 42–44; nineteenth century,
  67, 85, 90, 96, 111; North vs. South, 6;
  paintings, American Regionalist, 123;
  pie, pumpkin, 79, 104, 121
agricultural fairs: first, 61; nineteenth
  century, 88, 93, 98; "pumpkin shows,"
  86, 135, 167, 234n7
agriculture. *See* farming
American Agriculturalist, 61, 86
American Cookery, 52–54, 68, 160, 162. *See
  also* Simmons, Amelia
Anburey, Thomas, 46
apocolocyntosis (pumpkinification), 21, 25

apples: botany, 11; catalogs, seed, 61;
  cider, 51, 96, 180; colonial era, 32,
  48; as commodity, 191; cooked, 23,
  37, 53; as daily sustenance, 113; farm
  stands, 3, 180, 194; farming, 192; genre
  paintings, Dutch, 27; giant, 65; pie,
  48, 52, 54, 69, 103, 106; "pippins," 37;
  varieties, sweet pumpkin, 63; "vine
  apples" (summer squash), 13
Arata Pumpkin Farm (CA), 112, 116, 130,
  138, 165, 175, 190
Arcimboldo, Giuseppe (*Autumn*), 25–26,
  40, 25
Atlantic Canning Company (IL), 115

B

Bailey, Liberty, 219n64
Barlow, Joel, 48
Barnesville Pumpkin Festival (OH), 168
Bartram, John, 18, 20
Baum, L. Frank, 127
beans: as export, 39; as food, 36. *See also*
  corn, beans, and squash
Beecher, Henry Ward, 97, 106–7
beer, pumpkin: colonial era, 50–51, 59;
  twentieth century, 158–59, 254n87
bees: in literature, 107; pollination, 13, 188
Behmer's Pumpkin Fantasyland (IL), 180
Beuckelaer, Joachim, 27–29, 28

feed, livestock, 69, 87, 88; benefits, 57, 62–63; declined use, 112, 116, 139; new retail market, late twentieth century, 185–86; and pie, pumpkin, 69, 110; seeds, 226n28; USDA study, 114; zoos, 186

Fessenden, Thomas, 61

festivals, farm, 138, 175, 190; agrarianism, 174, 184; attractions, 178, 179; and children, 182; community building, 165, 183–84; economic benefits, 192–93, 194–95; "entertainment farming," 177, 178; entry fees, 178; goods for sale, 180–81; impact on rural economies, 184, 194–95; locations, 177–78; nostalgia, 177, 179, 180, 181, 182; origins and development, 174, 175–76; picking pumpkins, 174, 181–82, 182. *See also* direct farm marketing; farms, family; farm stands; pick-your-own farms

festivals, harvest, 100, 173; colonial era, 9, 47–48; Harvest Home, 34, 48, 52; "harvest social," 120; Succot, 34; without pumpkins, 55, 136. *See also* festivals, farm

festivals, town, 3; 165–74, 256n10; agrarianism, 136, 167, 174; origins, 135–36. *See also individual town festivals*

field pumpkins (*Cucurbita pepo*), 10, 11, 12; botanical classifications, 21–23, 24, 29, 45, 219n64; "Connecticut field," 62, 147, 149, 162; in farm stands, 134–35, 135, 136; in genre paintings, American, 75–76, 94–95, 94; in genre paintings, Dutch, 27, 28, 30; Indians, American, 13, 14, 20, 35; in Italy, art, 25–26, 41, 25; jack-o'-lantern, origins as, 90; melons, identified with, 21–23, 22, 35; as old-fashioned and of little worth, 60, 61–64, 226n20; Pankow's Field, 147; sales tax, Iowa, 267n136. *See also* varieties

Florida, 30–31, 190; Thanksgiving, 34

flowers, pumpkin: bees, 13, 188; botany, 11, 45; female, 13, 29, 152; as food, 18; in Italy, art, 24; in literature, 106–7

folklore: African Americans, 77, 82; giant pumpkins, 66–67, 228n56, 228n59; Jonathan, 60; numbskulls, 76, 109. *See also* Indians, American; oral traditions; *individual folktales*

foods: colonial era, 36–38, 46–54; Europeans, 23–24; Indians, American, 16–18; industrialization, 98–99; nineteenth century, 59, 87; processed, 195; twentieth century, 117–18, 119, 126, 161

foods, pumpkin: baked, 17–18, 23, 24, 33, 67; boiled, 18, 23, 24, 49; breads, 18, 32, 50, 67, 158; desserts, 119–20, 160; dried, 18, 50, 52, 67; at festivals, 165, 169, 172; fried, 23; Godiva, 157; for pioneers, midwestern, 67; "pompion chips," 50; pumpkin-shaped, 139, 157–58, 159, 195; "pumperkin" vinegar, 51; roasted, 17–18, 49; as seasonal, 158; soups, stews or sauces (puddings), 17–18; 34, 37–38, 49, 68; as sweetener, 50, 67, 229n67; tarts, 49; versatility, 37, 48, 49, 68. *See also* pies

Fourth of July. *See* Independence Day

France, 66; cooking, 49, 102–5; Huguenots, 34

Frey Farms (IL), 187, 190

Frost, Robert ("Roadside Stand"), 133, 134

Fuchs, Leonhard, 22–23, 22, 31

G

Gancarz, Edward, 155, 157

genre paintings: American, 93, 94–95, 95, 97; Dutch, 26–29, 28, 30, 74

Georgia, 47, 68, 220n73; Pumpkin Pile (GA), 68

Gerarde, John, 23, 35, 39

turkeys: colonial era, 30, 31; in genre paintings, American, 103; in genre paintings, Dutch, 30; in numbskull cartoon, 109; in poetry, 94; and pumpkin pie, 121; Thanksgiving dinner, 79, 102, 106, 108, 160

Turner, Frederick Jackson, 90, 111

turnips, 9, 27, 44; Halloween, 42

U

"Ugly Pumpkin," 143

U.S. Department of Agriculture (USDA): farm, family, definition, 174; feed, livestock, study, 114; Jack-Be-Littles designation as non-food item, 148; New Deal, programs, 116

U.S. Department of Agriculture, *Census of Agriculture*: origins, 87; statistics, 110, 117, 139, 185, 187–88, 193–94, 239–240n16

U.S. Farm Security Administration (FSA), 116; photograph division, 113, 122–23, 124–25, *124*, *125*, *129*, *135*, *135*, *136*, *139*

U.S. Food and Drug Administration, 118

U.S. Supreme Court, caricature, 96

U.S. Works Progress Administration, post office murals, 122

V

Vala's Pumpkin Patch (NE), 180, 183, 192, 194

Vallandigham, Clement, 96

van Bogaert, Harman Meyndertsz, 33

van der Donck, Adrian, 51, 206n27

van Rijck, Pieter Cornelisz, 30

varieties (by name): Autumn Gold, 147, 149; autumn marrow, 58; Autumn Pride, 146; Baby Boo, 148, 149; Big Autumn, 147; Big Gold, 110; Bush Hybrid Spirit, 149; Casper, 148;

Cinderella, 148; Common New England, 63; crooknecks (cushaws), 10, 16, 53, 58, 134; custard, 58; Dickinson, 161, 185; early sugar, 110; Finest family, 110; Ghost Rider, 146; Golden Marrow, 110; Howden, 147; Hybrid Frosty, 148, 149; Jack-Be-Little, 148, 149, 182; Jonathan, 60; Libby's Select, 161, 172, 185; Nantucket, 58; Oz, 147, 182; Paint-A-Pumpkin, 148; Pankow's Field, 147; pie, 146; possum-nosed, 60; Pure Gold, 87; Quaker Pie, 110; Spirit, 147; Spooktacular, 146; sugar, 110, 116; 146, 181; sugar babies, 146; sweet, 110; Thanksgiving, 110, 173; twentieth century, 146–48.

varieties, ornamental (jack-o'-lantern): farming, 185–86, 187, 188, 189–90, 264n103; market value, 191, 193–94; percentage of annual crop, 116; shipping and transportation, 190–91, 192, 264n106; USDA classifications, 148. *See also* canned goods; Libby's

vines, pumpkin, 4, 36, 48, 73; and cookbooks, 106, *107*; and farming, 16, 64, 186, 189; in festivals, town, 168, 235n25; in folklore, 66–67, 228n56; giant pumpkins, 152, 235n25; in Linnaean classification, 45; in literature, 71–72, 80, 98

Virginia: beer, 50; colonial era, 37, 38–39, 49, 173; farm stands, 196–98, *197*; farming, pumpkins, 36, 46, 67, 192, 193; festivals, farm, *175*, 178–79, *179*, 180, 183; festivals, harvest, 48; giant pumpkins, 65; Hampton Institute, 108; Indians, American, 14–18, *17*, 33; Jamestown (VA), 34; Jefferson, Thomas, 55; "Pumperkin" vinegar, 51; Pumpkin (VA), 68; Thanksgiving, 34, 108; "Virginia Macocke or Pompion," 23

Vollmer Farm (NC), 180, 265n112

W

Ward, Edward, 36, 39, 40, 48
Ward, Nathaniel, 40
Warnock, Warren, 151, 153
Warren, Samuel, 77
Washington, DC, 145, 186, 194; bakeries, 119, 131, 160; farm stands, 13, 178–80
Washington, George, 44, 46; birthday, 99–100; Thanksgiving, 223n106
"When the Frost is on the Pumpkin," 94
White, John, 16, 17
Whittier, John Greenleaf: abolitionism, 82–83; Pilgrims, opinion of, 101; "Pumpkin," 78–81, 90, 106, 120, 121
Whittredge, Worthington (*In the Pumpkin Patch*), 97
wholesale: brokers, 190–91, 192, 193; dollar value in sales, 192, 193, 194; farmers switch to PYO, 175–76, 177; prices undercut small farmers, 130; quality of pumpkins, 264n106
wilderness. *See* nature, wild
Wiley, Harvey, 118, 119
will-o'-the-wisps, 77
Williams, Roger, 13
Wilson, Olivia Lovell, 97
Wilson, Samuel, 88
Windy Acres Pumpkin Patch (OR), 180–91, 183, 193
Winslow, Edward, 9–10, 33, 36
Winters, John, 38
Withers, George, 29
Wizard of Oz, 127
women: as bakers, 68, 105; as bakers with political purpose, 6, 55, 106, 125–26, 129; bewitched, 77; Ceres, 41, 95; Cinderella, 6, 73–74, 78–79, 97, 129, 145; cookbooks, 53; domestic advice books, 80; farm stands, 134–35, 136; in genre paintings, American, 94–95, 95; as giant pumpkin, 87; Halloween party organizers, 126; ideas about

nature and, 75; Indians, American, 15, 19, 33, 49, 68; magazines, 5, 92, 99, 119–20, 159; Mother Nature, 75; textile workers, 75; view of "pumpkin manhood," 96. *See also individual women*
women, sexuality, 84, 106–7: in botanical dictionaries, 29; festivals, harvest, 48; in genre paintings, Dutch, 26–29, 28, 30, 74; immorality, 78, 143; infidelity, 74–75, 145; "Jack O'Lantern Girl," 127–28; men's anxieties about, 74, 75, 128–29, 145; nickname, 145
Wood, Grant, 123
Wood, William, 30
World Pumpkin Confederation, 153, 155, 156
World War I, 114, 115, 123
World War II, 123, 124, 134, 137, 165
World's Columbian Exposition (1893: Chicago, IL), 87, 90, 111, 151
Worster, Donald, 116
Wyeth, Andrew, 249n20
Wyeth, James, 144, 144

Y

Yankee, 78, 80, 83; Thanksgiving, 81, 108, 119
yards. *See* decorations, yards

Z

Zahr, Nathan and Paula, 153

WEYERHAEUSER ENVIRONMENTAL BOOKS

Making Mountains: New York City and the Catskills by David Stradling
The Fishermen's Frontier: People and Salmon in Southeast Alaska by David F. Arnold
Shaping the Shoreline: Fisheries and Tourism on the Monterey Coast by Connie Y. Chiang
Dreaming of Sheep in Navajo Country by Marsha Weisiger
The Toxic Archipelago: A History of Industrial Disease in Japan by Brett L. Walker
Seeking Refuge: Birds and Landscapes of the Pacific Flyway by Robert M. Wilson
Quagmire: Nation-Building and Nature in the Mekong Delta by David Biggs
Iceland Imagined: Nature, Culture, and Storytelling in the North Atlantic
    by Karen Oslund
A Storied Wilderness: Rewilding the Apostle Islands by James W. Feldman
The Republic of Nature: An Environmental History of the United States by Mark Fiege
The Promise of Wilderness: American Environmental Politics since 1964
    by James Morton Turner
Nature Next Door: Cities and Their Forests in the Northeastern United States
    by Ellen Stroud
Pumpkin: The Curious History of an American Icon by Cindy Ott
Car Country: An Environmental History by Christopher W. Wells

WEYERHAEUSER ENVIRONMENTAL CLASSICS

The Great Columbia Plain: A Historical Geography, 1805–1910 by D. W. Meinig
Mountain Gloom and Mountain Glory: The Development of the Aesthetics of the Infinite
    by Marjorie Hope Nicolson
Tutira: The Story of a New Zealand Sheep Station by Herbert Guthrie-Smith
A Symbol of Wilderness: Echo Park and the American Conservation Movement
    by Mark Harvey
Man and Nature: Or, Physical Geography as Modified by Human Action
    by George Perkins Marsh; edited and annotated by David Lowenthal
Conservation in the Progressive Era: Classic Texts edited by David Stradling
DDT, Silent Spring, and the Rise of Environmentalism: Classic Texts edited
    by Thomas R. Dunlap
The Environmental Moment, 1968–1972 by David Stradling

CYCLE OF FIRE BY STEPHEN J. PYNE

Fire: A Brief History
World Fire: The Culture of Fire on Earth
Vestal Fire: An Environmental History, Told through Fire,
    of Europe and Europe's Encounter with the World
Fire in America: A Cultural History of Wildland and Rural Fire
Burning Bush: A Fire History of Australia
The Ice: A Journey to Antarctica